THE ISSUE WITH ANTIQUITY

The Issue with Antiquity

By Anatoly Fomenko

DELAMERE PUBLISHING

•

THE ISSUE WITH ANTIQUITY
By Anatoly Fomenko

Book 5 of *History: Fiction or Science?* series

Translated from Russian by Mikhail Yagupov
Design and layout by Paul Bondarovski
Project management: Franck Tamdhu
Cover image: © David Cuesta Azor | Dreamstime

Published by Delamere Resources LLC

CONTENTS

History is a pack of lies about events that never happened told by people who weren't there.

GEORGE SANTAYANA

Be wary of mathematiciens, particularly when they speak the truth.

ST. AUGUSTINE

History repeats itself; that's one of the things that's wrong with history.

CLARENCE DARROW

Who controls the past controls the future. Who controls the present controls the past.

GEORGE ORWELL, *1984*

From the Publisher

The consensual world history was manufactured in Europe in XVI–XIX centuries on political agenda of powers of that period on the basis of erroneous clerical chronology elaborated by the Kabbalist Jesuits Joseph Justus Scaliger and perfected by the Jesuit Dionysius Petavius.

By the middle of XVI century the prime political agenda of Europe that reached superiority in Sciences and Technologies, but was still inferior militarily to the Evil Empire of Eurasia, was to free Europe.

The concerted effort of European aristocracy, black and white Catholic clergy, Protestants, humanists and scientists in XVI–XVII centuries in creation and dissemination of fictional Ancient World served this agenda perfectly.

The fictional Ancient World of Antiquity was created by black and white Catholic clergy, Protestants, humanists, and scientists by representing events of XI–XVI centuries as ones that happened thousands of years before according to the famous ancient authorities they invented.

The European aristocracy, a considerable part of which were noble fugitives from Byzantine and/or the inheritors of Eurasian warlords, supported the myth of Ancient World to justify their claims to countries they ruled.

The black and white Catholic clergy, Protestants developed and supported the myth of Ancient World to justify their claims of being

9

more ancient and to separate themselves from orthodoxy in the countries ruled by European aristocracy and nobility.

The scientists supported the myth of Ancient World as safe cover for their research that produced results heretic from the point of view of Christianity. They justified their discoveries by authorities of ancient scientists they themselves invented and used as pseudonyms.

The humanists developed and supported the myth of Ancient World as convenient cover for their ideas that conflicted with Christianity and aristocracy. Humanists too justified their ideas with authorities of ancient authors of their own making and used as pseudonyms.

> *"Who controls the past controls the future.*
> *Who controls the present controls the past."*
> – George Orwell, *1984*.

'Antiquity' taught in schools and universities worldwide is pure fiction! We are told that 'Antiquity' was followed by many centuries of utter stagnation and decline with virtually nothing happening but wars and famine and the destruction of the priceless ancient monuments.

Then, during the Renaissance, the Classical authors reappear from oblivion, Latin and Greek become resurrected as the intelligentsia Esperanto of the Middle Ages, numerous manuscripts reappear from oblivion to be copied, enter wide circulation, and – vanish again, never to be found.

The learned crowd of humanists and clergy invented 'ancient' Greek and Latin languages, wrote 'antique' masterpieces under 'antique' sounding pseudonyms. The talented artists, painters, and sculptors of XV–XVIII century mass-produced required paraphernalia.

Renaissance was on! The demand of the European aristocracy, nobility and the burgers for 'antique' labeled articles prices was solid. 'Antiquity' paraphernalia fetched high prices and was sold to the public lock, stock, and barrel.

How preposterous would it be to suggest that *there were no Dark Ages* to separate the antiquity from the Renaissance; that the "Re-naissance" was, in fact, the *Naissance* of the Western European culture as we know it?

The mythical Classical Age came into being from misdating medieval events by hundreds and thousands of years. 'Antiquity' meme is planted into defenseless young brains. Kids love tales and don't ask teachers awkward questions…

Dr. Anatoly Fomenko is a Full Member of the Russian Academy of Sciences, Full Member of the Russian Academy of Natural Sciences, Full Member of the International Higher Education Academy of Sciences, Doctor of Physics and Mathematics, Professor, Head of the Moscow State University Department of Mathematics and Mechanics. Solved the classical Plateau's Problem from the theory of minimal spectral surfaces.

Franck Tamdhu
August 2017

Are History and Astronomy incompatible?

By Béla Lukács

History: Fiction or Science? is a most unusual book series, one that undermines the very foundations of History. According to the author and his team of researchers, History as it has been taught in Europe ever since the Renaissance is fundamentally false, verified history beginning around 1250 A.D. the earliest. Jesus Christ was born in 1053 and crucified in 1086, the First Crusade being an immediate reaction to his Crucifixion. Homer identifies an anonymous poet of the second half of XIII century A.D., and the event led to the creation of the *Iliad* had been the fall of the Latin Empire of Constantinople in 1261 A.D. The list goes on and on.

Historians generally oppose the author's views without making much commentary. The author is not a historian, period. He is only a leading differential geometrician (mathematician), successful and respected. A. T. Fomenko is also a corresponding member of the Russian Academy of Sciences; his main argumentation is of a statistical and astronomical nature. I happen to be a physicist myself and not a historian. However, astronomy and differential geometry are known to me well from the area of general relativity, and I cannot recommend this book enough, since its author approaches History, usually a highly emotional discipline ascribed to the field of humanities, armed with impartial mathematics.

History is collective memory; yet even our own memory errs at times, and no real memory extends beyond three generations.

There are written sources, but each one of those might easily prove a forgery. There are material remnants of archaeological nature, but they may be misinterpreted.

Astronomy is precise by definition, and a historical dating that can be calculated from information about eclipses should satisfy any researcher. Yet the XIX century astronomers did not use the lunar tidal friction term in the equations of lunar motion, which would make ancient lunar eclipses appear several hours off the mark and relocate several total eclipses of the sun geographically (assuming tidal friction has remained the same all the time but there is no reason to believe it hasn't). How could XIX century calculations have conformed to consensual history?

I must say that a methodical recalculation of ancient eclipse datings shall invariably bring surprises; in the unlikely case these datings are correct, we shall prove the existence of erratic changes in telluric rotation over the last 4,000 years instead. Both possibilities are highly alarming.

Fomenko demonstrates the incompatibility between consensual history and modern astronomy. This incompatibility is a sad fact. (He exposes a number of other contentious issues as well, but those do not fall into my professional scope.) Which is more reliable – history or hard-boiled scientific facts? Science cannot afford subjectivity; most of us would feel the same way about history as well.

Chronological problems are very serious indeed; Fomenko offers a viable solution to most of them, and a radical one at that – a "Copernican revolution" of history, no less. I am not using the term to predict the final and total victory of his version; that is a matter for a multitude of scientific and scholarly discussions to come. But the contradiction between history and astronomy that becomes graver with the day cannot and must not be tolerated, in the best interests of both history and the theory of telluric rotation.

Preface

By Anatoly T. Fomenko

The materials contained in this book correspond to the research that was started in 1973.

One might wonder why we should want to revise the chronology of ancient history today and base our revision on new empirical-statistical methods. It would be worthwhile to remind the reader that *in the XVI–XVII century chronology was considered to be a subdivision of mathematics*, prior to having gradually transformed into a field of historical studies considered complete in general, and only requiring minor eventual clarifications leaving the actual edifice of chronology intact. And yet we discover that the contemporary official version of the chronology of ancient history is full of prodigious contradictions and inconsistencies that deserve an attempt of partial clarification and rectification based on the methods of modern statistics at the very least.

One often hears the question about what could possibly motivate a mathematician into wanting to study a seemingly historical problem. The answer is as follows. My primary interests are those of a professional mathematician; they are thus rather distant from historical and chronological issues. However, in the early 70's, namely, in 1972–1973, I had to deal with the dates of ancient eclipses during my studies of one of the key problems in celestial mechanics (see *Chron1*, Chapter2 for more details). It had to do with computing the so-called coefficient D'' in the Theory of Lunar Motion. The parameter characterizes acceleration and is computed as a time function on a large historical interval. The computations were performed by Robert Newton, a contemporary American astronomer and astrophysicist. Upon their completion, he had made the unexpected discovery of parameter D" behaving in the most peculiar manner, namely, performing an inexplicable leap on the interval of VIII–X century A.D. This leap cannot be explained by conventional gravitational theory, and is improbable to the extent of making Robert Newton invent mysterious "extra-gravitational forces" in the Earth-Moon system that suspiciously refuse to manifest in any other way.

This inexplicable effect attracted the professional interest of the mathematician in me. The verification of R. Newton's work showed that his computations conformed to the highest scientific standards and contained no errors. This made the gap in the diagram even more enigmatic. A prolonged pondering of this topic led me to the idea of checking the exactitude of *datings* of the ancient eclipses that the D" parameter computations were based upon since they implicitly affected the result. This idea turned out to have been unprecedented for the scientists that had dealt with the problem previously. Robert Newton himself, an eminent expert in the field of astronavigation and theoretical dynamics of natural and artificial celestial bodies, trusted the ancient historical dates completely and attempted to explain the leap in the behaviour of parameter D" from within his professional paradigm. That is to say, without the merest hint of the very idea of questioning ancient chronology. I was more fortunate in that respect: I found out that N. A. Morozov, a renowned Russian scientist and encyclopaedist, had analyzed the datings of ancient eclipses and claimed most of them to be in need of revision. This happened as early as the beginning of the XX century. He offered new datings for a large number of eclipses that were considerably more recent. Having obtained his tables, I repeated Newton's calculations using Morozov's dates in lieu of the consensual ones as input data. I was amazed to discover that the D" graph altered instantly and drastically, transforming into a rather even horizontal line that had concurred with the conventional gravitational theory perfectly. The enigmatic leap disappeared along with the necessity to invent fictitious "extra-gravitational forces".

The satisfaction from having finished a body of scientific work successfully was accompanied by a sudden awareness of a very knotty point arising in this respect, one of great peculiarity and paramount importance. Namely, that of whether the consensual chronology of ancient history was to be trusted at all.

It was true that the new datings of many ancient eclipses offered by N. A. Morozov led to the equalization of the D'' function diagram, the elimination of a strange contradiction from celestial mechanics, and to the discovery of the conformance of an important parameter in the theory of lunar motion to perfectly normal patterns of behaviour.

It was equally true, however, that fitting something like the idea that the three ancient eclipses described in the *History* of the prominent ancient author Thucydides took place in the XI or even the XII century A.D. and not in the V B.C. as it is believed today into one's perception proved quite impossible. The issue here is that the dating of the "triad of Thucydides" can only correspond to these two astronomically precise solutions (see *Chron1*, Chapter 2). The inevitable question that arose in this respect was that of which discipline had been correct in this case, astronomy or contemporary chronology.

I had to address several distinguished historians with this issue, including the ones from our very own Moscow State University. Their initial reaction was that of polite restraint. According to them, there was no point whatsoever in questioning the consensual chronology of ancient history since all the dates in question can easily be verified by any textbook on the subject and were proved veracious a long time ago. The fact that the diagram of some parameter D'' started to look natural after revised calculations based on some flimsy new chronology was hardly of any relevance. Moreover, it would perhaps be better for the mathematicians to occupy themselves with mathematics and leave history to historians. The same sentiment was expressed to me by L. N. Gumilyov. I refrained from arguing with him.

The reply offered by the historians failed to satisfy me. Firstly due to the fact that chronology, being a problem of calculating dates, bears immediate relevance to applied mathematics. This includes astronomical calculations, the verification of their precision, calendar problems, the interpretation of old writings based on their frequency characteristics etc, and may present an extensive number of complex issues. Secondly, becoming familiar with the contemporary chronological tables soon proved that the ancient dates were quoted rather arbitrarily, with hardly any references at all given anywhere. At best, the first chronological tables get a quote – however, those were compiled *relatively recently*, in the XVI–XVII century. Delving deeper into the problem revealed that the version of chronology that we agree upon today wasn't the only one available historically. I found out that eminent scientists from various countries expressed the idea that ancient datings required a radical revision. I realized that the answer was the furthest thing from simple, and that shedding some light on the issue would require plenty of time and effort. This is how 1973 saw me commencing work in this direction, aided by colleagues – most of them professional mathematicians and physicists.

The research progressed rapidly. Over the years that passed since 1973 many points have been clarified and a great volume of interesting information obtained. A lot of it was published by myself and my colleagues in a number of books and scientific articles quoted in the bibliography. The first related publication saw light in 1980. It has to be noted that over the course of time our opinions on certain chronological problems have changed. Said alterations never concerned the general picture, but occasionally led to significant shifts in our perception of details. Today we feel that the empirical-statistical methods that our chronological research was based upon need to be formulated and coordinated again. This is how the books *Chron1* and *Chron2* came to existence.

Chron1 is based on the first book I wrote on the subject – *Methods of Statistical Analysis of Narrative Texts and their Application to Chronology (Identifying and Dating Dependent Texts, The Statistical Chronology of Ancient History, The Statistics of Ancient Reports of Astronomical Events)*. It was published by the Moscow State University in 1990; a further revised and extended edition appeared in 1996 under the title *Methods of Mathematical Analysis of Historical Texts and their Applications to Chronology* (Moscow, Nauka Publishing, 1996). *Chron1* contains the entire material in a revised, extended, and coordinated form. It contains an extended version of two of my books: *Global Chronology* (Moscow, MSU, 1993) and *The New Chronology of Greece: The Mediaeval Age of Classics* (Moscow, MSU, 1996).

Certain important results that get briefly mentioned in *Chron1* and *Chron2* were achieved with the aid of outstanding scientists – Professor V. V. Kalashnikov, Doctor of Physical and Mathematical

Sciences (Moscow State University and the National Research Institute for System Studies, Moscow, Russia), and the Senior Scientific Associate G. V. Nosovskiy, Candidate of Physical and Mathematical Sciences (the Department of Mathematics and Mechanics, Moscow State University) – experts in fields of probability theory studies and mathematical statistics. The formation of the author's concept of chronology is largely a result of his having collaborated with V. V. Kalashnikov and G. V. Nosovskiy for many years, and I would like to express my heartfelt gratitude to both of them.

I would like to state explicitly that over the period of time from 1981 and until presently our collaboration with G. V. Nosovskiy has been constant and very fruitful, as the two of us have published a number of what we consider to be milestones of the new chronology. The formulation of the main principles of reconstructing modern chronology and mediaeval history is a direct result of the work we have done together over these years, which adds particular importance to this period.

Let us briefly describe the structure of *Chron1* and *Chron2*. The consensual versions of chronology, as well as those of ancient and mediaeval history, had evolved completely by the XVII century A.D. and appear to contain major flaws. Many prominent scientists are aware of this and have discussed it for quite a while (see *Chron1*, Chapter 1). However, the creation of a new concept of history that would be free from inconsistencies proved a truly formidable task.

A group of mathematicians, most of them from the Moscow State University, commenced their research of the problem in 1974. The results were most captivating, and got covered in a number of monographs (see bibliography) and several dozens of publications in scientific periodicals. Let us emphasize that the new concept of chronology is based primarily on *applying methods of modern statistics* to the analysis of historical sources and *extensive cybernetic computations.*

The main subject of the books *Chron1* and *Chron2* is the research of new *empirical-statistical methods* of finding dependencies in historical texts and derived procedures of *dating* historical events.

The task of *recognizing the difference between dependent and independent texts* is really one of *identifying images.* One encounters it in various scientific paradigms including applied statistics, linguistics, physics, genetics, historical source studies, etc. Finding *dependent* texts is of great utility as applied to studying historical sources where they may be traced to a *common original* that had been lost before our time. It is also very useful to be able to tell which texts are *independent,* or derived from non-correlating sources.

The very concept of *text* can be interpreted in a wide variety of ways. Any sequence of symbols, signals, and codes can be referred to as "text" – the sequences of genetic code in DNA chains, for instance. The common problem of finding *dependent texts* is formulated as follows: one has to find "similar fragments" in long signal sequences – that is, fragments of text that duplicate one another.

There is a multitude of methods used for the recognition of dependencies and the identification of "similar images" available today. We offer several new empirical-statistical methods. They might be of use in analyzing historical chronicles, manuscripts, and archive materials as well as in finding the so-called homologous fragments in texts of a significantly different, more general nature.

This book is divided into several parts or topics for the reader's convenience. This should help us to securely differentiate between proven statistical facts and hypotheses. At the same time, one has to state that such topical division is rather artificial since the topics really have lots and lots of points in common.

The first topic

Solving the problem of statistical recognition of dependent and independent historical texts. Formulating new statistical models and hypotheses, as well as verifying them with extensive experimental material of actual historical chronicles. It turns out we're able to acquire general verification of the models offered. In other words, we have managed to discover interesting statistical tendencies that define the evolution of textual information over a period of time, such as what really happens to the data contained in the manuscripts during their duplication, etc.

The discovery of these tendencies is our first result.

The discovered trends are used as basis for the formulation of new methods of dating the events described in the chronicles. This is achieved by statistical comparison of the chronicles and documents pertinent to the research with the ones possessing confirmed datings.

The methods are verified by a large body of correctly dated materials. Their application to the chronicles and documents describing the events of the XVII–XX century appears to confirm the efficacy of these methods. Namely, the statistical datings that we got as a result of our research concur with the ones confirmed by traditional methods. The *a priori dependent* chronicle pairs turn out to be *dependent statistically* with the use of our methods. The ones that are *independent a priori* turn out to be in*dependent statistically* as well.

Experimental examination of veraciously dated chronicles describing the events of XVII–XX century A.D. led to the discovery of natural numeral coefficients that allow us to differentiate between *a priori dependent chronicles* and *a priori independent ones* in 1974–1979. Basically, these numbers are rather small for *a priori* dependent pairs and rather large for *a priori* independent ones. This means that nowadays we can compare arbitrary chronicles X and Y and find out whether their proximity coefficients are within the zone that refers to dependent chronicles or the one that refers to independent ones. It is needless to say that the boundaries of these zones were found experimentally.

The discovery of the hidden dependencies that define the evolution of information in rather large historical chronicles as well as the development and experimental verification of the new dating methods (currently comprising a total of eight) – is the *second principal result of our work*. The datings achieved by our methods cannot be regarded as finite, so we shall refer to them as "statistical datings" and nothing more. We shall occasionally drop the word "statistical" for the sake of brevity. The above is to say that we regard the empirical-statistical dates that we computed to be a result of applying statistical methods to historical materials. Nevertheless, the concurrence of these statistical datings with the ones verified a priori that we have discovered in the interval of XVII–XX century A.D. implies that our results are of an objective nature.

The second topic

It can also be referred to as *critical*. We analyze the traditional datings of events that occurred in ancient and mediaeval Europe, Asia, the Mediterranean countries, Egypt, and America. Bearing the reader's convenience in mind, we have collected various materials here that can be found scattered across all kinds of scientific literature and are known to specialists of various profiles, but *often remain beyond the awareness of the general public*. These materials illustrate serious difficulties that are presently inherent in the problem of scientific dating of historical events preceding the XIV century A.D.

We shall inform the reader of the fundamental research conducted by the prominent Russian scientist and encyclopaedist Nikolai Aleksandrovich Morozov (1854–1946), honorary member of the USSR Academy of Sciences, who was the first to have formulated the problem of confirming the ancient and mediaeval chronology with the means offered by natural sciences in its entirety in addition to having collected a great volume of critical materials and suggested a number of innovative hypotheses.

We shall also report the chronological research conducted by Sir Isaac Newton, who questioned many datings of historical events, and several other representatives of the critical current in history and chronology. We quote from eminent authorities in the fields of archaeology, source studies, and numismatics, and a variety of other well-known scientists, and extensively compare different points of view so that the readers could develop their own opinions of the problems in question.

The primary application of novel empirical-statistical methods is the analysis of dates of historical occurrences. This is why we were forced to analyze as many *dating versions* of events in question as we could find in this day and age. The issue here is that various ancient and mediaeval chronicles frequently demonstrate *significant discrepancies* in their datings of certain important events. Attempting to navigate in this chaos of mediaeval versions, we devote special attention to those reflected in the chronicles of XV–XVI century A.D. due to the fact that the chronologists of that epoch were closer in time to the events described than we are. Subsequent chronological versions of XVII–XX century are often revisions of *derivative* material, obscuring and heavily distorting the original mediaeval meaning.

Starting with XVI–XVII century A.D., the version of the chronology of ancient history that was created in the works of prominent mediaeval chronologists J.Scaliger and D. Petavius "rigidifies." The main points of the official version of contemporary chronology coincide with those of Scaliger and Petavius. Hence we are to use the term "Scaligerian chronology" and refer to the consensual datings of ancient events as to "Scaligerian datings".

We presume the reader to be more or less familiar with the traditional – Scaligerian *de facto* – chronology concepts familiar from school and university. We shall thus refrain from quoting the Scaligerian concept in detail, considering this knowledge to be in public domain. On the contrary, we shall be making a special emphasis on its inconsistencies. Further on, we shall give a brief analysis of traditional dating methods: datings based on historical sources, archaeological datings, radiocarbon datings, dendrochronology, etc. It is expedient to allow the reader the evaluation of the veracity and the precision of these methods as well as their application areas.

The third topic

In 1975–1979, the author compiled a table entitled *"Global Chronological Map"*, which may be referred to as GCM for the sake of brevity. It may be regarded as a rather complete "Scaligerian textbook" of ancient and mediaeval history. All the principal events of ancient history with their dates according to Scaliger (the ones used today), lists of main historical characters, etc., were placed along the horizontal axis of time. All the key original sources that have survived with descriptions of contemporary life were quoted for each epoch. The resulting chronological map contains tens of thousands of names and dates. The physical space it covers amounts to several dozen square metres. This map proved itself a priceless encyclopedia and a great guide for the edifice of contemporary – Scaligerian *de facto* – ancient and mediaeval chronology. Due to the large volume of the material, it made its way into *Chron1* and *Chron2* with many expurgations, as small tables and diagrams.

The fourth topic

In 1974–1979, the entire arsenal of the new empirical-statistical dating methods was applied to the factual material collected on the map of the Scaligerian chronology. This was done by inspecting all manner of pairs of historical epochs and the key original sources pertinent to them. These chronicles were processed statistically and then compared in pairs, and eventually the dependence coefficients of compared historical texts were computed.

If such coefficients for the two compared chronicles X and Y proved to belong to *the same* numeric order as those of the *a priori dependent* chronicles from the "certainty interval" of XVII–XX century A.D., we called them *statistically dependent*. In this case, both correlating epochs (temporal periods) were marked on the map with *the same* arbitrarily chosen symbol such as the letter R.

If the proximity coefficient (or measure) of the two compared chronicles X and Y proved to belong to *the same* numeric order as those of the *a priori independent* chronicles from the "certainty interval" of the XVII–XX century A.D., we called them *statistically independent*. In this case, both correlating epochs (temporal periods) were marked on the map with *different* arbitrarily chosen symbols such as the letters N and S.

As a result of statistical research, pairs of statistically dependent chronicles and epochs pertinent to them were found and exposed in the "Scaligerian history textbook". We called such chronicles and the sequences of events they described *statistical duplicates*.

We discovered that the results of using different empirical-statistical methods correlate very well. Namely, the chronicle pairs "statistically similar" according to one method turned out to be "statistically similar" according to all the others (if such methods were at all applicable to the chronicles in question). This result correlation is perceived as important.

It is vital that our empirical-statistical methods have found no unforeseen duplicates, or chronicles whose dependent nature we weren't aware of *a priori*, on the interval of XVII–XX century A.D.

At the same time, the same methods found a large number of new statistically similar chronicles (duplicates) that were previously considered underived, independent in every sense of the word and ascribed to various epochs before the XVII century A.D., preceding the XI century in particular. The compilation of the Scaligerian chronological map and the discovery of statistical duplicates therein amount to the third principal result of this book.

The fourth principal result is the division of the Scaligerian chronological map into a sum of the four chronicle layers discovered by the author. These chronicle layers are nearly identical, but they are shifted in time in relation to each other. These shifts amount to significant amounts of time and their correspondent chronicle layers may be regarded as "short chronicles" of sorts. *A very rough description of "The Contemporary Scaligerian Textbook of Ancient and Mediaeval History" would be calling it a sum, or a collage, of four copies of the same short chronicle, statistically speaking.*

A criticism of the Scaligerian chronology and the description of the four statistical results mentioned above comprise the main part of the present book. Its other parts are of a hypothetical and interpretational nature. They aid the formulation of a possible answer to the naturally occurring question about the meaning of all the discovered empirical-statistical facts, and what the history was "really like".

The fifth topic

This topic can be called interpretational. This is where we offer the hypotheses that may explain the trends we have discovered and the reasons why the "Scaligerian textbook of history" might contain duplicates. Neither this material, nor the "truncated history textbook" that we offer are to be considered finite in any way. They may only be regarded as offering a possible version that requires a great body of work to be conducted by experts of various profiles, and maybe even special research facilities.

*　　*　　*

The author's position on a significant number of points raised in *Chron1* and *Chron2* has formed as a result of interaction, collective research, and extensive discussions with specialists from a wide variety of fields, most notably, the field of mathematics and fellow mathematicians. Specifically, the new statistical models and the results we have achieved have all been presented and discussed over the span of the past twenty-plus years:

the Fourth and the Fifth International Probability Theory and Mathematical Statistics Conferences in Vilnius, Lithuania, 1981 and 1985;

the First International Bernoulli Society for Mathematical Statistics and Probability Theory Congress in Tashkent, Uzbekistan, 1986;

the Multidimensional Statistical Analysis and Probabilistic Modelling of Real-Time Processes seminar by Prof. S.A. Aivazyan at the Central Institute of Economics and Mathematics of the USSR Academy of Sciences;

several national seminars on Stochastic Model Continuity and Stability by Prof. V. M. Zolotaryov (The V. A. Steklov Mathematics Institute of the Russian Academy of Sciences) and Prof. V. V. Kalashnikov (The National Research Institute for System Studies);

Controllable Processes and Martingales seminars by Prof. A. N. Shiryaev (V. A. Steklov Mathematics Institute of the Russian Academy of Sciences) and Prof. N. V. Krylov (Department of Mathematics and Mechanics, Moscow State University);

Academician V. S. Vladimirov's seminar at the V.A. Steklov Mathematics Institute of the Russian Academy of Sciences;

Academician O. A. Oleinik's seminar at the Department of Mathematics and Mechanics, Moscow State University;

Academician A. A. Samarsky's seminar at the USSR National Mathematical Modelling Centre.

The author would like to give thanks to all of the participants of the discussion, and the members of the audience.

The author also expresses his gratitude to the following members of the Russian Academy of Sciences for their kind support and collaboration: Academician E. P. Velikhov, Academician Y. V. Prokhorov, Academician I. M. Makarov, Academician I. D. Kovalchenko, Academician A. A. Samarsky, and Academician V. V. Kozlov, as well as Corresponding Member S. V. Yablonsky.

Thanks to fellow mathematicians, as well as mechanicians, physicists, chemists, and historians, most of them members of the Moscow State University faculty: Prof. V. V. Alexandrov, Prof. V. V. Belokourov, Prof. N.V. Brandt, Prof. Y. V. Chepurin, Prof. V. G. Dyomin, Cand. Sci. M. I. Grinchouk, Prof. N. N. Kolesnikov, Prof. V. V. Kozlov, member of the Russian Academy of Sciences, Prof. N. V. Krylov, Prof. A. S. Mishchenko, Prof. V. V. Moshchalkov, Prof. Y. M. Nikishin, Prof. V.A. Ouspensky, Prof. V. I. Piterbarg, Prof. M. M. Postnikov, Prof. Y. P. Solovyov, Prof. Y. V. Tatarinov, and Prof. V. I. Trukhin, as well as Prof. V. M. Zolotaryov and Prof. A. N. Shiryaev, Corresponding Member of the Russian Academy of Sciences, both members of the V. A. Steklov Mathematics Institute of the Russian Academy of Sciences; faculty members of the National Research

Institute for System Studies of the Russian Academy of Sciences, Prof. V. V. Kalashnikov and Prof. V. V. Fyodorov; faculty member of the Central Institute Of Economics and Mathematics of the Russian Academy of Sciences, Prof. Y. M. Kabanov; faculty member of the National Institute of Scientific Research in Information Transfer Problems, Prof. A.V. Chernavsky; faculty member of the Moscow Oil and Gas Institute, Prof. I. A. Volodin; Prof. S. V. Matveyev, Chelyabinsk University Corresponding Member of the Russian Academy of Sciences; faculty member of the Kiev University, M.V. Mikhalevich, and Prof. V. V. Sharko, staff member of the Ukrainian Academy of Sciences Institute of Mathematics.

The author would like to express his heartfelt gratitude to all of them, along with S. N. Gonshorek for his collaboration and support.

Over various stages the participants of the New Chronology project included the representatives of a variety of scientific paradigms. In their midst: V. V. Bandourkin and Prof. D. Blagoevic (Belgrade University, Belgrade, Yugoslavia), Cand. Phys. Math. Sci. B. E. Brodsky, T. G. Cherniyenko, Y. S. Chernyshov, Prof. B. S. Darkhovski, Prof. I. V. Davidenko, D. V. Denisenko, Cand. Phys. Math. Sci. T. N. Fomenko, V.P. Fomenko, Cand. Tech. Sci. T. G. Fomenko, I. A. Golubev, N. Gostyev, Cand. Phys. Math. Sci. M. I. Grinchouk, Prof. V. D. Gruba, I. Y. Kalinichenko, Cand. Phys. Math. Sci. N. S. Kellin, G. A. Khroustaliov, Prof. A. Lipkovsky (Belgrade University, Belgrade, Yugoslavia), Prof. A. S. Mishchenko, N. A. Milyakh, A. V. Nerlinsky, Cand. Phys. Math. Sci. I. N. Nikitin, Prof. E. M. Nikishin, M. G. Nikonova, A. A. Onishchenko, Dr. Guillermo Peña Feria (Cuba, Spain), M.E. Polyakov, S. N. Popov, Prof. M. M. Postnikov, N. Z. Rakhimov, A. Y. Ryabtsev, D. K. Salakhutdinov, Prof. Y. N. Sergiyenko, Prof. Jordan Tabov (The Bulgarian Academy of Sciences Institute of Mathematics, Sofia, Bulgaria), Y. N. Torkhov, and Y. A. Yeliseyev.

The author would also like to thank Prof. V. K. Abalakin, V. V. Bandourkin, A. V. Bogdanov, M. A. Bocharov, Prof. R. L. Dobroushin, Prof. E. Y. Gabovitsch, Prof. M.I. Grossman, Prof. A. O. Ivanov, Cand. Phys. Math. Sci. V. Kossenko, Prof. Y. M. Lotman, Dr. Christoph Marx (Switzerland), Prof. A. A. Polikarpov, Prof. V. D. Polikarpov, Cand. Hist. Sci. S. A. Poustovoyt, Prof. M.L. Remnyova, Prof. S. N. Sokolov, and Prof. A. A. Touzhilin, for valuable discussions and insights.

Many thanks for the kind assistance of Professor Peter Gruber (The Technical University, Vienna, Austria) who proved to be most valuable indeed.

The author is indebted to all those who helped with statistical work on original sources, namely N.S. Kellin, P. A. Pouchkov, M. Zamaletdinov, A. A. Makarov, N. G. Chebotaryev, E. T. Kouzmenko, V. V. Bashe, B. A. Silberhof, M. Y. Stein, V. P. Fomenko, Cand. Tech. Sci. T. G. Fomenko, and Cand. Phys. Math. Sci. T. N. Fomenko.

Cand. Phys. Math. Sci. N. S. Kellin, Cand. Phys. Math. Sci. N. Y. Rives, Cand. Phys. Math. Sci. I. S. Shiganov, P. A. Pouchkov, M. Zamaletdinov, Cand. Phys. Math. Sci. S. Y. Zholkov, and A. V. Kolbasov have all provided much appreciated help with the creation of algorithms and programs, as well as statistical work on the material.

The author would further like to thank T. G. Zakharova, Director of the N. A. Morozov Museum at the Inland Water Biology Institute, RAS, the entire staff of the museum, as well as V. B. Biryukov for the exceptionally valuable help in archive studies related to N. A. Morozov and his scientific output they provided.

Starting in 1998, the development of the new chronology was aided by a number of specialists from a variety of unrelated fields and adhering to different cognitive paradigms. In 2001 and 2002 G. K. Kasparov voiced his support of the New Chronology in its critical part a couple of times, on the radio and the television; I wish to express my gratitude to him. I am also grateful to Professor A. A. Zinoviev (MSU), the eminent writer, logician and sociologist, for active support and fruitful discussions. My thanks also go to the IAELPS Academician M. K. Moussin, a merited employee of the oil and gas industry, and all the members of his family who actively took part in the "New Chronology" project. Special thanks to I. R. Moussina for her help in compilation of the Dictionary of Interlingual Parallelisms. The project development was greatly helped by A. V. Podoinitsyn, the economist, and Prof. I. V. Davidenko, the geologist.

Disputes with various historians, philologists, and linguists have been a significant influence on the development of the new chronology.

The author is immensely grateful to the head of the Philological Department of the Moscow State University, Prof. M. L. Remnyova, for her kind assistance in allowing a reading of a special course in chronological problems and new mathematical methods in history and linguistics, which was read by G. V. Nosovskiy and the author, at the Philological Department of MSU in 1998. We would like to thank the Professor of the Philological Department, A. A. Polikarpov, who supervises the Laboratory of Computer Methods in Linguistics for his help in organizing this course and valuable discussions.

Thanks to the Freeborn Russia radio station (Moscow) for the informational support of the New Chronology project in 1998–1999, namely, a large series of special weeklies dedicated to our research. Y.S. Chernyshov brilliantly presented these programs. The second cycle of these programs appeared in 2001.

The author expresses gratitude to the dozens and dozens of people in complex chronological research, for their help and support.

A fond, special thanks to the author's parents, V. P. Fomenko and T. G. Fomenko, and his wife, T. N. Fomenko, Candidate of Physical and Mathematical Sciences, for the great and invaluable help in processing statistical materials and for their steady, unswerving support during all the years of robust and complex development of the new chronology.

I would like to re-emphasize that over the last couple of years our research has been getting active support of A. Zinoviev, the prominent thinker, logician, sociologist and writer. His support is all the more valuable to us since the period when it is being provided is that of the utmost controversy and difficulty in what concerns the acceptance of the New Chronology by the community of scientists. A. Zinoviev had pointed out the mechanisms used for the falsification of recent history (the XIX–XX century). His concept of "virtual reality" – the one created and deliberately planted for the distortion of one's perception of reality and the creation of "the official myth of the days of yore" concurs well with the results of our research which have helped to remove the veil obscuring the creation of the Scaligerian version of history in the XVI–XVIII century. Many of A. Zinoviev's ideas concerning the necessity of introducing the methods of modern constructive logic (including the logical methods created by himself) into sociology and history gain paramount actuality nowadays. The actual idea of translating our seven-volume work into foreign languages in order to increase the involvement of foreign scientists into the discussion of ancient chronology, as well as the organizational initiative, belong to none other but him. We are most grateful to A. Zinoviev for his support and the numerous scientific disputes covering a great scope of issues including those relevant to chronology. We consider it a great honour and privilege to be able to commune with one of the most eminent thinkers of the XX–XXI century.

The present publication of the seven volumes of *Chronology* only became feasible due to the creation of a special project for the translation and publication of our works on chronology by Youri Filippov. One has to emphasize that the translation of such a great bulk of complex scientific material is a most grandiose endeavour per se. We would like to express our sincere gratitude to Y. N. Filippov for the gigantic amount of labour invested, and also to the translators and editors for their hard and highly professional work.

*   *   *

The book is dedicated to the memory of Nikolai Aleksandrovich Morozov, brilliant scientist, encyclopaedist, and author of the most profound œuvres on chemistry, physics, mathematics, astronomy, and history. He was the first to have fully formulated the problem of finding scientific basis for ancient and mediaeval chronology using natural sciences, and obtaining fundamental results in this direction.

The author would like to express the wish for this seven-volume edition to provide an impetus for the development of new empirical-statistical methods of studying historical texts so that the problems of ancient chronology can be solved in their entirety.

A. T. Fomenko,
March 2002

PART ONE

The Middle Ages referred to as the "Antiquity".

Mutual superimposition of the Second and the Third Roman Empire, both of which become identified as the respective kingdoms of Israel and Judah

1.

Identifying the Second and the Third "ancient" Roman Empire as the same state. A chronological shift of 330 years

1.1. A dynastic description of the Second and the Third Roman Empire

Let us recall that under the First Roman Empire we understand the "ancient" kingdom as founded by Romulus and Remus, presumably about 753 B.C. ([72]). It had ended with the reign of the Roman King Tarquin the Proud, sometime around the alleged year 509 B.C. ([72]).

The Second Roman Empire is the kingdom which was actually founded by Lucius Sulla in the alleged years 83–82 B.C. and ended with the reign of Emperor Caracalla in the alleged year 217 A.D.

Under the Third Roman Empire we understand the newly founded kingdom that is supposed to have been "restored" by Emperor Lucius Aurelian in the alleged year 270 A.D. and ended with King Theodoric in the alleged year 526 A.D.

The comparison of the Second and Third Roman Empires reveals dynastic currents twined by an explicit dynastic parallelism, q.v. in Fig. 1.1. See also *Chron1*, Chapter 6. The chronological shift that separates those empires approximately equals 330 years. In this case, a dynastic current from the Second Empire includes virtually every ruler of the empire. The respective dynastic current from the Third Empire comprises the best-known rulers of the Third Roman Empire. We provide complete lists of both dynastic currents below.

N. A. Morozov had been the first to point out the parallels between

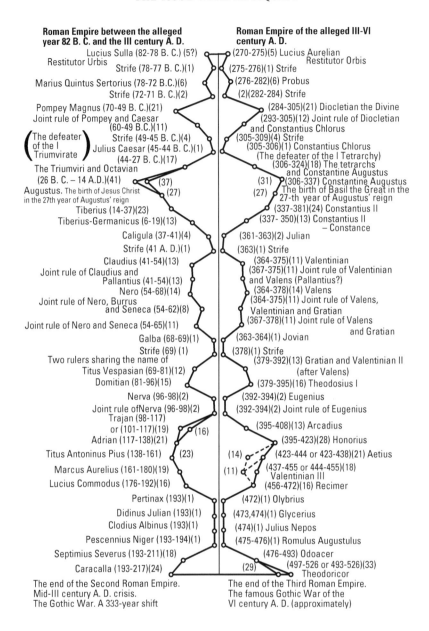

Roman Empire between the alleged year 82 B. C. and the III century A. D.

Lucius Sulla (82-78 B. C.) (5?)
Restitutor Urbis
Strife (78-77 B. C.)(1)
Marius Quintus Sertorius (78-72 B.C.)(6)
Strife (72-71 B. C.)(2)
Pompey Magnus (70-49 B.C.)(21)
Joint rule of Pompey and Caesar
(60-49 B.C.)(11)
(The defeater of the I Triumvirate) Strife (49-45 B. C.)(4)
Julius Caesar (45-44 B. C.)(1)
(44-27 B. C.)(17)
The Triumviri and Octavian
(26 B. C. – 14 A.D.)(41)
Augustus. The birth of Jesus Christ in the 27th year of Augustus' reign
Tiberius (14-37)(23)
Tiberius-Germanicus (6-19)(13)
Caligula (37-41)(4)
Strife (41 A. D.)(1)
Claudius (41-54)(13)
Joint rule of Claudius and Pallantius (41-54)(13)
Nero (54-68)(14)
Joint rule of Nero, Burrus and Seneca (54-62)(8)
Joint rule of Nero and Seneca (54-65)(11)
Galba (68-69)(1)
Strife (69) (1)
Two rulers sharing the name of
Titus Vespasian (69-81)(12)
Domitian (81-96)(15)
Nerva (96-98)(2)
Joint rule ofNerva (96-98)(2)
Trajan (98-117)
or (101-117)(19)
Adrian (117-138)(21)
Titus Antoninus Pius (138-161)
Marcus Aurelius (161-180)(19)
Lucius Commodus (176-192)(16)
Pertinax (193)(1)
Didinus Julian (193)(1)
Clodius Albinus (193)(1)
Pescennius Niger (193-194)(1)
Septimius Severus (193-211)(18)
Caracalla (193-217)(24)
(37)
(27)
(23)
(16)
(23)

The end of the Second Roman Empire.
Mid-III century A. D. crisis.
The Gothic War. A 333-year shift

Roman Empire of the alleged III-VI century A. D.

(270-275)(5) Lucius Aurelian
Restitutor Orbis
(275-276)(1) Strife
(276-282)(6) Probus
(2)(282-284) Strife
(284-305)(21) Diocletian the Divine
(293-305)(12) Joint rule of Diocletian and Constantius Chlorus
(305-309)(4) Strife
(305-306)(1) Constantius Chlorus
(The defeater of the I Tetrarchy)
(306-324)(18) The tetrarchs and Constantine Augustus
(306-337) Constantine Augustus
The birth of Basil the Great in the 27-th year of Augustus' reign
(337-381)(24) Constantius II
(337- 350)(13) Constantius II – Constance
(361-363)(2) Julian
(363)(1) Strife
(364-375)(11) Valentinian
(367-375)(11) Joint rule of Valentinian and Valens (Pallantius?)
(364-378)(14) Valens
(364-375)(11) Joint rule of Valens, Valentinian and Gratian
(367-378)(11) Joint rule of Valens and Gratian
(363-364)(1) Jovian
(378)(1) Strife
(379-392)(13) Gratian and Valentinian II (after Valens)
(379-395)(16) Theodosius I
(392-394)(2) Eugenius
(392-394)(2) Joint rule of Eugenius
(395-408)(13) Arcadius
(395-423)(28) Honorius
(423-444 or 423-438)(21) Aetius
(437-455 or 444-455)(18) Valentinian III
(456-472)(16) Recimer
(472)(1) Olybrius
(473,474)(1) Glycerius
(474)(1) Julius Nepos
(475-476)(1) Romulus Augustulus
(476-493) Odoacer
(497-526 or 493-526)(33) Theodoricor
(31)
(27)
(14)
(11)
(29)

The end of the Third Roman Empire.
The famous Gothic War of the
VI century A. D. (approximately)

Fig. 1.1. The dynastic parallelism between the Second "ancient" Roman Empire of the alleged years 82 B. C. – 217 A. D. and the Third "ancient" Roman Empire of the alleged years 270-526 A. D.

the Second and the Third Roman Empire in [544]. However, lacking a prejudice-free methodology for the selection and comparison of parallel dynastic currents, he had to contend himself with mere selection. As a result, the sequences of kings proposed by him prove to be far from optimal, and happen to be outright erroneous at times. The author of the present book found the optimal parallel dynastic currents whose details differ from the parallels proposed in [544]. Moreover, it soon became clear that the parallel between the Second and Third Roman Empires was by no means basic. It is of a secondary nature, that is, both empires themselves are phantom reflections of a much later mediaeval kingdom. Nevertheless, we decided to begin our list, which contains the most important dynastic parallelisms with this example, since it is a sufficiently vivid one, and also useful for further understanding.

Let us recall the parallelism table (see *Chron1*, Chapter 6). The rulers of the Second Roman Empire are listed in the first position, and the respective rulers of the Third Roman Empire that they're identified as, in the second. All the reign durations are indicated in parentheses (see also [72], pages 236–238). Besides reign durations, the table contains other curious numeric data, which were not taken into account in the calculation of the proximity coefficient c *(a, b)* – we were only proceeding from reign durations.

The Scaligerian history considers the first three emperors of the Second Roman Empire – Sulla, Pompey and Caesar – to have been "fictitious emperors", bearing the title of emperor just formally, as if something about it had been "out of the ordinary". However, this opinion is at odds with a number of "ancient" sources calling those rulers emperors very perspiciously. See Plutarch, for instance ([660], Volume 2, pages 137–138).

1*a. Lucius Sulla,* ruled for 4 years: 82–78 B.C.
■ 1*b. Aurelian (Lucius Domitian Aurelian)* ruled for 5 years: 270–275 A.D.

2*a. Strife,* less than 1 year: 78–77 B.C.
■ 2*b.* Strife, less than 1 year: 275–276 A.D.

3a. *Marius Quintus Sertorius,* 6 years: 79–72 B.C.

■ 3*b. Probus (Marcus Aurelius Probus)*, 6 years: 276–282 A.D.

4*a. Strife*, 2 years: 72–71 B.C.
■ 4*b. Strife*, 2 years: 282–284 A.D.

5*a. Gnaeus Pompey the Great*, 21 years: 70–49 B.C.
■ 5*b. Diocletian the Divine (Caius Aurelius Valerius Diocletian)*,
   21 years: 284–305 A.D.

6*a.* Joint rule of *Pompey* and *Julius Caesar* (first triumvirate), 11
   years: 60–49 B.C.
■ 6*b.* Joint rule of *Diocletian* and *Constantius I Chlorus* (first
   tetrarchy), 12 years: 293–305 A.D.

7*a. Strife*, 4 years: 49–45 B.C.
■ 7*b. Strife*, 4 years: 305–309 A.D.

8*a. Julius Caesar,* the conqueror of the first triumvirate, 1 year:
   45–44 B.C.
■ 8*b. Constantius I Chlorus (Marcus* or *Caius Flavius Valerius
   Constantius)*, the conqueror of first tetrarchy, 1 year: 305–
   306 A.D. or 13 years: 293–306 A.D.

9*a. Triumvirate*, 17 years: 44–27 B.C.
■ 9*b. Tetrarchy*, 18 years: 306–324 A.D.

10*a. Augustus (Caius Julius Octavian Augustus),* the conqueror of
   the second triumvirate, 41 years: from 27 B.C. to 14 A.D., or
   37 years: from 23 B.C. to 14 A.D.
■ 10*b. Constantine I (Caius Flavius Valerius Constantine Augustus)*, the conqueror of the second tetrarchy, 31 years:
   306–307 A.D., or 24 years: 313–337 A.D., with the defeat
   of *Licinius* taking place in 313 A.D., or 13 years: 324–337
   A.D., where year 324 A.D.marks the death of *Licinius*.

10'*a.* The birth of *Jesus Christ* in the 27th year of *Octavian Augustus*.
■ 10'*b.* The birth of *Saint Basil the Great* (The Great King) in the
   27th year of *Constantine I*.

11*a. Tiberius (Tiberius Claudius Nero Julius)*, 23 years: 14–17 A.D.
■ 11*b. Constantius II*, 24 years: 337–361 A.D., or 21 years: 340–361 A.D.

12*a.* Struggle between *Tiberius* and *Germanicus* (assassination of *Germanicus*), 13 years: 6–19 A.D.
■ 12*b.* Struggle between *Constantius II* and *Constans* (assassination of *Constans*), 13 years: 337–350 A.D.

13*a. Caligula (Caius Julius Caligula Germanicus)*, 4 years: 37–41 A.D.
■ 13*b. Julian*, 2 years: 361–363 A.D.

14*a.* The strife after the death of *Caligula* (brief unrest with the emperor present), less than 1 year: 41 A.D.
■ 14*b.* The strife after the death of *Julian* (brief unrest with the emperor present), less than 1 year: 363 A.D.

15*a. Claudius (Tiberius Claudius Nero Drusus Germanicus)*, 13 years: 41–54 A.D.
■ 15*b.* Valentinian I, 11 years: 364–375 A.D.

16*a.* "Joint rule" of *Claudius* and *Pallas* within the "triumvirate": *Claudius, Pallas, Narcissus;* not more than 13 years: 41–54 A.D.
■ 16*b.* "Joint rule" of *Valentinian I* and *Valens* within the "triumvirate": *Valentinian I, Valens, Gratian;* 11 years: 367–375 A.D.

17*a. Nero (Lucius Domitian Ahenobarbus Tiberius Claudius Drusus Germanicus Nero)*, 14 years: 54–68 A.D.
■ 17*b. Valens*, 14 years: 364–378 A.D.

18*a.* Joint rule of Nero with Burrus and Seneca, 8 years: 54–62 A.D.
■ 18*b.* Joint rule of Valens with Valentinian I and Gratian, 11 years: 364–375 A.D.

19*a.* Joint rule of *Nero* and *Seneca*, 11 years: 54–65 A.D.
■ 19*b.* Joint rule of *Valens* and *Gratian*, 11 years: 367–368 years A.D.

20*a. Galba (Servius Sulpicius Galba)*, 1 year: 68–69 A.D.

■ 20*b. Jovian*, 1 year: 363–364 A.D.

21*a. Strife*, less than 1 year: 69 A.D.
■ 21*b. Strife*, less than 1 year: 378 A.D.

22*a.* Two *Tituses Flaviuses Vespasians* (the names are completely
   identical), 12 years: 69–81 A.D.
■ 22*b. Gratian* and *Valentinian II* (after the death of *Valens*), 13 years:
   379–392 A.D.

23*a. Domitian (Titus Flavius Domitian)*, 15 years: 81–96 A.D.
■ 23*b. Theodosius the Great*, 16 years: 379–395 A.D.

24*a. Nerva (Marcus Cocceius Nerva)*, 2 years: 96–98 A.D.
■ 24*b. Eugenius*, 2 years: 392–394 A.D.

25*a.* Joint rule of *Nerva*, 2 years: 96–98 A.D.
■ 25*b.* Joint rule of *Eugenius*, 2 years: 392–394 A.D.

26*a. Trajan (Marcus Ulpius Trajan Nerva)*, 19 years: 98–117 A.D.,
   or 16 years: 101–117 A.D.
■ 26*b. Arcadius*, 13 years: 395–408 A.D.

27*a. Hadrian (Publius Aelius Hadrian Trajan)*, 21 years: 117–138 A.D.
■ 27*b. Honorius*, 28 years: 395–423 A.D.

28*a. Antoninus Pius (Titus Aurelius Fulvius Boionius Arrius
   Antoninus Hadrian)*, 23 years: 138–161 A.D.
■ 28*b. Aetius*, 21 years: 423–444 years A.D., or 14 years: 423–438
   the years A.D.

29*a. Marcus Aurelius (Marcus Annius Catilius Severus Aelius
   Aurelius Verus Antoninus)*, 19 years: 161–180 A.D.
■ 29*b. Valentinian III*, 18 years: 437–455 A.D., or 11 years:
   444–455 A.D., or 32 years: 423–455 A.D.

30*a. Commodus (Lucius Marcus Aurelius Commodus Antoninus)*,
   16 years: 176–192 A.D., or 12 years: 180–192 A.D.

- *30b. Recimer*, 16 years: 456–472 A.D.

31a. Pertinax (Publius Helvius Pertinax), less than 1 year: 193 A.D.
- *31b. Olybrius*, less than 1 year: 472 A.D.

32a. Didius Julian (Marcus Didius Severus Julian), less than 1 year: 193 A.D.
- *32b. Glycerius*, less than 1 year: 473–474 A.D.

33a. Clodius Albinus (Decimus Clodius Albinus Septimius), less than 1 year: 193 A.D.
- *33b. Julius Nepos*, less than 1 year: 474 A.D.

34a. Pescennius Niger (Caius Pescennius Justus Niger or Nigrus), 1 year: 193–194 A.D.
- *34b. Romulus Augustulus*, 1 year: 475–476 A.D.

35a. Septimius Severus (Lucius Septimius Severus Pertinax), 18 years: 193–211 A.D.
- *35b. Odoacer*, 17 years: 476–493 A.D.

36a. Caracalla (Septimius Bassianus Marcus Aurelius Antoninus Caracalla), 24 years: 193–217 A.D., or 6 years: 211–217 A.D.
- *36b. Theodoric the Great*, 29 years: 497–526 A.D., or 33 years: 493–526 A.D.

Besides reign durations, this table contains additional data irrelevant for the calculation of the *VSSD* = *c (a, b)* proximity coefficient, and hence not taken into account in computation. $VSSD = 10^{-12}$ in the statistical model that we present and prove correct in *Chron1*, Chapter 5; it indicates a manifest dependence between the discovered dynastic currents.

Aggregate timelines of the empires under comparison are somewhat different. Namely, the Second Empire spans 299 years. This figure equals 256 years in case of the Third Roman Empire, q.v. in fig. 1.2. Although a 43-year difference is minute as compared with the total timeframe, it should be taken into account nevertheless. The Second Empire turns to have zero joint rules of any significance,

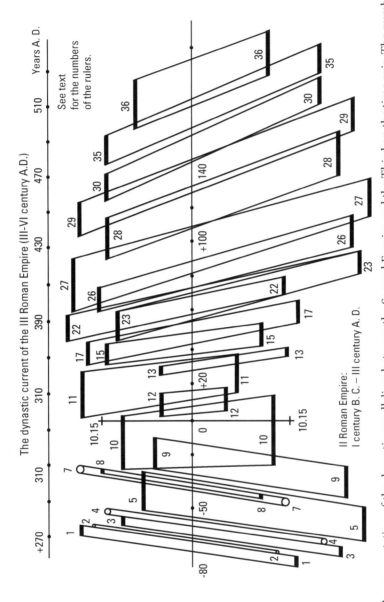

Fig. 1.2. A representation of the dynastic parallelism between the Second Empire and the Third on the time axis. The numbers on the graph correlate to the numbers given to the rulers on the previous illustration as well as in the table from Chapter 6 of *Chron1*.

by which we mean joint rules comparable to the duration of the corresponding reign, while the Third Empire has four pairs of such rulers (8, 9), (12, 13), (16, 17) and (19, 20).

Let us present both dynasties on the time axis. If every ruler is represented by a section whose beginning and end would correspond to the beginning and the end of said ruler's reign, four "major joint rules" shall separate the Third Empire into five blocks. What would happen to the chart of the Third Empire if we eliminated these joint rules – as in dividing the respective pairs of emperors and placing them one after the other in succession instead? Let us perform these four unidirectional shifts by the length of respective joint rules, keeping the individual sections unchanged. After such separation, the reign tables of the Second and the Third Empire turn out to be virtually identical, q.v. in fig. 1.2. The calculation of joint reign durations separated by the authors of the present book (with ruler number 29 made redundant, q.v. in the list) yields the exact difference of 43 years between the durations of the empires' existence. Thus, the difference became accumulated due to four prominent joint rules. Having made the distinction between the co-rulers, we find that the difference disappears, the durations of empires begin to coincide, and the two dynasties become virtually identical.

The mechanism of duplication becomes clear. Two different chroniclers would ascribe "extra age" to two different copies of the same mediaeval dynasty of the X–XIII or XIV–XVI century. Or, alternatively, one of the chroniclers, whilst transposing a mediaeval dynasty into the past, would separate its co-rulers, recording them in succession for the sake of simplicity; another chronicler would do the contrary and "combine rulers" by superimposing them one over the other, thus reducing the total timeframe of the entire dynasty. This was how the two phantom duplicates – namely, the Second and Third Roman Empires – had come into existence.

As we have already mentioned, the dynastic current of the Second Empire included in the parallelism virtually covers the entire *Second Empire*. Namely, it is only the following four emperors that remain outside the parallelism:

- *Otho (Marcus Salvius Otho)*, 69 A.D.,
- *Vitellius (Aulus Vitellius Germanicus)*, 69 A.D.,

- *Lucius Verus (Lucius Ceionnius Commodus Verus Aelius Aurelius),* 161–169 A.D.,
- *Geta (Lucius or Publius Septimius Geta),* 209–212 A.D.

It is clear why they had fallen out of the parallelism. They had all ruled jointly with political figures of greater prominence included in the parallelism. Namely, Lucius Verus is "covered" by Marcus Aurelius (161–180), and Geta by Caracalla (193–217). Both Otho and Vitellius had ruled for less than a year.

Let us now consider the Third Roman Empire and produce a complete list of its emperors, with all versions of their rules, and the strife periods. We use the data from [767], [327], [76], [579]. The list uses CAPITAL LETTERS for highlighting the emperors covered by the parallelism.

1) Tetricus, 270–273 A.D.,
2) LUCIUS AURELIAN, 270–275,
3) Tacitus, 275–276,
4) STRIFE, 275–276,
5) Florian, 276 year,
6) PROBUS, 276–282,
7) STRIFE, 282–284,
8) Carus, 282–283,
9) Julian, 283,
10) Carinus, 283–285,
11) Numerian, 283–284,
12) Carausius, 286–293,
13) DIOCLETIAN, 284–305,
14) Allectus, 293–296,
15) Maximian, 286–305,
16) Constantius I Chlorus, 293–306, first version,
17) Galerius 293–311, first version,
18) CONSTANTIUS I CHLORUS, 305–311, second version,
19) Flavius Severus, 306–307,
20) Galerius, 305–311, second version,
21) STRIFE, 305–309,
22) Maximinus Daia or Daza, 306–313,
23) Maxentius, 307–312,

24) Alexander, 308–311,

25) TETRARCHY, 306–324,

26) Licinius, 308–324, first version,

27) Licinius, 313–324, second version,

28) CONSTANTINE I, 306–337, first version,

29) Constantine I, 313–337, second version,

30) Constantine I, 324–337, third version,

31) Constantine II, 337–340,

32) Constans, 337–350,

33) CONSTANTIUS II, 337–361, first version,

34) Constantius II, 340–361, second version,

35) Magnentius, 350–353,

36) JULIAN, 361–363,

37) JOVIAN, 363–364,

38) VALENTINIAN I, 364–375,

39) VALENS, 364–378,

40) Gratian, 367–383, first version,

41) STRIFE, 378,

42) GRATIAN, 379–383, second version,

43) Valentinian II, 375–392, first version,

44) VALENTINIAN II, 379–392, second version,

45) Magnus Maximus, 383–388,

46) Flavius Victor, 384–388,

47) THEODOSIUS THE GREAT in the West and in the East, 379–395,

48) EUGENIUS, 392–394,

49) ARCADIUS in the West and in the East, 395–408,

50) HONORIUS, 395–423,

51) Marcus, 407 year,

52) Gratian II, 407,

53) Constantine III, 407–411,

54) Priscus Attains, 409–410, first version,

55) Heracleon, 409–413,

56) Jovian, 410–413,

57) Priscus Attains, 414, second version, second attempt to seize power,

58) Constantius III, 421,

59) John, 423, first version,

THE ISSUE WITH ANTIQUITY

60) John, 423–425, second version,
61) AETIUS, 423–444, first version,
62) Aetius, 423–438, second version,
63) Valentinian, III 423–455, first version,
64) VALENTINIAN III, 437–455, second version,
65) Valentinian III, 444–455, third version,
66) Petronius Maximus, 455,
67) Avitus, 455–456,
68) Majorian, 457–461,
69) RECIMER, 456–472,
70) Libius Severus, 461–465,
71) Anthemius Procopius, 467–472,
72) OLYBRIUS, 472,
73) GLYCERIUS, 473–474,
74) Anarchy and strife, 472–475,
75) JULIUS NEPOS, 474 or 474–475?,
76) ROMULUS AUGUSTULUS, 475–476,
77) ODOACER, 476–493,
78) Theodoric the Goth, 493–526, first version,
79) THEODORIC THE GOTH, 497–526, second version.

Many of the emperors that remained outside the parallelism are
the so-called "short-term" ones, in other words, they had ruled for
1–2 years each, and some are only known from coins. Furthermore,
some of them did not rule in Rome, but rather in the Roman provinces – Gaul, Africa, etc.

1.2. Biographical parallelism between the Second and Third Roman Empires. The 330-year shift

Alongside the statistical superimposition, there are amazing
biographical parallels which all but identify the map-codes of these
two dynasties as one another. We feel obliged to reiterate that the
detection of a separate isolated pair of "similar biographies" certainly does not mean anything. However, the occurrence of two long
sequences of such biographies spanning a total of several hundred
years gives one plenty of food for thought.

The biographic parallels that we have discovered, or the proximity
of the relevant map-codes (see *Chron1*, Chapter 5), compelled us to

44

compile a number of rather extensive tables and to compare them to each other. In order to save space, we shall only list the focal points of this multi-centenarian parallelism. Naturally, the royal biographies that we have compared were written by different scribes. These scribes would sometimes contradict each other in their evaluation of a given ruler's endeavours to a great extent. One scribe would praise an emperor, while another would pour scorn over said figure. However, the most remarkable fact in this long chain of coincidences is that all of them were discovered as a result of a continuous formal comparison of kings that had possessed identical numbers in their dynasties over the length of nearly three hundred years.

A) The parallelism between the Second and Third Roman Empires begins with prominent political figures. They both bear the name of Lucius as well as similar, almost identical, honourable titles, not applied to anyone else in these empires: Restitutor Urbis and Restitutor Orbis.

B) The parallelism ends with prominent political figures that accomplish fairly similar deeds. For instance, both of them had granted civil rights to the entire free populace.

C) Superimposition transforms empires and periods of joint rule into near-clones. Official collective joint rules, like triumvirates, are identified as similar joint rules, such as tetrarchies.

D) The "biographic parallelism", which often surprises us by the amazing uniformity of "conspiracy backbones", lasting for nearly 300 years.

The letter "*a*" stands for the Second Empire, and the letter "*b*" – for the Third.

1*a. Lucius Sulla.*
■ 1*b. Lucius Aurelian.*

1.1*a. Second Empire.* The official title of Sulla: Restitutor Urbis, or "the restorer of the city". This title was given to no one else in the *Second Empire.* First name, *Lucius.*
■ 1.1*b. Third Empire.* The official title of *Aurelian:* Restitutor Orbis, or "the restorer of the world" (the state). This title was given to no one else in the *Third Empire.* First name, *Lucius.* The names coincide.

1.2*a. Second Empire.* Sulla is a *Roman Emperor*, according to Plutarch, for instance ([660], Vol. 2, pages 137–138). In the Scaligerian history, Sulla is not formally considered an emperor [327]. This, however, does not conform to direct references of the "ancient" authors who distinctly refer to Sulla by his *emperor's* title, q.v. in Plutarch's work ([660], Vol. 2, pages 137–138). Modern historians believe the emperor's title to have had a "different meaning" when applied to Sulla ([660], Vol. 2, page 514, commentary 61).

■ 1.2*b. Third Empire.* Aurelian – a *Roman Emperor*, according to the Scaligerian history ([76]).

1.3*a. Second Empire.* Sulla becomes emperor as a result of a civil war ([327]), being the most successful military leader. It was one of the bloodiest wars seen by the *Second Empire*. It had raged on for many years ([327], page 197).

■ 1.3*b. Third Empire.* Aurelian seizes power as a result of a war against the Goths ([327]), being the most capable military leader. The war with the Goths is one of the bloodiest wars seen by the *Third Empire*. It had also lasted for many years ([327]).

1.4*a. Second Empire.* The war is predominantly civil and external to a lesser degree ([327]). The *troops* crown Sulla emperor ([660], Volume 2). The senate pronounces Sulla the dictator ([327]).

■ 1.4*b. Third Empire.* The war is both civil and external. It completes a major civil war in Italy thet dates to the middle of the alleged third century A.D. The *troops* pronounce Aurelian the emperor ([327]). The Roman senate approves the election of Aurelian under the pressure of the troops ([327]).

1.5*a. Second Empire.* Sulla *actually establishes* the Second Roman Empire after a period of anarchy and republican rule. He is thus the *first* emperor, *regnant for 4 years:* 83–78 B.C., or 82–78 B.C. The beginning of Sulla's reign is dated back to either 83 B.C. ([327], page 197) or 82 B.C. – the year of his victory at the walls of Rome ([327], pages 197–202).

■ 1.5*b. Third Empire.* Aurelian *"restores"* the Roman Empire after a severe period of strife. He is the *first* emperor of the *Third Empire.* He *rules for 5 years:* 270–275 A.D.([327] and [76], table 15). The two reign durations are of a virtually *similar length.*

2*a. Period of strife.*
■ 2*b. Period of strife.*

2.1*a. Second Empire.* After the death of Sulla, the *civil war* flares up again – actually, a series of wars fought by Pompey et al. *Two* brilliant military leaders gain prominence – Junius Brutus and Marcus Aemilius Lepidus. The troops of both leaders are *defeated.*

■ 2.1*b. Third Empire.* After the death of Aurelian, the stability of the state is lost again, and a *mutiny* begins. Tacitus, the successor of Aurelian, is murdered. Two new emperors gain prominence: Florian and Probus. The troops of one of the military leaders (Florian) are *defeated.*

2.2*a. Second Empire.* The strife lasts for *approximately 1 year:* 78–77 B.C. ([327], pages 207–208).

■ 2.2*b. Third Empire.* The strife lasts for *approximately 1 year:* 275–276 A.D. ([327], pages 446–447). The lengths of the periods coincide.

3*a. Marius Quintus Sertorius.*
■ 3*b. Probus.*

3.1*a. Second Empire.* After the death of Sulla and a brief period of strife, Marius Quintus Sertorius – the emperor of the troops, comes to power. However, he gets *murdered* as a result of a *plot.*

■ 3.1*b. Third Empire.* After the death of Aurelian and a period of anarchy, Probus becomes emperor. Soldiers *riot* against Probus and *murder* him.

3.2*a. Second Empire.* Sertorius *rules for 6 years:* 78–72 B.C. ([327], pages 208–209).

■ 3.2*b. Third Empire.* Probus *rules for 6 years:* 276–282 years
A.D.([327], page 413). The two reign durations coincide.

4*a. Period of strife.*
■ 4*b. Period of strife.*

4.1*a. Second Empire.* After the death of Sertorius in 72–71 B.C. a
great embroilment begins, marked by the uprising of Spartacus
in particular. Over the course of these two years, *two military
leaders* attain prominence – Pompey and Crassus. The two are
the most brilliant warlords of those years.

■ 4.1*b. Third Empire.* The death of Probus in 282–284 A.D. was
followed by a *violent civil unrest.* In the course of these two
years, *two military leaders* manage to distinguish themselves –
Aurelius Carinus and Numerian. The two are the most
eminent public figures of the period, who are identified as
the duplicates of Pompey and Crassus.

4.2*a. Second Empire.* The strife *lasts for 2 years:* 72–71 B.C. ([327],
page 215).

■ 4.2*b. Third Empire.* The strife *lasts for 2 years:* from the end of
282 to the beginning of 284 A.D. ([327], pages 647–648, and
[76], table 15). The durations of the periods *coincide.*

5*a. Gnaeus Pompey Magnus,* the organizer of the first triumvirate.
■ 5*b. Diocletian the Divine,* the organizer of the first tetrarchy.

5.1*a. Second Empire.* After the strife 70 B.C. the power passes into the
hands of the Emperor Pompey the same year. He enjoys a splen-
dorous triumph and becomes honoured with the consul's title
([660], V. 2, p. 338). The period of Pompey's reign is known as the
epoch of *Pompey's Principate* ([767], V. 1, Ch. XI). For Pompey,
the situation with his imperial title is similar to Sulla's. Although
contemporary historians do not consider Pompey to have been
"an actual emperor", Plutarch uses the title to refer to him without
any hesitation whatsoever, q.v. in [660], V. 2, p. 338. There are
also numerous ancient inscriptions in existence that call Pompey
emperor without any double-talk at all ([873], p. 91, No. 34).

■ 5.1*b. Third Empire.* After the strife of 284 A.D., Diocletian is crowned emperor ([76]). With Diocletian coming to power, "a new epoch begins in the history of the Roman Empire – *The Epoch of Dominate*" ([327], page 413).

5.2*a. Second Empire.* Pompey is one of the *most famous rulers* in the history of Rome. He accomplishes large-scale democratic reforms, in particular, the reformation of the court and the troops ([327], page 277). Pompey was *declared divine* in his lifetime ([767], Volume 1, p. 279).

■ 5.2*b. Third Empire.* Diocletian is one of the *most eminent rulers* in Roman history and the initiator of several important democratic reforms. He reforms the court as well as the military bodies; he is also the author of a monetary reform ([767], Volume 2, page 649 etc). Diocletian was also *deified* in his lifetime ([327], pages 422–424).

5.3*a. Second Empire.* In the alleged year 49 B.C., the Roman senate strips Pompey of all his powers. This marks the end of Pompey's reign; he dies in several years.

■ 5.3*b. Third Empire.* In the alleged year 305 A.D., Diocletian abdicates, which marks the end of his reign ([327], page 424). He dies a few years after that.

5.4*a. Second Empire.* Pompey *ruled for 21 years:* 70–49 B.C. ([76]).

■ 5.4*b. Third Empire.* Diocletian *ruled for 21 years:* 284–305 A.D. The reign durations *coincide.*

6*a. Joint rule of Pompey and Julius Caesar. The First Triumvirate.*

■ 6*b. Joint rule of Diocletian and Constantius I Chlorus. The First Tetrarchy.*

6.1*a. Second Empire.* a) Pompey, b) Julius Caesar, c) the first triumvirate, d) Crassus. At the peak of his fame in 60 B.C., Pompey founded the *First Triumvirate* to resist his enemies. For this purpose he had granted authority to two important military leaders, entering an agreement with them – Julius Caesar and Crassus ([327], p. 227).

■ 6.1*b. Third Empire.* a) Diocletian, b) Constantius Chlorus, c) the first tetrarchy, d) Maximian. At the peak of his popularity, allegedly in 293*a.d.*, Diocletian creates the *First Tetrarchy* to hold his opponents at bay. Three major political figures rise to positions of authority as a result – Constantius I Chlorus, Caius Galerius, and Maximian ([327], page 420).

6.2*a. Second Empire.* Pompey signs a pact with Crassus first, and then they include Julius Caesar in the coalition. This coalition is officially called the *First Triumvirate* in historical literature ([327], page 227).

■ 6.2*b. Third Empire.* Diocletian unites with his co-ruler, Maximian. Then they include Constantius I Chlorus in the group, and later on, Galerius. However, Galerius played no important part under Diocletian. In Roman history, this coalition is called the *First Tetrarchy* ([327]).

6.3*a. Second Empire.* In terms of popularity and importance, Julius Caesar is considered to rank second after Pompey, leaving Crassus behind ([327], pages 226–228). With Pompey being overthrown, the power passes on to Julius Caesar, his co-ruler.

■ 6.3*b. Third Empire.* In the hierarchy of power, Constantius I Chlorus (Julius Caesar's double) is considered to rank second after Diocletian (the double of Pompey) and leave Maximian (the double of Crassus) behind. After the abdication of Diocletian, Constantius I Chlorus, his co-ruler, comes to power.

6.4*a. Second Empire.* The joint rule of Pompey and Julius Caesar *lasts for 11 years*: 60–49 B.C.

■ 6.4*b. Third Empire.* The joint rule of Diocletian and Constantius I Chlorus *lasts for 11 years*: 293–305 A.D. The durations *coincide.*

COMMENTARY. Fig.1.3 shows "the statue of Pompey, at the foot of which, as they assume, Caesar had been killed". (Rome, Palazzo Spada – see [304], Volume 1, page 464). Fig.1.4 shows an "ancient" bust of Diocletian, Pompey's double, kept in the Capitol museum ([304], Volume 1, page 565). However, it is difficult to expect any semblance between the two sculptures, since they were hardly portraits in the contemporary sense. Moreover, they were most likely made as late as in the XVI–XVIII century to serve as "visual aids" for the "new Scaligerian history" introduced in that epoch – the epoch of Reformation.

Fig. 1.3. The "ancient" statue of the emperor Pompey (the Second Empire). Kept in the Palazzo Spada, Rome. Taken from [304], Volume 1, page 464.

7a. Period of strife.

■ 7b. Period of strife.

7.1a. Second Empire. Pompey becomes overthrown in 49 B.C., and a great *strife* begins, one that *lasts for 4 years:* 49–45 B.C. ([327], pages 244–247). The strife covers the entire period of Julius Caesar's rule and the *Second Triumvirate*, ending with the rise of Octavian Augustus ([327], pages 244–247).

■ 7.1b. Third Empire. Diocletian abdicates in 305 A.D., which leads to a *four-year period* of strife (305–309 A.D., q.v. in [767] and [327]). The strife covers the entire rule of Constantius I Chlorus (Julius Caesar's double) and the *Second Tetrarchy.* Towards

Fig. 1.4. The "ancient" sculpture of his double – emperor Diocletian (the Third Empire). Kept in the Capitol Museum. Taken from [304], Volume 1, page 565.

the end of the period of strife, Constantine I gains prominence ([767], Volume 1, pages 330–332, and [76], table 12). The durations of the two strife periods coincide.

8a. Julius Caesar, the conqueror of the First Triumvirate.
■ *8b. Constantius I Chlorus, the conqueror of the First Tetrarchy.*

8.1a. Second Empire. Julius Caesar comes to power after a strife and a dynastic struggle, destroying his former companions-in-arms. In the Scaligerian history, Julius Caesar, likewise Sulla and Pompey, is considered to have been "an irregular emperor". However, Plutarch, for example, explicitly calls Julius Caesar *King* ([660], Volume 1, pages 486–487). There are also "ancient" coins and "ancient" inscriptions in existence that refer to Julius Caesar as to *Emperor*, and sans hesitation at that ([873], page 184, No.137).

■ *8.1b. Third Empire.* Constantius I Chlorus seizes power during the strife. A party struggle destroyed many of his former friends and supporters. He was honoured with the title Augustus.

8.2a. Second Empire. Julius Caesar adopts and elevates the nineteen-year-old Octavian. Octavian soon becomes the famous Augustus, ranking amongst demigods.

■ *8.2b. Third Empire.* Constantius I Chlorus enthrones his twenty-year-old son, Constantine. Note the similarity between respective ages of nineteen and twenty years. Constantine I soon becomes the famous Augustus, declared a saint and a demigod.

8.3a. Second Empire. Julius Caesar *ruled for 1 year:* 45–44 B.C.

■ *8.3b. Third Empire.* Constantius I Chlorus *ruled for 1 year:* 305–306 A.D. We shall remind the reader that he was pronounced Augustus in 305 A.D.

9a. The triumvirs and the increasing importance of one of their number – Caius Julius Caesar Octavian (Augustus).
■ *9b. The tetrarchs and the increasing importance of one of their number – Caius Flavius Valerius Constantius I (Augustus).*

9.1*a. Second Empire.* After the death of Julius Caesar, the *nineteen-year-old* Octavian, *adopted* by Caesar and supported by his troops, claims the throne for himself and soon attains it. In doing so, he relies on the Roman *legions* that he was tremendously popular with.

■ 9.1*b. Third Empire.* After the death of Constantius I Chlorus, allegedly in 306 A.D., the *twenty-year-old* Constantine, *son* of Constantius I Chlorus, is appointed the Caesar of the West. It is the support of his *troops* that earned Constantine the title of Caesar.

9.2*a. Second Empire.* After a certain period of time, the *Second Triumvirate* is created with the participation of Octavian Augustus. Antonius, a member of this triumvirate, initially *despises* Octavian.

■ 9.2*b. Third Empire.* The *Second Tetrarchy* with the participation of Constantine I is soon formed. Galerius, a member of this tetrarchy, also treats Constantine, the son of Constantius I Chlorus, *with disdain* at the beginning.

9.3*a. Second Empire.* Antony, considering the influence of Octavian Augustus' army and his popularity in Rome, is forced to negotiate and make peace with Octavian. The end of the *Second Triumvirate:* Octavian defeated Antony and Cleopatra in a *sea battle* and became the *sole ruler* of the Second Empire.

■ 9.3*b. Third Empire.* Galerius, "considering the strength of the Gallic army and Constantine's popularity among the Gallic aristocracy... was forced to recognize him as the Caesar" ([327], page 424). End of the *Second Tetrarchy:* in a *sea battle* of 324, Constantine crushes the fleet of his enemies, remaining the *sole emperor* of the Third Empire. It is possible that "Gaul" might have formerly been used to refer to both the territory of France and *Galicia.*

9.4*a. Second Empire.* The duration of the strife and the reign of the triumvirs *equals 17 years:* 44–27 B.C. ([767], Volume 1, pages 346, 351–352, 424–425).

THE ISSUE WITH ANTIQUITY

■ 9.4*b. Third Empire.* The duration of the strife and the tetrarchy *equals 18 years:* 306–324 A.D. ([327], pages 249–258, 289–291). The durations are similar.

10*a. Caius Julius Caesar Octavian Augustus. Conqueror of the Second Triumvirate.*

■ 10*b. Caius Flavius Valerius Constantine Augustus. Conqueror of the Second Tetrarchy.*

10.1*a. Second Empire.* In the *sea battle* of Accium, Octavian Augustus defeats Antony, his *last* enemy, completely. With this victory, "the period of civil wars in the history of Rome ends" ([327], page 259). Octavian Augustus is one of the *most widely known* emperors of Rome in its entire history. First name, *Caius.*

■ 10.1*b. Third Empire.* In the *sea battle* of Adrianopolis, Constantine I finally defeats Licinius, his *last* competitor. This victory marks the end of the civil war epoch in the alleged III century A.D. ([327], page 429). Constantine I Augustus is one of the *most famous* rulers in the history of Rome. First name, *Caius.* The names of the doubles coincide.

10.2*a. Second Empire.* Antony, defeated by Octavian, had been his close *friend and co-ruler* initially, subsequently having become Octavian's worst *enemy.* Before his coronation, Octavian had served in the troops in the *East.*

■ 10.2*b. Third Empire.* Defeated by Constantine I, Licinius, who had earlier been his *companion-in-arms and co-ruler,* later became Constantine's *enemy.* Before his coronation, Constantine I had served in the troops in the *East.*

10.3*a. Second Empire.* At the beginning of Octavian's career, the key position of power was occupied by the *Second Triumvirate,* whose members had plotted against him. Then Octavian Augustus became *canonized* ([579], page 339). A *new stage* in Roman history is considered to begin with Augustus. It is often written that "this moment [27 B.C. – A.F.] signifies the very beginning of the Roman Empire" ([579], page 339).

■ 10.3*b. Third Empire.* In the biography of Constantine I Augustus (the *Second Tetrarchy*), a political struggle ensues between its participants, known as one of the key events that had taken place at the beginning of his rule. Constantine I was pronounced a son of the God of the Sun ([767], Volume 1, page 674). Everything related to the person of the emperor in one way was declared divine. The Christian Church is considered to have recognized Constantine I as a *Saint* equal to the Apostles in his rank ([767], Volume 2, page 674). Constantine I is also believed to have initiated a *new stage* in the history of "the revived empire", sometimes called "the holy period". Christianity had got to enjoy the state support and grown considerably stronger – presumably, for the first time.

10.4*a. Second Empire.* Octavian Augustus concentrated all the important functions of military, civil and religious power in his hands ([579], page 339). Octavian's legislative activity was highly popular. Not only were new laws issued, but the former Roman codices also got "revised" ([767], Volume 2, page 408).

■ 10.4*b. Third Empire.* Constantine I is considered to have got hold of all military, civil and religious power ([767], Volume 2, page 668). Constantine's legislative activity is renowned in particular. He published new laws, and also restored the codices of the "pre-Diocletian epoch" ([767], Volume 2, page 669).

10.5*a. Second Empire.* Initially, Octavian Augustus hasn't got any permanent residence of any sort. After the end of the civil war, Augustus settles down in Rome and "transforms her into a new city". Rome is considered to have become a highly urbanized centre of paramount importance under Octavian Augustus ([767], Volume 2, page 408).

■ 10.5*b. Third Empire.* In the first years of his rule, Constantine I *has got no permanent capital.* He later transfers the capital of the Roman Empire from Rome to the *New Rome* on the Bosporus. "New Rome" is the official name of the new cap-

ital founded by Constantine I. The city received the name
of Constantinople a few years later ([327], page 436, [240],
page 26).

10.6a. *Second Empire.* Chronicles especially emphasize that
Augustus transformed Rome (allegedly in Italy) into a rich
city. "Under Augustus, Rome was rebuilt in marble instead of
wood and brick, having undergone a radical reorganization"
([767], Volume 2, page 408). Under Augustus, 82 temples had
been erected and restored ([767], Volume 2). The foundation
of the New Rome on the Bosporus is mentioned as follows:
"Byzantium, with its seven hills, had looked very much like
Rome" ([240], page 225). However, the question would arise:
which one of the cities had really resembled the other? The
conclusions that ensue from the decomposition of the global chronological map into a sum of four chronicles, q.v. in
Chron1, Chapter 6, suggest that it had most likely been the
Italian Rome that was built in the XIII–XV century A.D. in
the image of Czar-Grad on the Bosporus.

■ 10.6b. *Third Empire.* Constantine I transforms the New Rome
into a luxurious capital city ([240], page 26). The city was
built as a "capital of stone" and a powerful sea fortress. The
settlement of Byzantium located at that site underwent a
radical reconstruction. A specific administrative structure
was introduced, which is known to have existed in the Italian Rome. Constantine had built a large number of palaces,
a hippodrome, and a great many temples ([327], page 436).

10.7a. *Second Empire.* In the *27th year* of the rule of Octavian
Augustus, Jesus Christ was born. It is from his birth that we
count "the new era" nowadays.

■ 10.7b. *Third Empire.* In the *27th year* of the rule of Constantine
I, the famous Saint Basil the Great was born, apparently a
reflection of Jesus Christ. The parallelism between Jesus
and Basil was first pointed out by N.A. Morozov ([544]).

10.8a. *Second Empire.* Augustus had ruled for 41 or 37 years.
There are two versions of the beginning of his reign – either

the year 27 or 23 B.C. Let us note that the year 23 B.C. marks the beginning of the absolute power period for Augustus: he is granted dictatorship, a lifelong consulate, and unlimited legislative powers ([327] and [579], page 304).

■ 10.8*b. Third Empire.* Constantine I had ruled for 31 years. We have three reign duration versions in his case. We consider the basic version here: 306–337 A.D. The reign durations are similar.

COMMENTARY. Fig.1.5 shows a triumphal statue of Emperor Octavian Augustus, located in Rome. On fig.1.6 we sees an enormous "ancient" statue of Constantine I, the double of Octavian Augustus, in a portico of the Lutheran basilica in Rome ([304], Volume 1, page 572). We shall repeat what we have said about the statues of Pompey and Diocletian. Most likely, the statues of Augustus and Constantine, as well as every similar sculptural image of "antiquity", are not lifetime representations at all, but rather were made in the XVII–XVIII century, the epoch of Reformation, as "visual aids" illustrating Scaligerian history introduced en masse at that time.

11*a. Tiberius.*
■ 11*b. Constantius II.*

11.1*a. Second Empire.* "Right after the death of Augustus, who had left *no direct heir*... the issue of succession arose immediately" ([767], Volume 2, page 412). A struggle for power begins. In face of the uncertainty concerning the identity of his successor, Tiberius, having acceded to the throne, had to fight other pretenders, Germanicus in particular, "on equal terms".

■ 11.1*b. Third Empire.* Constantine I leaves *no direct heir*, but "dividing the empire between his three sons and two nephews" ([327], page 438). Naturally, after the death of Constantine I, a furious power struggle had flared up. Constantine I had brought major confusion afoot, since he had specified no single successor to the throne. Constantius II, having captured "Constantinople, exterminated the families of the two stepbrothers of Constantine" ([327], page 438).

11.2*a. Second Empire.* A while ago Tiberius was *adopted* by Octavian Augustus ([767], Volume 2, page 412). Tiberius is known to have died being "strangled with blankets" [767], Volume 2, page 423. In a sense, this death may be considered *unexpected.*

■ 11.2*b. Third Empire.* Constantius II is the *son* of Constantine I ([327], page 438). Constantius II, as historians tell us, "died *unexpectedly*" ([327], page 440).

11.3*a. Second Empire.* Tiberius *ruled for 23 years:* 14–37 A.D.

■ 11.3*b. Third Empire.* Constantius II had *ruled for 24 years:* 337–361 A.D. The reign durations of the duplicates are similar.

12*a. Struggle between Tiberius and Germanicus. The assassination of Germanicus.*

■ 12*b. Struggle between Constantius II and Constans. The assassination of Constans.*

12.1*a. Second Empire.* Tiberius and Germanicus appear on the political scene simultaneously, as of 6 A.D.([767],

Fig. 1.5. The triumphal statue of emperor Octavian Augustus made of bronze (Rome, Via dei Fori Imperiali). Nowadays it is considered to be a copy from an "ancient" marble original which is kept in the Vatican Museum (see photograph in *Chron1*, Chapter 7). However, a comparison between the "original" and the "copy" demonstrates the two to be ostensibly different from each other. Apparently, in the XVII–XVIII century the manufacture of such "visual aids to the Scaligerian history textbook" assumed the character of mass production, and there was little care about such trifles as similarity between copies and originals. A possible reason may be that the creators were well aware of the fact that there hadn't been any originals anymore – most of them faced destruction in the Reformation epoch of the XVI–XVII century. Taken from [1242], page 60.

Volume 2, page 414). Both come from royal families. Germanicus is Tiberius' *nephew* ([767], Volume 2, page 414). Their destinies are inseparable, with Tiberius playing the *key part*.

- 12.1*b. Third Empire.* Constantius II and Constans appear in the political life of the empire virtually at the same time, namely, in 337 A.D. Constans is the co-ruler of his *brother* Constantius II in the West ([327], page 439). Constantius II had always been *dominant* in this pair ([327]).

Fig. 1.6. The "ancient" statue of Constantine I, the double of Octavian Augustus, from the portico of the Lateran Basilica in Rome ([304], Volume 1, page 572).

12.2*a. Second Empire.* At the beginning of his career, Germanicus had accomplished several great victories over barbarians ([767], V. 2, p. 414). He had fought in the West. The ensuing competition and struggle between Tiberius and Germanicus result in Tiberius accusing Germanicus of plotting against him ([767], V. 2, p. 417).

- 12.2*b. Third Empire.* At the beginning of his political career, Constans defeats the barbarians several times ([327]). Likewise Germanicus, he fights successfully in the West. Then a great discord flares up in the empire, allegedly one of a religious nature. As a result, Constantius II and Constans find themselves in *different camps* ([327], page 439).

12.3*a. Second Empire.* Germanicus was soon *assassinated* by Piso, governor-general in Syria. Tiberius, presumably wishing to ward off suspicions of Germanicus' assassination, had arranged a trial over Piso and *executed* him.

■ 12.3*b. Third Empire*. Constans was soon *assassinated* by Magnentius the impostor ([327]). Constantius II launched a campaign against Magnentius in retribution against the assassin of Constans. He took him prisoner and *executed* him ([327]).

12.4*a. Second Empire*. The joint rule of Tiberius and Germanicus *lasted for 13 years*: 6–19 A.D.

■ 12.4*b. Third Empire*. The joint rule of Constantius II and Constans *lasted for 13 years*: 337–350 A.D. The lengths of the duplicates' reigns coincide.

13*a. Caius Caesar Caligula.*

■ 13*b. Caesar Julian.*

13.1*a. Second Empire*. Information about Caligula is scarce ([767], Volume 2). It is known, though, that he had suffered from some mental disease, imagined himself to be a *deity incarnate*, and pursued correspondent behaviour by extremely insalubrious means ([327], page 300, [767], Volume 2, pages 423–422).

■ 13.1*b. Third Empire*. Information about Julian, on the contrary, is plentiful. He is considered to have been an important reformer of religion. However, the actual data concerning the nature of his reforms are rather contradictory. Some Byzantine historians even called him *"The Lord Incarnate"* ([327]). Julian is considered to have been the "restorer of pagan worship". His reforms ended in a failure.

13.2*a. Second Empire*. Caligula is *assassinated* as a result of a plot ([327], page 301). The details of the plot are unknown. Legend has it that Caligula had received his name – "Caligula", or, allegedly, *"Soldier's Boot"*, for having worn *soldier's boots* as a child.

■ 13.2*b. Third Empire*. Julian is *assassinated* on a march, allegedly with a dart. The assassin remains unknown. By and large, there are many legends about his death ([327], page 441). Julian is considered to have been an ardent worshipper of Mithras, and a priest of this god. One of important distinguishing features of the Mithraist priests was that the latter had worn red *soldier's (!) boots,* or *caligulae* ([260], page 69).

13.3*a. Second Empire.* Caligula had *ruled for 4 years: 37–41 A.D.*
■ 13.3*b. Third Empire.* Julian had *ruled for 2 years: 361–363 A.D.* We see similar reign durations.

14*a. Strife after Caligula's death. Short strife under the emperor.*
■ 14*b. Strife after Julian's death. Short strife under the emperor.*

14.1*a. Second Empire.* In 41 A.D., *after Caligula's death, a civil discord begins* in the Second Roman Empire. The *troops* elect Claudius as emperor ([327], page 301).
■ 14.1*b. Third Empire.* In 363 A.D., *after Julian's death, a strife begins* in the Third Roman Empire. The *legionaries* elect Jovian as emperor ([327], page 441).

14.2*a. Second Empire.* The strife lasts for *several months only.* The senate fails to resist the will of the troops ([327], page 301).
■ 14.2*b. Third Empire.*Jovian had "ruled" for *7 months maximum,* and only in the East, as he had had no time for returning to the capital of the empire. We shall recall that at the moment of the election he was on a march ([327], page 441, [76], table 16). The reign durations are thus similar.

15*a. Claudius.*
■ 15*b. Valentinian I.*

15.1*a. Second Empire.* During the *strife* that had lasted for several months, the troops pronounced Claudius emperor. *One year after* Claudius' accession, the *uprising* of Scribonianus flares up in the *northern provinces* of the empire ([327], page 301). This uprising is one of the *most famous* ones in the history of the Second Empire. Scribonianus is a governor-general in Illyria ([327], page 301).
■ 15.1*b. Third Empire.* After the *strife* related to the actions of Jovian in the East, far away from the capital, legions pronounce Valentinian I emperor. *One year after* the accession

of Valentinian I, the *uprising* of Procopius begins in the *northern and eastern provinces* of the empire ([327], page 442). This mutiny is one of the *most notorious* events in the history of the Third Empire. Procopius is a relative of Julian ([327], page 442).

15.2a. *Second Empire. Simultaneously* with the uprising of Scribonianus, a *plot organized by his supporters is uncovered in Rome* ([327], page 301). The troops of Scribonianus and the conspirators are *crushed.*

■ 15.2b. *Third Empire. Simultaneously* with the mutiny of Procopius, a *plot organized by his supporters was uncovered in Rome* ([327], page 442). The troops of Procopius and the conspirators were also *defeated.*

15.3a. *Second Empire.* Claudius begins mass repressions against the residents and the former administration of Rome ([327]). The repressions encounter serious opposition in the troops. The praetorians and the legionaries rebel. The Roman nobility, too, rises against Claudius ([327]). Claudius is *poisoned* ([327]).

■ 15.3b. *Third Empire.* Valentinian I launches the prosecution of large groups of the supporters of Procopius. As a response to the repressions, discontent in the troops flares up, involving "many strata of the society" ([327], page 442). The only report about the death of Valentinian I tells us that "he had *died unexpectedly*" ([327], page 442).

15.4a. *Second Empire.* Claudius had *ruled for 13 years:* 41–54 A.D.
■ 15.4b. *Third Empire.* Valentinian I had *ruled for 11 years:* 364–375 A.D. The reign durations are similar.

16a. *"Joint rule" of Claudius and Pallas within the "Triumvirate": Claudius, Pallas, Narcissus.*
■ 16b. *"Joint rule" of Valentinian I and Valens within the "Triumvirate": Valentinian I, Valens, Gratian.*

16.1a. *Second Empire.* The three characters mentioned above are normally ranked by their influence in this empire as follows:

1) Claudius, 2) Pallas, 3) Narcissus. Under Claudius, the "triumvirate" comes to power, namely, Claudius himself and his two influential minions – Pallas (Valens?) and Narcissus (Gratian?). They exert a great influence upon the policy of the empire ([767], Volume 2, page 426).

■ 16.1*b. Third Empire.* The ranking of these characters by their influence is as follows: 1) Valentinian I, 2) Valens, 3) Gratian. Valentinian I organizes the "triumvirate" in the following way: he appoints Valens his co-ruler, with Gratian assisting him in the West, from 367 and on ([327], pages 441–442). One cannot but note the similarity between the names of the duplicates: *Pallas* and *Valens.* The names of Gratian and Narcissus may also be related to each other in some way.

16.2*a. Second Empire.* The "joint rule" of Claudius and Pallas *does not exceed 13 years in duration.*

■ 16.2*b. Third Empire.* The "joint rule" of Valentinian I and Valens *lasts for 11 years.* The reign durations are similar.

17*a. Nero (Tiberius Claudius Nero).*
■ 17*b. Valens.*

17.1*a. Second Empire.* After the *poisoning* of Claudius, Nero, the stepson of Claudius, becomes emperor ([767], Volume 2, page 789). Nero is notorious for confiscations, persecutions and numerous murders that took place during his reign ([767], Volume 2, page 431). This notably distinguished Nero among the emperors of the Second Empire. He repeatedly replenished the treasury by means of mass expropriations.

■ 17.1*b. Third Empire.* After the *"unexpected death"* of Valentinian I in 375, Valens, Valentinian's brother, remains the sole ruler. He stands out for terrorizing the country: murders, persecutions and "political purges". Like Nero, he had often used mass confiscations in order to replenish the state treasury ([327]). Valens was also known as *Valens the Goth* ([269], p. 7).

17.2*a. Second Empire.* Nero's policy causes resentment in the Second Empire and results in the so-called "plot of 65". This *plot* is headed by the representatives of the empire's *supreme nobility* ([767], Volume 2, page 437). However, the plot becomes *uncovered*, and the would-be uprising suppressed. After this, Nero launches major repressions. This leads to mass denunciations ([767], Volume 2).

■ 17.2b. *Third Empire.* The cruel actions of Valens had increased tension in the Third Empire. A *plot* against Valens resulted in the uprising of Procopius to flare up. The plot was headed by the *supreme nobility* of the empire ([327], page 442). However, the plot was *uncovered* and the rebellion of Procopius got suppressed ruthlessly, with mass repressions coming in its wake. Numerous public denunciations followed as a result [327].

17.3a. *Second Empire.* Nero is known to have been a vehement *persecutor of the Christians*. They describe the ill-famed burnings of Christians – the so-called "Nero's torches of tar" ([767], Volume 2). Anti-Christian repressions were especially commonplace in Rome. At the end of Nero's rule, the position of the Second Empire is noted to have seriously worsened.

■ 17.3b. *Third Empire.* Valens persistently *persecutes Christians*. Certain sources consider him to have been an Aryan. During his reign, the famous Saint Basil the Great suffers from repressions (the "Passions" of St. Basil the Great, q.v. in [544], Volume 1). Since Basil the Great is a phantom reflection of Jesus Christ ([544]), it is possible that these events reflect the Gospels. In that case, "vicious Valens" is a reflection of the Evangelical "vicious King Herod".

17.4a. *Second Empire.* The *uprising* of Julius Vindex became the culmination of this troubled period ([327], page 306). It flared up in Aquitania, *on the border of the empire*. Let us note that there had been no conspiracy in Rome. The rebels sought help in the *western provinces* of the empire calling out to dethrone Nero ([767], Volume 2, page 438). Governor-generals of the Pyrenean peninsula provinces joined the uprising ([327], page 306).

■ 17.4b. *Third Empire.* The *insurrection* of the Goths on the river Danube in 376 is regarded as a special event of that troubled epoch ([327], page 443). The uprising took place *on the borders of the empire*. However, there was no conspiracy in Rome. The Goth rebels had sought help in the *western provinces* of the empire, calling for the dethronement of Valens ([767], Volume 2, page 443). Moesia and Thracia had joined in the insurrection ([767], Volume 2).

17.5a. Second Empire. Upper-German legions had destroyed Vindex, but turned against Nero right away, demanding a new emperor ([327], page 306). Nero *attempts to escape*, but *perishes* during the pursuit. Let us note that the full names of Nero and his predecessor, Claudius, *resemble each other*, q.v. above. The full names both contain *the same* formula: Claudius Tiberius Nero Drusus Germanicus ([72]).

■ *17.5b. Third Empire.* The rebels destroy the troops sent against them by the government ([767], Volume 2, page 443). Valens also *attempts to escape,* but *ends up killed* ([767], Volume 2, page 443). The names of Valens and his predecessor – Valentinian I – are very similar: *Valens* and *Valen*tinian.

17.6a. Second Empire. Nero *rules for 14 years:* 54–68 A.D.

■ *17.6b. Third Empire.* Valens *rules for 14 years:* 364–378 A.D. The reign durations coincide.

18a. Joint rule of Nero with Burrus and Seneca. Death of Burrus.

■ *18b. Joint rule of Valens with Valentinian I and Gratian. Death of Valentinian I.*

18.1a. Second Empire. In this empire, the three indicated characters are ranked by their influence as follows: 1) Nero, 2) Burrus, 3) Seneca. "Policy management in the first half of Nero's rule had been in the hands of philosopher Seneca and praetor prefect Burrus" ([767], Volume 2, page 430). At this time, Burrus had even held the key position in this "triumvirate", since he educated Nero ([327], page 305). But in reality Nero, the emperor, had been the key figure of authority.

■ *18.1b. Third Empire.* The ranking of these characters is as follows: 1) Valens, 2) Valentinian I, 3) Gratian. In the very beginning of the rule of Valens, Valentinian I had managed the policy as the elder. He is similar to Burrus in this respect. Thus, Valentinian I had been the first in the "triumvirate" during this period ([76], table 16). Gratian took the third place after Valens. But, of course, it is actually Valens the emperor who had been first there. Therefore, we list him first.

18.2a. *Second Empire.* Nero reigned jointly with Burrus for 8 years, 54–62 ([327], page 305). Seneca had been the co-ruler of Nero for most of his term as emperor, that is, 54 to 65 A.D.

■ 18.2b. *Third Empire.* Valens had ruled together with Valentinian I for 11 years: 364–375 ([327]). Gratian, the double of Seneca, had ruled together with Valens virtually throughout the entire term of Valens as emperor, 367 to 378. The reign durations are similar.

19a. *"Joint rule" of Nero and Seneca:* 54–65 A.D.

■ 19b. *Joint rule of Valens and Gratian:* 367–378 A.D. Both joint rules last for 11 years. Durations coincide.

20a. *Servius Sulpicius Galba.*

■ 20b. *Jovian.*

20.1a. *Second Empire.* Galba was pronounced emperor by the troops. He abolished nearly all the orders and decisions of his predecessor (767], Volume 2).

■ 20.1b. *Third Empire.* Jovian was declared emperor by the troops. He had decisively "broken with the past" and abolished the orders and decisions of his predecessor (767], Volume 2).

20.2a. *Second Empire.* Galba had ruled for about 1 year: 68–69 ([767], Volume 2, page 789, [327], page 208).

■ 20.2b. *Third Empire.* Jovian had ruled for about 1 year: 363–364 A.D. ([767], Volume 2, page 793). The durations are similar.

21a. *Strife.*

■ 21b. *Strife.*

21.1*a. Second Empire.* In the year of 69, after the death of Galba, a *civil* war breaks out. Its duration *does not exceed 1 year* ([327], page 309).

■ 21.1*b. Third Empire.* In the year 378, right after the death of Valens, a *civil* war breaks out. Its duration *does not exceed 1 year,* either ([327], page 443). The strife periods have similar durations.

22*a. Two Titus Flavius Vespasians:* Titus Flavius Vespasian and his successor, another Titus Flavius Vespasian.

■ 22*b. Gratian* – after the death of Valens; *Valentinian* II – also after the death of Valens.

22.1*a. Second Empire.* The names of these two rulers coincide. They are considered to have been father and son ([767], Volume 2, page 789; also [327], pages 309–310). This "double Titus" had ruled for a total of 12 years, 69–81, *in the West.*

■ 22.1*b. Third Empire.* After the death of Valens in 378, Gratian and Valentinian II remain the only rulers of the empire. Both *rule in the West.* The duration of their joint rule equals 13 years: 379–392 (see [767], Volume 2, page 793). The duplicate reigns have similar durations.

23*a. Titus Flavius Domitian.*

■ 23*b.* Theodosius I the Great.

23.1*a. Second Empire.* Domitian becomes emperor after the "double Titus". Chronicles ([327], page 313) emphasize the fact that he had concentrated enormous power in his hands. Domitian demanded that "he, when addressed, was to be called Lord and God" ([327], p. 319).

■ 23.1*b. Third Empire.* Theodosius I the Great comes to power in the east of the empire while the pair of emperors – Gratian and Valentinian II – rules in the west. He acquires enormous influence throughout the empire, and considerably enhances its influence in the east ([327], p. 444, and [767], V. 2, p. 793). Theodosius I is known to have been an extremely pious ruler, also in full control of the ecclesiastical power in the empire [327].

23.2a. Second Empire. Under Domitian, "the Roman provinces *of the Balkan Peninsula* had found themselves threatened" ([327], page 314). The Dacian rebellion had made the frontier troops of Domitian suffer bitter defeat ([327]). The Second Empire enters a lengthy and hard war against Dacians thereafter.

■ *23.2b. Third Empire.* Under Theodosius I, the uprising of the Visigoths set the Roman provinces *of the Balkan Peninsula* in turmoil. The troops dispatched by Theodosius I were put to rout ([327]). The Third Empire had started arduous and prolonged war against the Visigoths.

23.3a. Second Empire. Domitian negotiates a *truce* with the Dacians, which is considered to be unfavourable for the Second Empire. Although the Dacians were considered "allies" at that time, relations between the two parties remained extremely strained ([327], page 316). Nevertheless, this peace pact with the Dacians is regarded as one of the *most important* ones ever signed by the Second Empire ([327]). The truce in question was signed in *the eighth year* of Domitian's rule.

■ *23.3b. Third Empire.* Theodosius I had bribed the Goths and signed a *peace treaty* with them ([327], page 444). The treaty is considered to have been unsuccessful for the Third Empire, since the Goths "formed a semi-independent state within the Roman Empire" thereafter ([327], page 444). The treaty with the Goths also ranks among the *key treaties* of the Third Empire ([327]). The treaty was signed in *the seventh reign year* of Theodosius I ([327], page 444). Thus, if we superimpose the Second Empire over the Third, we shall see that a very important treaty had been signed the same year. This, among other things, identifies the *Dacians* as the *Visigoths*.

23.4a. Second Empire. The war of the Second Empire against the Dacians was followed by a domestic uprising – the plot of Saturninus etc. Severe repressions had followed as Domitian's response. The emperor had died in the atmosphere of discontent and confusion that prevailed throughout the Second Empire ([327]).

■ *23.4b. Third Empire.* After the war against the Visigoths, unrest flares up in the Third Empire, allegedly of a religious origin; we see reports of massacre, plunder, and arson ([327], page 444). Theodosius commences sweeping repressions. He dies in the atmosphere of overall civil unrest and rumblings in the Third Empire ([327]).

23.5a. *Second Empire. Domitian had ruled for 15 years:* 81–96 ([327], pages 444–445; also [767], Volume 2, page 793).

■ 23.5b. *Third Empire. Theodosius I had ruled for 16 years:* 379–395 ([76], table 16). The reign durations are similar.

24a. *Marcus Cocceus Nerva.*
■ 24b. *Eugenius.*

24.1a. *Second Empire.* Immediately after the death of Domitian, Nerva becomes emperor in the west. His reign *lasts for 2 years:* 96–98 ([327], page 317).

■ 24.1b. *Third Empire.* After Theodosius I, Eugenius becomes emperor in the West. He *rules for 2 years:* 392–394 ([767], Volume 2, page 793). The reign durations coincide.

25a. *Joint rule of Nerva.*
■ 25b. *Joint rule of Eugenius.*

25.1a. *Second Empire.* Throughout his entire reign, Nerva had ruled jointly with Trajan, and the famous emperor eventually "outshone" Nerva. The duration of this joint rule is *2 years:* 96–98.

■ 25.1b. *Third Empire.* Throughout his entire reign, Eugenius had ruled jointly with Theodosius I the Great – the famous emperor that had "stolen Eugenius' thunder". This joint rule lasts for *2 years:* 392–394. Durations coincide.

26a. *Marcus Ulpius Trajan.*
■ 26b. *Arcadius.*

26.1a. *Second Empire.* Trajan's rule is considered to have been the beginning of the "golden age" in the Second Empire ([327], page 317). While still in power, Trajan wages *three major wars.*

■ 26.1*b. Third Empire.* In 395, Emperor Arcadius (the name translating as "joyful") assumes power over "the rich and civilized East" ([327], page 445). Arcadius also wages *three major wars* during his reign.

26.2*a. Second Empire.* Trajan's enemy in the Balkans is Decebalus, a well-known chieftain of the *Dacians* ([327]). The war against Decebalus is Trajan's *first* one, one he had waged right after his accession – or, more precisely, in the third year of his rule. As we stated above, little is known about the first three years of Trajan's rule. Decebalus is a well-known commander in the history of the Second Empire. His name may possibly hail back to "Daci-bella", or the war with the Dacians.

■ 26.2*b. Third Empire.* The famous Alaric, chief of the Visigoths, is Arcadius' enemy in the Balkans. Again, *we identify Visigoths as the Dacians,* as seen in paragraph 23 above. The war against Alaric is the *first* one waged by Arcadius, one that started immediately after his accession ([767], Volume 2). Alaric is a legendary commander in the history of the Third Empire. His name might possibly have been pronounced "Ala-Rex". Thus, Decebalus and Alaric may have not been names in the contemporary sense – aliases, more likely.

26.3*a. Second Empire.* The Great Roman Army of Trajan engages in an all-out war with Decebalus, one that had lasted for *2 years* ([327] and [767], Volume 2). Finally, the Second Empire forged a truce with Decebalus ([767], Volume 2, page 789). Decebalus had taken advantage of this armistice to consolidate his army, and became the commander of a large body of troops in several years' time. Then he violated the truce by having started the second war against the Dacians.

■ 26.3*b. Third Empire.* A large Roman army, headed by Roman general Stilicho, had been fighting Alaric for *two years.* As a result, the Third Empire had signed a peace treaty with Alaric [767], Volume 2, page 793. During the armistice, Alaric had built up his strength and formed a powerful army in several years. Afterwards, he also violated the truce, and started the second war with the Goths.

26.4a. *Second Empire.* The second war against the Dacians rages for *several years.* The outcome of the war is rather uncertain. Rome arranges for another armistice. After a short lull, a *third* war begins, this time against Parthia; this one also takes a few years to finish.

■ 26.4b. *Third Empire.* The second war against the Visigoths rages on for *several years.* The outcome of the war is uncertain. The empire forges another truce with the Visigoths. After a fairly calm period, the *Third Gothic War* flares up, also lasting for several years.

26.5a. *Second Empire.* The empire loses the third war. Rome suffers a bitter defeat ([767], Volume 2). We can conclude by saying that Trajan's main enemy had been Decebalus in *the Balkans.*

■ 26.5b. *Third Empire.* The Third Empire loses the last war as well. Moreover, this had been an actual defeat of Rome, since it was Stilicho, the Roman commander that loses the war. Thus, Arcadius's main enemy had been Alaric, who also came from the *Balkans.*

26.6a. *Second Empire.* Trajan had ruled for either *19 years:* 98–117, or *16 years:* 101–117. It has to be noted that very little is known about the first three years of his rule ([327], page 318; also [767], Volume 2).

■ 26.6b. *Third Empire.* Arcadius had ruled for *13 years:* 395–408 ([767], Volume 2, page 793; also [76], tables 16–17). Reign durations are similar.

27a. *Publius Aelius Hadrian.*
■ 27b. *Honorius.*

27.1a. *Second Empire.* Hadrian was adopted by Trajan, his predecessor. Let us also note that Adrian is a relation of the emperor Trajan's wife ([327], page 322).

■ 27.1b. *Third Empire.* Honorius and Arcadius, his predecessor, had been *brothers* ([327]).

27.2a. *Second Empire.* Under Hadrian, the Roman army falls into

71

utter decline ([327], page 324). As one can see below, similar events take place under Honorius, the duplicate of Hadrian. Moreover, these two processes of armies sliding into decline – under both Hadrian and Honorius – are so similar that the contemporary books on the history of Rome describe them *in virtually the same words*. We shall cite two such descriptions to illustrate. This is how historians describe the decay of the Roman army in Hadrian's epoch: "Seeing as how many Roman citizens had refused to serve in the legions, Hadrian introduced the practice of reinforcing the ranks of legionaries by representatives of a different social stratum than the residents of the provinces, who had the rights of Roman citizenship, namely, common free provincials. The legionaries had finally lost their "Roman" character and turned into a multinational force, which had been armed with Roman weapons and used Latin as the official language" ([327], page 324). This is how the Roman army had disintegrated under *Hadrian*.

■ *27.2b. Third Empire*. Let us now cite the description of the Roman army in the time of *Honorius*: "The Roman troops of the time had looked nothing like the legions of early empires. Although they had carried on calling themselves legions, both the armament and the organization of the Roman army had changed completely after the massacre at *Adrian*ople. They had transformed into an army of barbarian soldiers… Most of the military commanders were barbarian chieftains bearing Roman military ranks" ([327], page 324). Nowadays, the rout of the Roman troops near *Adrian*ople, in the alleged year 378, is linked to this deterioration in the state of army affairs. Thus, the name of *Hadrian* appears in the biography of his doppelganger Honorius precisely "in the right place", manifest as "the massacre of Adrianople". This is how a very demonstrative parallelism between the Second and Third Roman Empires appears on the pages of contemporary historical books, not recorded as a system previously.

27.3a. Second Empire. Hadrian had been afflicted by a *serious illness*. He was a very suspicious person, and had sired no children ([327], pages 322–325). A brief example of how he had treated his military leaders is as follows: having suddenly suspected a plot among his commanders, he inflicted a series of harsh repressions upon them. Chronicles mention no names, and only refer to schemers "among the supreme officers of the army" ([327], page 322).

■ *27.3b. Third Empire.* Honorius had been notorious for his *frail health*, and also considered weak-minded. He had left no children ([327], page 449; also [64], page 33). The attitude of Honorius to his commanders exposes his paranoid tendencies. In the alleged year of 408, he treacherously murdered his best military leader Stilicho, who had been accused of plotting against Honorius. All of this "plotting" is supposed to have been slander ([767], Volume 2, page 793).

27.4a. Second Empire. Hadrian had forged his most important *truce* with Parthia. Let us recall that the war against Parthia is identified as the war against *Alaric* in the Third Empire, q.v. above.

■ *27.4b. Third Empire.* Honorius had signed a very important *peace treaty* (by the order of Arcadius), namely, the treaty with *Alaric*.

27.5a. Second Empire. Hadrian had *ruled for 21 years:* 117–138 A.D.
■ *27.5b. Third Empire.* Honorius had *ruled for 28 years:* 395–423. Reign durations are fairly similar. The above data are taken from [327], page 325, [767] (Volume 2, page 793), and [76]. Let us note that old chronicles would normally preserve nothing but a number of scraps and extracts from the rulers' biographies. Therefore, sometimes even minor facts that have managed to survive by sheer accident acquire great importance as the only evidence of the past, and should by no means remain neglected.

28a. Antoninus Pius.
■ *28b. Aetius.*

28.1a. Second Empire. Emperor Antoninus Pius succeeds Hadrian: 138–161 ([767], Volume 2, page 789).

■ 28.1*b*. *Third Empire.* After Honorius, the 6-year-old Valentinian III is proclaimed Emperor in the west. However, he did not actually rule at all, having been in the custody of Placidia, his mother, who, in turn, had obeyed the will of Aetius. It is said that Placidia "had fallen under the influence... of commander Aetius, a barbarian by birth" ([64], pp. 33, 40). Aetius thus becomes acknowledged as *the official custodian* of Valentinian III ([767], V. 2, p. 757). For many years Aetius remained *the autocrat* of the Third Empire. Theodosius II, his co-ruler in the east, is considered to have been an insignificant figure without any actual influence on the policy of the empire ([64], p. 35).

28.2*a*. *Second Empire.* The reign of Antoninus Pius was a raging storm. Numerous chaotic wars – against the Dacians, the Germans, and in the East of the Empire ([327], page 326) – had raged all across the land during his reign. Antoninus Pius is known to have been a most successful general indeed. Despite the great number of his enemies, he had managed to guard the borders of the empire with a great deal of efficiency.

■ 28.2*b*. *Third Empire.* The epoch of Aetius was also filled with wars and conflicts. Waves of "barbarian hordes" had repeatedly raided the Third Empire over that period ([767], Volume 2). Chronicles also describe Aetius as an excellent professional commander. He had been the triumphant leader of the Empire's numerous military campaigns ([64], page 34).

28.3*a*. *Second Empire.* Antoninus Pius was extremely resourceful in his domestic policy, considering the general instability of the Second Empire. In particular, he would make advances to the lowest strata of society, give away stocks of food, and curb the rights of masters over their slaves ([327], page 325; also [767], Volume 2, page 789).

■ 28.3*b*. *Third Empire.* Due to his barbarian origin, Aetius had been under pressure to keep fortifying his position in Rome. His domestic policy was very flexible. He had also won the sympathies of the most diverse strata of the Roman populace. He is known to have been a prominent Roman politician in an epoch of civil unrest ([64]).

28.4a. *Second Empire.* Antoninus Pius had *ruled for 23 years:* 138–161 ([767], Volume 2, page 789).

■ 28.4b. *Third Empire.* Aetius had *ruled for 21 years:* 423–444 (or 14 years: 423–437, according to another version). Mark the fact that in 437 the authority of Aetius was dealt a heavy blow by Valentinian III, whose custody had then come to its end, and who had become a de facto ruler ([64], p. 486). Nevertheless, Aetius had enjoyed a formal influence until the year 444; however, after the loss of several important battles in 444, his falling out of grace had become irreversible ([64], p. 486).

29a. *Marcus Aurelius.*
■ 29b. *Valentinian III.*

29.1a. *Second Empire.* After Antoninus Pius, the power passes on to Aurelius – *the adopted son* of Antoninus Pius ([327], page 326). Marcus Aurelius *rules jointly* with Lucius Verus ([327]). Moreover, Lucius Verus *is younger* than Marcus Aurelius [327].

■ 29.1b. *Third Empire.* After Aetius, the power goes to Valentinian III – the "adopted son" of Aetius. Let us recall that Aetius was *the custodian* of Valentinian III. Valentinian III *rules jointly* with Theodosius II, who governs over the east of the empire. Although Theodosius II had been older than Valentinian III (q.v. in [327]), it was Theodosius II who was usually referred to as "the youngster" ([76]).

29.2a. *Second Empire.* Lucius Verus *is subordinate* to Marcus Aurelius. They say that "the empire had actually been ruled by the elder – Marcus Aurelius" ([327], page 326). Lucius Verus, his younger age notwithstanding, had died before the end of Aurelius's reign ([327], pages 326–327).

■ 29.2b. *Third Empire.* Initially, Valentinian III had been dependent on Theodosius II, but their roles became reversed subsequently ([327]). We see the scenario from the Second Empire recurring. Furthermore, Theodosius II also died *before* the rule of Valentinian III had ended.

29.3a. *Second Empire.* Marcus Aurelius faces a number of major difficulties that "transformed almost the entire period of their [co-rulers' – A.F.] principate... into a time of bloody wars and economic depression" ([327], page 326).

- ■ 29.3b. *Third Empire*. Valentinian III is also forced to face a number of serious challenges. His reign in the Third Empire is marked by truculent wars and economic troubles. The empire begins to slide into decline ([327] and [64]).

29.4a. *Second Empire*. Under Marcus Aurelius, a ferocious military campaign against the well-known King Vologaeses ([327]) begins – a long-drawn war with varying success. Finally, a peace treaty with Vologaeses is reached, in no way implying security for the *Second Empire*. Immediately after the signing of the treaty, a war against nomadic tribes, which broke through the Roman frontier fortifications, begins on the Danube ([327], p. 280).

- ■ 29.4b. *Third Empire*. Under Valentinian III, a bloody war against King Attila ([327]) begins – a protracted one, with success favouring both sides unevenly. The empire had negotiated a truce with Attila, which brought no real peace. Right after the signing of the truce, barbarians invade the empire, which subsequently becomes involved in a series of exhausting wars – in the west and in the east, at different times ([767], Volume 2, page 38).

We have approached the final phase of parallelism between the Second and the Third Roman Empire. In both empires, the hard and troubled times set in simultaneously. As we proceed, we shall primarily follow the events that had taken place in the west of the *Third Empire*. The ties between the east and the west are considered to have gradually weakened, from Theodosius II and on.

30a. *Commodus*.
- ■ 30b. *Recimer*.

30.1a. *Second Empire*. After the death of Marcus Aurelius, his son Commodus becomes emperor. The rule of Commodus *stands out* against others, since several *influential minions* had emerged in his time ([579], pages 405–406).

■ 30.1*b. Third Empire.* In 455, after the death of Valentinian III, a talented commander-in-chief by the name of Recimer works his way up to the very top of the Third Empire's hierarchy. He acquires enormous influence in Rome and becomes its actual ruler for several years. According to his contemporaries, "Recimer has by now become *the most powerful* person in Western Rome" ([579], page 487). The rule of Recimer has a *notable feature:* during his reign, there had been several *influential imperial minions,* all of them pawns of the Emperor de facto ([579], pages 487–490). The comparison of the two influential minion groups in the Second and the Third Empires exposes the two as duplicates.

30.2*a. Second Empire.* The *first* proxy ruler under Commodus was called Perennis. He had soon got killed, likewise his Third Empire double Petronius, q.v. below ([579], pages 405–406).

■ 30.2*b. Third Empire.* The *first* proxy emperor under Recimer had been Petronius Maximus. He was killed three months later ([579], page 487). The two names (Petronius and Perennis) may stem from the same root.

30.3*a. Second Empire.* The *second* proxy ruler under Commodus had borne the name of Cleander; he was withdrawn from his position of power by Commodus a short while later ([579], pages 405–406).

■ 30.3*b. Third Empire.* The *second* proxy ruler under Recimer was called Mecilius Avitus. Recimer had made him surrender the throne rather soon ([579], pages 486 and 488).

30.4*a. Second Empire.* The *third* proxy ruler under Commodus was named Eclectus; it doesn't take Commodus too long to strip him of his powers ([579]). Furthermore, we still have assorted data telling us about other proxy rulers under Commodus – a certain Marcia, for instance ([579]). This proxy co-ruler shuffling ends with the death of Commodus.

■ 30.4*b. Third Empire.* The *third* proxy emperor under Recimer was called Flavius Julian Majorian. Recimer had made him ruler, but soon revoked the rule ([579]). We also have rather sparse data concerning other creatures of Recimer's – such as Libius Severus and Anthemia ([579]). This endless changing of proxy co-rulers also ended with the death of Recimer in the Third Empire.

30.5a. Commodus had either *ruled for 16 years* (176–192 A.D.) or *12 years* (180–192 A.D.). 180 A.D. is the year when his father died.

■ 30.5b. *Third Empire.* Recimer *ruled 16 years* (456–472 A.D.). The durations coincide (for the first version of Commodus' reign).

31a. *Publius Helvius Pertinax.*
■ 31b. *Olybrius.*

31.1a. *Second Empire.* Pertinax had ruled for less than a year, in 193 A.D. We know very little of him; the complex situation in the Second Empire is pointed out ([579], pages 406–407).

■ 31.1b. *Third Empire.* Olybrius had reigned for less than a year in 472 A.D. There is hardly anything known about him. The Third Empire's situation is critical ([579], page 490). The reign durations all but coincide.

32a. *Marcus Didius Severus Julian.*
■ 32b. *Glycerius.*

32.1a. *Second Empire.* The reign of Didius Julian is shorter than a year and falls on 193 A.D. We hardly know anything about him at all. His rule is accompanied by a great embroilment ([579], page 407).

■ 32.1b. *Third Empire.* Glycerius had reigned for less than a year in 473 A.D. We know little about him; his rule was accompanied by a great strife ([579], page 490). The reign durations in both cases are virtually identical.

33a. *Decimus Clodius Albinus.*
■ 33b. *Julius Nepos.*

33.1a. *Second Empire.* Clodius Albin had reigned for less than a

year in 193 A.D. We don't know much about him; his entire
reign is accompanied by civil unrest ([579], p. 407).

■ 33.1*b. Third Empire.* Julius Nepos had reigned for less than one
year in 474 A.D. There is very little biographical information available of this ruler nowadays. His reign is marked by
embroilment ([579], p. 490). Reign durations are virtually
identical.

34*a. Gaius Pescennius Niger.*
■ 34*b. Romulus Augustulus.*

34.1*a. Second Empire.* Niger's reign had lasted *one year* – 193–194
A.D. He was *defeated* by Severus and *deposed* ([767], Volume
2, page 790; also [579], page 407).

■ 34.1*b. Third Empire.* Romulus Augustulus had only reigned for
one year in 475–476 A.D. Odoacer *defeated* and *dethroned* him
([767], V. 2, p. 794; also [579], p. 490). Reign durations coincide.

35*a. Lucius Septimius Severus.*
■ 35*b. Odoacer.*

35.1*a. Second Empire.* Severus was proclaimed emperor after
Niger, and is related to *Germany*, where had been crowned
([579], page 408). Severus had defeated Pescennius Niger, the
double of Romulus Augustulus from the Third Empire. Niger
got *killed* after the battle – cf. Orestes, the father of Romulus,
from the Third Empire.

■ 35.1*b. Third Empire.* Odoacer, leader of the *German* Heruls in the
Roman army, was crowned emperor after Romulus Augustulus. Constantinople recognizes his authority ([767], Volume
2, page 760. Odoacer had crushed the troops of Romulus
Augustulus led by Orestes, the father of Romulus. Orestes was
murdered. Odoacer deposed Romulus ([579], page 493).

35.2*a. Second Empire.* Severus had been "a strong ruler … this
leader was prudent and earnest" ([579], page 409). The rule of
Severus "is an important breakpoint in many regards" ([579],
page 409). We are approaching the end of the Second Empire.

■ *35.2b. Third Empire.* Odoacer is known to have been a sensible and modest ruler. He had tried to restore the unity of the Third Empire that kept falling apart ([579]). The reign of Odoacer is also considered a *breakpoint* in Roman history marking the end of the "purely Roman" dynasty. We see the first symptoms of the Third Empire's decline. Its last two rulers had been foreign – Odoacer the German and Theodoric the Goth.

35.3a. Second Empire. Severus had fought a single war, albeit an arduous one, struggling against the Parthian king Vologaeses IV. The course of the war kept changing: "The North was forced to suppress the Northern peoples that had lived close to the border, which had also been a formidable task" ([579], page 410).

■ *35.3b. Third Empire.* Odoacer's only enemy had been Theodoric the Goth; the war between the two went down in history as long, violent and wearisome. Success would favour both parties unevenly. Finally the Goths led by Theodoric invaded the Empire from the North. Odoacer was defeated and surrendered in one of the battles. He had been made a co-ruler initially, but his assassination followed before too long ([579], page 493).

35.4a. Second Empire. Severus had *reigned for 18 years* between 193 and 211.

■ *35.4b. Third Empire.* Odoacer had *reigned for 17 years* (476–493 A.D.). Reign durations are similar.

36a. Caracalla.
■ *36b. Theodoric the Goth (the Great).*

36.1a. Second Empire. Caracalla had been a *co-ruler* of Severus and reigned in the *West.* He had constantly struggled against his co-ruler Publius Septimius Geta. Both brothers "hated one another and sowed permanent discord amidst the troops, likewise in the court; they had even thought of *dividing the state*" ([579], page 410).

- ■ *36.1b. Third Empire.* Theodoric had been the *co-ruler* of Odoacer in the *West*. The reign of Theodoric is accompanied by very abrasive relations between himself and his eastern co-ruler Anastasius. This opposition would often break out into military conflicts ([579], pages 495–496). Both co-rulers already rule in the *divided* Third Empire – the Western and the Eastern.

36.2a. Second Empire. The domestic policy of Caracalla is characterized by the chronicles as rather lenient. His efforts to make the army obedient resulted in the *corruption* of the latter which, in turn, had impaired the discipline, according to [579]. Caracalla "granted *full civil rights* to each and every imperial community" ([579], page 410).

- ■ *36.2b. Third Empire.* Theodoric's domestic policy was also known for its great flexibility and religious tolerance. He was renowned a patron of the arts, and had also greatly indulged in the *bribery* of the troops due to his status of a foreigner in Rome and his ambition to secure support for himself amongst wider society strata ([579]). Theodoric had made foreigners *equal to Romans in rights* and instigated large-scale migrations on imperial territory.

36.3a. Second Empire. In 217 A.D. Caracalla was *preparing a campaign* against the Parthians and died at the peak of the preparations ([579]).

- ■ *36.3b. Third Empire.* In 526 Theodoric *launches a campaign* against the barbarians but dies before the preparations are over ([579], page 495).

36.4a. Second Empire. Caracalla had *reigned for 24 years* (193–217 A.D.) or *6 years* (211–217 A.D.), 211 A.D. being the year of Severus' demise.

- ■ *36.4b. Third Empire.* Theodoric's *reign lasts 29 years* (497–526 A.D.) or *33 years* (493–526 A.D.). Theodoric came to power in 493, the year of Odoacer's death – however, it was only in 497 A.D. that Zeno in Constantinople had acknowledged his rule ([579], p. 494). The durations are close enough (first versions).

This is where the dynastic currents of the Second and the Third Empire end. However, amazingly enough, the parallelism that binds them together can be traced further, spanning the alleged years 217–235 A.D. and 526–536 A.D.

37a. *Second Empire* ceases to exist in a blaze of warfare and anarchy. The period of 217–270 A.D. is officially known as that of "political anarchy of the middle of the III century, or the time of 'soldier emperors'" in Scaligerian history ([327], page 406). This prolonged period of anarchy is a unique phenomenon in the history of the Second Empire.

■ 37b. The decline of the *Third Empire* (in the West) was accompanied by bloody wars and social discord. The period of 526–552 A.D. is officially known as one of "political anarchy in the middle of the III century. The Ostrogothic rule in Italy" ([579]). This epoch of strife and embroilment is also unique in the history of the Third Empire. As we can see, these two periods (duplicates, as we understand it now) are characterized in the same words by Scaligerite historians.

38a. *Julia Maesa.*
■ 38b. *Amalasuntha.*

38.1a. *Second Empire.* After the death of Caracalla, the power in the Second Empire is inherited by Julia Maesa in 217 (after a very brief reign of Macrinus, a former slave) – see [327], pages 404–406. Julia Maesa is a *relation* of Caracalla's ([327]). Near Julia Maesa we see her *daughter* Mamea, occupied with matters of secondary importance.

■ 38.1b. *Third Empire.* After the death of Theodoric (the double of Caracalla), Amalasuntha inherits the power in the Third empire ([579], pages 498–499). Amalasuntha is one of the most famous women in the entire history of Rome ([196]). She is the *daughter* of Theodoric ([579]). Her sister Matasuntha played a secondary part as her ally. Let us emphasize that the two duplicates (Julia Maesa and Amalasuntha) are the most prominent female rulers in the history of both empires. They were the only ones who had the power to crown Roman Emperors. Their unvocalized names (MSL for Maesa Julia and MLSNTH for Amalasuntha) might be derived from the same root.

38.2a. *Second Empire.* Julia Maesa enthrones her elder son – Varius Avitus Bassianus (Marcus Aurelius Atoninus) known as Heliogabalus ([327], pages 405–406), who *obeys her every word.* He *dies a violent death.* Heliogabalus had *reigned for 4 years* (218–222 A.D.; see [327]).

■ 38.2b. *Third Empire.* Amalasuntha enthrones her son Amalaric ([579], pages 405–406), who *obeys her every word.* He *dies a violent death.* Amalaric had *reigned for 5 years* between 526 and 531 A.D. We observe similar reign durations.

38.3a. *Second Empire.* Julia Maesa hands the reins of power over to Alexander Severus, a meek and indecisive man and an obedient creature of Julia Maesa ([327]). The reign length of Alexander Severus equals *13 years* (222–235 A.D.).

■ 38.3b. *Third Empire.* In the Third Empire we observe Athalaric, the second minion of Amalasuntha, come to power. He had been perfectly obedient to Amalasuntha ([579]). Athalaric had *reigned for 8 years* (526–534 A.D.) – see [76], table 18.

Reign durations differ, but they don't affect the general correlation of the entire current of events that characterize the Second and the *Third Empire.*

38.4a. *Second Empire.* Julia Maesa was killed in 234 A.D. The end of her reign is marked by the war with the *Persians* in the East of the Empire ([327]). 3 years after the death of Julia Maesa, a large-scale war against the *Goths* breaks out – the *Gothic war* of 238–251 A.D. ([64]).

■ 38.4b. *Third Empire.* Amalasuntha was killed in 535 A.D. At the end of Amalasuntha's reign, a war against the Orient breaks out – namely, with the *Persians* and with Constantinople. This is how the famous *Gothic war* of the VI century A.D. began ([579]).

Thus, in order to conclude the parallelism, we compare the period of the alleged years 217–234 A.D. at the end of the Second empire to that of the alleged years 526–535 A.D., when the Third Roman Empire ceased to exist in the West. The parallelism does in fact span subsequent epochs as well; however, it is rather difficult to relate, since we enter parallel epoch of violent civil wars, and their history is fragmentary and extremely vague; we shall therefore end our comparison table here.

However, we must point out the following important fact. Once we reach the last days of the Second Empire (the alleged year 270 A.D.), we discover having approached the first days of the Third Empire. Let us remind the reader that this is the very year that marks the superimposition of the Third Empire over the Second. The period of the alleged years 240–270 A.D. that separates the Second Empire from the Third is considered the heyday of political anarchy in Scaligerian history. It is written that "by the time Claudius II came to power [in 268 A.D. – A. F.] there had de facto been no united empire" ([327], page 410). Thus, 270 A.D., the year we discover to correspond to the beginning of the Third Empire, needed to be referred to as one of the empire's "reconstruction" after a presumed period of utter disarray. However, this very "disarray" is of a fictitious nature, and only became recorded in historical sources as a result of an erroneous chronology.

2.

The correlation between two different dating methods illustrated by the superimposition of two epochs from the history of Roman Papacy one over the other. A brief scheme

The dating method based on the principles of frequency damping and duplication was applied to the dynastic current of the Roman Popes that begins in the alleged I century A.D. with Paul the Apostle and exists until the present day. We have used the chronological tables of J. Blair ([76]) and the list of popes given in [544].

The time interval in question (amounting to some 1900 years) was divided into short 10-year intervals. Then we compiled an exhaustive list of all the names of Popes who occupied the Holy See between the alleged I century A.D. and 1700 A.D. 89 different papal names were ordered in accordance with the sequence of their first appearance in papal currents. After that, a rectangular matrix sized 89 × 170 was constructed by the author of the present book assisted by A. Makarov. Each row of the matrix possesses the length of 170 units and represents the frequency evolution of a single name out of the list of 89. The matrix contains 89 rows and 170 columns altogether. Each papal name is marked as corresponding to the decade of said pope's ascension. The row numbered 53, for instance, lists all the decades when the Holy See was occupied by a pope named *John*. They fall on the following years: 523–526, 532–535, 560–573, 640–642, 685–686, 704–707, 872–882, 898–900, 914–928, 931–936, 956–963, 965–972, 983–984, 985–996, 997–998, 1003, 1003–1009, 1024–1033, 1285–1287, 1316–1334, 1410–1415.

Afterwards, the duplicate localization method based on the calculation and processing of frequencies $K(Q, T)$ was applied to the resultant rectangular frequency matrix. As a result, a square frequency matrix sized 170 × 170 was built. Each of its rows numbered Q contains the values of $K(Q, T)$ demonstrating the manifestation frequency of names that first appeared in decade Q in the subsequent decade T as well as the exact amount of times a certain name is manifest. The value of $K(Q, Q)$ stands for the papal names from decade Q that we haven't come across in the papal list as to yet.

A study of the papal name frequency matrix immediately reveals several circumstances of the utmost interest. For example, we learn that the names of the I century popes (such as Linus, Anacletus, Clement and Evaristus) are unexpectedly "revived" in the XI century A.D., which corresponds perfectly well to the chronological shift of 1000–1050 years.

Similarly, other duplicates spawned by the chronological shift of 333 years approximately are also manifest in the frequency matrix. Higher concentrations of the name John, for instance (q.v. above) fall on the middle of the VI century A.D., the end of the VII century, the X century and the end of the XIII century. As we shall demonstrate below, this corresponds excellently to how the phantom duplicates of the T series that we discovered in the "Scaligerian history textbook" are distributed along the time axis, q.v. in fig. 1.7. The matter is that John happens to be one of the key names in history of the XIII century war and its duplicates.

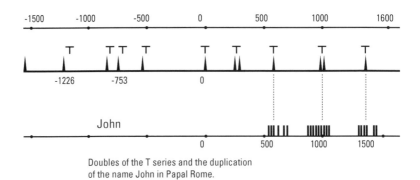

Doubles of the T series and the duplication
of the name John in Papal Rome.

Fig. 1.7. Phantom duplicates of the T series and the duplication of the name John in Papal Rome between the I and the XVI century. Let us point out that higher concentrations of the name fall directly over the duplicates of the T series.

Further studies of name frequency matrices (as built for lists containing the names of Popes, Byzantine Pontifices, Roman and Byzantine emperors etc.) were subsequently carried out by the author together with G. V. Nosovskiy. The results are related in our scientific publications ([593], [594], [595], [596] and [597], in particular); see also the Annexes to *Chron7*. These works contain a great body of numerical material as well as frequency matrices, and also a modification of the frequency damping principle formulated in terms of a "card deck shuffling" problem.

All of our results correspond to the facts discovered with the use of the dynastical parallelism method. In Chapter 6 of *Chron1* we indicate two isomorphic "parallel" Papal dynasties that we have discovered. Bear in mind that the list of the Pope, likewise the Imperial list, is considered to be the "spinal column" of Roman and European chronology. The modern list of Popes is based on the *Book of the Pontifices* whose origins cannot be traced further back than the XIII century A.D. ([196]).

The biography of the first pope (Peter the Apostle) and his seven successors up until St. Hyginus (137–141 A.D.) is considered quite vague in the modern "Scaligerian textbook". S. G. Lozinskiy, for instance, wrote that "in reality, we only encounter veracious information about the Episcopes of Rome [as the Popes were called in the alleged first centuries of the new era – A. F.] starting with III A.D. – and even this information contains many gaps… the mythical character of pre–120 A.D. pontifices is also recognized by the Protestant theologists" ([492], page 312).

Our method of dynastic parallelisms led us to the discovery that the Roman Episcopate period of 140–314 A.D. duplicates that of 314–532 A.D., q.v. in *Chron1*, Chapter 6. VSSD coefficient here equals 8.66×10^{-8}. In particular, they turn out to be phantom reflections of a later mediaeval list of popes. Out of the 47 popes that we find in the period of 141–532 A.D., 43 are covered by the parallelism, leaving just 4 short-term popes beyond it ([76]). Both duplicates are therefore extremely representative.

It is important that this collation of ecclesiastical Roman chronicles concurs perfectly well with the independent secular collation of imperial chronicles that we mention above.

3.

The superimposition of the Israelite (Theomachist) kingdom over the Third Roman Empire in the West.
A shift of circa 1230 years

This parallelism was also discovered by the VSSD calculation method, confirming the claim made in [544] that the "ancient" kingdoms of Israel and Judea can be identified as the "early mediaeval" Roman empire. VSSD here equals $c(a, b) = 1.3 \times 10^{-12}$.

One must be aware of the fact that the name Israel translates as Theomachist ([544], Volume 1, pages 416 and 437) – God's warrior, in other words, or a fighter against foreign gods. Therefore, the word "Israelite" can also be translated as "Theomachist", as we shall be doing from time to time. The word Judean translates as "Theocratic" ([544]); it may have been used for referring to priests. There is hardly any point in delving deep into translation details, since they are of no importance to us.

In the Scaligerian chronology, the Israelite kingdom between Jeroboam I and Uzziah is dated to the alleged centuries X–VII B.C., or years 922–724 B.C. ([72], page 192). Since the Third Roman Empire is dated to the alleged IV–V century B.C. by the Scaligerites (don't forget that the dynastical current from this empire that is of interest to us presently dates to the alleged years 306–476 A.D.), the chronological shift (or superimposition) that we discovered between the Biblical and Roman kingdoms roughly equals 1230 years here. In other words, "ancient" history of Israel and Judea needs to be moved forward in time by 1230 years at the very least – and even this result will be far from final, as we already demonstrated in *Chron1*,

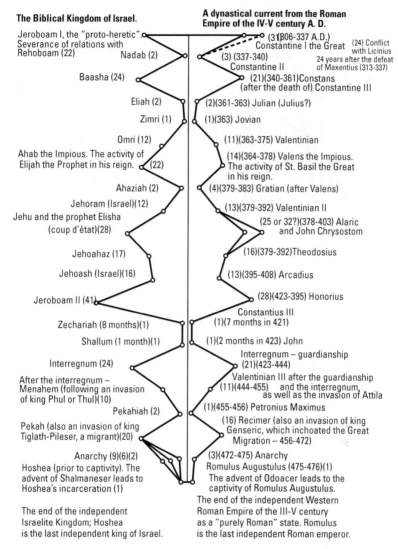

The Biblical Kingdom of Israel.

Jeroboam I, the "proto-heretic".
Severance of relations with
Rehoboam (22)   Nadab (2)

Baasha (24)

Eliah (2)

Zimri (1)

Omri (12)

Ahab the Impious. The activity of
Elijah the Prophet in his reign.   (22)

Ahaziah (2)

Jehoram (Israel)(12)
Jehu and the prophet Elisha
(coup d'état)(28)

Jehoahaz (17)

Jehoash (Israel)(16)

Jeroboam II (41)

Zechariah (8 months)(1)

Shallum (1 month)(1)

Interregnum (24)

After the interregnum –
Menahem (following an invasion
of king Phul or Thul)(10)
Pekahiah (2)

Pekah (also an invasion of king
Tiglath-Pileser, a migrant)(20)

Anarchy (9)(6)(2)
Hoshea (prior to captivity). The
advent of Shalmaneser leads to
Hoshea's incarceration (1)

The end of the independent
Israelite Kingdom; Hoshea
is the last independent king of Israel.

**A dynastical current from the Roman
Empire of the IV-V century A. D.**

(306-337 A.D.)
Constantine I the Great   (24) Conflict
(3) (337-340)   with Licinius
Constantine II   24 years after the defeat
                      of Maxentius (313-337)
(21)(340-361)Constans
(after the death of) Constantine III

(2)(361-363) Julian (Julius?)

(1)(363) Jovian

(11)(363-375) Valentinian

(14)(364-378) Valens the Impious.
The activity of St. Basil the Great
in his reign.

(4)(379-383) Gratian (after Valens)

(13)(379-392) Valentinian II

(25 or 32?)(378-403) Alaric
and John Chrysostom

(16)(379-392)Theodosius

(13)(395-408) Arcadius

(28)(423-395) Honorius

Constantius III
(1)(7 months in 421)

(1)(2 months in 423) John

Interregnum – guardianship
(21)(423-444)
Valentinian III after the guardianship
(11)(444-455)   and the interregnum,
                as well as the invasion of Attila
(1)(455-456) Petronius Maximus

(16) Recimer (also an invasion of king
Genseric, which inchoated the Great
Migration – 456-472)

(3)(472-475) Anarchy
Romulus Augustulus (475-476)(1)
The advent of Odoacer leads to the
captivity of Romulus Augustulus.
The end of the independent Western
Roman Empire of the III-V century
as a "purely Roman" state. Romulus
is the last independent Roman emperor.

Fig. 1.8. The reign correlation of the "ancient" Biblical kingdom of Israel and the Third "ancient" Roman Empire.

Chapter 6. Biblical history needs to be moved forward by another 600 years at the very least.

According to the Bible, the kingdoms of Israel and Judea represent the two dynastical branches of a state that had initially been united, which is similar to the division of the formerly united Roman Empire into the Western and the Eastern parts. The first three Biblical kings (Saul, David and Solomon) had ruled a united state, which fell apart immediately after Solomon. Jeroboam I becomes the first independent Theomachist king, and Rehoboam – the first independent king of the Theocrats.

We already mentioned the fact that the Bible contains a "double entry system" that allows for easy conversions between respective Israelite and Judaic reigns, q.v. in *Chron1*, Annex 6.4. These data shall be used in the present section as well. Bear in mind that the parallelism between the Israelite Kingdom and the Third Roman Empire is of a secondary nature, being but a reflection of more fundamental parallelisms that we shall relate in the chapters to follow.

Let us cite two parallel dynastic currents of a secondary nature, using a single number to indicate two "parallel rulers", q.v. in fig. 1.8.

1*a. Jeroboam I* – reigned for 22 years.
■ 1*b. Constantine I* had reigned for 24 after his victory over Maxentius – 313–337 A.D.

2*a. Nadab* – 2 years.
■ 2*b. Constantine II* – 3 years (337–340 A.D.).

3*a.* Baasha – 24 years.
■ 3*b. Constantius II* – 21 years (340–361 A.D.).

4*a.* Ilas – 2 years.
■ 4*b. Julian* – 2 years (361–363 A.D.).

5*a. Zimri* – less than 1 year.
■ 5*b. Jovian* – less than 1 year in 363 A.D.

6*a. Omri* – 12 years.
■ 6*b. Valentinian* – 11 years (364–373 A.D.).

7*a. Achab* (and Elijah the Great Prophet) – 22 years.
■ 7*b. Valens* (and the famous St. Basil the Great) – 14 years (364–378 A.D.)

8*a. Achaziah* – 2 years.

■ *8b. Gratian* – 4 years (379–383 A.D.)

9a. Joram of Israel – 12 years.
■ *9b. Valentinian II* – 13 years (379–392 A.D.)

10a. Jehu and Elijah the Prophet (28 years).
■ *10b.* A lacuna (or, according to another version – *Alaric* and
   John Chrysostom the prophet (25 years – 378–403 A.D.)

11a. Jehoahaz – 17 years.
■ *11b. Theodosius* – 16 years (379–395 A.D.)

12a. Jehoash of Israel – 16 years.
■ *12b. Arcadius* – 13 years: 395–408 A.D.

13a. Jeroboam II – 14 years.
■ *13b. Honorius* – 28 years (395–423 A.D.)

14a. Zechariah – less than 1 year (6 months).
■ *14b. Constantius III* – less than 1 year (7 months) – 421 A.D. or
   423 A.D.

15a. Shallum – less than 1 year (1 month).
■ *15b. John* – less than 1 year (2 months) – 423 A.D.

16a. Interregnum – 24 years.
■ *16b. Interregnum/custody* – 21 years (423–444 A.D.)

17a. Menahem – 10 years.
■ *17b. Valentinian III* – 11 years (444–445 A.D.)

18a. Pekahiah – 2 years.
■ *18b. Petronius Maximus* – 1 year (455–456 A.D.)

19a. Pekah – 20 years.
■ *19b. Recimer* – 16 years (456–472 A.D.)

20a. Anarchy – 2, 6 or 9 years (three versions).

■ 20*b. Anarchy* – 3 years (472–475 A.D.)

21*a. Uzziah* (before falling captive to Shalmaneser) – 1 year or 3 years.
■ 21*b. Romulus Augustulus* (before falling captive to Odoacer) – 1 year (475–476 A.D.)

A) The emperors of the Third Roman Empire that ended up in this dynastical current have reigned in the West for the most part – presumably, in Italian Rome. Those of the emperors listed whose primary residence had been in Constantinople had been so powerful that they played a dominant role in the West of the empire as well, often even with a Roman co-ruler present. Let us further point out that the kingdom of Israel is covered by this parallelism *completely*.

B) Both dynasties begin with prominent political and religious leaders. In particular, we have Jeroboam I, the famous progenitor of "Jeroboam's heresy". His double, Constantine I Augustus (or "Holy") is presumed to be the first patron of Christianity. The naissance and the establishment of Arianism (a possible analogue of Jeroboam's heresy) take place in his reign.

Jeroboam I struggled against Rehoboam of Judah, who had *broken away* from him, while Constantine I battled against Licinius, who had also *initiated a secession*.

Under Jeroboam I the formerly united Biblical kingdom becomes *divided in two* – the kingdoms of Judah and Israel. The same happens under Constantine I when the formerly united Roman empire becomes *divided* into two parts, the Western and the Eastern. Constantine I went so far as to move the imperial capital from Rome in Italy to New Rome on the Bosporus.

The united Biblical kingdom had been ruled by *three prominent kings* – Saul, David and Solomon. The Third Roman Empire also has *three famous rulers* at its very beginning – Aurelian = Sulla, Diocletian = Pompey, and Constantius I Chlorus = Julius Caesar. They are the duplicates of the Biblical Saul, David and Solomon.

According to the Bible, the Israelites were *divided into 12 tribes*. Likewise, under Constantine I the Roman empire was divided into 12 dioceses, or regions. In the kingdom of Israel, a *thirteenth* tribe joined the other twelve eventually – the offspring of Dinah. The same thing happened in the Roman Empire under Constantius II, the son of Constantine I, when a *thirteenth* diocese was added to the abovementioned twelve ([544], Volume 7).

C) Both dynasties end with rulers who fall under the power of a foreign king. In the kingdom of Israel it's Uzziah who becomes Shalmaneser's (Czar Solomon's?) captive, whereas in the Third Roman Empire we have Romulus Augustulus deposed by Odoacer, also a foreign king. Shalmaneser is King of *Assyria*, whereas Odoacer is a *German* king. What we have is the "ancient" Assyria superimposed over the mediaeval Germany (or Prussia, = White Russia?). See more on this subject in *Chron5*.

Both of the dynasties under comparison cease their existence under these duplicate kings. Bear in mind that the last two emperors of the Third Roman Empire (Odoacer and Theodoric) aren't Roman anymore – they are foreigners. Among other things, they are said to have practised a different religion. This circumstance may have played a certain role in how they became reflected on the pages of the Bible, which is a distinctly religious source.

D) The anarchy and interregnum periods coincide for both dynasties.

E) There are many stunning parallels in the "biographical" currents of the Israelite and Roman rulers. The form-codes of these dynasties coincide.

We must point out that we give the translations of the Biblical names according to [544].

1*a. Jeroboam I* (Protector of the People).
■ 1*b. Constantine I Augustus.*

1.1*a. Israel.* The name "Jeroboam" could have stood for "The *Holy Clarion*" in Greek pronunciation ([544], Volume 7, page 338). Jeroboam I came to power together with Rehoboam (1 Kings 11:43, 12:2–3 and 19–20). They shared the formerly united kingdom between the two of them.
■ 1.1*b. Third Empire.* The name "Augustus" of Constantine I also stands for *"Holy"*. Constantine I was declared a saint equal to the Apostles in rank. He and Licinius acquire absolute power in the East and in the West, respectively ([327], page 429).

1.2a. *Israel.* Jeroboam I *"rebelled"* against Rehoboam in the first year of his reign, *severing all relations between the two* (1 Kings 12:19–20). The Bible proceeds to tell us that *"there was war between Rehoboam and Jeroboam all their days"* (1 Kings 14:30).

■ 1.2b. *Third Empire.* Constantine I *severs all ties* with Licinius at the very beginning of his reign, after the victory over Maxentius in 313. This leads to a war between them ([327], page 429). Licinius "was *assaulted* by his co-ruler Constantine already in 314" (*ibid.*). Constantine I wages constant wars against Licinius.

1.3a. *Israel.* Under Jeroboam, "Israel rebelled against the house of David unto this day" (1 Kings 12:19). Jeroboam I *transferred the capital* of the state to the city of Sechem (1 Kings 12:25). Let us point out that Jeroboam I is the *only* king of Israel who had moved the capital city as a result of the foundation of a new state.

■ 1.3b. *Third Empire.* Around 330, Constantine I *moves the imperial capital* from Rome in Italy to New Rome on the Bosporus. This important event signified the beginning of the Roman Empire's division into two parts – the Eastern and the Western. Constantine I is the *only* emperor of the Third Empire to transfer the capital; this coincided with the foundation of the new Eastern Roman Empire.

1.4a. *Israel.* In order to prevent the restoration of Rehoboam's rule, Jeroboam I also seceded from him ecclesiastically. *He had founded a new religious movement* known as "Jeroboam's heresy" (1 Kings 12:28 and 12:31). This "heresy" was adhered to by all of the subsequent Israelite kings. It played a major part in the entire history of the Theomachist Israelites. Bible refers to "Jeroboam's heresy" in the biography of each Israelite king after Jeroboam.

■ 1.4b. *Third Empire.* Constantine I Augustus (The Holy) is occasionally called the *founder of Orthodox Christianity* in Christian sources. Modern historians acknowledge the only fact out of the numerous legends about Constantine, namely, that he had founded a certain cult, possibly of a "heretical" nature. The fact that he had been a Christian is often disputed. It was under Constantine I that Arius, the founder of *Arianism*, had first emerged with his teaching ([579], pages 466–467). Arianism is a well-known Christian "heresy" that had made a significant impact on the entire history of the Third Roman Empire ([579]).

1.5a. *Israel.* The reign duration of Jeroboam I equals *22 years* (1 Kings 14:20).

■ 1.5b. *Third Empire.* Constantine I had reigned for *24 years* between 313 and 337, counting from the beginning of his joint rule and the struggle against Licinius, after the defeat of Maxentius. Other versions claim his reign duration to have equalled 13 or 31 years, q.v. above. The durations are rather close to each other.

2a. *Nadab* (The Generous).
■ 2b. *Constantine II.*

2.1a. *Israel.* Nadab is the son of Jeroboam I (1 Kings 15:25). Nadab came to power immediately after the death of his father (ibid). The Bible emphasizes that King Nadab *adhered to Jeroboam's heresy*: "And he did evil in the sight of the Lord, and walked in the way of his father" (1 Kings 15:26).

■ 2.1b. *Third Empire.* Constantine II was the son of Constantine I ([327]). Constantine II came to power *immediately after the death of his father* ([327]). He successfully *carried on with the religious policy of Constantine I* ([327]). The Biblical author may well have regarded this as "walking in the way of his father".

2.2a. *Israel.* Nadab was killed by Baasha, who had seized the throne of Israel (1 Kings 15:28). Baasha became the next king. "Even in the third year of Asa king of Judah did Baasha slay him, and reigned in his stead" (1 Kings 15:28). Asa, king of Judah, might simply be a reflection of Jesus Christ.

■ 2.2b. *Third Empire.* Constantine II had launched a campaign

THE ISSUE WITH ANTIQUITY

against his brother Constans and got killed in a battle ([327], page 438). Constans, the killer of Constantine II, becomes the next Roman emperor, ruling jointly with the third brother – Constantius II ([327]). This happens immediately after the death of Constantine II in 340 ([767], Volume 2, page 468). The joint rule of the three brothers began in 337; Constantine II was killed in either the *fifth* or the *seventh* year of St. Basil the Great, or The Great King (basileus = king), who is most likely to be a reflection of Andronicus, or Jesus (Asa?) from the XII century A.D. Let us point out that there are two versions for the birth date of Basil the Great. The most common one cites the year 333; the other one insists on 335 ([544], Volume 1). We see a very good concurrence of these data with the Biblical indications.

2.3*a*. *Israel*. Nadab's reign lasted *2 years* (1 Kings 15:25).

■ 2.3*b*. *Third Empire*. Constantine II had reigned for *three years* between 337 and 340 ([327], page 792; also [767], Volume 2, page 468). Reign durations are similar.

3*a*. *Baasha* (The Creator).

■ 3*b*. *Constantius II*.

3.1*a*. *Israel*. Baasha came to power as the killer of his predecessor Nadab, King of Israel. King Baasha *was following Jeroboam's heresy*, or "walked in the way of Jeroboam" (1 Kings 15:34). Baasha *initiated a massacre* of his fellow tribesmen: "And it came to pass, when he reigned, that he smote all the house of Jeroboam; he left not to Jeroboam any that breathed, until he had destroyed him" (1 Kings 15:29). Baasha chose *Tirzah* as his capital; the name might actually refer to *Turkey*.

■ 3.1*b*. *Third Empire*. Constantius II came to power as one of the killers of his predecessor Constantine II. Historians report that "Constantius united the entire state under his rule once again. *Church disputes, which he took part in*, had played an important part in his reign" ([579], page 469). Constantius II had *massacred the kin* of Constantine I, the double of the Biblical Jeroboam I. He had *killed all the family members* of the two half-brothers of Constantine ([327], page 438). Constantius II resided in Constantinople, and had lived in Asian provinces for a long time; he relocated to *Turkey* in 335 ([327]). This is basically what the Bible tells us, q.v. above.

3.2*a*. *Israel*. Baasha's reign duration equals *24 years* (1 Kings 15:33).
- 3.2*b*. *Third Empire*. Constantius II reigned for *21 years*, between 340–361 (after the death of Constantine II). Another version dates his reign to 337–361 (*24 years*), from the moment that his joint rule with Constantine II began ([327]). Reign durations are similar.

4*a*. *Elah* ("The God", or "The Sun").
- 4*b*. *Julian* ("The Lord").

4.1*a*. *Israel*. Elah was the *son* of Baasha (1 Kings 16:8). It has to be pointed out that the Biblical formula "son" often refers to religious succession and not actual kinship. The name Elah ("The Lord") concurs well with the name of his "Roman double" Julian.
- 4.1*b*. *Third Empire*. Julian is presumed to have been a *cousin* of Constantius II, the double of the Biblical Baasha. Constantius II had no children ([579]). Julian was *deified* while still alive; he is known as a religious reformer.

4.2*a*. *Israel*. Despite the fact that King Elah had possessed such a grandiloquent name ("The God"), the Bible hardly tells us anything about him at all. This is all the more egregious when compared to the detailed "biographies" of the Israelite kings whose names were a great deal more "modest". Let us remind the reader that the Bible is a religious source that pays a lot of attention to the religious policies of the rulers referred to therein.
- 4.2*b*. *Third Empire*. Julian ("The God") became reflected in ecclesiastical history under the alias of "The Apostate". He is considered to have been the archenemy of Christianity and a restorer of paganism. The information on this emperor found in the Christian sources is extremely sparse and

very negative. On the other hand, secular Roman historians (Marcellinus, for instance) dedicate voluminous exalted pan-egyrics to Emperor Julian, glorifying his deeds ([579]).

4.3a. *Israel.* King Elah was killed by Zimri, his *command-er-in-chief* (1 Kings 16:10). The Bible gives us no details of the murder. Elah's reign lasted for *2 years* (1 Kings 16:8).

■ 4.3b. *Third Empire.* Emperor Julian was killed during a cam-paign in the East under uncertain circumstances. The next emperor is Jovian, who had been the *commander-in-chief* of Julian's army ([579], page 472). Julian's reign lasted for *2 years* (361–363, see [767], Volume 2, page 793; also [579] and [327]). Reign durations coincide.

5a. *Zimri* ("Singer of hymns").

■ 5b. *Jovian.*

5.1a. *Israel.* Zimri was the *commander-in-chief* in the army of his predecessor Elah, whom he had killed (1 Kings 16:9–16:10). Zimri came to power *in the 27th year* of Asa (Jesus?), king of Judah (1 Kings 16:10).

■ 5.1b. *Third Empire.* Jovian was the *commander-in-chief* in the army of Emperor Julian, his predecessor, and had accom-panied him in the Persian campaign ([579], page 472). There are many legends about the murder of Julian. At any rate, Jovian had been Julian's successor. One of the versions claims Julian to have been a victim of a plot. Jovian ascended to the throne in 363, *in the 30th year* of St. Basil the Great – possibly a duplicate of Asa (Jesus). Bear in mind that Basil is presumed to have been "incarnated" in 333, which gives us $30 = 363 - 333$.

5.2a. *Israel.* Zimri followed Jeroboam's heresy: "For his sins which he sinned in doing evil in the sight of the Lord, in walking in the way of Jeroboam, and in his sin which he did, to make Israel to sin." (1 Kings 16:19). Also: "In the twenty and seventh year of Asa king of Judah did Zimri reign seven days in *Tir-zah.*" (1 Kings 16:15). Thus, Zimri's reign lasted *7 days*.

- **5.2b.** *Third Empire.* "Jovian was a Christian" ([579], page 472).
  This might be why the Bible mentions that he had "walked
  in the way of Jeroboam". Jovian's reign began in the East, near
  Turkey, during the campaign. He had reigned for *less than
  one year* ([767], Volume 2, page 793; also [327]). The entirety
  of this brief period was spent on the march when Jovian was
  returning to the imperial capital. According to some of the
  sources, he never reached it. Reign durations are similar.

6a. Omri ("The Head").
- **6b.** *Valentinian I.*

6.1a. *Israel.* Omri, the successor of Zimri, had been the *commander-in-chief* in the army of his predecessor (1 Kings 16:16).
  Omri's *reign began in the 31st year* of Asa, King of Judah
  (Jesus?) (1 Kings 16:23).
- **6.1b.** *Third Empire.* Valentinian I, who became emperor after
  Jovian, had been the *commander-in-chief* in the army of the
  latter ([327], page 441. Having ascended to the throne in
  364, Valentinian I *became emperor in the 31st year* of St. Basil
  the Great, the reflection of Jesus Christ – or, possibly, Asa of
  Judah, considering how 364 – 333 = 31. In both cases we see
  that the ascension to the throne takes place *in the 31st year.*

6.2a. *Israel.* Omri waged a violent war against Tibni who had
  claimed his right to the throne of Israel (1 Kings 16:21–22).
  Omri ended up *winning* the war (1 Kings 16:22). Tibni the
  claimant was *killed* (1 Kings 16:22).
- **6.2b.** *Third Empire.* Valentinian I *battled* against Procopius, a
  relation of Julian who had claimed his right for the Roman
  throne. Valentinian I *won* this war ([327] and [767], Volume
  2). Procopius was *killed* ([327], page 442).

6.3a. *Israel.* Omri had *transferred* his residence to the city of
  Samaria located *on a hill or near a hill* (1 Kings 16:24). Omri
  had been renowned for *cruelty*: "But Omri wrought evil in the
  eyes of the Lord, and did worse than all that were before him"
  (1 Kings 16:25).

■ 6.3*b*. *Third Empire.* Valentinian I *transferred* his residence to Rome in the west. One must bear in mind that there is a famous *mountain* near Rome – the volcano Vesuvius. Valentinian I was *distrustful and cruel.* Together with his brother Valens they created a very tense political climate in Rome, especially after the defeat of Procopius. Valentinian I had executed a large number of Romans ([327], page 442).

6.4*a*. *Israel.* Omri wasn't killed, but rather "slept with his fathers" peacefully (1 Kings 16:26–28). His reign had lasted 12 years (1 Kings 16:23).

■ 6.4*b*. *Third Empire.* Valentinian I may have died a natural death; it is however reported that "his death came suddenly" ([327]). His reign duration equals 11 years (364–375, q.v. in [327] and [767], Volume 2; also [76]).

7*a*. *Ahab* ("The Uncle"). Elijah, the great prophet, was active during his reign.

■ 7*b*. *Valens.* The famous prophet and saint (Basil the Great) was active in his reign.

7.1*a*. *Israel.* King Ahab is described in the Bible at length (3 Kings 17–22). He is one of the most notorious kings of Israel, and one of the most rigorous ones as well (1 Kings 22). The Bible characterizes Ahab as a particularly "impious king". Apart from following "Jeroboam's heresy" he also "went and served Baal, and worshipped him" (1 Kings 16:31–33). The term "Ahab the impious" became denominative in later literature.

■ 7.1*b*. *Third Empire.* Valens is one of the most notorious Roman emperors. In particular, he is presumed to have been one of the cruellest rulers of the Empire. Bear in mind that his duplicate from the Second Empire is another notorious and cruel ruler – Nero. Valens is described very negatively in Christian sources. He was a "devout Arian" – a heretic, as it were ([579], page 674). The wickedness of Valens and his duplicate Nero is reflected in Christian literature as a classical embodiment of all negative qualities.

7.2*a. Israel.* The famous Biblical prophet Elijah begins his career under Ahab (1 Kings 21:17 ff). The name Elijah translates as "God" ([544], Volume 7). The relations between Ahab and Elijah the prophet are hostile (1 Kings 21: 17–29). Opposition between them soon leads to *direct confrontation* (1 Kings 21:20–23).

■ 7.2*b. Third Empire.* Basil the Great, the famous Christian Saint, is active in the reign of Valens. Legends about him are identical to the ones told about Jesus Christ. The relationship between Basil and Valens is a very strained one, and eventually leads to an *open conflict*, q.v. in the *Menaion* ([544], Volume 1).

7.3*a. Israel.* The "biography" of Ahab as related in the Bible is the story of his interactions with the prophet Elijah for the most part (1 Kings 21:17–29). The Bible, being a religious source, naturally pays attention to such facts. Ahab had been scared of Elijah, "and went softly" (1 Kings 21:27).

■ 7.3*b. Third Empire.* Fragments of the biography of Valens as presented in the *Menaion* are covered as the story of opposition between Valens and St. Basil the Great. Valens had been "afraid of Basil". Quotation given according to [544], Volume 1.

7.4*a. Israel.* Ahab wages war against "the King of Syria" (1 Kings 22). Ahab's army is defeated. Ahab himself gets seriously wounded during his escape from the battlefield, and soon dies (1 Kings 22:37–38).

■ 7.4*b. Third Empire.* Valens fights the Goths ([327]). Once again we see the Biblical *Syrians*, or Assyrians, identified as the mediaeval *Goths*. The troops of Valens are crushed; he gets killed as he flees the battlefield, likewise his double Nero from the Second Roman Empire ([327] and [767], Volume 2).

7.5*a. Israel.* The Bible portrays the notorious Jezebel, Ahab's wife, in the most unfavourable manner: "the dogs shall eat Jezebel" (1 Kings 21:23). Ahab's reign duration equals 22 years (1 Kings 16:29).

■ 7.5b. *Third Empire.* Since Basil the Great is most likely to be
a phantom reflection of Jesus Christ from the XII century,
Valens can probably be identified as "King Herod" from the
Gospels. The Gospels describe him very negatively, likewise
his wife Herodias. Valens reigned for 14 years (364–378, q.v.
in [327]). A propos, the pair of emperors (Valens + Valentinian I) had reigned for 25 years (14 + 11 = 25). Reign durations are similar in the second version.

8a. *Ahaziah* ("The Lord's Owner").
■ 8b. *Gratian.*

8.1a. *Israel.* Ahaziah is Ahab's successor (1 Kings 22:51). Ahaziah
had reigned in Samaria (1 Kings 22:51). His reign duration
equals 2 years (1 Kings 22:51).
■ 8.1b. *Third Empire.* After the death of Valens in 378, his co-ruler Gratian remains regnant in the West of the empire until
his death in 383 ([327]). Gratian rules in Rome; once again
we see the city identified as the Biblical Samaria. Gratian's
reign duration equals 4 years (379–383) or 5 years (378–383,
q.v. in [327], page 444). The reign durations of the two are
similar. Let us point out that although formally Gratian
remained the sole ruler of the empire from 378 and on, the
entire year 378 was marked by embroilment after the death
of Valens. Gratians's stable reign begins in 379, after the end
of the strife and the civil war, likewise the reign of Theodosius, who was appointed in 379.

9a. *Jehoram* ("The Lord's Archer").
■ 9b. *Valentinian II.*

9.1a. *Israel.* Jehoram had reigned for *12 years* (2 Kings 3:1).
■ 9.1b. *Third Empire.* The reign of Valentinian II lasted *13 years*
after the death of Valens and the civil unrest of 379 (379–
392, q.v. in [767], Volume 2, page 793). Reign durations are
similar.

10a. *Jehu* and the prophet *Elisha.*

■ 10*b*. Lacuna. No duplicate emperor here. One could think
that the parallelism were interrupted here; however, it has
to be pointed out that the gap instantly gets filled once we
turn to the events of the alleged IV–V century that involve
the famous warlord *Alaric*. Thus, we have *Alaric* and *John
Chrysostom* the prophet.

10.1*a*. *Israel.* We see a troubled period in history of the Israelite
kingdom – the *invasion* of Jehu. Elijah's successor in ecclesiastical power is the famous Biblical prophet Elisha (2 Kings
2:9). He is the inspirer and the organizer of a great religious
upheaval in the kingdom of Israel.

■ 10.1*b*. *Third Empire.* The famous troubles in the Third Roman
Empire – Alaric's *invasion*. John Chrysostom inherits ecclesiastical power from Saint Basil the Great. He is a famous
religious figure in the history of the Christian church of the
alleged IV–V century and the initiator of a powerful religious movement in the Third Empire ([542]).

10.2*a*. *Israel.* Jehu the warlord is active in the epoch of the prophet Elisha (2 Kings 9). The name Jehu can be regarded as a
distorted version of *"Jehovah"* ([544], Volume 7, page 344). The
invasion of Jehu is described in the Bible as a barbaric invasion, likewise the rebellion that he leads. Jehu does not belong
to the regnant dynasty of Israelite kings, and is summoned
into the country by Elisha (2 Kings 9). Elisha and Jehu had
ruled in the Kingdom of Israel together (2 Kings 9–10).

■ 10.2*b*. *Third Empire.* The military leader Alaric is active in the
epoch of St. John Chrysostom ([327]). Some sources inform
us of his mediaeval alias *"Wrath of Lord"*. His invasion was
regarded as the advent of Jehovah angered by the sins of the
people ([544], Volume 7, page 345; also [64]). Alaric's rebellion, as well as his invasion, are barbaric in nature. Alaric
was the military commander of the Roman Empire (likewise
the Biblical Jehu), but not the formal leader of the empire
([327]). Apparently, the imperial policy was largely affected
by John Chrysostom in 399–400; Emperor Arcadius is supposed to have acted in accordance with John's advice ([544]).

10.3*a. Israel.* Elisha the prophet castigated Jezebel and finally destroyed her by proxy of Jehu (2 Kings 9). Jezebel was killed (2 Kings 9:30–33). She had been a king's daughter (2 Kings 9:34). At the same time, several Christian authors (Eusebius, for instance) had used the word "wife" for referring to a confession.

■ 10.3*b. Third Empire.* John Chrysostom had vehemently criticised the official church; however, the parallel here isn't quite clear.

10.4*a. Israel.* According to the Bible, Jehu had "*reigned* over Israel" (2 Kings 10:36), anointed by Elisha the prophet (2 Kings 9:6). The allegedly *pagan cult of Baal was overthrown* under Elisha (2 Kings 10:28). "And they brought forth the images out of the house of Baal, and burned them. And they brake down the image of Baal, and brake down the house of Baal, and made it a draught house unto this day" (2 Kings 10:26–27). This is the passage where the Bible condemns and forbids the cult of Baal.

■ 10.4*b. Third Empire.* The invasion of Alaric had stunned the entire Roman Empire. He took Rome in 410. Alaric became *King* of the Goths in 396 ([327], page 446). The *pagan cult becomes downtrodden* in the empire under John Chrysostom. In the alleged year 391 the imperial edict comes out that forbids sacrifices. The last Olympic games take place in 393; all the Olympian temples are *destroyed* the same year ([327], page 444–445). The famous statue of Zeus is taken to Constantinople; pagan religious services are outlawed ([327]).

10.5*a. Israel.* Jehu took part in this religious struggle personally as the persecutor of Baal's cult. Jehu's reign duration equals *28 years* (2 Kings 10:36).

■ 10.5*b. Third Empire.* Alaric also took part in the religious struggle of this period in the Roman Empire. He had been an Arian and persecuted Orthodox Christians ([327]). The "reign" of Alaric and John Chrysostom lasted for either *25 or 32 years.* It has to be explained that the activity of Chrysostom begins in the alleged year 378, after the death of Valens and Basil the Great, the double of the Biblical Elijah.

The *rebellion of the Goths* takes place the same year ([327], p. 443). Chrysostom dies in the alleged year 403. Alaric becomes famous in the alleged year 385, and becomes King of the Goths in 398 ([327], p. 446). Alaric died in the alleged year 410 or 411. Thus, we get the 15 years as the period of 396–411 (Alaric), 32 years as the period of 378–410 (the Gothic rebellion followed by Alaric's reign), or 30 years as the period of 378–407 (Chrysostom).

11a. *Jehoash* ("The Lord's Property")
■ 11b. *Theodosius I.*

11.1a. *Israel.* Jehoash followed Jeroboam's heresy, or "walked in the sins of Jeroboam" (2 Kings 13:2), likewise the previous kings of Israel excepting Jehu. His name can be translated as "the Lord's own". He may have been considered "son of God" (Jehu, or Jehovah?). See [544], Volume 4.

■ 11.1b. *Third Empire.* Theodosius I was a *fanatical* Christian ([327], page 444). Furthermore, from the point of view of an ecclesiastical chronicler, he may have been called "the Lord's own", since the Goths led by Alaric ("Wrath of God") attacked him when they first rebelled in 378.

11.2a. *Israel.* The reign of Jehoash is marked by a single, yet arduous, war against Hazael, king of *Syria* (2 Kings 13:3). The Bible describes Hazael's invasion as barbaric (2 Kings 13). Jehoash lost the war (2 Kings 13:3), but signed a peace with Hazael (2 Kings 13:5). Jehoash *reigned for 17 years* (2 Kings 13:1).

■ 11.2b. *Third Empire.* The war against the *Goths* accompanies the entire rule of Theodosius I. This war was violent, bloody, and arduous. Roman chronicles regarded the invasion of the *Goths* as a barbaric intrusion. In 386, Theodosius I manages to negotiate a truce with the Goths ([327]; also [767], Volume 2). We see another identification of the biblical *Arameans* with the mediaeval *Goths*. Theodosius I had *reigned 16 years: 379–395* ([767], Volume 2, page 793). The reign durations are similar.

12*a. Jehoash of Israel* (God's Fire).

■ 12*b. Arcadius.*

12.1*a. Israel.* Jehoash is the *son* of Jehoahaz (2 Kings 13:10). Next to Jehoash we see the eminent prophet St. Elisha, whose orders were good as law for Jehoash (2 Kings 13:14–20). "Elisha had died… *And now* Moabite raiders invaded the country" (2 Kings 13:20).

■ 12.1*b. Third Empire.* Arcadius is a *son* of Theodosius I ([327], page 445). Next to Arcadius we find a well-known saint, John Chrysostom, whose advice Emperor Arcadius allegedly followed in 400–401 ([542]). St. John Chrysostom *died* in 407. The next year, in 408, Alaric re-invaded the empire.

12.2*a. Israel.* Jehoash wages wars against *two* kings – Hazael and Ben-Hadad (2 Kings 13:3–7, 13:22–25). The Bible calls Hazael King of *Aram* (2 Kings 13:22). Ben-Hadad is his son (2 Kings 13:25). Jehoash *did not succeed* in destroying Hazael completely (2 Kings 13:19).

■ 12.2*b. Third Empire.* Arcadius wages wars against *two* kings – Alaric and Radagaisius. Arcadius *did not succeed* in destroying Alaric's troops completely ([327], page 447). Alaric and Radagaisius were the respective leaders of the *Goths* and the *Germans* [327]. Thus, we encounter another superimposition of the biblical *Arameans* over the medieval *Goths* and *Germans* – probably *Prussians.*

12.3*a. Israel.* Jehoash had continuously been at feud with the king of Judah, who ruled jointly with him (2 Kings 13). Eventually, a war between Jehoash and his co-ruler of Judah broke out (2 Kings 13:12). Jehoash died in the capital and not on the battlefield. His reign duration equals *16 years* (2 Kings 13:10).

■ 12.3*b. Third Empire.* Arcadius had been at feud with his co-ruler Honorius; he'd also had a hated private fiend by the name of Stilicho, the personal commander of Honorius ([327], pages 446–447). In the epoch of the co-rulers Arcadius and Honorius, "a war between Western and Eastern Rome began" ([579], page 478). Arcadius doesn't die on the battlefield, but rather in the capital. His reign lasted for *13 years:* 395–408 [327].

13*a. Jeroboam II* (Protector of People).
■ 13*b. Honorius.*

13.1*a. Israel.* Jeroboam II rules in Samaria (2 Kings 14:23) and fights against the *Arameans*, who attack the kingdom of Israel ceaselessly (2 Kings 14).

■ 13.1*b. Third Empire.* Honorius rules in Rome. Once again we see the already familiar identification of the biblical Samaria as the mediaeval Rome. The rule of Honorius, likewise that of his co-ruler Arcadius, is accompanied by continuous wars against the *Goths* and *Germans.* We observe yet another superimposition of the biblical Arameans over the medieval *Goths* and *Germans* (possibly *Prussians*).

13.2*a. Israel.* Jeroboam II arranges for a short *ceasefire* in this protracted invasion (2 Kings 14: 25–27). "He [Jeroboam – A. F.] *had restored the boundaries* of Israel" (2 Kings 14:25). It must have been the defeat of his enemies, Hazael and Ben-Hadad, described in the following passage of the Bible: "I will send fire upon the house of Hazael [Alaric? – A. F.] that will consume the fortresses of Ben-Hadad [Radagaisius? – A. F.]" (Amos 1:4).

■ 13.2*b. Third Empire.* Honorius manages to *stop* the invasion, arranging for a truce with Alaric in 395 ([327] and [767], Volume 2). In spite of the short duration of the ceasefire, it had led to an *expansion* of the state. Stilicho, the military commander of Honorius, drove the *Goths* back, away from the original boundaries of the Roman Empire ([327], pages 446–447). The troops of Honorius, led by Stilicho, defeated Alaric once again in the alleged year 402. Radagaisius is supposed to have been killed in 405 A.D. Thus, the defeat had been temporary for Alaric and final for Radagaisius ([327]).

13.3*a. Israel.* The "biography" of Jeroboam II mentions Hazael, King of Aram, although, according to the 2nd Book of Kings 13:24, Hazael had died in the times of Jehoash of Israel – the predecessor of Jeroboam II. This probably indicates that Jeroboam II and Jehoash of Israel were *co-rulers.*

■ 13.3*b. Third Empire.* Honorius, the double of Jeroboam II, and Arcadius, the double of Jehoash the Israelite, are considered to have been *co-rulers* in Roman history. The reign of Arcadius covers the period of 395–408, and that of Honorius - 395–423 ([327] and [767], Volume 2).

13.4*a. Israel.* During the rule of Jeroboam II, the prophet St. Jonah gains prominence – an envoy of God who liberates the land from enemies (2 Kings 14:25–27). It is most likely that *Jonah* is a slightly distorted version of the name *John.* Jonah is one of the key figures in the reign of Jeroboam II. It is through Jonah that God helps the kingdom of Israel (2 Kings 14:25). The reign of Jeroboam II *lasts for 41 years* (2 Kings 14:23).

■ 13.4*b. Third Empire.* St. John Chrysostom was active in the time of Honorius and his co-ruler Arcadius. Let us point out that Radagaisius, the duplicate of the Biblical Ben-Hadad, had died in the alleged year 405 A.D. Furthermore, Alaric, the duplicate of the Biblical Hazael, had perished in 410 A.D. Since both Radagaisius and Alaric had died in the epoch of Honorius (The Biblical Jeroboam II), the year 407, when *St. John Chrysostom*, the duplicate of the Biblical *Jonah*, had ceased his activity, actually coincides with the end of the invasion as described in the Bible. Honorius had *reigned for 28 years*: 395–423. Reign durations differ considerably, but it does not appear to influence the correlation of entire dynasties.

14*a. Zechariah* (The Lord's Memory).
■ 14*b. Constantius II.*

14.1*a. Israel.* Little is known of Zachariah. *He is presumed to have reigned for 6 months* (2 Kings 15:8).

■ 14.1*b. Third Empire.* There is virtually no information available about Constantius II. *He had reigned for 7 months* in either 421 or 423 A.D. ([767], Volume 2, page 793). He was proclaimed Augustus in 421, being a co-ruler of Honorius. Their respective reign durations are rather close.

15*a*. *Shallum* or *Selom* (Peaceful).

■ 15*b*. *John.*

15.1*a*. *Israel.* Very little is known of Shallum (2 Kings 15:10, 15:13). *He had reigned for 1 month* (2 Kings 15:13).

■ 15.1*b*. *Third Empire.* We know virtually nothing of John, who had reigned for 2 months in 423 ([579], page 482). Reign durations are similar.

COMMENTARY: Available sources reflect the downfall of the Western Roman Empire in a fragmentary and contradictory manner; this confusion is observable in contemporary monographs as well. For instance, [767], Volume 2, gives us the following years for Emperor John's reign: 423–425 A.D., without any comments whatsoever. Therefore we have been using an older text that was nevertheless a great deal more complete [579], which relates the events of this period (albeit briefly) specifies the duration of John's rule as equalling two months ([76]).

16*a*. *Interregnum* in the Kingdom of Israel.

■ 16*b*. *"Interregnum-guardianship"* in the West of the Third Roman Empire.

16.1*a*. *Israel.* After the death of Jeroboam II, a 24-year long period of strife begins. Menahem accedes under unclear circumstances. The 2nd Book of Kings (15:17) indicates that Menahem had ascended the throne in the 39th year of Azariah, the king of Judah, and *reigned* for 10 years. On the other hand, Menahem is supposed to have "attacked Shallum, the son of Jabesh" (2 Kings 15:14). That is to say, Menahem replaced Shallum (Selom). Shallum had *reigned* for 1 month, and his predecessor Zechariah - for 6 months only, q.v. below. Thus, Menahem ascended the throne 7 months after Zachariah's co-ruler or predecessor – Jeroboam II. In other words, no gap is indicated between any of these three kings. However, Jeroboam II had died in the 14th year of Azariah of Judah, as mentioned above, since: "In the twenty-seventh year of Jeroboam, king of Israel, Azariah, son of Amaziah, king of Judah, began his reign" (2 Kings 15:1). Moreover, Jeroboam II had *reigned* for 41 years, q.v. above. Thus, 24 years went missing between the end of Shallum's rule and the beginning of Menahem's rule. See also the "double entries" as described in *Chron1*, Annex 6.4. Chronologists have long ago noted this fact and called it an interregnum. See also the survey in [544], Volume 7. Thus, the interregnum had *lasted for 24 years*.

■ 16.1*b. Third Empire.* As we have noted earlier, the period of 423–444 A.D. had been the time of guardianship-inter-regnum in the Roman Empire. Young Valentinian III was formally under the guardianship of his mother, Placidia, but actually Aetius ([64], page 33). The guardianship had *lasted 21 years*. Durations are similar.

17*a. Menahem* (Gift to People).
■ 17*b. Valentinian III.*

17.1*a. Israel.* During Menahem's rule, an important event takes place – the troops of Phul, king of *Assyria*, invade the Israeli kingdom (2 Kings 15:19) *near the end* of Menahem's rule (2 Kings 15:19, 15:21–22).

NOTE: In the Russian Bible used here by A. T. Fomenko (and in several other Slavonic Bibles), king of Assyria is called FUL. In the NIV, however, this king's name is **PUL**. Therefore, the next sentence is provided in two versions – translation of the actual sentence by A.T. Fomenko and a suggestion on how to deal with the varying spelling. This difference influences some of the further paragraphs, q.v. below.

A.T. Fomenko: Since the sounds F (phita) and T were often subject to flexion, the name *Ful* might also have been pronounced as *Tul*.

SUGGESTION: Since the sounds P, F, and T were frequently subject to flexion, the name *Pul* might have also been pronounced as *Ful* or *Tul*.

■ 17.1*b. Third Empire.* The rule of Valentinian III is marked by a major invasion. The troops of the famous *Attila* invade the

Roman Empire ([64]) in the alleged year 452 – towards *the end of the reign* of Valentinian III. Let us recall that he had reigned between the alleged years 444 and 455. The name *Attila* is virtually identical with the biblical name Tul. What we get sans vocalizations is TTL – TL. Thus, by reporting the intrusion of Ful – Tul, the Bible explicitly indicates *Attila*. Attila is considered to have been the leader of the *Huns*.

COMMENTARY: The fact is that whenever the Bible reports a Syrian (occasionally also *Aramean*) or *Assyrian* invasion, we immediately see either *Germans* (*Prussians*), or *Goths*, or *Huns* invade the Third Roman Empire from the north. As for the word Ashur or Ashr, ("Assyrian") in [544], Volume 2, the following translation was offered: leader-mentor. *Ashur* and *Ashri* means "to walk straight", "to lead others", similar to the German form "Führer" – leader. In the Biblical Books of Kings, *Assyrians* are described as a powerful militant nation. In *Chron5* we have formulated the hypothesis that the country described in the Bible under the name of *Assyria* is the medieval Russia, providing argumentation in its support. Thus the biblical names:

- *Assiria* or *Assur*, same as
- *Asur* or *Syria*, same as
- *Ashur* – being simply the reverse spelling of the three famous medieval names of the country:
- *Rossiya* (modern name of Russia) = *Assiria* or *Assur*,
- *Russ* (the archaic name of *Russia*) = *Asur* or *Syria*,
- *Russia* = *Ashur*.

Let us point towards the fact that the English name for the country (Russia) is virtually identical to "Ashur" reversed phonetically. See also *Chron6*.

17.2a. *Israel.* Under the threat of suffering a complete rout, Menahem gave Pul "a thousand silver talents... Menahem exacted this money from Israel. Every wealthy man had to contribute... to the king of Assyria. So the king of Assyria withdrew and stayed in the land no longer" (2 Kings 15:19–20). Menahem had *reigned for 10 years* (2 Kings 15:17).

■ 17.2b. *Third Empire.* On the verge of a crushing military defeat,

Valentinian III tempts Attila the Hun (Khan?) with a large sum of money, agreeing to pay a yearly levy. This event takes place in the alleged year 452 ([64], page 37). The sum of said levy is not specified, though it is said to have been large. Valentinian III had reigned for 14 years, q.v. above. Reign durations are similar.

18a. *Pekahiah* (The Lord's Watchful One).

■ 18b. *Petronius Maximus.*

18.1a. *Israel.* Pekahiah had replaced Menahem (2 Kings 15:23). He was *murdered by his minions* after a plot (2 Kings 15:25). He *had reigned* in Samaria (2 Kings 15:23). Menahem had *reigned for 2 years* (2 Kings 15:23).

■ 18.1b. *Third Empire.* Petronius Maximus had replaced Valentinian III and "got murdered during a flight *by his own minions*" ([579], page 487). He *had reigned* in Rome ([579]). We see another identification of the biblical Samaria as the mediaeval Rome. However, this does not imply the Italian Rome bears any relation to the events in question at all. Petronius Maximus had *reigned for less than 1 year* ([579], pages 487–488). Reign durations are similar.

19a. *Pekah* or *Thahash* (The Watchful One).

■ 19b. *Recimer.*

19.1a. *Israel.* Under Thahash, the kingdom of Israel (Theomachist) was attacked by Tilgath-Pilneser, king of *barbarians* (2 Kings 15:29) – or king of *Assyria* (2 Kings 15:29). N. A. Morozov noted that his name (Tilgath-Pilneser), can be translated as "*migrant* monster" ([544], Volume 7, page 356).

■ 19.1b. *Third Empire.* Under Recimer the Roman Empire had suffered from the invasion of Genzeric, the leader of *barbarians* ([579], pages 487–488). In Scaligerian history, the invasion of Genzeric is considered to have been the beginning of the Volkswanderung [579], pp.487–488. Several years later, another barbarian ruler, a "migrant monster", will appear in the Third Empire – Theodoric king of Goths. He is believed to have performed massive relocations, shuffled the population of Italy and mixed it with Goths and Germans. We will see Theodoric described on the pages of the Bible as well, under the name "Tiglath-Pileser".

19.2a. *Israel.* Thahash = Pekah *reigns* in Samaria (2 Kings 15:27). The duration of his reign equals *20 years* (2 Kings 15:27).

■ 19.2b. *Third Empire.* Recimer *reigns* in Rome. Again, we see that the biblical Samaria can be identified as the mediaeval Rome. We have already mentioned that Recimer was the actual ruler who had replaced several "short-term" emperors on the Roman throne. Recimer's reign lasted for *16 years*: 456–472, q.v. above. The reign durations of the two are similar.

20a. *Anarchy* in the kingdom of the Israelites.

■ 20b. *Anarchy* in the Third Roman Empire in the West.

20.1a. *Israel.* Different researchers of the Bible estimate the duration of this anarchy in the kingdom of Israel in different ways, to be equal to some value between 6 and 9 years ([544], Volume 7, page 303, table XVII). Our analysis of the Bible yields two versions: 2 and 9 years (2 Kings 15:30). See the "double entry" method as described in *Chron1*, Appendix 6.4. We put all three versions down: 2, 6, 9 years.

■ 20.1b. *Third Empire.* Recimer died in the alleged year 472 A.D. The country had been in anarchy until the alleged year 475, when, after a lengthy struggle, the patrician Orestes enthroned his son Romulus Augustulus in Rome ([579], page 490). The duration of the anarchy period equals 3 years.

21a. *Uzziah* (the Saviour, or Son of God).

■ 21b. *Romulus Augustulus.*

21.1a. *Israel.* After the anarchy, Uzziah ascends the throne of Israel in Samaria (2 Kings 17:1). The sacred title of the Saviour, of the Son of God was possibly given to Uzziah as a mockery.

Indeed, virtually from the very beginning of his rule, Uzziah had been under the influence of a foreign king called Shalmaneser, remaining de facto deprived of real power himself (2 Kings 17:1–4).

■ 21.1b. *Third Empire.* After the anarchy (again we see a superimposition of the biblical Samaria over the medieval Rome), the 15-year-old Romulus Augustulus ascends the Roman throne. His name "Augustulus" is derived from the famous name Augustus. Historians note: "The population of Italy gave to the adolescent "emperor" a mocking nickname 'Augustulus', which stands for 'Little Augustus' or 'Augustus Junior'" [327], page 450.

21.2a. *Israel.* Almost immediately after the beginning of Uzziah's rule, the state was attacked by Shalmaneser, a foreigner. "Uzziah had been his vassal and had paid him tribute" (2 Kings 17:3). Shalmaneser is a king of *Assyria* (2 Kings 17:3). Shalmaneser *"had seized him* [Uzziah - A. F.] ... *and put him into prison"* (2 Kings 17:4).

■ 21.2b. *Third Empire.* In the alleged year 476, the foreigner Odoacer destroys the troops of Rome led by Orestes and claims the royal throne for himself, displacing Romulus Augustulus ([579]). This event concludes the "purely Roman" dynasty in the west of the Third Empire. Odoacer is a German military commander ([579], pages 490–491). Again we see the Assyrians identified as Germans (Prussians, or P-Russians). Odoacer *banishes* Romulus Augustulus to his estate in Campagnia, where the latter ends his days under house arrest ([579], pages 490–491).

21.3a. *Israel.* Uzziah had *reigned as an independent king for less than 1 year* (2 Kings 17). Although he formally *reigned* for 9 years (2 Kings 17:1), at the very beginning of Uzziah's story (2 Kings 17:3) the Bible tells us that Uzziah became subject to a king of Assyria.

■ 21.3b. *Third Empire.* Romulus Augustulus had *reigned for a single year as an independent emperor* in the alleged years 475–476 ([579], pages 490–491). Reign durations coincide.

21.4*a*. *Israel.* Shalmaneser arranges for a mass migration of the Israelites (2 Kings 17:6). Then the Bible describes radical changes – not only in the state system of the theomachist kingdom under the rule of a foreign king, but the religious cult as well. Uzziah's rule marks the end of the independent kingdom of Israel.

■ 21.4*b*. *Third Empire.* Odoacer had arranged for a major migration to Italy. German mercenaries settled throughout the country. They were given a third of the entire land. The Western Roman Empire ceased to exist as a "purely Roman" state; it was governed by two conqueror kings – the foreigners Odoacer and Theodoric. A German-Gothic kingdom emerges, and the country receives an infusion of new customs and new religion. In Scaligerian history, the Third Empire in the west is considered to have finally collapsed after Theodoric as a result of the Gothic War of the alleged VI century.

Thus ends the biblical history of the kingdom of Israel and the "royal purity period" in the history of the Third Roman Empire in the west.

4.
Identifying the theocratic Kingdom of Judah as the Third Roman Empire in the East. A shift of circa 1230 years (short diagram)

Since the Kingdom of Israel of the alleged years 922–724 B.C. can be identified as the Third Roman Empire of the alleged years 306–476 A.D. in the west, it is a natural assumption that the kingdom of Judah of the alleged years 928–587 B.C. should be superimposed over the Eastern Empire of the alleged years 306–700 A.D. This assumption is confirmed by the method of dynastic parallelisms as described in Chapter 6 of *Chron1*. Let us reiterate that *these parallelisms* are actually of a *secondary* nature – that is, *they are but derivatives* of the *main* parallelisms with the German and the Roman coronations of the Sacred Empire of the X–XIII century A.D. and the empire of the Habsburgs (Nov-Gorod?) of the XIV-XVI century.

The Theomachist Kingdom of Israel duplicates the Roman coronation sequence of the Holy Roman Empire in the alleged X–XIII century A.D., q.v. in Chapter 6 of *Chron1*.

The Theocratic Kingdom of Judah duplicates the German coronations in the Holy Roman Empire of the alleged X–XIII century A.D., q.v. in Chapter 6 of *Chron1*. Ergo, both kingdoms of Israel and Judah are, to a substantial extent, phantom *reflections of the Habsburg Empire* of XIV–XVI century A.D., q.v. in *Chron1*, Chapter 6.

Thus, a general diagram of these triple reflections is as follows:

---

1 **DUPLICATE:** The *Roman* coronation sequence of the Holy Roman Empire in the alleged X–XIII century A.D., which is

116

a partial reflection of the XIV–XVI century Habsburg (Nov-Gorod?) Empire.

2 DUPLICATE: The Biblical Theomachist (Israelite) kingdom of the alleged years 922–724 B.C. ([72], p. 192).

3 DUPLICATE: The Third Roman Empire in the West (the alleged years 306–476 A.D.).

---

1 DUPLICATE: The *German* coronation sequence of the Holy Roman Empire in the alleged X–XIII century A.D., which is a partial reflection of the XIV–XVI century Habsburg (Nov-Gorod?) Empire.

2 DUPLICATE: The Biblical Theocratic = Judaic kingdom of the alleged years 928–587 B.C. ([72], page 192).

3 DUPLICATE: Third Roman Empire in the East. The alleged years 306–700 A.D.

Biographical parallelisms between the Theocratic = Judaic kingdom of the alleged years 928–587 B.C. and the phantom Third Roman Empire in the east dating to the alleged years 306–700 A.D. are related in greater detail in *Chron2*, Chapter 4, as a part of our analysis of the Bible.

5.

Saint Basil the Great in the alleged IV century A.D. and his prototype in the XII century A.D. – Jesus Christ. The resulting shift of 820 years

Let us relate an interesting parallelism between the respective biographies of Saint Basil the Great (The Great King), who had lived in the alleged IV century A.D., and Jesus Christ, who had lived in the alleged first century A.D. According to our research, q.v. in our book entitled *The King of the Slavs,* the Emperor Andronicus (Christ) is most likely to have lived in the XII century A.D. His reflection is Pope Gregory VII Hildebrand from the alleged XI century.

In Greek, the word "Christ" means "the anointed one", or "the initiate" ([544], Volume 1, page 109). People initiated into the mysteries of sciences are presumed to have been named Christ after a ceremonial anointment with holy oil. The Hebraic translation of the Greek "Christ" is "Nazarene" ([544], Volume 1, page 109). The Gospel does occasionally refer to the Saviour as Jesus "the Nazarene" (Matthew 2:23). Joshua (Jesus) – allegedly Joshua, son of Nun ([240]), is buried upon the Beykos mountain near the outskirts of Istanbul, which is also named "Hazreti," or "Holy" in Turkish ([1181]). The words "Nazarene" and "Hazreti" may have the same meaning, q.v. in *Chron5.*

A propos, let us recall that the famous Orthodox Apostolic Creed had first been adopted by the Nicaean Council in the alleged year 325 A.D. (the edicts of the council haven't reached our age), but later edited and supplemented by the Constantinople Council in the alleged year 381 A.D. (the of that council did not survive until

Fig. 1.9. St. Basil the Great. Icon from the iconostasis of the Blagoveshchensky Cathedral of the Muscovite Kremlin ([114], page 253).

our day, either). This is exactly the epoch over which Jesus Christ of the XII century A.D. becomes superimposed, likewise his reflection – Gregory Hildebrand, (shift value equalling 820 years, q.v. in *Chron1*, Chapter 6).

Stories collected in *The General Menaion* (Monthly Readings hagiography) are of a certain interest if we study the history of the cult. We quote them after [544], Volume 1.

Let us recollect which saint's holy day the European New Year begins with. The first page reads, *"January 1st. Saint Basil the Great."* "Basil" is the Greek for "King" ("Basileus"). That is to say, the Christian year begins with a Saint Great King. Who is he? Why does he occupy this honorary position? Why is he considered to have been "the great father of the church"? ([849], page 176.) Basil was born in the alleged year 333 A.D.; N. A. Morozov collected a vast body of intriguing materials to demonstrate parallels between St. Basil the Great and Jesus Christ ([544], Volume 1). We have composed a short table of this parallel's form-codes.

1a. *Jesus Christ.* Jesus is the King of the Jews, according to the Gospels (Matthew 27:11) and (John 19:21). He is also the founder of a new religion. Christian crucifixes are often adorned with the letters INRI, which stand for "Iesus Nazarenus Rex Iudaeorum" (Jesus Nazarene, King of the Jews).

■ 1b. *St. Basil the Great.* Basil the Great = The Great King. Basil, or Basileus, translates as "king". He is one of the most important Christian saints. On fig. 1.9 we can see an image of St. Basil the Great on the iconostasis of the Annunciation Cathedral in the Muscovite Kremlin ([114], page 253). On fig. 1.10 we see an icon from the first half of the XVII century depicting St. Basil the Great.

Fig. 1.10. St. Basil the Great. An icon. The Andrei Roublyov Central Museum of Art. First half of the XVII century ([114], page 460).

2a. *Jesus Christ.* A famous legend from the Gospel according to Luke: "After three days they found Him in the temple courts, sitting among the teachers, listening to them and asking them questions. Everyone who heard Him was amazed at His understanding and His answers" (Luke 2:46–47).

■ 2b. *St. Basil the Great.* At the age of 5, St. Basil could comprehend the entire body of philosophical works available at that epoch; since 12, he had been taught by scribes, amazing them with the profundity of his understanding. Quoted after [544], Volume 1.

3a. *Jesus Christ.* The wanderings of Jesus before He began his ministration. See, in particular, the time Jesus had spent in the desert (Matthew 4:1–11), (Mark 1:12).

■ 3b. *St. Basil the Great.* St. Basil had also left for Egypt and lived there, "feeding on water and vegetables." Quoted according to [544], Volume 1.

4a. *Jesus Christ.* Jesus returns from his wanderings with a group of twelve followers known as the Apostles (Matthew 10:1–5).

■ 4b. *St. Basil the Great.* The Great King also returns from his travels surrounded by students. Quoted after [544], Volume 1.

5a. *Jesus Christ.* Jesus and his disciples (the Apostles) enter Jerusalem preaching asceticism and poverty, (Matthew 21:10).

■ 5b. *St. Basil the Great.* St. Basil and his disciples do likewise.

They are said to have "given their property away to the indigent and gone to Jerusalem dressed in white". Quoted after [544], Volume 1.

6a. *Jesus Christ.* The famous scene of Jesus baptized by his Precursor – Prophet St. John the Baptist (Matthew 3:13–16). In the Orthodox tradition, St. John the Baptist is usually called "Saint John the Great".

■ 6b. *St. Basil the Great.* Here, Maximus, or "The Greatest" baptises St. Basil the Great = The Great King in the Jordan. This version may have called St. John the Baptist Maximus, or "the Greatest". Quoted after [544], Volume 1.

7a. *Jesus Christ.* The scene of the baptism of Jesus is described as follows: "At that time Jesus came... and was baptized by John in the Jordan. As Jesus was coming up out of the water, he saw heaven being torn open and the Spirit descending on Him like a dove. And a voice came from heaven" (Mark 1:9–11).

■ 7b. *St. Basil the Great.* We see the exact same scenario repeated! During the baptism of The Great King, "a kind of fiery lightning came down on him, and a *dove* flew out of it, which descended upon the Jordan, troubled the water and flew back to heaven. And those standing on the shore, upon seeing this, were frightened with a great fear and glorifying God". Quoted after [544], Volume 1. The lightning must have been accompanied by "a voice like thunder".

8a. *Jesus Christ.* The key elements of the plot are as follows: baptism, the Jordan, a dove and a voice from heaven.

■ 8b. *St. Basil the Great.* This myth is based on the same elements: baptism, the Jordan, a dove and a lightning (possibly, a voice from heaven).

9a. *Jesus Christ.* The scene of the transfiguration of Jesus: "After six days Jesus took with Him, Peter, James and John ... and led them up a high mountain by themselves. There he was transfigured before them. His face shone like the sun ... Just then there appeared before them Moses and Elijah, talking with

Jesus... When the disciples heard this, they fell facedown to the ground, terrified" (Matthew 17:1–3, 17:6).

■ 9b. *St. Basil the Great.* The scene of the transfiguration of the Great King is just the same: the King prayed the God to bestow His grace upon him. He had made a sacrifice: he was calling upon the Lord for *six days,* and "all the high clergy saw the celestial light shed upon the altar, and men in bright garments surrounding the Great King. Those who saw it fell facedown". Quoted after [544], Volume 1, page 125.

10a. *Jesus Christ.* Thus, the essence of the myth is as follows: six days, prayer, transfiguration, celestial light, prophets appearing and the disciples in fear ("falling facedown").

■ 10b. *St. Basil the Great.* The essentials of the myth are absolutely the same: six days, prayer, celestial light, men appearing and spectators in fear ("falling facedown" as well).

11a. *Jesus Christ.* A close companion of Jesus is called Simon Peter; he is said to have been *older* than Jesus.

■ 11b. St Basil the Great. Next to the Great King we see his close companion Eubulus, whose name translates as "Good Advice"; he is the Great King's *senior.* Quoted after [544], Volume 1.

12a. *Jesus Christ.* Next to Jesus we see *St. Peter* the Apostle. He is a *married man* (Mark 1:29), (Luke 4:38).

■ 12b. *St. Basil the Great.* Next to the Great King, we also see *Peter,* a high priest. He is *married* and has children (possibly, a double of Eubulus). Quoted after [544], Volume 1. The names of the doubles coincide.

13a. *Jesus Christ.* Jesus performs many miracles (such as exorcising malignant spirits, healing lepers, and raising the dead.

■ 13b. *St. Basil the Great.* Virtually the same list of miracles is attributed to the Great King [544], Volume 1.

14a. *Jesus Christ.* The devil tempts Jesus (Luke 4:1–13).

■ 14b. *St. Basil the Great.* We learn of a similar temptation of the Great King by the devil. Quoted after [544], Volume 1.

15a. *Jesus Christ.* The famous Mary Magdalene had been living a life of sin for a long time; however, when she had met Jesus, she was absolved of her sins and accompanied him as an ardent worshipper (Luke 7:36–50, 8:1–2).

■ 15b. *St. Basil the Great.* Here, a certain rich widow had been living a dissolute life for a long time - however, when she'd met the Great King, she begged him for an absolution. She received the absolution and became a worshipper of the King. Quoted after [544], Volume 1. The plot is very similar.

16a. *Jesus Christ.* Jesus is said to have known the secret thoughts of people: when he had met an unfamiliar Samaritan woman, he told her that she'd had five husbands, and that the man she had been with when they met wasn't in fact her husband (John 4:15–19).

■ 16b. *St. Basil the Great.* An identical plot: upon meeting a stranger by the name of Theognia, the Great King had told her that the man who was accompanying her as a husband hadn't been such. Quoted after [544], Volume 1.

17a. *Jesus Christ.* State authorities begin repressions against Jesus, willing to make him adhere to the previous cult. Jesus, aided by a number of the Apostles, heads an oppositional religious movement.

■ 17b. *St. Basil the Great.* Valens the Roman Emperor assaults the Great King, willing to make him adhere to Aryanism. The Great King resists and, accompanied by his followers, heads the opposition. Quoted after [544], Volume 1. We see an evident parallelism: both Jesus and the Great King step up against the Roman authorities.

18a. *Jesus Christ.* The Pharisees, sworn enemies of Jesus, form a group supported by the state (John 7:32).

■ 18b. *St. Basil the Great.* Aryanists are sworn enemies of the Great King. They also enjoy the support of the emperor's authority. Quoted after [544], Volume 1.

19a. *Jesus Christ.* The trial of Jesus and His Crucifixion (John 18–19).

■ 19*b. St. Basil the Great.* In the alleged year 368 A.D. Valens initiates a trial over the Great King, willing to sentence him to exile. Quoted after [544], Volume 1.

20*a. Jesus Christ.* Jesus is crucified at the age of 33. His ministration began when he had been about thirty years of age (Luke 3:23).

■ 20*b. St. Basil the Great.* The Great King was born in the alleged year 333 A.D.; therefore, at the time of Valens' trial, in the alleged year 368, he had been 35 [544], Volume 1.

21*a. Jesus Christ.* Pontius Pilate, the chief Roman magistrate, refuses to judge Jesus and "washes his hands". "When Pilate saw that he was getting nowhere, but that instead an uproar was starting, he took water and washed his hands in front of the crowd" (Matthew 27:24).

■ 21*b. St. Basil the Great.* Roman emperor, Valens wants to sign the sentence, but the cane "breaks in his hand" and he, frightened, tears his decree to pieces. Quoted after [544], Volume 1.

22*a. Jesus Christ.* The trial over Jesus takes place at the place of Pontius Pilate, that is, Pilate of Pontus. The word "pilat" used to mean "hangman, tormentor", in the old Russian language – hence Russian word "pilatit – to torture, tyrannize" (V. Dal – [223], see "pilatit"). Thus, Pontius Pilate is the Hangman from Pontus, or the Tormentor from Pontus. It is therefore possible that, rather than being a name, the word "Pilate" stands for occupation in the Gospels. Pilate of Pontus is merely the judge of Pontus, or the state official who administers justice and manages hangmen. According to the Gospels, there are two rulers on the historical scene: King Herod and the judge Pontius Pilate, a Roman governor.

■ 22*b. St. Basil the Great.* The trial over the Great King takes place at the residence of the high priest of Pontus. Here we also see two influential rulers: Emperor Valens and a judge – the high priest of Pontus. Quoted after [544], Volume 1.

23*a. Jesus Christ.* King Herod hands Jesus over to Pontius Pilate (Luke 23:8–11).

- *23b. St. Basil the Great.* Emperor Valens hands the Great King to the high priest of Pontus. Quoted after [544], Volume 1.

24a. Jesus Christ. The court sentences Jesus to death (Luke 23:13–5).
- *24b. St. Basil the Great.* The Great King is also sentenced to death according to [544], Volume 1.

25a. Jesus Christ. After the execution, or the Crucifixion, a miracle takes place, namely, the Resurrection of Jesus Christ (Matthew 28:5–20).
- *25b. St. Basil the Great.* A miracle saves the Great King from death (see [544], Volume 1). It is interesting that neither the "biography" of the Great King, nor that of Hildebrand (another reflection of Jesus Christ) should mention the execution itself – that is, the crucifixion *is not actually described at all.*

26a. Jesus Christ. After His Resurrection, Jesus "appears before many" - his disciples in particular (Matthew 28:16–17). The Gospel tells us nothing of the further fate of Jesus Christ.
- *26b. St. Basil the Great.* After the "resurrection" (having been on the verge of death, but not executed), the Great King had lived for 10 years and died in the alleged year 378 A.D., vested in the great authority of being a religious leader ([544], Volume 1).

27a. Jesus Christ. Before the "death", or the Crucifixion, Jesus distinguishes his youngest and most beloved disciple during the Last Supper – St. John the Apostle (John 13:23 and on).
- *27b. St. Basil the Great.* Before his death, the Great King transfers his authority to his disciple *John.* He is said to have baptized his disciple and "communicated to him the divine Mysteries… Only then… has he committed his soul into the hands of God". Quoted after [544], Volume 1.

28a. Jesus Christ. Jesus is considered the founder of Christianity.
- *28b. St. Basil the Great.* The Great King is the progenitor of the Christian mysteries ([544], Volume 1). The most important

element of the cult is the so-called *Liturgy of St. Basil the Great* ([544], Volume 1).

29*a. Jesus Christ.* Jesus is the head of the Holy Family, a group of Christian saints.

■ 29*b. St. Basil the Great.* The Great King was canonized as a Christian saint together with his brothers and sisters.

30*a. Jesus Christ.* There are two traditional points of view on how old Jesus was at the moment of his "death": 33 years, according to the most common version (Luke 3:23), and approaching 50 – "You are not yet fifty years of age" (John 8:57).

■ 30*b. St. Basil the Great.* The "ecclesiastical age" of the Great King, who was born in the alleged year 333 A.D., can calculated in two ways: 1) either 35 years, up to Valens' trial that allegedly took place around 368 A.D., or 2) 45 years, up to his death allegedly in 378 A.D. [544], Volume 1. We see sufficient conformity.

31*a. Jesus Christ.* The feast of the Nativity of Christ (Christmas) is the most important Christian holy day.

■ 31*b. St. Basil the Great..* The feast of the Nativity of Christ is considered to have appeared among the followers of the famous Christian sect of *Basilidians* ([744], page 47). Today they are presumed to have been the followers of the notorious heretic Basilides ([744], page 47). It is however possible that the tale of "Basilides the Heretic" was just another version of the legend about St. Basil the Great.

Thus, St. Basil the Great appears to have been a phantom reflection of Jesus Christ, or Emperor Andronicus from the XII century A.D.

PART TWO

The famous reform of the Occidental Church in the XI century by "Pope Gregory Hildebrand" as the reflection of the XII century reforms of Andronicus (Christ).

The Trojan War of the XIII century A.D.

6.
"Pope Gregory Hildebrand" from the XI century A.D. as a replica of Jesus Christ (Andronicus) from the XII century. A chronological shift of 100 years. The Scaligerite chronologists have subsequently moved the life of Christ 1050 years backwards, into the I century A.D.

The great ecclesiastical reform of the XI century, conceived and initiated by the famous Pope Gregory Hildebrand, is a well-known event in the history of Western Europe and the Occidental Christian Church. It is supposed to have radically altered the life of the Europeans. As we shall demonstrate in the present chapter, the XI century "Pope Gregory Hildebrand" is really a phantom reflection of Andronicus (Christ) from the XII century A.D.

Let us explain in more detail. The decomposition of the "Scaligerian history textbook" into the sum of four shorter chronicles shifted against each other implies the existence of an erroneous mediaeval tradition that dated Christ's lifetime to the XI century A.D. This fact had initially been discovered by the author in his study of the global chronological map (the 1053-year shift that superimposes the phantom I century A.D. over the XI century A.D.). This erroneous point of view that the ancient chroniclers had adhered to was further rediscovered by G. V. Nosovskiy in his analysis of the Mediaeval calculations related to the Passover and the calendar, q.v. in *Chron6* and Annex 4 to *The Biblical Russia*.

One should therefore expect a phantom reflection of Jesus Christ to manifest in the "Scaligerian XI century". This prognosis is confirmed, and we shall demonstrate the facts that confirm it in the present chapter.

Our subsequent analysis of the ancient and mediaeval historical chronology demonstrated that the epoch of Christ, which is presumed to be at a distance of 2000 years from today, to have been 1100 years closer to us, falling over the XII century A.D. See our book entitled *King of the Slavs* for further reference. Apparently, despite the fact that the mediaeval chronologists have shifted Christ's life as reflected in the chronicles into the I century A.D., having "removed" it from the XII century, an "intermediate reflection" of Emperor Andronicus (Christ) remained in the XI century as the biography of "Pope Gregory VII Hildebrand".

This statement, which is of a purely chronological nature, is often misunderstood by religious people. This stems from the false impression that the re-dating of the Evangelical events that we offer contradicts the Christian creed. This is not so. The re-dating of the years of Christ's life that we offer taken together with the alternative datings for other events recorded in ancient and mediaeval history has got absolutely nothing to do with Christian theology.

The same can be said about the parallels between the Evangelical descriptions of Christ's life and the biography of "Pope" Gregory Hildebrand.

A parallelism doesn't imply that Hildebrand's biography is based on reality and the Gospels are a myth that duplicates it. On the contrary, in our works on chronology we demonstrate our discovery that the history of the Italian Rome (where Pope Hildebrand is supposed to have been active in the XI century, according to Scaligerian history) only commences from the XIV century. Also, up until the XVII century it had differed from the consensual version substantially. Ergo, real history tells us that there could have been no Roman Pontiff by the name of Hildebrand in the XI century Italy – if only due to the non-existence of Rome itself at that epoch.

What are the origins of "Pope Hildebrand's" biography, and why does it contain duplicates of a number of Evangelical events? This issue requires a separate study. It is of great interest in itself, and remains rather contentious. In any case, if we are to assume a purely chronological stance, we shall certainly become interested in the fact that the Scaligerian history of the XI century contains a distinctive parallelism with the Evangelical events.

6.1 Astronomy in the Gospels

6.1.1 The true dating of the evangelical eclipse

The issue of dating the evangelical events through the study of the eclipse described in the Gospels and other early Christian sources (Phlegon, Africanus, Synkellos etc) has a long history – it has been repeatedly discussed by astronomers and chronologists alike. There is controversy in what concerns whether the eclipse in question was solar or lunar – we shall therefore consider both possibilities. Let us ponder the possibility of a lunar eclipse first. The Scaligerian chronology suggests 33 A.D. as a fitting solution – see Ginzel's astronomical canon, for instance ([1154]). However, this solution doesn't quite fit, since the lunar eclipse of 33 A.D. was all but unobservable in the Middle East. Apart from that, the eclipse's phase was minute ([1154]). Nevertheless, the eclipse of 33 A.D. is still persistently claimed to confirm the Scaligerian dating of the Crucifixion – the alleged year 33 A.D.

N. A. Morozov suggested another solution: 24 March 368 A.D. ([544], Volume 1, page 96. However, if we are to consider the results of our research that had demonstrated the "Scaligerian History Textbook" to fall apart into four brief chronicles collated to each other, this solution is nowhere near recent enough to satisfy our requirements. Morozov considered the Scaligerian chronology to be basically correct in the new era; therefore, he only got to analyze the eclipses that "preceded the VIII century – that is, from the dawn of history to the second half of the Middle Ages – I decided going any further back would be futile [sic! – A. F.]" ([544], Volume 1, page 97).

We have thus extended the time interval to be searched for astronomical solutions into the epochs nearer to the present, having analyzed all the eclipses up until the XVI century A.D. It turns out that there is an eclipse that satisfies to the conditions – the one that occurred on Friday, 3 April 1075. The coordinates of the zenith point are as follows: + 10 degrees of longitude and – 8 degrees of latitude. See Oppolzer's canon, for instance ([1315]). The eclipse was observable from the entire area of Europe and the Middle East that is of interest to us. According to the ecclesiastical tradition, the Crucifixion and the eclipse were simultaneous events that took place two days before the Easter. This could not have preceded the equinox. The eclipse dating to 3 April 1075 A.D. precedes Easter (which falls on Sunday, 5 April that year) by two days, as a matter of fact. The phase of the 1075 eclipse is 4"8 – not that great. Later on, in our analysis of Gregory Hildebrand's "biography", we shall see that the eclipse of 1075 A.D. corresponds well with other important events of the XI century which may have become reflected in the Gospels.

Let us now consider the solar eclipse version. According to the Gospels and the ecclesiastical tradition ([518]), a new star flared up in the East the year the Saviour was born (Matthew 2:2, 2:7, 2:9–10), and a total eclipse of the sun followed in 31 years, in the year of the Resurrection. The Gospel according to Luke (23:45) tells us explicitly that the sun "hath darkened" during the Crucifixion. Ecclesiastical sources also make direct references to the fact of the Resurrection being accompanied by a solar eclipse, and not necessarily on Good Friday. Let us point out that an eclipse, let alone a total eclipse, is a rare event in that part of the world. Although solar eclipses occur every year, one can only observe them from the narrow track of lunar shadow on the Earth (unlike lunar eclipses that one can observe from across an entire hemisphere). The Bible scholars of the XVIII-XIX century decided to consider the eclipse to have been a lunar one, which didn't help much, since no fitting lunar eclipse could be found, either (q.v. above). However, since then the consensual opinion has been that the Gospels describe a lunar eclipse and not a solar one. Let us adhere to the original point of view that is reflected in the sources, namely, that the eclipse was a solar one.

We learn that such combination of rarest astronomical events as a nova explosion and a full eclipse of the sun following it by roughly 33 years did actually occur – however, in the XII century A.D., and not the first! We are referring to the famous nova explosion roughly dated to 1150 and the total eclipse of the sun of the 1 May 1185. We relate it in detail in our book *King of the Slavs*.

Thus, astronomical evidence testifies to the fact that the Evangelical events are most likely to have taken place in the XII century

A.D. – about 1100 later than the Scaligerian "dating" ([1154]), and 800 years later than the dating suggested by N. A. Morozov ([544], Volume 1).

However, later chronologists have shifted the supernova explosion (the Evangelical star of Bethlehem) 100 years backwards, declaring it to have taken place in 1054. What are the origins of this version? It is possible that the desperate attempts of the mediaeval chronologists to find a "fitting" eclipse in the XI century played some part here. A total eclipse of the sun took place on the 16 February 1086, on Monday ([1154]). The shadow track from this eclipse covered Italy and Byzantium. According to Ginzel's astronomical canon ([1154]), the eclipse had the following characteristics: the coordinates of the beginning of the shadow track were –76 degrees of longitude and +14 degrees of latitude (these values are –14 longitude and +22 latitude for the track's middle, and +47 longitude with latitude equalling +45 degrees for its end). The eclipse was total. Having erroneously declared this eclipse to have been the one that coincided with the Crucifixion, the XIV-XV century chronologists had apparently counted 33 years (Christ's age) backwards from this date (approximately 1086 A.D.), dating the Nativity to the middle of the XI century. They were 100 years off the mark.

Let us linger on the ecclesiastical tradition that associated the Crucifixion with a solar eclipse.

6.1.2. The Gospels apparently reflect a sufficiently advanced level of astronomical eclipse theories, which contradicts the consensual evangelical history

The Bible scholars have long ago taken notice of the claim that the eclipse had lasted about three hours made by the authors of the Gospels.

Matthew tells us the following: "Now from the sixth hour there was darkness *all over the land* unto the ninth hour" (Matthew 27:45).

According to Luke, "… it was about the sixth hour, and there was a darkness all over the earth until the ninth hour. And *the sun was darkened…*" (Luke 23:44–45)

Mark informs us that "… when the sixth hour was come, there was darkness all over the whole land until the ninth hour".

John hasn't got anything to say on the subject.

The numerous commentators of the Bible have often been puzzled by the fact that the evangelists report a solar eclipse ("the sun was darkened") with its unnaturally long three-hour duration, since a regular solar eclipse is only observable for several minutes from each particular location. We consider the explanation offered by Andrei Nemoyevskiy, the author of the book *Jesus the God* ([576]) a while ago, to make perfect sense. He wrote: "we know that a solar eclipse could not have lasted for three hours and covered the entire country [it is usually assumed that the country in question is the diminutive area around Jerusalem – A. F.]. Its maximal duration could not have possibly exceed 4–8 minutes. The evangelists apparently were well familiar with astronomy and could not have uttered any such nonsense … Luke (XXIII, 44) … Mark (XV, 33) … and Matthew (XXVII, 45) … tell us that "there was darkness *all over the land*", which really could have lasted for several hours. The duration of the *entire* solar eclipse that occurred on 6 May 1883 equalled 5 hours and 5 minutes; however, the *full* eclipse lasted for 3 hours and 5 minutes – exactly the time interval specified in the Gospels" ([576], page 23).

In other words, the three hours specified by the evangelists referred to *the entire duration of the lunar shadow's movement across the surface of the Earth* and not the time a single observation point was obscured – that is, the duration of the eclipse from the moment of its beginning (in Britain, for instance) and until its end in some place like Iran. It took the lunar shadow three hours to cover the entire track that ran "all over the land", inside which "there was darkness". The phrase *"all over the land"* was thus used deliberately.

Naturally, such interpretation of the Gospels implies a sufficiently advanced level of their authors' understanding of the eclipses, their mechanics et al. However, if the events in question took place in the XII century and were recorded and edited in the XII-XIV century the earliest, possibly a lot later, there is hardly any wonder here. Mediaeval astronomers already understood the mechanism of solar eclipses well enough, as well as the fact that the lunar shadow slides across the surface of the Earth ("all over the land") for several hours.

Let us point out that this high a level of astronomical knowledge from the part of the evangelists is an absolute impossibility in the reality tunnel of the Scaligerian chronology. We are told that the evangelists were lay astronomers at best, and neither possessed nor used any special knowledge of astronomy.

We shall consider the issue of the "passover eclipse" that occurred during the Crucifixion once again. Many old ecclesiastical sources insist the eclipse to have been a *solar* one. This obviously contradicts the Gospels claiming that the Jesus Christ was crucified around the time of the Passover, which also implies a full moon. Now, it is common knowledge that no solar eclipse can occur when the moon is full, since the sun and the moon face *opposite* sides of the Earth. The sun is located "behind the back" of the terrestrial observer, which is the reason why the latter sees the entire sunlit part of the moon – a full moon, that is.

All of the above notwithstanding, we have discovered a total eclipse of the sun that took place on 1 May 1185 falling precisely on the year of the Crucifixion, q.v. in the *King of the Slavs*. Let us remind the reader that a full solar eclipse is an exceptionally rare event for this particular geographical area. Centuries may pass between two solar eclipses observed from this region. Therefore, the eclipse of 1185 could have been eventually linked to the moment of the Crucifixion. Hence the concept of the "passover eclipse". This shouldn't surprise us since in the Middle Ages a clear understanding of how the locations of celestial bodies were related to one another had been a great rarity, even among scientists.

In fig. 2.1 we can see an ancient miniature of the Crucifixion taken from the famous Rhemish Missal. At the bottom of the miniature we see a solar eclipse that accompanies the Crucifixion (fig. 2.2). Modern commentary runs as follows: "the third scene in the bottom field depicts the apocryphal scene of the eclipse observed by Dionysius Areopagites and Apollophanes from Heliopolis" ([1485], page 54. We see the Sun is completely covered by the dark lunar disc, with the corona visible underneath. The sky is painted black, since "there was darkness all over the whole land". Numerous spectators look at the sky in fear while the two sages point their fingers at the eclipse and the Crucifixion, q.v. near the top of the picture.

In fig. 2.3 we see the fragment of a New Testament frontispiece from *La Bible historiale*, a book by Guiart des Moulins ([1485], ill. 91). We see the Crucifixion accompanied by a total eclipse of the sun; we actually see a sequence of two events in the same miniature –

Fig. 2.1 A miniature from the *Rhemish Missal* (Missale remense. Missel à l'usage de Saint-Nicaise de Reims) dating to the alleged years 1285–1297. We see the Crucifixion accompanied by a total eclipse of the sun. Taken from [1485], ill. 25.

Fig. 2.2 A close-in of the fragment depicting a total solar eclipse on the miniature from the *Rhemish Missal* ([1485], ill. 25).

136

on the left of the cross the sun is still shining bright, whereas on the right it is completely obscured by the blackness of the lunar disc. This method was often used by mediaeval artists for a more comprehensive visual representation of sequences of events – "proto-animation" of sorts.

Yet another miniature where we see the Crucifixion accompanied by a solar eclipse can be seen in fig. 2.4 – it dates to the end of the alleged XV century ([1485], ill. 209). We see two events in a sequence once again. The sun is still bright on the left of the cross, and it is beginning to darken on the right where we see it obscured by the moon, which is about to hide the luminary from sight completely. We see a starlit sky, and that is something that only happens during a total eclipse of the sun.

It is interesting that the traces of references to Christ in mediaeval chronicles relating the XI century events have even reached our day. For instance, the 1680 Chronograph ([940]) informs us that Pope Leo IX (1049–1054) was visit-

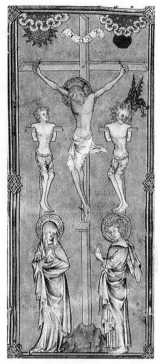

Fig. 2.3. Frontispiece fragment from an edition of the New Testament that dates to the end of the alleged XIV century with a Crucifixion scene accompanied by a total solar eclipse. Taken from [1485], ill. 91.

ed by Christ himself: "It is said that Christ had visited him [Leo IX] in his abode of repose, disguised as a beggar" ([940], sheet 287). It is important that there are no similar references anywhere else in the Chronograph ([940]) except for the renditions of the Gospels. In the next section we shall discover evangelical parallels in the biography of Pope Gregory VII, who had died in 1085. It is possible that Gregory VII is a reflection of Jesus Christ, or Emperor Andronicus, due to the fact that the Romean history of Constantinople was relocated to Italy as reflected by historical records.

This is why the first "A.D." year mentioned in a number of chronicles could have erroneously referred to 1054 A.D. This eventually gave birth to another chronological shift of 1053 years. In other words, some of the mediaeval chronologers were apparently accustomed to dating the Nativity to either 1054 or 1053 (instead of 1153, which is the correct dating).

A propos, the beginning of the first crusade – the one that had the "liberation of the Holy Sepulchre" as its objective – is erroneously

Fig. 2.4. An ancient miniature from the book entitled *Heures de Rolin-Lévis. À l'usage de Paris.* We see the Crucifixion as well as a total eclipse (the visibility of stars being a unique characteristic of the latter). Taken from [1485], ill. 209.

dated to 1096 ([76]) instead of circa 1196. On the other hand, one should pay attention to the mediaeval ecclesiastical sources, such as *The Tale of the Saviour's Passions* and *Pilate's Letter to Tiberius.* They often relate the events involving Christ in greater detail than the Gospels. And so, according to these sources, Pilate had been summoned to Rome immediately after the Resurrection and executed there, and the Caesar's troops marched towards Jerusalem and captured the city. Nowadays all of this mediaeval information is supposed to be of a figmental nature, since no Roman campaign against Jerusalem that took place in the third decade of the first century A.D. is recorded anywhere in the Scaligerian history. However, if we are to date the Resurrection to the end of the XII century, this statement that one encounters in mediaeval sources immediately assumes a literal meaning, being a reference to the crusades of the late XII – early XIII century, and particularly the so-called Fourth Crusade of 1204, which resulted in the fall of Czar-Grad.

Later chronologists, confused by the centenarian chronological shift, have moved the dates of the crusades of the late XII – early XIII century to the end of the XI century. This resulted in the phantom crusade of 1096, for instance, which is presumed to have led to the fall of Jerusalem ([76]).

6.2. The Roman John Crescentius of the alleged X century A.D. as a reflection of the Evangelical John the Baptist from the XII century A.D. A biographical parallelism

As we demonstrate in our book *King of the Slavs,* John the Baptist had lived in the XII century A.D. In the present section we shall discuss the correlation between his two phantom reflections in the I and the X century A.D.

The chronicles that tell us about the origins of the Second Roman Empire dating from the alleged I century A.D. include a detailed description of the great ecclesiastical reform implemented by Jesus Christ and partially instigated by his precursor John the Baptist. This is what the Gospels tell us. As one can see in Chapter 6 of *Chron1,* most of these events can be linked to the dawn of the X-XIII century Roman Empire – namely, the XII century A.D. One has to bear in mind that these events took place in the New Rome, or Czar-Grad on the Bosporus. The identification of the Second Empire as that

THE ISSUE WITH ANTIQUITY

of the X-XIII century is a consequence of the chronological shift of roughly 1053 years. It can be represented as the formula P = T + 1053, where T is the Scaligerian B.C. or A.D. dating of the event, and P – the new one suggested by our conception. Thus, if T equals zero (being the first year of the new era), the P date becomes equal to 1053 A.D. In other words, the results related in Chapter 6 of *Chron1* formally imply the existence of a mediaeval tradition dating the beginning of the new to 1053 A.D. in modern chronology.

Thus, the initial dating of Christ's lifetime to the XI century made by the mediaeval chronologists was 100 years off the mark. The real date of the Nativity falls on 1152, q.v. in our book entitled *King of the Slavs*.

We have observed the effects of the chronological shift (P = T + 1053) on the millenarian Roman history. If we are to move forward in time along this parallelism, we shall eventually reach the "beginning of the new era". What discoveries await us here? The answer is given below in numerous biographical collations and identifications. The "a" points of our table as presented below contain numerous references to the book of F. Gregorovius ([196], Volume 3).

In our relation of the parallelism we shall concentrate on its "mediaeval half", since the content of the Gospels is known to most readers quite well, unlike the mediaeval version. From the point of view of the parallelism that we have discovered, the mediaeval version is important as yet another rendition of the evangelical events. One should also bear in mind that nowadays the events related to Crescentius and Hildebrand are supposed to have happened in the Italian Rome. This is most probably untrue. The events described in the Gospels took place in Czar-Grad on the Bosporus, and got transferred to Italy on pages of later chronicles when the Italian Rome emerged as the new capital in the XIV century A.D. This young city had been in dire need of an "ancient history", which was promptly created.

COMPARISON TABLE FOR THE MEDIAEVAL JOHN CRESCENTIUS AND THE "ANCIENT" JOHN THE BAPTIST

a. John Crescentius. The alleged X century Rome (possibly the XII century Czar-Grad).

■ *b. John the Baptist.* The alleged I century A.D. See the Gospels for reference.

1*a. John Crescentius.* X century Rome, possibly the XII century Czar-Grad. The name is John Crescentius ([196], Volume 3).

■ 1*b. John the Baptist.* The name is John the Baptist (Matthew 3:1). The Russian version of the name is *Krestitel*; we hardly need to be surprised by their phonetic proximity. Apparently, the tale of John Crescentius was imported to the Italian Rome from the New Rome as recently as approximately the XIV century A.D. In *Chron7* one can find our definition of "Classical Latin".

2*a. John Crescentius.* X century Rome, possibly the XII century Czar-Grad. John Crescentius is a hero of the secular mediaeval Rome and a fighter for freedom from the foreign German rule. He presided the National-Patriotic party of Rome, which was founded around 960 A.D. He is said to have been "an eminent Roman... for several years John Crescentius had managed to hold the seat of Roman power... as the head of the National party" ([196], Volume 3, pages 325–326). Crescentius is the most famous representative of the mediaeval Crescentii family. He was "the secular ruler of Rome, but in no way an independent monarch" ([196], Volume 3, pages 326–327.

■ 2*b. John the Baptist.* John the Baptist is the famous prophet and extirpator who had fought against King Herod and his clan (Herod and his brother Philip – Mark 6:17).

3*a. John Crescentius.* X century Rome, possibly the XII century Czar-Grad. John Crescentius overthrows Pope John XV in Rome and thus seizes *ecclesiastical power* in Rome ([196], Volume 3, pages 325–343.

■ 3*b. John the Baptist.* The leadership of the contemporary religious movement is his to a large extent. He is a greatly respected prophet and the precursor of Jesus Christ.

4*a. John Crescentius.* X century Rome, possibly the XII century Czar-Grad. John Crescentius is supposed to have taken vows in 972 or 981 ([196], Volume 3, page 335).

■ 4b. John the Baptist. John the Baptist leads an ascetic monastic life. "And the same John had his raiment of camel's hair, and a leathern girdle about his loins; and his meat was locusts and wild honey" (Matthew 3:4).

5a. *John Crescentius.* X century Rome, possibly the XII century Czar-Grad. John Crescentius is supposed to have ruled in Rome. Most possibly the city in question was really the New Rome, or Czar-Grad, q.v. in *Chron1*, Chapter 6. According to geographical identifications that we suggest in *Chron5*, the evangelical "Jordan river" could really have been Danube (R + DAN). The Czar-Grad region can thus prove to be the biblical "region round about Jordan".

■ 5b. *John the Baptist.* John's sermons made a lot of people congregate around him: "Then went out to him ... all the area round about Jordan, and were baptized of him in Jordan, confessing their sins" (Matthew 3:5–6).

6a. *John Crescentius.* X century Rome, possibly the XII century Czar-Grad. As we have already pointed out, mediaeval chronicles would often identify Jerusalem as Rome or the New Rome.

■ 6b. *John the Baptist.* John the Baptist also preaches in Jerusalem (Matthew 3:5) – Judea remains under the Roman rule all the while.

7a. *John Crescentius.* X century Rome, possibly the XII century Czar-Grad. The emperor Otho III is John's main opponent. In 985 John Crescentius became the ruler of Rome in the absence of Otho III, who had been away from Rome at the time. Crescentius formally recognized the German rule as represented by Otho ([196], Volume 3, page 328). In 991, after the death of empress Theophano, John Crescentius "finally began to rule the city all by himself" ([196], Volume 3, page 342). Otho had launched a campaign against Rome in 996 and conquered the city. Crescentius remained head of the party, but no longer an independent governor.

■ 7b. *John the Baptist.* King Herod is the opponent of John the Baptist (Mark 6:27–28).

8a. *John Crescentius.* X century Rome, possibly the XII century

Czar-Grad. Being a German emperor, Otho was crowned Emperor of Rome in 996. "This had brought an end to the patrician authority of Crescentius" ([196], Volume 3, p. 346). "After a period of 13 years when there had been no one to bear the title of emperor, the walls of Rome finally saw the new Augustus" ([196], Volume 3, p. 346).

■ 8b. *John the Baptist.* King Herod is the ruler of the country (Matthew 2:1); John the Baptist has to recognize the secular power of King Herod.

9a. *John Crescentius.* X century Rome, possibly the XII century Czar-Grad. The relations between John Crescentius and Otho must have been neutral initially, despite their mutual political opposition. John remained head of the Roman National party ([196], Volume 3, page 346).

■ 9b. *John the Baptist.* The relationships between John the Baptist and King Herod had been neutral initially. "... for Herod feared John, knowing that he was a just man and an holy, and observed him; and when he heard him, he did many things, and heard him gladly" (Mark 6:20).

10a. *John Crescentius.* X century Rome, possibly the XII century Czar-Grad. The Pope's name is Bruno, he's the religious leader of Rome and a *cousin* of Emperor Otho. We learn that Otho had made his cousin Pope to replace Pope John XV, who was banished by Crescentius ([196], Volume 3, pages 343 and 346).

■ 10b. *John the Baptist.* The name of the ruler is Philip, and he's King Herod's *brother* (Mark 6:17).

11a. *John Crescentius.* X century Rome, possibly the XII century Czar-Grad. Bruno was *of royal blood* – namely, a grandson of Emperor Otho I (the Great – see [196], Volume 3, page 343).

■ 11b. *John the Baptist.* Philip the ruler is *of royal blood,* and he's the King's brother (Mark 6:17).

12a. *John Crescentius.* X century Rome, possibly the XII century Czar-Grad. Romans, especially members of the National party led by Crescentius, are *hostile* towards the Germans Otho and

THE ISSUE WITH ANTIQUITY

Bruno. On the contrary, Crescentius becomes a *national hero* of Rome and remains such for the next couple of centuries to follow ([196], Volume 3). "The Pope, likewise the Emperor... were relations, and both of German origin... Romans eyed these fair-haired Saxons who had come to rule their city and the entire Christian world with animosity, and the young tramontanes failed to instil due respect of their authority into the Romans" ([196], Volume 3, page 346).

■ 12*b*. *John the Baptist.* The Gospels mention both Herod and his brother Philip in a negative light, and treat John the Baptist with exalted reverence. The Gospels made Herod's name a derogatory denominative in many languages.

13*a*. *John Crescentius.* X Century Rome, possibly the XII century Czar-Grad. John Crescentius struggles against the rule of Otho's and Bruno's clan.

■ 13*b*. *John the Baptist.* John the Baptist is a freedom fighter, a vehement opponent of Herod and Philip, and their clan in general.

14*a*. *John Crescentius.* X century Rome, possibly the XII century Czar-Grad. John Crescentius is arrested, brought to trial and sentenced to banishment at the order of Otho, the Roman Emperor. "After the ascension of the Pope [Bruno – A. F.], who had been of the same blood as the emperor, the city needed pacification... Renegade Romans who had banished John XV were tried... Some of the popular leaders [of the rebellion – A. F.] were sentenced to banishment, among their number Crescentius" ([196], Volume 3, page 347).

■ 14*b*. *John the Baptist.* The arrest and incarceration of John the Baptist by King Herod. "For Herod himself had sent forth and laid hold upon John, and bound him in prison..." (Mark 6:17).

15*a*. *John Crescentius.* X century Rome, possibly the XII century Czar-Grad. Official amnesty given to John by Otho (and Bruno). John remains in Rome, albeit withdrawn from political power – a house arrest of sorts ([196], Volume 3, page 347.

- **15b. *John the Baptist.*** "Amnesty" given to John by Herod and
  Philip. Indeed, although John remains incarcerated, he isn't
  executed – moreover, King Herod still respects him, after a
  manner (Mark 6:20 and 6:26).

16a. *John Crescentius.* X century Rome, possibly the XII century
Czar-Grad. The "insult" to Pope Bruno credited to John Crescentius: John banishes Bruno from Rome ([196], Volume 3,
page 351). The banishment of Pope Bruno, Otho's placeman
and cousin, was clearly an insult to their entire clan.
- **16b. *John the Baptist.*** John the Baptist "insults" the clan of Philip, accusing Herod and Herodias, Philip's wife, of being in
  an unlawful liaison: "For John had said unto Herod, It is not
  lawful for thee to have thy brother's wife" (Mark 6:18).

17a. *John Crescentius.* X century Rome, possibly the XII century
Czar-Grad. The name of John's wife is Stephanie; however,
according to several mediaeval legends, she was Otho's concubine [Otho himself being a possible double of the Biblical
King Herod] ([196], Volume 3, p. 404).
- **17b. *John the Baptist.*** The daughter of Herodias (Mark 6:22)
  takes part in these events, being also a relation of King
  Herod (Mark, 6:17–22). Let us remind the reader that Herodias was the name of Herod's wife.

18a. *John Crescentius.* X century Rome, possibly the XII century
Czar-Grad. Stephanie is supposed to have "hexed" Otto
(which is a legend of a latter mediaeval epoch). The chronicles of the Middle Ages tell us that after the death of John
Crescentius Stephanie was given to mercenaries "as prey" –
however, Gregorovius tells us that "this tale is nothing but
pure fiction stemming from national pride and hatred of the
Romans. There is another legend of an altogether different
nature where Stephanie plays the fairylike role of the concubine of John's conqueror [becomes Otto's lover, that is – A. F.],
q.v. in [196], Volume 3, page 404.
- **18b. *John the Baptist.*** The daughter of Herodias "charms" King
  Herod with her dances: "Herod on his birthday made a

supper to his lords ... the daughter of Herodias came in, and danced, and pleased Herod... the king said unto the damsel, Ask of me whatsoever thou wilt, and I will give it thee" (Mark 6:21–22).

19a. *John Crescentius.* X century Rome, possibly the XII century Czar-Grad. The events in Rome take a turn that is to prove catastrophic for John Crescentius eventually, for he becomes the leader of an uprising ([196], Volume 3, page 352). "Having established his judicatory in the Eternal City, and having calmed the Romans by his amnesty, Otho III... had returned to Germany. His withdrawal had soon served as a signal for the Romans to rebel: the National party had made another desperate attempt to rid the country from the German yoke... Crescentius plots against the German Pope and his minions. The folk had reasons to be discontent – these foreigners were unfamiliar with Roman laws and appointed judges who weren't subsidized by the state and were corrupt and inequitable... there was an uprising, and the Pope had to flee on 29 September 996... the bold rebel [John Crescentius – A. F.] hurried to stabilize his position of power in Rome... when the Pope had fled, the Roman government was revolutionized completely... Crescentius declared himself a patrician and a consul of the Romans once again" ([196], Volume 3, pages 348–352). In 998 Otho and his troops approached the Roman fortifications. The city had capitulated, except for the Castle of St. Angelus where John Crescentius and his supporters decided to "make their last stand to the bitter end... Otho had demanded that Crescentius lay down his weapons" ([196], Volume 3, page 355). Having received a defiant reply, Otho commanded to storm the castle, which was conquered on 29 April 998.

■ 19b. *John the Baptist.* Events take a fatal turn for John: Herodias demands his execution. Her daughter "went forth and said unto her mother, What shall I ask? And she said, The head of John the Baptist. And she came in straightway with haste unto the king, and asked, saying, I will that thou give me by and by in a charger the head of John the Baptist" (Mark 6:24–25).

20*a. John Crescentius.* X century Rome, possibly the XII century Czar-Grad. The execution of Crescentius at the order of Otho ([196], Volume 3, pages 358–359).

■ 20*b. John the Baptist.* The execution of John the Baptist at the order of King Herod: "And immediately the king sent an executioner, and commanded his head to be brought: and he went and *beheaded* him in the prison, and brought his head in a charger, and gave it to the damsel: and the damsel gave it to her mother" (Mark 6:27–28).

21*a. John Crescentius.* X century Rome, possibly the XII century Czar-Grad. The severed head of John Crescentius became an important narrative element in the mediaeval chronicles of the X century. There were many legends about the death of Crescentius ([196], Volume 3, pages 358–359). "Crescentius was beheaded, thrown on the ground, and then hanged... Italian chroniclers tell us that prior to this Crescentius had been blinded with his every limb broken, and he was then dragged across the streets of Rome on the hide of a cow" ([196], Volume 3, pages 358–359).

■ 21*b. John the Baptist.* The severed head of John the Baptist became a popular mediaeval subject, which was extensively used in Christian paintings and mediaeval art (John's head on a dish).

22*a. John Crescentius.* X century Rome, possibly the XII century Czar-Grad. "It is even said that he [John Crescentius – A. F.] became disillusioned in further resistance due to its futility, and *took the vows*" ([196], Volume 3, page 358).

■ 22*b. John the Baptist.* "And the same John had his raiment of camel's hair, and a leathern girdle about his loins" (Matthew 3:4). John the Baptist had led a *monastic* life.

23*a. John Crescentius.* X century Rome, possibly the XII century Czar-Grad. John Crescentius is a famous martyr in the Roman history of the X century A.D. "His [John's – A. F.] demise after a brief but valiant stand served to cover his name in glory ... the Romans had wept for the unfortunate Crescentius for a long time; in the municipal acts of the XI century *we come across the name Crescentius extremely often* [sic! – A. F.], which was for a good reason – many families called their sons after Crescentius. This must have been a tribute to the memory of the intrepid Roman freedom fighter. The epitaph on the grave of Crescentius has survived until our day, and it is one of the most remarkable mediaeval Roman epitaphs" ([196], Volume 3, page 360).

■ 23b. *John the Baptist.* John the Baptist is a famous Christian saint and martyr of the alleged I century A.D. The chronological shift here equals about a thousand years.

24a. *John Crescentius.* X century Rome, possibly the XII century Czar-Grad. The Scaligerian chronology informs us of a great "evangelical upsurge" of the late X – early XI century A.D. It coincides with the beginning of the crusade epoch (in reality, all of this took place later – in the late XII – early XIII century). The Gospels are the main ideological weapon of the time. There is even a special term – "the evangelical *Renaissance* of the X-XI century A.D."

■ 24b. *John the Baptist.* The story of John the Baptist is one of the main evangelical legends. These texts served as a basis for the "evangelical" movement, or early Christianity of the alleged I century A.D. A chronological shift of 1053 years places this epoch exactly at the end of the X – beginning of the XI century. Thus, the shift in question identifies the two main "evangelical upsurges" in the Scaligerian history as two doubles. This "peak" can really be dated to the end of the XII – beginning of the XIII century, q.v. in our book entitled *King of the Slavs.*

25a. *John Crescentius.* X century Rome, possibly the XII century Czar-Grad. The legend of treachery that resulted in the death of John Crescentius. In this mediaeval version we see "treachery" from the part of the emperor Otho (the evangelical King Herod?) himself: "there was no shortage in versions that ascribed the fall of Crescentius to despicable perfidy demonstrated by Otho" ([196], Volume 3, pages 358–359). It is said

that Otho traitorously offered Crescentius a free pardon via
Tammus the knight, and when John had trusted him and capitulated, Otho gave orders to execute him as a proditor. The execution of Crescentius proved a political event serious enough
to tie the death of the emperor Otho that ensued in 1002 to the
name of John Crescentius in legends ([196], Volume 3, p. 404).
- 25b. *John the Baptist.* Above we have referred to the evangelical tale of perjury that led to the death of John the Baptist.
  According to the Gospels, John's death was the result of
  treachery from the part of Herodias, who had used her cun-
  ning to get the prophet executed with the assistance of her
  daughter (Mark 6:21–28).

26a. *John Crescentius.* X century Rome, possibly the XII century
Czar-Grad. Stephanie is *blamed for the death of Otho,* and
considered to have been *the wife of John Crescentius.* Other versions of the story call her emperor Otho's concubine.
When we compare the Gospels to the mediaeval Roman
chronicles, we see that they use the term "wife" in all the
wrong places; there is definitely confusion in the plot. This
must have led to the fact that the husband was confused for
his opponent. "The death of Otho... soon took on the hues
of a legend. It was told that the new Medea incarnate as the
widow of Crescentius managed to get Otho under her spell [a
parallel with the Gospels telling us about Herod charmed by
the daughter of Herodias – A. F.]; she is supposed to have pre-
tended that she wanted to heal the emperor, and, according
to various sources, had either wrapped him up in a poisoned
deer hide, poisoned his drink, or put a poison ring on his
finger" ([196], Volume 3, page 404).
- 26b. *John the Baptist.* St. Mark the evangelist directly refers to
  Herodias as *the one to blame for the death of John the Baptist*
  (Mark 6:24–25). Let us remind the reader that Herodias had
  allegedly been the wife of King Herod (the double of Otho?).

27a. *John Crescentius.* X century Rome, possibly the XII century
Czar-Grad. It is possible that Gregory Hildebrand was born
in the time of John Crescentius. Below we shall demonstrate

a very vivid parallelism between the mediaeval reports of the famous "Pope" Gregory VII Hildebrand and the evangelical story of Jesus Christ. The period when Hildebrand had been politically active in Rome falls on the epoch of 1049–1085 A.D. He is supposed to have been born in 1020 ([64], page 216), which is very close to the epoch of Crescentius (991–998 A.D.). One has to point out that there is another Crescentius in the Scaligerian history of Rome, namely, "John Crescentius the Second" ([196], Volume 3). He had allegedly been the son of "John Crescentius the First" whose biography we have studied above. This "son" is said to have ruled in Rome between 1002 and 1012. We know very little about him except for the fact that he "followed in his father's footsteps". This "John Crescentius Junior" may prove to be a second version of the same old legend about the first Crescentius, in which case the activities of Crescentius (the Baptist) precede the birth of Hildebrand immediately. Such a "duplication" of Crescentius shouldn't really surprise us. Above we have demonstrated the two duplicates of the war that broke out in the XIII century A.D., which were placed in the X century A.D. by the chronologists. They are shown on the global chronological map in *Chron1*, Chapter 6, as the two black triangles that mark the X century A.D. This narrative duplication of the war could have duplicated John Crescentius as well.

■ 27b. *John the Baptist.* Jesus Christ is said to have been born in the time of John the Baptist who had baptized Jesus (Matthew 3:1–3 and 3:13).

28a. *John Crescentius.* X century Rome, possibly the XII century Czar-Grad. Hildebrand's death *follows* the death of John Crescentius. Hildebrand "carries the banner" of John. We shall return to this below (see [196], Volume 3).

■ 28b. *John the Baptist.* The death of Jesus Christ *follows* the death of John the Baptist. Christ carries on with what was started by John the Baptist, who is therefore called his precursor. John used to preach "saying, There cometh one mightier than I after me, the latchet of whose shoes I am not worthy to stoop down and unloose. I indeed have baptized you with water: but he shall baptize you with the Holy Ghost" (Mark 1:7–8).

29a. *John Crescentius.* X century Rome, possibly the XII century Czar-Grad. The epoch of John Crescentius falls on the end of the X century. He had been in a mature enough age when he died; his activity (political and religious reforms) had started substantially earlier than 990 – somewhere in the middle of the alleged X century ([196], Volume 3).

■ 29b. *John the Baptist.* Major religious events in the history of the mediaeval states were connected with the name of John the Baptist. Let us point towards the well-known *baptism* of Russia somewhere around 980–990 A.D.

30a. *John Crescentius.* X century Rome, possibly the XII century Czar-Grad. If John the Baptist had something to do with the naissance of the rite of baptism, this rite must have had few "Jesus elements" around that time (allegedly the late X – early XI century; XII century in reality), since the epoch of Jesus Christ, or Andronicus (who became reflected in the Roman history as Hildebrand) was just dawning. It falls over the second half of the XII century.

■ 30b. *John the Baptist.* The main rite recorded in the chronicles telling us about the baptism of Russia refers to a *water baptism*. However, this rite had been introduced by John the Baptist before Jesus. By the way, this also implies that the baptism of Russia in the alleged X century (the XII century in reality), as well as the crusades of the alleged XI-XIII century (late XII – early XIII century really) didn't "wait for a thousand years to happen", but had rather proved a fast and immediate reaction to the principal religious events of that age.

6.3. "Pope" Gregory VII Hildebrand from the Roman chronicles dated to the XI century A.D. as the reflection of Jesus Christ (Andronicus) from the XI century A.D. A biographical parallelism

In the present section we demonstrate the famous "Pope Hildebrand" from the alleged XI century A.D. to be a phantom reflection of Andronicus (Christ) from the XII century A.D.

Scaligerian history considers "Pope" Hildebrand to have been the most eminent reformist of the mediaeval Christian church in the west. He is counted amongst the greatest European popes; his name is most commonly associated with the greatest reform of the mediaeval Christian church in the Western Europe that had made a tremendous political impact. "Contemporaries compare the renowned votary to Marius, Scipio and Caesar" ([196], Volume 4, p. 119).

Hildebrand is considered to have been the author of the famous celibacy edict that led to large-scale upheavals all across Western Europe. He had been the first to conceive of the crusades and make this concept a reality, which had defined the style and character of the three centuries to follow ([196], Volume 4). These "reborn Gospels" were the official ideological documents to serve as foundations of this crucial XI century reform; Scaligerian history dates them to the I century A.D. which precedes this epoch by a millennium.

This reform was enforced *manu militari* and led to a violent struggle between the devotees of the old church and the supporters of the new confession (the so-called reformist or evangelical church in the West) that had raged across the Western Europe for fifty years on end. Despite the fact that influential strata of European society had opposed his actions vehemently, Hildebrand made both the ecclesial and secular authorities conform to the new doctrine. He is considered the first organizer of the church in its evangelical format ([196], Volume 4).

One mustn't get the idea that Hildebrand's "biography" really pertains to the XII century A.D. It had most probably been compiled a great deal later, around the XIV-XVI century A.D. – especially since the very foundation of the Italian Rome as a capital can be relatively safely dated to the XIV century. This consideration stems from our discovery that the First Roman Empire, or Livy's "Imperian Rome", can be identified as the Holy Roman Empire of the X-XIII century A.D. and the Habsburg (Nov-Gorod?) Empire of the XIV-XVI century A.D.

Let us relate in brief the parallels between the biographies of Jesus Christ (Andronicus) and "Pope Hildebrand". They became identified as one and the same person by formal methods described in *Chron1*, Chapter 6. Let us point out that the name Hildebrand can be a derivative of "Ablaze with Gold" ("Hilde" being related to such words as "gilded", "golden" etc; as for "Brand" – the igneous connotations of the word are obvious enough). Bear in mind that Christ would also

152

be referred to as "The Sun", q.v. in fig. 2.9. The name *Hilde-Brand* may also be a reference to the Slavic word *Kolyada* – another name of Christ, q.v. in our book entitled *King of the Slavs*.

COMPARISON TABLE FOR HILDEBRAND AND JESUS CHRIST (ANDRONICUS)

a. Hildebrand (Ablaze with Gold). Presumably XI century Rome, possibly the XII century Czar-Grad.

■ *b. Jesus Christ* (Andronicus). The alleged I century A.D. (the XII century in reality). Active in Jerusalem, or Czar-Grad.

1*a. Hildebrand.* XI century Rome, possibly the XII century Czar-Grad. The approximate date of Hildebrand's birth is 1020 ([64], page 216) – the 12th year of the reign of Henry II the Holy, or Augustus, q.v. above – the emperor who is identified as none other but Octavian Augustus in the parallelism between the Roman Empire of the X-XIII century and the Second Roman Empire. Pope Octavian is another reflection of this character, q.v. below.

■ 1*b. Jesus Christ* (Andronicus). According to the Scaligerian chronology, Jesus Christ (Andronicus) was born on the 23rd reign year of Octavian Augustus in the Second Roman Empire (or the 27th year, according to another version – see [76]). The discrepancy between this date and the 12th year of Henry II the Holy equals a mere 5–10 years if we are to consider the 1053-year shift. We see a very good date correlation.

2*a. Hildebrand.* XI century Rome, possibly the XII century Czar-Grad. The death of Hildebrand in the alleged year 1085 ([196], Volume 4).

■ 2*b. Jesus Christ* (Andronicus). The death of Jesus Christ (Andronicus) in the alleged year 33 ([76]). We give a comparison of dates with the effects of the 1053 year shift taken into account. The latter can be expressed by the formula $P = T + 1035$. Thus, the death of Jesus Christ (Andronicus) in the alleged year 33 A.D. ([76]) occurs right in 1086, since

33 + 1053 = 1086. The death of both these characters occurs in the same year – 1085–1086 A.D. We must point out that Andronicus (Christ) was really crucified a century later, in 1185 (q.v. in our book entitled *King of the Slavs*).

3*a. Hildebrand.* XI century Rome, possibly the XII century Czar-Grad. Hildebrand arrives in Rome in 1049. This moment marks the beginning of his ecclesiastical reformist activity, and can therefore be considered the year of his making into the greatest reformer even seen in the ranks of the clergy ([196], Volume 4, page 57). Another important date in Hildebrand's biography is 1053, q.v. below.

■ 3*b. Jesus Christ* (Andronicus). A 1053 shift forwards in time shall transpose the birth of Jesus Christ (Andronicus) to 1053 A.D. This date differs from 1049 A.D., the date of Hildebrand's arrival to Rome, by a mere 4 years. The same shift moves the date of Christ's death (33 years later according to the Gospels) to 1086 A.D., whilst Hildebrand's death is dated to 1085 A.D. We see that the discrepancy only equals one year. Therefore, *a 1053 year shift makes the principal dates virtually identical.* Let us point out that the main date related to Jesus Christ (Andronicus) is usually considered to be the date of his death (Crucifixion, or the Passions). The date of his birth was calculated somewhat later, with the date of the Crucifixion used as source information. It is said that a monk by the name of "Dionysius Exiguus" (Dionysius the Little) had first calculated the year of Christ's death, and then subtracted 33 years to obtain the date of the Nativity according to the Gospels, q.v. above. Therefore the brilliant correlation between the dates of the Crucifixion and Hildebrand's death with a shift of 1053 years is extremely important to us. We are led to the idea that the A.D. chronological scale only actually begins in the year referred to as 1053 A.D. nowadays. A deliberate or accidental 1053-year shift buried it under a load of many additional years. Thus, one gets the idea that, according to the erroneous mediaeval tradition, the "new era" had really been counted from the phantom year 1053 in modern chronology for some time. It was only in the XVI-

XVII century that the phantom year 1053 "travelled backwards in time" as a result of another deliberate or accidental
chronological shift of 1053 years. This is how "year zero" of
the new era was calculated (with a 1100-year discrepancy).

4a. *Hildebrand.* XI century Rome, possibly the XII century Czar-
Grad. 1053 is a famous date in global ecclesiastical history. The
notorious schism between the Occident and the Orient, or the
"ecclesial schism", which exists to this day, took place in 1053 or
1054. This is considered to be the moment when a new epoch
began for Western Europe ([196], Volume 4).

■ 4b. *Jesus Christ* (Andronicus). The "dawn of the new era" is the
time the new church was born – the Christian (Evangelical)
one. This "evangelical hue" of the epoch corresponds very
well with the XI century "Evangelical Renaissance" if we are
to consider the 1053-year shift. The crusades are of a particular interest to us since their ideological basis was defined by
the Gospels.

5a. *Hildebrand.* XI century Rome, possibly the XII century Czar-
Grad. Hildebrand is considered to have been "the son of a carpenter" ([196], Volume 4, page 139). Mediaeval chronicles give
us a distinctly divine description of Hildebrand (Ablaze with
Gold) as an infant: "there were flames of fire coming from his
head" etc ([196], Volume 4, page 179, comment 1). Chronicles
mention no other pope who'd be the "son of a *carpenter*". This
is a characteristic as unique as its evangelical counterpart in the
biography of Jesus.

■ 5b. *Jesus Christ* (Andronicus). The Gospels tell us that Christ's
father had been a carpenter: "Is not this the carpenter's son?"
(Matthew 13:55). Mark calls Jesus himself a carpenter: "Is not
this the carpenter, the son of Mary?" (Mark 6:3). The birth of
Christ is described as an incarnation of God in the Gospels.

6a. *Hildebrand.* XI century Rome, possibly the XII century Czar-
Grad. We didn't manage to find any information about Hildebrand's mother; however, his maternal uncle is supposed to
have been the abbot of St. Mary's monastery ([196], Volume 4,

p. 139). Moreover, Hildebrand is supposed to have lived in the monastery of St. Mary ([459], Volume 1, page 64). This may be a distorted reflection of the fact that Jesus had been the son of Mary. "Hildebrand's biography" made Mary the mother disappear; however, a reference to living in St. Mary's monastery has taken its place.

■ 6b. *Jesus Christ* (Andronicus). The mother of Jesus was called Mary (Matthew 1:18) – thus, the name "accompanies" the birth of both characters in question. In figs. 2.5 and 2.6 we see some interesting mediaeval artwork – namely, a mediaeval relief depicting Our Lady with *two long braids* ([992], pages 20, 21 and 211). This is a XII-XIII century relief from the Liebfrauenkirche church in Halberstadt (Germany). "Likewise her close relation from Hildesheim, Our Lady of Halberstadt belongs to the well-known Romanesque iconographic type of *Our Ladies with braids*" ([992], page 23).

Fig. 2.5. A statue of Our Lady with two long braids. A relief from the Liebfrauenkirche church in Halberstadt, Germany. Taken from [992], page 20, ill. 15.

Fig. 2.6 Blessed Virgin Mary with braids. A fragment of the previous photograph.

7a. *Hildebrand*. XI century Rome, possibly the XII century Czar-Grad. The consensual opinion is that Hildebrand had been born in Italy ([196], Volume 4). There is a town in Italy by the name of Palestrina – the name must date to XIV century or a later epoch, when the legends of Jesus Christ (Andronicus) (under the alias of Hildebrand) came to these parts. The evangelical Christ is said to have been active in Palestine (White Camp or Babylonian Camp?). Furthermore, ever since the XIII century the Catholic Church has been claiming that Archangel Gabriel came to Mary the Mother of Christ who had allegedly lived in the town of Loreto (or Loretto) in Italy ([444], page 198). Christ's mother may have really lived in Italy – however, this legend is most probably a planted one and reflects the transposition of events that took place in the New Rome to the Italian Rome, founded rather recently (in the XIV century), an in urgent need of an "ancient history" at the time. An indirect proof of this can be found in the rather remarkable mediaeval tradition telling us that Mary's house used to be in an altogether different place and was *brought* to Loreto later. This tradition is manifest in such works of art as the ancient painting by Cesare Nebbia (circa 1536–1614) and his apprentices, titled candidly and unequivocally "The Holy House of Our Lady Carried to Loreto" (The Geographical Card Gallery, Vatican – vaulting artwork detail). The picture shows angels *carrying* Mary's house to Italy (fig. 2.8).

Fig. 2.7. "The Holy House of Our Lady Carried to Loreto" by Cesare Nebbia and apprentices, depicting angels carrying Mary's house to Italy. This may be a reflection of the "paperwork migration" of Constantinople events to Rome in Italy during the epoch when the "ancient history" of this city was being created. Taken from [713], page 438, ill. 417.

Fig. 2.8. A fragment of the picture entitled "The Holy House of Our Lady Carried to Loreto" by Cesare Nebbia and apprentices. Taken from [713], page 438, ill. 417.

■ *7b. Jesus Christ* (Andronicus). "The angel Gabriel was sent from God unto a city of Galilee, named Nazareth, to a virgin … and the virgin's name was Mary" (Luke 1:26–27). Let us remind the reader that Nazareth may well have the same meaning as the Turkish word Nazreti – "holy" ([1181]).

8a. Hildebrand. XI century Rome, possibly the XII century Czar-Grad. Hildebrand's reforms were preceded by the endeavours of John Crescentius, q.v. above. Both were focussed on the same goal: the glorification of Rome and the foundation of a new church whose influence would spread across the entire Europe ([196], Volumes 3 and 4).

■ *8b. Jesus Christ.* Christ's precursor is John the Baptist. Both of them have contributed to the creation of the new religion to some extent – see the comparison table for the biographies of Crescentius and John the Baptist above.

9a. Hildebrand. XI century Rome, possibly the XII century Czar-Grad. Hildebrand is the author of a radical ecclesiastical reform in the Middle Ages, as well as the organizer and supervisor of its implementation. He was a vehement antagonist of the old cult and its devotees ([196], Volume 4).

■ *9b. Jesus Christ* (Andronicus). Jesus is the founder of a new religion that led to a radical reform in the old church. He had also opposed those who followed the Orthodox Judaic tradition. Some of the reforms implemented by Jesus and Hildebrand are very similar, q.v. below.

10a. Hildebrand. XI century Rome, possibly the XII century Czar-Grad. The well-known decree against simony, or the sale of ecclesial positions ([196], Volume 4.

■ *10b. Jesus Christ* (Andronicus). Jesus banishing vendors from the temple. "And he went into the temple, and began to cast out them that sold therein, and them that bought" (Luke 19:45).

11a. Hildebrand. XI century Rome, possibly the XII century Czar-Grad. Hildebrand's activity is allegedly confined to Rome for

158

the most part, likewise that of his precursor John Crescentius ([196], Volume 4). We have already mentioned the identification of Rome as Jerusalem above – see *Chron2*, Chapter 1.

■ 11*b. Jesus Christ* (Andronicus). Christ preaches in the same geographical area as his predecessor John the Baptist – Jerusalem, Judea and Samaria. According to our reconstruction, the Jerusalem mentioned in the Gospels is really Czar-Grad on the Bosporus.

12*a. Hildebrand.* XI century Rome, possibly the XII century Czar-Grad. Hildebrand had "served" the church between 1049 (the year he first came to Rome) and 1085 (the year of his death – see [196], Volume 4). If we are to consider 1054, the year of the Great Schism, to have marked the beginning of his ministry, the correlation with the datings valid for Jesus (shifted by 1100 years) becomes ideal given the 1053-year shift, q.v. below.

■ 12*b. Jesus Christ* (Andronicus). Jesus had lived for 33 years – that is, between 0 and 33 A.D. in Scaligerian chronology ([76]). A 1053-year shift forward in time gives us the interval between 1053 and 1086 A.D. Theology differentiates between the two periods of Christ's ministry: the first one starting from his birth and ending with his death, and the other covering the period between his 30th year and the Crucifixion.

13*a. Hildebrand.* XI century Rome, possibly the XII century Czar-Grad. Hildebrand initiated the ecclesial reform in 1049, when he had been 29 or 30 years of age ([196], Volume 4). Let us remind the reader that he was born in the alleged year 1020 ([64], page 216).

■ 13*b. Jesus Christ* (Andronicus). Luke the Evangelist tells us that "Jesus himself began to be about thirty years of age" (Luke 3:23). We see a perfect correlation with the "Hildebrand" dates.

14*a. Hildebrand.* XI century Rome, possibly the XII century Czar-Grad. Hildebrand was "born twice": in 1020 de facto, with his initiation into priesthood occurring in either 1049 or 1053.

This provides us with the following versions of his age: 32 or 36 as the age his ecclesial career began, or 65 years of actual age.

■ 14*b*. *Jesus Christ* (Andronicus). The Gospels also provide two versions of Christ's age: 33 years and approaching 50. The former version is considered to have higher authority, q.v. above. The second is derived from St. John's indication saying "Thou art not yet fifty years old" (John 8:57). A comparison with "Hildebrand" tells us that 33 years of Christ are very similar to "Hildebrand's" 32, and "not yet fifty" may also refer to the age of 65.

15*a*. *Hildebrand*. XI century Rome, possibly the XII century Czar-Grad. The official beginning of Hildebrand's reform and the ecclesiastical schism are usually dated to 1054 ([196], Volume 4). All of this is supposed to follow the death of the Roman emperor in 1039 by roughly 15 years – or in the 15th year of the *autocracy* of Henry III the Black in Rome. Let us remind the reader that he had been a co-ruler of Conrad II prior to that date, q.v. in Table 8, which is to be found in Chapter 6 of *Chron1*.

■ 15*b*. *Jesus Christ* (Andronicus). Christ's reforms begin when he is 30 years of age (Luke 3:23) – right in the 15th year of the reign of Tiberius, the "Black Emperor" (see Table 8 in Chapter 6 of *Chron1*). Now, according to the Scaligerian chronology, Tiberius ascended the throne in 14 A.D. Thus, Christ's 30th year falls exactly over the 15th year of Tiberius' reign. Another important fact is that an independent dynastic superimposition of the Second Roman Empire over the Roman Empire of the X-XIII century identifies Tiberius as Henry the Black, no less! We see perfect date correlation for Christ and "Hildebrand".

16*a*. *Hildebrand*. XI century Rome, possibly the XII century Czar-Grad. Roman chronicles dated to the XI century nowadays contain numerous references to a well-known ally of Hildebrand – Countess Matilda, whose influence and finances had always been ready at hand whenever support was called for.

She is said to have owned half of Italy [!] All of her estate was at Hildebrand's disposal ([196], Volume 4, pages 148 and 192.

■ 16*b. Jesus Christ* (Andronicus). The Gospels tell us a lot about the woman who had accompanied Jesus Christ (Andronicus) constantly – Mary Magdalene, the repentant sinner. She is always found by his side ready to support him: "and certain women ... Mary, called *Magdalene* ... and many others, which ministered unto him *of their substance*" (Luke 8:2–3).

17*a. Hildebrand.* XI century Rome, possibly the XII century Czar-Grad. We learn that Countess Matilda's name is spelt MATHILDA ([196], Volume 4, page 180, comment 12. A slightly distorted reading could make this name sound like "Madgilda" (MDGLD without vocalizations), or "Magdalene".

■ 17*b. Jesus Christ* (Andronicus). The name of Christ's ally is Magdalene. MGDLN without vocalizations, which corresponds well with the MDGLD version offered above.

18*a. Hildebrand.* XI century Rome, possibly the XII century Czar-Grad. F. Gregorovius tells us there were no findings of coins from the Papal Rome that can be dated to the period between 984 A.D. and Leo IX (mid-XI century). F. Gregorovius points out specifically that "it is all the more surprising that not a single coin from the period of Gregory VII was to be found anywhere" ([196], Volume 4, page 74, comment 41). We shouldn't be surprised - as we're beginning to understand, there has never been any pope by the name of Hildebrand, since he is a mere reflection of the XII century figure of Jesus Christ (Andronicus). Hence the absence of "Pope Hildebrand's" coins – no one ever minted them.

■ 18*b. Jesus Christ* (Andronicus). We learn that there are mediaeval coins with Jesus Christ (Andronicus) bearing respective inscriptions. One of them can be seen in fig. 2.9. Jesus Christ (Andronicus) has a halo around his head, and the reverse of the coins says "Jesus Christ (Andronicus) Basileus" (King). The coin is presumed to have been minted under John I Tsimisces (taken from [578], Volume 1, page 177, ill. 153). In

Fig. 2.9 A mediaeval coin depicting Jesus Christ (with the words "Jesus Christ Basileus" on the flip side). Taken from [578], Volume 1, page 177, ill. 153.

fig. 2.10 we can see another such coin ([684], table 21). As V. M. Potin points our, images of Christ are "characteristic for mediaeval coins". In this case we see Jesus Christ (Andronicus) at the bottom, and two mediaeval rulers on top of the flip side. They are allegedly Leo VI and Constantine VII, and their portraits on the coin are those of "Christ's legates" who had received their power from him.

19a. Hildebrand. XI century Rome, possibly the XII century Czar-Grad. Hildebrand comes to Rome in 1049 with the party of Leo IX, which can be considered the beginning of "Hildebrand's ministry" ([196], Volume 4). He was about 30 years of age at the time. Commentators compare this advent of the reformer-to-be to an apostolic advent, or the Evangelical "entry into Jerusalem". According to Gregorovius, "in February 1049 the new pope [Leo IX – A. F.] arrived in Rome and proceeded along the streets barefoot, reading prayers in humility, accompanied by a very modest entourage. A sight as uncommon as this couldn't fail to leave the Romans completely flabbergasted. It seemed as though an apostle…

Fig. 2.10 A mediaeval coin depicting Jesus Christ. Taken from [684], table 21.

had entered the city... no aristocrat was seen in his party – this bishop came as a simple pilgrim who knocked on the doors of the Romans asking them whether they desired to accept him in the name of Christ... But one of his satellites had such spiritual power that its beacon had shone a great deal brighter than that of any royalty... it was Hildebrand" ([196], Volume 4, page 57).

■ 19b. *Jesus Christ* (Andronicus). The entry of Jesus and his disciples into Jerusalem is the beginning of "Christ's ministry". He was about 30 at the time (Luke 3:23). As Jesus was entering Jerusalem, "many spread their garments in the way: and others cut off branches off the trees, and strawed them in the way... And Jesus entered into Jerusalem" (Mark 11:8 and 11:11).

20a. *Hildebrand.* XI century Rome, possibly the XII century Czar-Grad. At the peak of the reforms, a certain Cencius tries to assassinate Hildebrand in 1075. We thus see an *attempt to assassinate "Hildebrand"* ([196], Volume 4, page 155).

■ 20b. *Jesus Christ* (Andronicus). A plot against Christ is organized in Jerusalem by Judas Iscariot, one of the apostles. The plot results in the arrest of Jesus and his subsequent crucifixion.

21a. *Hildebrand.* XI century Rome, possibly the XII century Czar-Grad. Roman chronicles of the XI century refer to Cencius with the utmost scorn and distaste ([196], Volume 4, pages 126–127). According to Gregorovius, "the chronicles of the time [the ones dated to the XI century nowadays, if we are to be more precise – A.D.] portray Cencius as ... a godless robber and philanderer... this unflattering characteristic of the head of Cadalus' party might well be the furthest thing from exaggeration" ([196], Volume 4, pages 126–127).

■ 21b. *Jesus Christ* (Andronicus). The Gospels characterize Judas in a very negative manner, and his name transformed into a negative denominative in the entire Christian tradition.

22a. *Hildebrand.* XI century Rome, possibly the XII century Czar-Grad. Cencius had initially participated in Hildebrand's reformist activities, and been in a close bond with Hildebrand's party ([196], Volume 4, page 126). Stefan, the father of Cencius, had been a Roman prefect and maintained good relationships with the allies of "Hildebrand" the reformist. Moreover, Cencius belonged to the family of Crescentii ([196], Volume 4) – that is, the same family as John the Baptist – the precursor of Christ, whose identification with the "Roman" John Crescentius is related above in detail.

■ 22b. *Jesus Christ* (Andronicus). Judas was related to Jesus in the most direct manner possible, having been his disciple – one of the twelve Apostles.

23a. *Hildebrand.* XI century Rome, possibly the XII century Czar-Grad. Cencius soon heads the Roman party of malcontents, which opposes "Hildebrand" ([196], Volume 4, page 155).

■ 23b. *Jesus Christ* (Andronicus). A short while later, Judas betrays his teacher and joins the ranks of those in Jerusalem who are dissatisfied by the reforms of Jesus. Judas makes a deal with the high priests, or "Pharisees".

24a. *Hildebrand.* XI century Rome, possibly the XII century Czar-Grad. The alleged chronicles of Rome relate further actions from the part of Cencius as a betrayal of Hildebrand. Cencius is portrayed as a detestable ingrate – as early as around the beginning of 1075 Cencius was plotting against Hildebrand. The plot had proved a failure, and the city prefect launched a process against Cencius – however, the latter had received the unexpected support of Hildebrand himself, likewise Countess Matilda (MDGLD). Only the protection of the great reformist had secured Cencius' freedom ([196], Volume 4, page 155).

■ 24b. *Jesus Christ* (Andronicus). The Gospels describe the actions of the former Apostle Judas as a betrayal of Jesus and his cause. Judas treats Jesus with the utmost ingratitude, hence the numerous negative connotations of the name that is used as a denominative nowadays.

25a. *Hildebrand.* XI century Rome, possibly the XII century Czar-Grad. "For the meantime, he [Cencius – A. F.] was plotting his

revenge. Seeing that a severance of relations between the Pope
[Hildebrand – A. F.] and Henry was inevitable, Cencius had
thought up a plan to dethrone Pope Gregory. He had made
Henry [the emperor – A. F.] an offer on behalf of the Romans
to seize Rome, promising to capture Gregory and hand him
over to Henry as a captive" ([196], Volume 4, page 155).

■ 25b. *Jesus Christ* (Andronicus). "Then one of the twelve, called
Judas Iscariot, went unto the chief priests, and said unto
them, What will ye give me, and I will deliver him unto
you?" (Matthew 26:14–16). "And he went his way, and
communed with the chief priests and the captains, how he
might betray him unto them" (Luke 22:4). See also (Mark
14:10–11).

26a. *Hildebrand.* XI century Rome, possibly the XII century Czar-
Grad. "The scene that took place on Christmas Day in 1075
is one of the most gruesome episodes in the entire history of
mediaeval Rome. On Christmas eve the Pope [Hildebrand –
A. F.] had been preparing to say mass in the subterranean
church of S. Maria Maggiore; suddenly, there were cries and
weapon noises all over; the church was invaded by Cencius,
who brandished a sword in his hands, surrounded by aristocratic intrigants" ([196], Volume 4, page 155).

■ 26b. *Jesus Christ* (Andronicus). "And immediately, while he
[Jesus – A. F.] yet spake [bear in mind that Jesus was reading a sermon to his disciples, or saying mass in a way – A.
F.], cometh Judas, one of the twelve, and with him a great
multitude with swords and staves, from the chief priests and
the scribes and the elders" (Mark 14:43). Let us re-emphasize that, likewise Hildebrand, Jesus was giving orders to his
disciples when the enemy came.

27a. *Hildebrand.* XI century Rome, possibly the XII century Czar-
Grad. "Having seized the bruised and battered Pope [Hilde-
brand – A. F.] by the locks, Cencius dragged him out of the
church, heaved him onto a horse and hurried to his castle
through the dormant streets of Rome" ([196], Volume 4, page
155). All of this happens *at night.*

■ 27b. *Jesus Christ* (Andronicus). "And they laid their hands on him, and took him (Mark 14:46). "And some began to spit on him, and to cover his face, and to buffet him, and to say unto him, Prophesy: and the servants did strike him with the palms of their hands" (Mark 14:65). All of the above also takes place *at night*.

28a. *Hildebrand*. XI century Rome, possibly the XII century Czar-Grad. "The whole city was immediately agitated – bells rang out in alarm, people grabbed their weapons, and priests locked up their altars in horror" ([196], Volume 4, pages 155–156). However, there is no direct military conflict. Hildebrand forgives Cencius (likewise Jesus who is supposed to have "forgiven" Judas the betrayal).

■ 28b. *Jesus Christ* (Andronicus). "When they which were about him saw what would follow, they said unto him, Lord, shall we smite with the sword? And one of them smote the servant of the high priest, and cut off his right ear. And Jesus answered and said, Suffer ye this far." (Luke 22:49–51). There is no armed conflict.

29a. *Hildebrand*. XI century Rome, possibly the XII century Czar-Grad. "Roman" chronicles tell us nothing about either the trial of Hildebrand or his "crucifixion" ([196], Volume 4). Recently, in 2004, we discovered ancient data clearly demonstrating that at the end of Hildebrand's "biography" one can find vivid Evangelical scenarios pertaining to the Crucifixion of 1185 A.D. We shall relate this in detail in our subsequent publications.

■ 29b. *Jesus Christ* (Andronicus). The Gospels describe the trial and crucifixion of Jesus (his so-called Passions). The parallelism breaks out of synch here.

30a. *Hildebrand*. XI century Rome, possibly the XII century Czar-Grad. The following is told about the fate of Cencius the betrayer: "In his attempts to catch Gregory unawares, this vengeful Roman kept thinking up new plots until his *sudden death* in Pavia" ([196], Volume 4, page 170).

■ 30*b*. *Jesus Christ* (Andronicus). The following is said about
   Judas: "And he cast down the pieces of silver in the temple,
   and departed, and went and hanged himself" (Matthew
   27:5).

31*a*. *Hildebrand*. XI century Rome, possibly the XII century Czar-
   Grad. The second most important leader of the reformist (or
   Evangelical) movement of Hildebrand is the well-known *Peter
   Damiani*, Hildebrand's right hand. He was born in 1007 and
   "had the reputation of an extraordinarily gifted individual"
   ([196], Volume 4, page 84). As we already understand, this
   Peter is most probably a reflection of Peter the Apostle, the
   closest ally of Jesus. Peter Damiani became head of the hermit
   army in the XI century - these hermits were just about as influential as Peter – their influence "was *a mystery in what concerned the strength of its manifestation* – they weren't equalled
   by anyone in this respect, with the possible exception of *the
   Old Testament prophets*" ([196], Volume 4, pages 84–85).

   This mystery is but a side effect of the Scaligerian chronology that
transferred the Evangelical boom into the I century A.D. from the
XII. F. Gregorovius proceeds to tell us that "Damiani had been the
very heart of this church [the church of Hildebrand, that is – A. F.]"
([196], Volume 4, pages 88–89). Damiani's banner was immediately
picked up by Peter the Stylite: "he became a folk hero, a prophet of
sorts – someone who received his authority of a crusade leader from
Christ himself" ([196], Volume 4). These two Peters are the only
well-known characters in the XI century Rome bearing that name.
They may have been reflected in the collective evangelical character
by the name of "Peter Simon the Apostle". The names Simon and
Damian may have been interchangeable.

■ 31*b*. *Jesus Christ* (Andronicus). Peter Simon is considered the
   main figure among the apostles of Christ – he is called the
   founder of the new Roman church. The Papal throne is
   still referred to as the Throne of St. Peter. According to the
   official formula, Peter had been the keystone of the Catholic
   Church.

32a. *Hildebrand.* XI century Rome, possibly the XII century Czar-Grad. According to some mediaeval Russian chronicles, Russia was baptized by Andrew the Apostle, an actual disciple of Jesus Christ (Andronicus) ([208], pages 121–122). At the same time, according to the Scaligerian-Romanovian chronology, Russia was baptised in late X – early XI century, that is, allegedly *a thousand years later than Christ had lived.* More details concerning the fact that Andrew the Apostle is really yet another reflection of the XII century Emperor Andronicus can be found in our book entitled *King of the Slavs.*

■ 32b. *Jesus Christ* (Andronicus). One of the apostles of Jesus was called Andrew (Mark 1:16). As well as the other apostles, he had walked the Earth preaching the doctrine of Jesus. The Scaligerian chronology places him in the I century. How could he have baptized Russia in the XI century?

COMMENTARY. The Scaligerian-Romanovian version tells us about Andrew the Apostle and his baptism of Russia in the X–XI century A.D., which contradicts the same Scaligerian dating of Andrew's lifetime (I century A.D.). However, this baptism corresponds to our new chronology and the year 1053 (considering the 1153-year shift) perfectly. Indeed, when we transpose the evangelical events from the phantom I century into the real XII century, everything falls into place. We begin to understand why the "evangelical boom" falls on the XII–XIII century, as well as "the heyday of baptisms". It becomes perfectly clear that Russia didn't have to wait a whole millennium so that it could "finally" get baptized – the baptism followed the naissance of the new religion in the XII century almost immediately. The legend about Andrew the Apostle baptizing Russia also begins to make sense. By the way, the Scaligerian-Romanovian history shall doubtlessly assure us that the legend of Andrew the Apostle baptizing Russia is a "later addition" to the famous *Povest Vremennyh Let* ([208], p. 121). Nevertheless, in the XVI century John IV the Terrible, being unaware of the Scaligerian chronology, which was introduced after his death, "used to point out that the Russians were baptized by Andrew the Apostle himself, and didn't import Christianity from Greece. That was the very same thing that Hieromonk Arseniy Soukhanov, the emissary in Greece … had told the Greeks a century later" ([208], p. 121).

Mind that a 720-year chronological shift backwards in time (its value equalling the subtraction residual of the two primary shifts: 720 = 1053 – 333) superimposes Hildebrand over a well-known Christian saint – Basil the Great (or "The Great King" in translation). The year 1053 is shifted backwards and transforms into the year 333 A.D., since 1053 – 720 = 333. *This happens to be precisely the year Basil the Great was born according to the Scaligerian chronology.*

This fact instantly explains the vivid and explicit parallelism between Jesus Christ (Andronicus) and Basil the Great that was already pointed out by N. A. Morozov in [544], Volume 1. Thus, the XII century Jesus (Andronicus) became reflected in history twice – as "Pope Hildebrand" and St. Basil the Great.

As we have already mentioned, the hagiographies of St. Basil the Great devote plenty of attention to his conflict with the Roman emper-or Valens "the Unholy" – the double of the Evangelical King Herod. In the alleged IV century A.D. St. Basil the Great "instilled horror into Valens" and broke his spirit in a way. We see another "secular trace" of this scenario in the alleged XI century – the well-known opposition between "Pope Hildebrand" and the Roman Emperor Henry. We are referring to the well-known scene that took place in Canossa in 1077 A.D., when Hildebrand had humiliated Henry.

We have to bear in mind that when the struggle against the secular authorities had reached its apogee in the alleged XI century, "Pope" Gregory had excommunicated Emperor Henry. "The clerical excommunication that Gregory

Fig. 2.11 A mediaeval picture of Emperor Henry IV genuflecting before Margravess Matilda in Canossa. Taken from the parchment manuscript entitled *The Life History of Matilda* by Doniso the Coenobite written in the monastery of Canossa. The manuscript is dated to 1114 and is kept in the Vatican Library. Taken from [304], V. 2, pp. 184–185.

sentenced the most powerful Christian monarch to had left the entire world amazed. Not a single excommunication that preceded it had ever made such a tremendous impact" ([196], Volume 4, page 162). Henry had to beg for absolution on his knees. "The poor king had to stand in front of the inner gate of the castle begging to open it, dressed in the clothes of a repentant sinner" ([196], Volume 4, page 168. "This bloodless victory of the coenobite [Hildebrand – A. F.] is more wonderful than all the victories of Alexander the Great" ([196], Volume 4, page 167). Henry would eventually revenge himself and his humiliation upon Gregory.

On fig. 2.11 we can see a mediaeval picture of "the scene in Canossa" which was painted in the alleged year 1114. Emperor Henry IV kneels before Margravess Matilda ([304], Volume 2, pages 184–185).

6.4. The Bethlehem Star of the alleged I century and the famous supernova explosion of circa 1150 (subsequently shifted to 1054 by the chronologists)

Let us turn to some fascinating astronomical data that prove our reconstruction according to which Jesus Christ (Andronicus) had lived in the XII century A.D. In our book entitled *King of the Slavs* we demonstrate that the famous supernova explosion dated to 1054 nowadays really took part a century later, in circa 1150, and became reflected in the Gospels as the Star of Bethlehem.

We shall proceed to cite the list of Scaligerian datings pertaining to the so-called nova and supernova flashes as reflected in "ancient" chronicles. The list was compiled by M. Zamaletdinov according to [978] and [703]. Let us emphasize that the list in question is a *complete* collection of all the flashes whose veracity isn't doubted.

The datings are as follows: the alleged years 2296 B.C., 2241 B.C., 185 A.D., 393, 902, 1006, 1054, 1184 and 1230 A.D. followed by several XVI century flashes, q.v. in Kepler's list. We shall point out the flash of 11 November 1572 that was mentioned by Tycho Brahe – the so-called "Tychonian Supernova" ([395], pages 124–125). This list is usually complemented by the so-called "Christian Supernova", or the famous Star of Bethlehem as described in the Gospels and allegedly dating to the I century A.D. This flash marked the birth of Jesus Christ (Andronicus). The Oriental Magi were asking: "Where is he that is born King of the Jews? For we have seen his star in the East... Then Herod, when he had privily called the wise men, enquired of them diligently what time the star appeared... and, lo, the star which they saw in the east, went before them... when they saw the star, they rejoiced with exceeding great joy" (Matthew 2:2, 2:7, 2:9–10). In fig. 2.12 we see a mediaeval picture of the Star of Bethlehem from the book by S. Lubienietski ([1257]).

Fig. 2.12 A mediaeval picture of the Evangelical "Star of Bethlehem" from the *Historia universalis omnium Cometarum* by Stanislaw Lubienietski ([1257]). Taken from [543], page 13, ill. 4.

Amongst the scientists who delved into the research of the astronomical environment as it had been in the I century A.D. was, amongst others, the eminent astronomer J. Kepler. The same "Star of the Magi" enjoyed a great deal of attention from the part of the chronologist Ludwig Ideler ([426], pages 128–129).

Let us now try a different approach to the issue. As we are beginning to understand, the list of nova and supernova flashes can (and must) contain duplicates. In other words, the number of flashes observed wasn't that great – however, they were "multiplied" when some of the chronicles had to "travel backwards in time". Let us compare the nova flash dates for the Second Roman Empire and the Roman Empire of the X-XIII century (see table below).

THE NOVA FLASH DATES FOR THE SECOND ROMAN EMPIRE AND THE ROMAN EMPIRE OF THE X-XIII CENTURY

a. Middle Ages (Roman Empire of the X–XIII century A.D.)
■ *b. "Antiquity"* (The Second Roman Empire of the I–III century A.D.)

1*a*. We give a *complete* list of all nova and supernova flashes reflected in the documents of the X-XIII century empire epoch:

1) The flash of 1006 A.D.
2) The famous flash of 1054.
3) The flash of 1184.
4) The flash of 1230.

■ 1*b*. Below find a *complete* list of all nova and supernova flashes reflected in the documents of the Second Empire (the alleged I–III century A.D.):
1) ?
2) The evangelical flash of 1 A.D.
3) ?
4) The famous flash of 185 A.D.

COMMENTARY. As we have already seen, a chronological shift of 1053 years leads to the mutual superimposition of the events that took place in the Second Roman Empire over those of the Holy Roman Empire that existed in the alleged X-XIII century, identifying them as each other's duplicates.

It would be interesting to find out whether a shift of 1053 years should give a superimposition of star flash dates, or phantom reflections of the flashes that were observed in the X-XIII century Roman Empire.

The answer happens to be in the positive (see fig. 2.13).

2*a*. The flash of the alleged year 1054 A.D.
■ 2*b*. The flash of the alleged year 1 A.D.

COMMENTARY. The dates of these flashes correlate ideally if we're to consider the 1053-year shift.

3*a*. The flash of 1054 was visible "in the eastern sky", according to mediaeval chronicles. Quoting by [703].
■ 3*b*. The flash of 1 A.D. was visible "in the East", according to the Gospels (Matthew 2:2 and 2:9). Concurs well with the Middle Ages' data.

4*a*. The flash of 1230.
■ 4*b*. The flash of 185.

COMMENTARY. These flashes get superimposed over each other if we're to consider a 1053-year shift, the difference being a mere 8 years.

5*a*. The flash of 1230 lasted for 6 months ([703]).

■ 5*b*. The flash of 185 lasted for 7 months ([703] and [978]).

COMMENTARY. Thus, we discover that the entire list of flashes with their characteristics as given for the Second Roman Empire is derived from several flashes observed in the Holy Roman Empire of the X-XIII century shifted 1053 years backwards in time. Thus, half of mediaeval flashes observed in this epoch drifted backwards in time and ended up in the "antiquity" instead of the Middle Ages (see fig. 2.13)

6*a*. The famous supernova flash of 1054 was observed in the Taurus constellation (The Great Soviet Encyclopaedia, 3rd edition, Volume 23, page 53). "A most amazing example of what supernova explosion remnants may look like is the Crab nebula

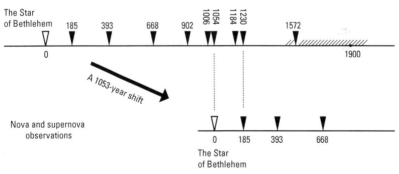

Fig. 2.13 Nova and supernova flash chronology according to the Scaligerian chronology. It is plainly visible that a 1053-year shift shall identify the Evangelical Star of Bethlehem as the famous supernova explosion dated to 1054 A.D., by the modern historians, for instance. The real explosion took place in mid-XII century, around 1152 A.D. It was subsequently misdated to 1053 A.D. by the mediaeval chronologists who were of the opinion that Christ wasn't born in 1152 A.D., but rather 1052 A.D. (q.v. in our book entitled *King of the Slavs*. The Nativity date was then shifted by an additional 1000 years, transforming into 1 A.D. Taken from [395], [703] and [978].

which is located where the Chinese and Japanese chronicles reported a bright supernova explosion in 1054" (GSE).

■ 6*b*. The famous flash – the Star of Bethlehem that could be observed when Jesus Christ (Andronicus) was born (Matthew 2). Representations of this star can often be found in Christian iconography, as well as mediaeval art and literature in general. Many chronologists tried to date the Nativity with the aid of this outstanding and scarce astronomical phenomenon, but to no avail, since they were looking for the star in the wrong century; as for the XI – there hardly is any point in looking for it here, it is known quite well already. In reality, this flash took place a century later, around 1150, q.v. above. Mediaeval chronologists have first misdated it to the XI century instead of the XII, and then aggravated the error, dating it to the I century A.D.

We have demonstrated the parallelism between the "biographies" of Jesus Christ (Andronicus) from the XII century and "Pope Gregory Hildebrand" from the XI. Let us reiterate that Italian Rome had apparently not been founded yet, and the events known as "Roman" nowadays really took place in the New Rome on the Bosporus, or Constantinople. Later on, when Byzantine events migrated westwards (on paper), Jesus Christ (Andronicus), who had preached in the New Rome in the XII century A.D. and suffered there, became reflected in Italian history as "Pope Hildebrand".

COROLLARY. Jesus Christ, also known as the Byzantine emperor Andronicus who had lived in the XII century A.D., became reflected in the Scaligerian version of Roman history as "Pope Hildebrand" from the alleged XI century.

6.5. The Crucifixion of Jesus on Mount Beykos, or the evangelical Golgotha, which is located outside Constantinople, near the shore of the Bosporus

Where did the events described in the Gospels really take place? Let us point out a very interesting and important fact directly related to this issue.

The Turkish historian Jalal Assad in his book entitled *Constanti-*

nople ([240]) tells us that right outside Constantinople, on the Asian coast of Bosporus straits, one finds "the tallest hill of the Upper Bosporus. On top of this hill (180 metres above the sea level) there is *the grave of Joshua son of Nun, or Ioushah*" ([240], page 76).

However, according to our reconstruction, Joshua son of Nun is merely another name of Jesus Christ (Andronicus), q.v. below; one can thus suggest that this tallest hill of the Upper Bosporus might really be the famous Golgotha where they crucified Christ.

Since we doubt that all of our readers have heard or read about the "grave of Joshua son of Nun", we shall tell its story in brief. Jalal Assad, the famous Muslim author of the XIX century tells us that "if one is to follow the Asian coast of the Bosporus, one comes to a small bunder by the name of Sutluge, which is where the path to the tallest hill of the Upper Bosporus. On top of this hill (180 metres above the sea level) there is *the grave of Joshua son of Nun, or Ioushah...* There are many different superstitions concerning this *gigantic grave,* which is four metres long and half a metre wide. According to one opinion, this used to be the bed of Heracles; some others deem this to be the grave of Amycus killed by Polydeuces [Polydes, or Pilates? – A. F.]. Muslims believe this to be the grave of Joshua, son of Nun. Many travel there... in hope of curing their ills.

One sees some Byzantine ruins on the top of this hill – possibly the ruins of the Church of St. Pantaleimon, as well as a holy spring... in the Byzantine epoch this place was called the Bed of Heracles... the renowned village of Beykos is located at the foot of this hill; this is where the Argonauts came to replenish their supply of food, and also the place where *king Amycus was killed*" ([240], pages 76–77).

Our reconstruction is as follows. Mount Beykos is most probably the famous Christian Golgotha. The "murder of king Amycus" at the foot of the hill would thus become identified as the crucifixion upon the Golgotha. The church, whose ruins we see on the hill, is none other but the famous Church of Resurrection that had been built on top of the Golgotha, according to the ecclesial tradition. It is well understood why the Argonauts – or, as we already understand, the crusaders – had to stop at this particular location.

This "grave" exists until the present day, and is considered a holy place. Locals call it the grave of saint Jushah, or Ioushah. That may well mean Jesus. What we see here nowadays is a flat 17 by 2 metre

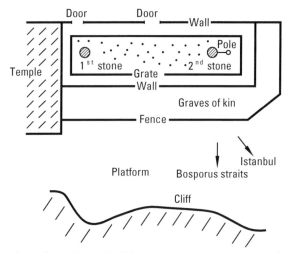

Fig. 2.14 A plan of Jesus' (Ioushah's) grave on top of Mount Beykos just outside Istanbul (modern condition).

field. The graves of his kin are of a regular size and can be found all around this gigantic "sepulchre". The plan of the "grave of Jesus" in its modern condition can be seen in fig. 2.14; one can also find the legends of St. Ioushah in [1181].

However, this account of ours is far from being exhaustive. Near the grave of St. Ioushah, or Jesus, one finds three more gigantic graves about 7 or 8 metres long. One of them is the grave of Kirklar Sultan, and it is concealed within a mausoleum of sorts, unlike the other two burial grounds, which one finds out in the open – the graves of the holy Uzun Elviya Leblebici Baba and Akbaba Sultan.

Apart from that, as some Beykos locals had told the author in 1995, there are 5 or 6 more of similar gigantic graves of saints on the other (European) side of the Bosporus. Could these "graves" be real or symbolic sepulchres of some of the Apostles of Jesus? We still know nothing of where most of them had been buried, after all.

So, could this "grave of St. Ioushah", or Joshua, be the place

Fig. 2.15 The Golden Gate of Czar-Grad (Constantinople). Taken from [240], inset between pages 128–129.

Fig. 2.17 A close-in with the Ottoman crescent upon a spire. Taken from [745], Volume 7, page 339.

Fig. 2.16 Jesus Christ enters Jerusalem. One can clearly see the Ottoman crescent on the spire at the background. Taken from [745], Volume 7, page 339. A 1693 Aprakos Evangelium. BAS archive #339, page 568, reverse.

where Jesus was crucified and the place where the Holy Sepulchre stood – the one sought by the crusaders?

It may be for some reason that "the main street of Constantinople led from the Forum of Arcadius and the first wall of the city to the Golden Gate, presently Isa-Kapusu, or the Gate of Jesus" ([240], page 67; see fig. 2.15). Could this be an indication that the evangelical events really took place in the New Rome? See more on the subject in *Chron5* and *Chron6*.

In *Chron6* we analyze the description of Daniel's voyage to the Golgotha in the Middle Ages. As we point out, in Daniel's rendition the place is closer to "the scene of the events" than to a real grave of Jesus. He calls in the "spot of the Crucifixion". Therefore, what we can find on Mount Beykos is a monument that tells us Jesus was crucified on *this very spot* – possibly rebuilt; its survival is truly a mystery. The exceptional size of the grave is also easily explained by the fact that the fenced area doesn't surround the actual grave, but rather the place where the events took place. In this case, the 17 by 2 metre size is easily understood.

Our conception of evangelical events really taking place in the New Rome = Czar-Grad = Constantinople is confirmed by the established mediaeval tradition of painting the evangelical Jerusalem as a city with Ottoman crescents. In fig. 2.16, for instance, we see a mediaeval painting of Christ entering Jerusalem ([745], Volume 7, page 339; The Aprakos Gospel, 1693). We see the city of Jerusalem in the background, with a distinct *Ottoman crescent* topping one of the spires, q.v. in fig. 2.17.

In fig. 2.18 we see a mediaeval picture of Pilate's trial of Jesus ([745], Volume 7, page 356 – The Aprakos Gospel, 1693). We see a turban with an Ottoman crescent on Pilate's head.

We shall keep coming across the fact that a crescent with a star used to be the ancient symbol of Czar-Grad, or Constantinople. It is possible that it symbolized the Moon, which had obscured the Sun in the year of the crucifixion, together with the Star of Bethlehem that had flared up around 1150 and was misdated to 1054 by later chronologists. The crescent could symbolize the moon, or, alternatively, partially obscured solar disc during the eclipse.

Let us mention another fact that is of interest to us. In figs. 2.20 ([745], Volume 7, page 155) and 2.21 ([745], Volume 8, page 326) we see two mediaeval pictures of the evangelical Jerusalem (the Aprakos Gospel, 1693). We see tall chimneys over the rooftops. This implies the existence of furnaces in the evangelical Jerusalem – most probably heaters used to keep houses warm, which doesn't quite concur with the Scaligerian version that tells us Jerusalem was situated on the territory of modern Palestine, which is tropical enough to render heating unnecessary – however, it does occasionally snow in Istanbul, and it can get rather cold. At any case, smoke from chimneys indicates the evangelical Jerusalem to have been situated somewhat further to the north than the Scaligerian version insists.

Let us conclude with a peculiar detail. Apparently, the true XII century dating of the Crucifixion had been recorded in various literary sources, which were later declared apocryphal and remained such for a considerable amount of time. In particular, the legend of Andrew the Apostle baptizing Russia near the end of the alleged X century (the XII century in reality) could be related to the recent Crucifixion. This tradition was reflected in the famous novel *Master and Margarita* by M. A. Bulgakov, who had studied various apocryphal tales of Christ, which he had incorporated into his work. The fact that we are about to relate was pointed out to us by our readers, and it fits well into our reconstruction. The last 32nd chapter of Bulgakov's novel entitled "Forgiveness and Eternal Abode" mentions

LEFT: Fig. 2.18. Pilate's Judgement. Pilate is wearing a crescent-shaped turban. Taken from [745], Volume 7, page 356. A 1693 Aprakos Evangelium. BAS archive # 339, p. 646. CENTER: Fig. 2.20 A mediaeval illustration with a view of the Evangelical Jerusalem. The city has tall chimneys installed for heating purposes. Taken from [745], Volume 7, page 155. A 1693 Aprakos Evangelium. BAS archive # 339, page 241. RIGHT: Fig. 2.21 A similar view of Jerusalem with smoking chimneys. Taken from [745], Volume 8, page 326. A 1693 Aprakos Evangelium. BAS archive # 339, page 725, reverse.

Boland leaving Moscow accompanied by his entourage and paying a visit to the Roman Procurator of Judea Pontius Pilate, who was serving his penance as a hermit perched upon a rock in a desolate land; Margarita expressed her amazement at the long term of this amercement in the following words: "Isn't twelve thousand moons for a single moon a little too much?" The events are supposed to take place in the late 1930's – the novel itself was finished in 1940.

Moons have been well known to stand for the so-called lunar or synodal months, which have passed since a certain event. Such a month equals 29.5 calendar days ([797], page 792). However, in

179

this case we find 12,000 moons counted backwards from 1940 to equal 970.8 years and give us 969 A.D. as the approximate dating of the Crucifixion. If we are to think that a "moon" really equals a stellar lunar month equalling 27.3 calendar days ([797], page 792), this date shall be 1043 A.D. One way or another, the tradition which was voiced by M. A. Bulgakov in a somewhat clandestine manner indicates the Crucifixion to have occurred in either the X or XI century. This mediaeval tradition is some 100–150 years off the mark, since it indicates the phantom XI-century dating instead of the real XII-century one. This circumstance proves nothing per se, but becomes understandable enough if we are to consider some of the facts that are known to us.

7.
Identifying Livy's "ancient imperial Rome" as the Third Roman Empire after a 1053-year shift

In the preceding paragraphs we have given brief descriptions of several dynastic parallelisms that emerge from the "Scaligerian History Textbook", which are really the manifestations of the chronological shifts with values equalling 333, 1230 and 1053 years. We shall carry on with our discussion of the 1053-year shift. We shall relate this method of restoring the correct datings in more detail below – a brief version can be found in Chapter 6 of *Chron1*.

Let us regard the history of "ancient" and mediaeval Rome. The parallelism that we are about to relate covers 1300 years, no less. It serves to "identify" the mediaeval Rome as its "ancient" double. We learn that one has to move the "ancient" dating of Rome's foundation (around the alleged year 753 A.D.) forwards in time by 1053 years, which transposes it to approximately 300 A.D. This is how the 1053-year shift manifests itself; bear in mind that the hypothesis about Diocletian, who is supposed to have ruled in the alleged years 284–305 A.D., was already suggested by N. A. Morozov in [544]. However, this hypothesis had proved erroneous. Our hypothesis shows that this millenarian shift forward in time is far from sufficient. We shall have to move it even closer to our age – by a further 1000–1050 years. Therefore, the true dating of the foundation of Rome in Italy shall fall on the XIV century A.D. See *Chron6* for more details. However, we aren't concerned with this shift at the moment – let us just concentrate on the very first step, which is interesting by itself and deserves to be covered separately.

So as not to bind ourselves by any additional hypotheses, we shall be formal enough in the demonstration of the parallelism that we have discovered. We shall simply superimpose Livy's *ab urbe condita* date (counted off the alleged foundation of Rome in Italy) over 300 A.D. (instead of the 753 B.C. dating prevalent in Scaligerian history). We shall then proceed forwards along the chronology of events as reflected in "ancient" and mediaeval sources, comparing them to one another with the aid of the same universal chronological formula that we shall abbreviate to T = X + 300. X stands for the *ab urbe condita* dating according to Titus Livy and other "ancient" sources, whereas T represents the Scaligerian A.D. dating. We thus suggest considering the date of Rome's foundation to be 300 A.D. This "uniform rigid formula" was discovered when we were processing form-codes and compiling the global chronological map.

In other words, the formula that we transcribe as T = X + 300 is a somewhat different representation of the same chronological shift of 1053 years.

It is extremely important that the superimposition of the "ancient" Roman history over its mediaeval original as suggested by this formula is confirmed by the discovered parallelism of compared events. That is, "ancient" and mediaeval Roman events that the "Scaligerian

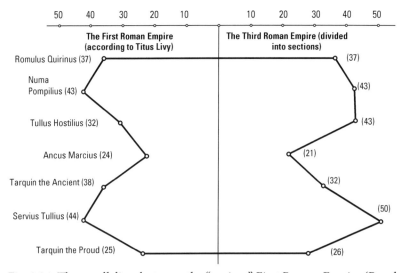

Fig. 2.24. The parallelism between the "ancient" First Roman Empire (Regal Rome as described by Titus Livy) and the "ancient" Third Roman Empire.

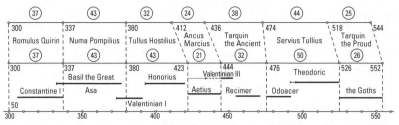

Fig. 2.25 A superimposition of the "ancient" First Roman Empire and the "ancient" Third Roman Empire with a rigid shift of roughly 1050 years.

textbook" separates by a period of about 1053 years turn out to be extremely similar to each other. A more formal way of putting it would be to say that these events possess extremely similar form-codes; this ongoing parallelism turns out to cover a very long time interval very methodically – an interval of 1300 years, to be precise.

A) According to the $T = X + 300$ formula, all 244 years of Livy's "Ancient Royal Rome" ([482]), or the First Roman Empire in our terminology, become identified as the interval that covers the alleged years 300–552 A.D. – that of the Third Roman Empire in the West.

B) The seven kings described by Titus Livy ([482]) are really a collection of generalized aliases, or terms used for referring to the seven consecutive epochs of the Third Roman Empire. We find out that every such epoch is represented in Livy's work by a biography or two from the imperial history of the Third Empire. As we find out, Livy concentrates on these emperors and hardly mentions any other rulers from the epoch in question, either ignoring or being ignorant of them.

C) We learn that the form-codes of the First and the Third Roman Empire demonstrate a very obvious parallelism.

We shall present the seven epochs (Livy's "kings") below, also providing their "translations" into the terms of the Third Roman Empire, q.v. in figs. 2.24 and 2.25. See the discussion of dates and reign durations for the emperors of the Third Roman Empire in *Chron2*, Chapter 1.

1a. *Romulus Quirin:* the alleged years 300–337 A.D. after a shift of 1053 years.

■ 1b. *Constantine I the Great.*

2a. Numa Pompilius: the alleged years 380–423 A.D. after a shift of 1053 years.

■ *2b. St. Basil the Great,* or the Great King (since Basil = Basileus, or simply "King").

3a. Tullus Hostilius: the alleged years 380–423 A.D. after a 1053-year shift.

■ *3b. Valentinian II + Honorius.* Alternatively, we can take *Theodosius I* – the co-ruler of Valentinian.

4a. Ancus Marcius: the alleged years 423–444 A.D. after a 1053-year shift.

■ *4b. Aetius.*

5a. Tarquin the Ancient: the alleged years 444–476 A.D. after a 1053-year shift.

■ *5b. Valentinian III + Recimer.*

6a. Servius Tullius: the alleged years 476–526 A.D. after a 1053-year shift.

■ *6b. Odoacer + Theodoric.*

7a. Tarquin the Proud: the alleged years 526–552 A.D. after a 1053-year shift.

■ *7b. The royal Gothic dynasty:* from Amalasuntha to Teia.

The comparison of reign durations with the numbers indicated by Titus Livy ([482], Book 1) shall give us the following: 37–37, 43–43, 32–43, 24–21, 38–32, 44–50 and 25–26. A calculation of proximity coefficients gives us 10–4. Let us compare the general duration of the "Regal Rome" epoch as described by Livy with the length of the Third Empire period that we are considering presently (300–552 A.D.). This duration equals 252 or 246 years if we are to begin counting from the first reign year of the first Emperor – Constantine I the Great. Livy indicates the duration of 244 years. Thus, the two durations – 244 according to Livy and 252 – differ from 246 by a mere 3%.

One cannot fail to notice that the special attention received from the part of Livy by some of the epochs we discovered correlates quite unequivocally with their division into intervals bordering on periods of *great civil unrest*. We have already considered these intervals in our comparison of the Second Empire with the Third. If we are to calculate the amount of years covered by the abovementioned emperors of the Third Empire in the epoch of 300–552, we shall get the duration of 242 years as a result! Titus Livy reckons the period to equal 244 years. The reign duration correlation is virtually ideal. We see that Livy had simply summed up the reign durations of the Third Empire's rulers that we mention.

Let us now cite a brief table of this biographical parallelism, only pointing out its most important moments. See more details concerning the rulers of the Third Roman Empire as well as the kings of Israel and Judea above – in Chapter 1 of *Chron2*. We use the letter "a" to denote Livy's "Regal Rome", or the First Empire; "b" stands for the Third Roman Empire, and "c" – for the Biblical Israelite reign and the Kingdom of Judea.

1a. *The First Roman Empire.* The epoch of Romulus Quirin according to Livy.

■ 1b. *The Third Roman Empire.* The alleged years 300–337 A.D. The main representative of the epoch is Constantine I the Great: the alleged years 306–337 A.D.

■ ■ 1c. *Israel and Judea.* The epoch of Jeroboam I and Rehoboam.

1.1a. *The First Empire.* Livy tells us that the founder of Rome was called Romulus ([482], Book 1:7, page 11). Eutropius the historian also writes that "having founded Rome, the city that he had named after himself, Romulus proceeded to do the following…" ([269], page 8). Thus, the capital is named after its founder: RM = RML sans vocalizations. Apart from that, Romulus had a brother by the name of Remus, whose name is virtually identical to the word "Rome". We shall also mark that there were no other capital foundations in the history of the Regal Rome after Remus.

■ 1.1b. *The Third Empire.* Constantine I founds the new capital

185

THE ISSUE WITH ANTIQUITY

that he calls New Rome (allegedly moving it to that site from elsewhere). This city is supposed to have been called Constantinople in the Middle Ages. Here we see another case of a capital named after its founder (Constantine). It is very noteworthy that mediaeval chronicles actually mention the parallelism between Constantine the Great and the "ancient" Romulus, calling the Temple of Constantine I in Rome the Temple of Romulus ([196]). See more details above in *Chron1*, Chapter 7. There were no other capitals founded in the Third Empire (300–552) after Constantine.

■ ■ *1.1c. Israel-Judea.* Jeroboam I, the double of Constantine I, moves the capital of the state to the town of Sichem and thus becomes the founder of a new capital, q.v. above, in Chapter 1 of *Chron2*. No other capitals were founded in the Kingdom of Israel after Jeroboam I.

1.2a. The First Empire. Romulus rules jointly with his brother Remus ([482], Book 1:6–7). Romulus kills Remus subsequently ([482], Book 1:6–7, page 11). After the murder of Remus, Romulus remains the single head of state ([482]). Mark that the non-vocalized versions of the names of the two founders, Romulus and Remus, are rather similar: RML and RM.

■ *1.2b. The Third Empire.* Constantine I rules together with Licinius. Soon Constantine I makes Licinius suffer bitter defeat at Hellespont, and the Licinius is killed during his battle with Constantite the Great. After the death of Licinius Constantine remains the sole ruler of the state, q.v. in *Chron2*, Chapter 1. The names of Constantine and Licinius bear no semblance to each other.

■ ■ *1.2c. Israel-Judea.* Jeroboam I rules together with Rehoboam. They had been at war basically all the time of their joint rule, q.v. in *Chron2*, Chapter 1. Unvocalized names of Jeroboam and Rehoboam, the finders of the kingdoms of the Israelite and Judea are virtually the same: RBM and RBM.

1.3a. First Empire. The notorious "rape of the Sabines" happens under Romulus (the Romans were short of wives, and are thus forced to abduct women from a neighbouring tribe). This event occurs in the epoch of Rome's foundation.

■ *1.3b. Third Empire.* We find no such event in the Third Empire.

■ ■ *1.3c. Israel-Judea.* Right before the beginning of the Israelite reign the Bible contains the well-known legend of "the rape of the daughters of Shiloh (Judges 21:21–25). This event is perfectly analogous to the Roman "rape of the Sabine women". The sons of Benjamin also had a shortage of wives; then this tribe of Israel carried off the women of another tribe. A more detailed comparison of the Biblical description of this event with the Roman shall be given below.

1.4a. First Empire. Romulus Quirin was deified alive ([482], Book 1:16). One should remember that "quirin" translates as "divine" ([544]). Quirin was rapt up into heaven when he died. Livy tells us "everybody praises Romulus as a divine entity and a son of a deity [sic! – A. F.], King and Founder of Rome; he is often addressed in prayers" ([482], Book 1:16, page 27). This point of view is manifestly Christian and evangelical – suffice to remember Christ rapt into heaven, q.v. in the Gospels.

■ *1.4b. Third Empire.* Constantine the Great was also proclaimed divine while alive (see *Chron2*, Chapter 1). Christian church ranks him among its saints. Arianism, the Christian analogy of "Jeroboam's heresy", flowers in his lifetime, q.v. above. St. Basil the Great was born around 333 A.D., near the end of Constantine's life (who is supposed to have died in 337 – see [544], Volume 1. Legends about him are virtually identical to what we know about Jesus Christ ([544], Volume 1). Therefore, the "phantom biographies" of St. Basil the Great and Constantine I cast an evangelical glow over each other.

■ ■ *1.4c. Israel-Judea.* The Biblical "double entry" system (see *Chron1*, Annex 6.4) of the kingdoms of Judah and Israel allows us to estimate that the Judaic king Asa, the double of St. Basil the Great, began his reign two years before the rule of Jeroboam I had ended. In other words, when Jeroboam I, the double of Romulus and Constantine I, was nearing death. Therefore, the Bible also tells us Asa

(Jesus?) had lived in the epoch of the first "great king" Jeroboam I.

1.5a. *First Empire.* Sometime after his ascension into heaven, Romulus "comes down to Earth all of a sudden" ([482], Books 1:16 and 26) and appears before a Roman by the name of Proculus Julius. Romulus pronounces a hortation before his disciples, and then returns to heaven. Livy tells us that "he had uttered those words and ascended into the heavens" ([482], Book 1:16, page 27).

■ 1.5b. *Third Empire.* No ascension into heavens is mentioned in St. Basil's "biography".

■ ■ 1.5c. *Israel-Judea.* Gospels tell us about Jesus returning to Earth after the Crucifixion. "After these things [the ascension, that is – A. F.] Jesus shewed himself again to the disciples" (John 21:1). Jesus, who has returned to Earth, converses with his disciples, and ascends into heavens again, this time for good. "And it came to pass, while he blessed them, he was parted from them, and carried up into heaven" (Luke 24:51).

COMMENTARY. Thus, we see that the legends placed at the end of the biography of Romulus by Titus Livy are of an evangelical nature, and may contain references to both Jesus and Constantine the Great. Let us now give a more detailed comparison of the two stories: Livy's, which tells us about the rape of the Sabines, and the Biblical legend of the daughters of Shiloh.

1.6a. *First Empire.* The events take place in the recently founded city of Rome, in the reign of King Romulus, the epoch of Regal Rome's naissance (according to Livy), or the very beginning of the First Roman Empire in our terminology. There was a shortage of women in Rome, which had made the prospects of progeny and procreation look grim ([482], Volume 1, pages 15–16).

■ ■ 1.6c. *Israel-Judea.* The event precedes the formation of the Israelite Kingdom immediately: "In those days there was no king in Israel" (Judges 21:35). The tribe of Benjamin lost its women in a war, and was thus on the brink on extinction (Judges 21:16–25).

1.7*a. First Empire.* Romulus sends delegations to neighbouring tribes and asks those to send some of their women to Rome ([482], Book 1). The ambassadors face a hostile reception; none of the nations in the vicinity of Rome concede to provide the Romans with wives ([482], Book 1).

■ ■ 1.7*c. Israel-Judea.* The Bible tells us that all the tribe's elders had gathered together in order to decide what to do about wives for the tribe of Benjamin, having asked other tribes of Israel for help (Judges 21). Their pleas didn't lead anywhere: "Then the elders of the congregation said… we may not give them wives of our daughters: for the children of Israel have sworn, saying, Cursed be he that giveth a wife to Benjamin" (Judges 21:16, 21:18).

1.8*a. First Empire.* The Romans proceeded to organize festivities and invite the inhabitants of nearby settlements together with their wives and children. Livy writes that "the entire Sabine tribe came together with their wives and their offspring" ([482], Volume 1, Book 1:9, page 16). The ulterior motivation behind the feast had been the abduction of women. There may be a proximity pattern between the unvocalized "Sabine" and "Benjamin" – SBN and BNMN without vocalizations, respectively.

■ ■ 1.8*c. Israel-Judea.* According to the Bible, "there is a feast of the Lord in Shiloh yearly… Therefore they commanded the children of Benjamin, saying, Go and lie in wait in the vineyards… and, behold, if the daughters of Shiloh come out to dance in dances… catch you every man his wife of the daughters of Shiloh" (Judges 21:19–21).

1.9*a. First Empire.* In the middle of the celebrations the Romans seize foreign women and abduct them. This is how they obtained wives and secured a legacy, and this is also the beginning of how the Romans began to dwell in their new City ([482], Book 1:9). According to Livy, the Rape of the Sabines took place in Italy ([482], Book 1). Furthermore, Livy is of the opinion that the founders of Rome were the offspring of the Trojans who had initially disembarked at Sicily after having fled Troy, which was destroyed by the Greeks ([482], Book 1:1, pages 3–4). Therefore, the founders of Rome could be referred to as "the sons of Sicily" or "Sicilians". We should also bear in mind that the "ancient" authors Hellanicus and Damastes claimed Rome to have been founded by Odysseus and Aeneas ([579], page 23).

■ ■ 1.9c. *Israel-Judea.* The Bible tells us that "the sons of Benjamin did so, and took them wives, according to their number, of them that danced, whom they caught: and they went and returned unto their inheritance, and repaired the cities, and dwelt in them" (Judges 21:23). N. A. Morozov suggests that it might be possible to identify the Biblical tribes as the mediaeval European nations in [544]; his localization of said tribes differs from the Scaligerian to a large extent. The "sons of Benjamin" thus became identified as the inhabitants of Italy and Sicily; is it therefore possible that the "daughters of Shiloh" were really the "daughters of Sicily".

2a. *The First Roman Empire.* The epoch of Numa Pompilius according to Livy. It is possible that "Pompilius" conceals the name of Julian or Elias and that Livy is really referring to Julian the Great.

■ 2b. *The Third Roman Empire.* The epoch of the alleged years 337–380 A.D. The absolute protagonist of this epoch is St. Basil the Great, or the Great King (the alleged years 333–378). This happens in the reign of the Roman emperor Julian who allegedly reigned in 361–363. A biographical parallelism between Julian and St. Basil can be found in [544].

■ ■ 2c. *The Bible.* Here we have Asa, king of Judah (Jesus?) As we have already mentioned, he appears to be the double of Basil the Great. See more about the superimposition of the Kingdom of Judah over the Third Roman Empire in the East in *Chron1*, Chapter 6.

2.1a. *First Empire.* Livy characterizes Numa Pompilius as a just and pious ruler, and tells us that "Numa... was a man most experienced in laws secular as well as ecclesial" ([482], Book 1:18, pages 30–31). Numa became enthroned in Rome as a result of divine intervention from the part of Jupiter ([482], Book 1:18). Titus Livy relates Numa's affairs of the state at length; all of them appear to be of a conspicuously ecclesiastical character ([482], Book 1).

■ 2.1b. *Third Empire.* St. Basil the Great (or the Great King) is considered to be one of the central figures in Christian hagiography. He is said to have instigated the modern procedure of officiation – the so-called "Liturgy of St. Basil the Great". As we already pointed out above, Basil is very likely to be a double of Jesus Christ who had lived in the XII century. Legends of Basil the Great usually mention his ecclesiastical activities and their impact on the history of the Third Empire.

■ ■ 2.1c. *Israel-Judea.* Jesus Christ is sent to Earth by the Almighty Father with a mission of ministration. The Gospels are focused on Christ's religious activities primarily; the tales of "Pope" Gregory VII Hildebrand (one of the XI century reflections of the XII-century Jesus) are all of a similar nature.

2.2a. *First Empire.* Numa Pompilius manages to implement a major calendar reform. He divides the year into 12 months, having also introduced intermediate months so as to make the calendar conform to climatic changes and the solar year ([482], Book 1:19). What this reform resembles the most is the introduction of the Julian calendar with its leap year system. According to Livy, "it was he who had made the distinction between days when there was service, and those when there was none" ([482], Book 1:19). This may be a reference to the Sundays introduced into the week. "The death of Numa led to an interregnum" ([482], Book 1, page 36). It is peculiar that Livy tells us nothing of Numa's death. The reason may be that Livy had already assigned these details (including the "ascension into heaven" to the final period of Romulus' reign.

■ 2.2b. *Third Empire.* Scaligerian history is of the opinion that the Julian calendar was introduced by Julius Caesar in the alleged I century B.C., or at the very dawn of the Second Roman Empire. However, due to the parallelism between the Second Empire and the Third, the introduction of the Julian calendar falls onto the epoch of Constance I Chlorus, the double of Julius Caesar – the alleged years 305–306 A.D. This date is close to the epoch of the alleged years 333–378 – the "reign" of St. Basil the Great. We should also keep in mind the partial superimposition of Julian Caesar (the alleged years 361–363) over Julius Caesar. The death of Basil the Great in the alleged year 378 led to a period of *interregnum* – there was an upheaval that year, q.v. in *Chron2*, Chapter 1. What we see is a parallelism between the events contemporary to Numa as described by Livy, and the ones that were happening at the foundation of the Third Empire. We shall emphasize that none of these events could have happened before the XII century A.D., according to the global chronological map as presented in Chapter 6 of *Chron1*.

3a. *The First Roman Empire.* The epoch of Tullus Hostilius according to Livy.

■ 3b. *The Third Roman Empire.* The epoch of the alleged years 380–423 A.D. Valentinian II (378–392) or Theodosius I (379–395) and Honorius (395–423).

3.1a. *First Empire.* The beginning of Tullus' reign is marked by a series of wars with the Alvanoi ([482], Book 1:23, page 37). The Alvanoi attack the Roman region with a great number of troops. Tullus launches a campaign against the "perfidious" Alvanoi ([482], Book 1:23). The Alvanoi are then united by the dictator Mettius Fufetius ([482], Book 1:23, page 37).

■ 3.1b. *Third Empire.* The parallelism between the Third Empire and the Second tells us that the double of Theodosius I in the Second Empire is Emperor Domitian. At the very beginning of his reign, Theodosius (Domician) enters his first large-scale military conflict with the "Albanians". We learn that "the Roman provinces of the Balkan peninsula were under threat of invasion" ([327], page 314). The Albanians (or Dacians) rebelled. Under Theodosius I the Albanian Goths did likewise. The Dacian Goths unite under the leadership of Decebel. "Decebel", or "Dacibel" might be derived from "Dacians" and the word "bellum", or war.

3.2a. *First Empire.* The "ancient" Alvanoi soon sign a truce with Tullus ([482], Book 1:24–25, page 40). However, they break the pact soon enough, initiating a second war with Rome, which leads to a defeat of the Alvanoi ([482], Book 1:29–30, page 50).

■ 3.2b. *Third Empire.* The Albanians, or the Dacian Goths, negotiate a truce with Theodosius-Domitian (under Valentinian II, q.v. in [327], page 444). A short while later, the Albanians (Dacians-Goths) denounce the truce, and another war with Rome begins under Honorius. This time the famous Alaric comes from the Balkans ([767], Volume 2, page 793).

3.3a. *First Empire.* Towards the end of Tullus' reign – under Honorius, if we're to bear the parallelism in mind, or in the alleged years 395–423 A.D. – "one would often observe *stones hailing from the skies* near the Alvanoi Mount ... people were sent to study this miracle ... indeed, there were rocks falling from the sky ... they heard *a terrifying voice* from the grove that stood on top of the mountain that ordered the Alvanoi to occupy themselves with holy ceremonies ... impressed by this miracle, the Romans themselves made sacrifices for nine days in a row" ([482], Book 1:31, pages 52–53). According to the Scaligerian version of the story, the Alvanoi Mountain is in Italy. Apparently, Livy refers to a volcanic eruption that took place somewhere upon that peninsula. There is indeed a volcano here, a single one on the mainland – the Vesuvius.

■ 3.3b. *Third Empire.* One of the famous eruptions of the Vesuvius took place in the alleged year 79 A.D. The parallelism between the Second Empire and the Third places this eruption into the epoch of Honorius (395–423), making it cover the interval between the alleged years 409 and 420 A.D. – most probably in 412 A.D. Vesuvius is the famous volcano in Italy that is located near Rome. This powerful eruption had led the town of Pompeii to an untimely demise. If we're to count 79 years forwards starting from 333 A.D., or the "date of birth" of Basil the Great, the double of Jesus Christ (also known as the beginning of the "new era"), we shall come up with the year 412, or the very end of the epoch of king Tullus, according to Titus Livy. It is however necessary to state it explicitly that the eruptions of the alleged years 79 or 412 are really phantom reflections of a *later* eruption of Vesuvius. It is possible that the archetypal eruption had been the one that occurred in 1138–1139 A.D. The chronological shift here equals exactly 1053 years. However, the real prototype of the "Pompeian eruption" must have been the more recent eruption of the Vesuvius dating to either 1500 or even 1631, q.v. below.

4*a. The First Roman Empire.* The epoch of "Ancus Marcius" (according to Livy).

■ 4*b. The Third Roman Empire.* The epoch of the alleged years 423–444 A.D. Aetius.

4.1*a. First Empire.* After King Tullus, the Roman throne is succeeded by Ancus Marcius ([482]). However, a short while later a certain Lucumon appears in Rome, who soon changes his name to L. Tarquin the Ancient, alias Tarquin Priscus ([269], page 9). He is reckoned to have been of "an Etruscan origin" ([269], page 319). Also see Livy, Book 1:34 Tarquin began to gather great influence in Rome ([482], Book 1:34, pages 58–59). One has to point out that the name of Ancus Marcius might be close to the name Aetius.

■ 4.1*b. Third Empire.* Aetius becomes the de facto ruler in the West of the Third empire between the years of 423 and 444, q.v. in *Chron2*, Chapter 1. However, the balance of powers in Rome slowly but steadily shifts in favour of the young Valentinian III, who had been in custody of Aetius ([767], Volume 2; also [64]).

4.2*a. First Empire.* L. Tarquin the Ancient subsequently becomes king of the "ancient" Rome and succeeds Ancus Marcius on the throne, having successfully shifted the power balance in his own favour ([482], Book 1). We see two characters here: the Roman Ancus Marcius, and L. Tarquin the Ancient – an alien or a "barbarian", since he came from another country far away ([482], Book 1:34).

■ 4.2b. *Third Empire.* Valentinian III subsequently becomes the Emperor of Rome and seizes power. He eventually pushes his custodian Aetius away from the throne. What we see here is another pair of political leaders whose destinies are twined: the first one is Aetius, a "barbarian by birth" ([64], pages 33 and 40). He came to Rome from a distant land. The other character is the Roman Valentinian III. When we compare this with Livy's description, we notice that in this particular manifestation of the parallelism the terms "Roman" and "barbarian" are obviously swapped.

4.3a. *First Empire.* L. Tarquin the Ancient had been accompanied by his wife Tanaquil, "a patrician by birth" ([482], Book 1:34, page 59). She had a great influence on L. Tarquin the Ancient. Tanaquil was very eager to seize power in Rome, and kept impelling her husband to engage in this activity. Livy tells us that "his pride was constantly fuelled by his wife Tanaquil... who would not allow the position of her husband to be any lower than that of her own family" ([482], Book 1:34, page 59).

■ 4.3b. *Third Empire.* We observe the same thing to happen in the Third Empire. Next to Valentinian III we see his mother and official custodian Placidia, who had herself been under the influence of Aetius. Placidia is the Emperor's mother, her family is therefore aristocratic by definition, as Livy duly notes when he describes her as "Tanaquil".

4.4a. *First Empire.* According to Livy, "he [L. Tarquin the Ancient – A. F.] soon transformed his acquaintance with the king into a strong friendship ... being his advisor at meetings social as well as private, civil as well as military" ([482], Book 1:34, page 60). Also: "Tried and tested in every which way, he [L. Tarquin the Ancient – A. F.] even became ... the custodian of the King's children" ([482], Book 1:34, page 60).

■ *4.4b. Third Empire.* It is natural that the relationship between the young Valentinian III and his custodian Aetius had initially been very much like a family bond; Livy is correct to call him the custodian of the royal offspring since Valentinian III is the son of Placidia. Historians tell us that "until Valentinian III had reached the age of 27 years (in 444), no one ever doubted the right of Aetius to rule the state" ([64], page 35). If we are to compare this version with Livy's, we shall see that the custodian and the child in custody have swapped places.

4.5a. First Empire. The very fact of such "custody" is unique for the history of the "Regal Rome". No other ruler of the First Roman Empire is characterized in this manner (according to Livy). Ancus Marcius had ruled for 24 years ([482]). This concurs perfectly with the Biblical information about his double, q.v. below.

■ *4.5b. Third Empire.* The custody in question as described above is a unique occurrence in the history of the Third Roman Empire. No other emperor of the Third Empire is described in this manner – that is, no one had ever been in custody of his mother and her powerful ally. Aetius had reigned for 21 years, q.v. in *Chron2*, Chapter 1. However, the Bible actually reports a 24-year interregnum that falls on this epoch, q.v. in *Chron2*, Chapter 1, and the "double entry" system as related in Annex 6.4 to *Chron1*. In other words, the lengths of this period according to the Bible and Titus Livy coincide! We are beginning to understand that Titus Livy had been more familiar with the Biblical version of Rome's history that its secular variety, and shall soon encounter more evidence to prove this.

4.6a. First Empire. Livy tells us that "at home as well as on the battlefield he [L. Tarquin the Ancient – A. F.] was accompanied by an experienced mentor, the king Ancus himself ... and so he had studied Roman law and... had been emulous of everyone ... including the king [sic! – A. F.]" ([482], Book 1:35, page 61).

■ 4.6b. *Third Empire.* Valentinian III continues to push Aetius aside, formally remaining in his custody. As Valentinian III grows older, the influence of Aetius diminishes.

4.7a. *First Empire.* L. Tarquin the Ancient finally seizes power in Rome. He addresses the Romans with a request [?] to elect him king instead of Ancus Marcius. Livy tells us that "the people voted in favour of vesting him with royal authority. This man... was pursued by the very same ambition when he came to the throne as had led him in his contest for the kingdom" ([482], Book 1:35, page 61).

■ 4.7b. *Third Empire.* Valentinian III finally seizes full power. In the alleged year 444 Aetius loses the last shreds of his influence after a series of military defeats. Valentinian III casts away the burden of custody ([64]). All of this happens while Aetius, or the "experienced mentor" (according to Livy) is still alive.

4.8a. *First Empire.* Titus Livy tells us nothing of how Ancus Marcius had lost his regal power. According to Livy, L. Tarquin the Ancient becomes emperor in a peaceful manner, with the consent of the people. For some reason, Livy tells us nothing about the death of Ancus Marcius ([482]). Eutropius the historian tells us that Ancus Marcius had "expired of a disease on the 24th year of his rule" ([269], page 8).

■ 4.8b. *Third Empire.* Valentinian III gets full power after a very peaceful procedure. There was no coup in 444, the year when the power of Aetius the custodian was no more. Having seized power, Valentinian III soon kills Aetius in Ravenna with his own hands ([579]). As we can see, Livy remained silent about this for some reason.

Commentary. It is supposed that Livy localizes all these events in Italy. On the other hand, when we begin to compare them to the ones that took place in the Third Roman Empire, we begin to find out that other chronicles reckon some of these events at least to have happened in the New Rome on the Bosporus, moving them to the East. This may be the aftermath of some confusion, or a deliberate distortion of history, when a lot of occurrences had migrated from Constantinople to Rome in Italy on paper.

5a. *The First Roman Empire.* The epoch of "Tarquin the Ancient" according to Livy.

■ 5b. *The Third Roman Empire.* The epoch of the alleged years 444–476 A.D. Valentinian III (444–455) and Recimer (456–472).

■ ■ 5c. *The Bible.* Menahem + Pekahiah = Pekah, acting as a double of Recimer here, q.v. in *Chron2*, Chapter 1.

5.1a. *First Empire.* Tarquin the Ancient fights just one war with the Sabines, but it's a hard and bloody one. The war progresses unevenly and ends in a truce ([482], Book 1).

■ 5.1b. *Third Empire.* Valentinian III fights a single war with the notorious Attila the Hun, which proves a long and hard one. Success favours both parties erratically; finally, Rome signs a pact of peace with Attila, paying him a large tribute, q.v. in *Chron2*, Chapter 1.

■ ■ 5.1c. *Israel-Judea.* The Biblical double of Valentinian III, Menahem, has just one war to fight with the king Phul or Thul, but this war is long and violent. Peace comes when Menahem pays tribute to Phul or Thul – as we have already pointed out, this barbaric king is most probably a double of Attila the Hun.

5.2a. *First Empire.* The end of the epoch of "Tarquin the Ancient" is abundant in political turmoil, as Livy tells us. Power struggle flares up in Rome; Tarquin the Ancient is assassinated in a conspiracy ([482], Book 1:40, pages 67–68).

■ 5.2b. *Third Empire.* In the Third Empire the end of this epoch (the alleged years 444–476) coincides with the reign of Recimer (456–472). This is one of the largest upheavals in the Third Empire. We see more power struggle, a series of temporary emperors on the throne shuffled by Recimer. After the death of Recimer (the alleged years 472–475), the Empire is shaken by a civil war, q.v. in *Chron2*, Chapter 1.

■ ■ 5.2c. *Israel-Judea.* According to the Bible, this epoch ends

with Pekah. "And Hoshea the son of Elah made a conspiracy agaist Pekah the son of Remaliah, and smote him,
and slew him" (II Kings 15:30). Once again we see Livy's
version to be closer to the Biblical version that to secular
Roman history.

6a. *The First Roman Empire*. The epoch of "Servius Tullius"
according to Livy.
■ 6b. *The Third Roman Empire*. The epoch of the alleged years
476–526 A.D. Odoacer (476–493) + Theodoric (493–526 or
497–526).

6.1a. *First Empire*. Mark the name of this ancient king, which is
"Servius". It obviously resembles the name Severus, which we
are about to encounter in the history of the Third Empire. Livy
describes Servius Tullius as a very level-headed, intelligent and
steadfast politician ([482]).
■ 6.1b. *Third Empire*. The name of Odoacer's double in the Second Empire is Septimus Severus, whose name is somewhat
similar to that of Servius. Both Odoacer and Theodoric
are known to have been prudent rulers, unlike the emperors of the preceding anarchical period. A propos, Severus
(Servius?) had a co-ruler by the name of Geta in the Second
Empire (209–212). In the Third Empire king Theodoric is a
Goth. Geta and Goth sound very similar.

7a. *The First Roman Empire*. The epoch of "Tarquin the Great"
according to Livy.
■ 7b. *The Third Roman Empire*. The epoch of the alleged years
526–552 A.D. Gothic dynasty.

The parallelism between these two last epochs that we have discovered is an extremely vivid and obvious one, and it is of great enough
importance for our analysis of the consensual global chronology
to make us allocate a separate section for its discussion, q.v. below.
    For the meantime, let us answer a question that one cannot evade
under these circumstances. Which part of Livy's book describes

Fig. 2.26 A page from an edition of Titus Livy's *Ab urbe condita* dating to the alleged XV century. "Ancient" Romans are portrayed as mediaeval knights; the pages of the book are all covered with mediaeval coats of arms – possibly belonging to the participants of the events described by Livy or their contemporaries. Vatican, Biblioteca Apostolica Vaticana, Arch. Cap. S. Pietro, page 132, fol. 65v. Taken from [1229], page 29.

events with parallels in the Third Roman Empire? In other words, how much of the information related by Livy remains unperturbed by all of the superimpositions listed above? In terms of form-codes, this question can be formulated as follows: what is the volume of section AK–34? See *Chron1*, Chapter 5.

Let us point out that Livy's texts consist primarily of isolated short stories. Each of those relates a single episode. Livy hardly ever returns to past episodes; ergo, the value of X = A/B is relatively easy to calculate, A being the volume (in pages, for instance) of the stories that contain parallelisms with the Third Empire, and B – the general volume of the fragment of Livy's *History* that we have been comparing to the Third Empire. We calculated the X value, which turned out to equal 67 per cent. In other words, *67% of Livy's text that describes the Regal Rome happens to be isomorphic with the history of the Third Empire.* It is possible that we have failed to discover all of the parallels. Apart from that, it is possible that the events related in the remaining 33% of Livy's text weren't reflected in any other mediaeval chronicles that our conception of the Third Roman Empire relies upon.

On fig 2.26 one sees a page from Livy's *Ab urbe condita* allegedly dating from the XV century ([1229], page 29). The illustrations look distinctly mediaeval, as well as the book in general. In the top left corner we see a battle between the "ancient" Romans, or the characters described by Titus Livy. All of them look like typical mediaeval knights in heavy armour and helmets with visors. Several mediaeval Christian coats of arms can be seen nearby, q.v. on the right and at the bottom. Historians are trying to convince us that mediaeval painters included these coats of arms into books with the sole objective of pandering to the tastes of their clients. However, these mediaeval coats of arms most probably reflect mediaeval reality – just like the pictures of mediaeval Roman knights found in the books of the mediaeval author Titus Livy.

About the Author

Fomenko, *Anatoly Timofeevich* (b. 1945). Full Member (Academician) of the Russian Academy of Sciences, Full Member of the Russian Academy of Natural Sciences, Full Member of the International Higher Education Academy of Sciences, Doctor of Physics and Mathematics, Professor, Head of the Moscow State University Section of Mathematics of the Department of Mathematics and Mechanics. Solved Plateau's Problem from the theory of minimal spectral surfaces. Author of the theory of invariants and topological classification of integrable Hamiltonian dynamic systems. Laureate of the 1996 National Premium of the Russian Federation (in Mathematics) for a cycle of works on the Hamiltonian dynamical systems and manifolds' invariants theory. Author of 200 scientific publications, 28 monographs and textbooks on mathematics, a specialist in geometry and topology, calculus of variations, symplectic topology, Hamiltonian geometry and mechanics, computer geometry. Author of a number of books on the development of new empirico-statistical methods and their application to the analysis of historical chronicles as well as the chronology of antiquity and the Middle Ages.

What mainstream historians say about the New Chronology?

The **New Chronology** is a fringe theory regarded by the academic community as pseudohistory, which argues that the conventional chronology of Middle Eastern and European history is fundamentally flawed, and that events attributed to the civilizations of the Roman Empire, Ancient Greece and Ancient Egypt actually occurred during the Middle Ages, more than a thousand years later. The central concepts of the New Chronology are derived from the ideas of Russian scholar Nikolai Morozov (1854-1946), although work by French scholar Jean Hardouin (1646-1729) can be viewed as an earlier predecessor. However, the New Chronology is most commonly associated with Russian mathematician Anatoly Fomenko (b. 1945), although published works on the subject are actually a collaboration between Fomenko and several other mathematicians. The concept is most fully explained in *History: Fiction or Science?* book series, originally published in Russian.

The New Chronology also contains *a reconstruction*, an alternative chronology, radically shorter than the standard historical timeline, because all ancient history is "folded" onto the Middle Ages. According to Fomenko's claims, the written history of humankind goes only as far back as AD 800, there is almost no information about events between AD 800–1000, and most known historical events took place in AD 1000–1500.

The New Chronology is rejected by mainstream historians and is inconsistent with absolute and relative dating techniques used in the wider scholarly community. The majority of scientific commentators consider the New Chronology to be pseudoscientific.

History of New Chronology

The idea of chronologies that differ from the conventional chronology can be traced back to at least the early XVII century. Jean Hardouinthen suggested that many ancient historical documents were much younger than commonly believed to be. In 1685 he published a version of Pliny the Elder's *Natural History* in which he claimed that most Greek and Roman texts had been forged by Benedictine monks. When later questioned on these results, Hardouin stated that he would reveal the monks' reasons in a letter to be revealed only after his death. The executors of his estate were unable to find such a document among his posthumous papers. In the XVII century, Sir Isaac Newton, examining the current chronology of Ancient Greece, Ancient Egypt and the Ancient Near East, expressed discontent with prevailing theories and proposed one of his own, which, basing its study on Apollonius of Rhodes's *Argonautica*, changed the traditional dating of the Argonautic Expedition, the Trojan War, and the Founding of Rome.

In 1887, Edwin Johnson expressed the opinion that early Christian history was largely invented or corrupted in the II and III centuries.

In 1909, Otto Rank made note of duplications in literary history of a variety of cultures:

> "... almost all important civilized peoples have early woven myths around and glorified in poetry their heroes, mythical kings and princes, founders of religions, of dynasties, empires and cities—in short, their national heroes. Especially the history of their birth and of their early years is furnished with phantastic [*sic*] traits; the amazing similarity, nay literal identity, of those tales, even if they refer to different, completely independent peoples, sometimes geographically far removed from one another, is well known and has struck many an investigator." (Rank, Otto. *Der Mythos von der Geburt des Helden.*)

Fomenko became interested in Morozov's theories in 1973. In 1980, together with a few colleagues from the mathematics department of Moscow State University, he published several articles on "new mathematical methods in history" in peer-reviewed journals. The articles stirred a lot of controversy, but ultimately Fomenko failed to win any respected historians to his side. By the early 1990s, Fomenko shifted his focus from trying to convince the scientific community via peer-reviewed publications to publishing books. Beam writes that Fomenko and his colleagues were discovered by the Soviet scientific press in the early 1980s, leading to "a brief period of renown"; a contemporary review from the journal *Questions of History* complained, "Their constructions have nothing in common with Marxist historical science." (Alex Beam. "A shorter history of civilization." *Boston Globe*, 16 September 1991.)

By 1996, his theory had grown to cover Russia, Turkey, China, Europe, and Egypt [Emp:1].

Fomenko's claims

According to New Chronology, the traditional chronology consists of four overlapping copies of the "true" chronology shifted back in time by significant intervals with some further revisions. Fomenko claims all events and characters conventionally dated earlier than XI century are fictional, and represent "phantom reflections" of actual Middle Ages events and characters, brought about by intentional or accidental misdatings of historical documents. Before the invention of printing, accounts of the same events by different eyewitnesses were sometimes retold several times before being written down, then often went through multiple rounds of translating and copyediting. Names were translated, mispronounced and misspelled to the point where they bore little resemblance to originals.

According to Fomenko, this led early chronologists to believe or choose to believe that those accounts described different events and even different countries and time periods. Fomenko justifies this approach by the fact that, in many cases, the original documents are simply not available. Fomenko claims that all the history of the ancient world is known to us from manuscripts that date from the XV century to the XVIII century, but describe events that allegedly happened thousands of years before, the originals regrettably and conveniently lost.

For example, the oldest extant manuscripts of monumental treatises on Ancient Roman and Greek history, such as *Annals* and *Histories*, are conventionally dated c. AD 1100, more than a full millennium after the events they describe, and they did not come to scholars' attention until the XV century. According to Fomenko, the XV century is probably when these documents were first written.

Central to Fomenko's New Chronology is his claim of the existence of a vast Slav-Turk empire, which he called the "Russian Horde", which he says played the dominant role in Eurasian history before the XVII century. The various peoples identified in ancient and medieval history, from the Scythians, Huns, Goths and Bulgars, through the Polyane, Duleby, Drevliane, Pechenegs, to in more recent times, the Cossacks, Ukrainians, and Belarusians, are nothing but elements of the single Russian Horde. For the New Chronologists, peoples such as the Ukrainians, Belarusians, Mongols, and others who assert their national independence from Russia, are suffering from a historical delusion.

Fomenko claims that the most probable prototype of the historical Jesus was Andronikos I Komnenos (allegedly AD 1152 to 1185), the emperor of Byzantium, known for his failed reforms; his traits and deeds reflected in 'biographies' of many real and imaginary persons (A. T. Fomenko, G. V. Nosovskiy. *Czar of the Slavs* (in Russian). St. Petersburg: Neva, 2004.). The historical Jesus is a composite figure and reflection of the Old Testament prophet Elisha (850-800 BC?), Pope Gregory VII (1020?-1085), Saint Basil of Caesarea (330-379), and even Li Yuanhao (also known as Emperor Jingzong, or "Son of Heaven", emperor of Western Xia, who reigned in 1032-1048), Euclides, Bacchus and Dionysius. Fomenko explains the seemingly vast differences in the biographies of these figures as resulting from difference in languages, points of view and time frame of the authors of said accounts and biographies.

Fomenko also merges the cities and histories of Jerusalem, Rome and Troy into "New Rome" = Gospel Jerusalem (in the XII and XIII centuries) = Troy = Yoros Castle (A. T. Fomenko, G. V. Nosovskiy. *Forgotten Jerusalem: Istanbul in the light of New Chronology* (in Russian). ?oscow: Astrel, AST, 2007). To the south of Yoros Castle is Joshua's Hill which Fomenko alleges is the hill Calvary depicted in the Bible.

Fomenko claims the Hagia Sophia is actually the biblical Temple of Solomon. He identifies Solomon as sultan Suleiman the Magnificent (1494–1566). He claims that historical Jesus may have been born in 1152 and was crucified around AD 1185 on the hill over-looking the Bosphorus.

On the other hand, according to Fomenko the word "Rome" is a placeholder and can signify any one of several different cities and kingdoms. He claims the "First Rome", or "Ancient Rome", or "Mizraim", is an ancient Egyptian kingdom in the delta of the Nile with its capital in Alexandria. The second and most famous "New Rome" is Constantinople. The third "Rome" is constituted by three different cities: Constantinople (again), Rome in Italy, and Moscow. According to his claims, Rome in Italy was founded around AD 1380 by Aeneas, and Moscow as the third Rome was the capital of the great "Russian Horde." Similarly, the word "Jerusalem" is actually a placeholder rather than a physical location and can refer to differ-ent cities at different times and the word "Israel" did not define a state, even not a territory, but people fighting for God, for example, French St. Louis and English Elizabeth called themselves the King/ Queen of Israel.

He claims that parallelism between John the Baptist, Jesus, and Old Testament prophets implies that the New Testament was writ-ten before the Old Testament. Fomenko claims that the Bible was being written until the Council of Trent (1545–1563), when the list of canonical books was established, and all apocryphal books were ordered to be destroyed. Fomenko also claims that Plato, Plotinus and Gemistus Pletho are one and the same person; according to him, some texts by or about Pletho were misdated and today believed to be texts by or about Plotinus or Plato. He claims similar duplicates Dionysius the Areopagite, Pseudo-Dionysius the Areopagite, and Dionysius Petavius. He claims Florence and the House of Medici bankrolled and played an important role in creation of the magnif-icent 'Roman' and 'Greek' past.

Specific claims

In volumes 1, 2, 3 and 4 of *History: Fiction or Science?* Fomenko and his colleagues make numerous claims:

- Historians and translators often "assign" different dates and locations to different accounts of the same historical events, creating multiple "phantom copies" of these events. These "phantom copies" are often misdated by centuries or even millennia and end up incorporated into conventional chronology.

- This chronology was largely manufactured by Joseph Justus Scaliger in *Opus Novum de emendatione temporum* (1583) and *Thesaurum temporum* (1606), and represents a vast array of dates produced without any justification whatsoever, containing the repeating sequences of dates with shifts equal to multiples of the major cabbalistic numbers 333 and 360. The Jesuit Dionysius Petavius completed this chronology in *De Doctrina Temporum*, 1627 (v. 1) and 1632 (v. 2).

- Archaeological dating, dendrochronological dating, paleographical dating, numismatic dating, carbon dating, and other methods of dating of ancient sources and artifacts known today are erroneous, non-exact or dependent on traditional chronology.

- No single document in existence can be reliably dated earlier than the XI century. Most "ancient" artifacts may find other than consensual explanation.

- Histories of Ancient Rome, Greece and Egypt were crafted during the Renaissance by humanists and clergy - mostly on the basis of documents of their own making.

- The Old Testament represents a rendition of events of the XIV to XVI centuries AD in Europe and Byzantium, containing "prophecies" about "future" events related in the New Testament, a rendition of events of AD 1152 to 1185.

- The history of religions runs as follows: the pre-Christian period (before the XI century and the birth of Jesus), Bacchic Christianity (XI and XII centuries, before and after the life of Jesus), Christianity (XII to XVI centuries) and its subsequent mutations into Orthodox Christianity, Catholicism, Judaism, and Islam.

- The *Almagest* of Claudius Ptolemy, traditionally dated to around AD 150 and considered the cornerstone of classical history, was compiled in XVI and XVII centuries from astronomical data of the IX to XVI centuries.

- 37 complete Egyptian horoscopes found in Denderah, Esna,

and other temples have unique valid astronomical solutions with dates ranging from AD 1000 and up to as late as AD 1700.

- The Book of Revelation, as we know it, contains a horoscope, dated to 25 September - 10 October 1486, compiled by cabbalistJohannes Reuchlin.
- The horoscopes found in Sumerian/Babylonian tablets do not contain sufficient astronomical data; consequently, they have solutions every 30–50 years on the time axis and are therefore useless for purposes of dating.
- The Chinese tables of eclipses are useless for dating, as they contain too many eclipses that did not take place astronomically. Chinese tables of comets, even if true, cannot be used for dating.
- All major inventions like powder and guns, paper and print occurred in Europe in the period between the X and the XVI centuries.
- Ancient Roman and Greek statues, showing perfect command of the human anatomy, are fakes crafted in the Renaissance, when artists attained such command for the first time.
- There was no such thing as the Tartar and Mongol invasion followed by over two centuries of yoke and slavery, because the so-called "Tartars and Mongols" were the actual ancestors of the modern Russians, living in a bilingual state with Turkic spoken as freely as Russian. So, Russia and Turkey once formed parts of the same empire. This ancient Russian state was governed by a double structure of civil and military authorities and the hordes were actually professional armies with a tradition of lifelong conscription (the recruitment being the so-called "blood tax"). The Mongol "invasions" were punitive operations against the regions of the empire that attempted tax evasion. Tamerlane was probably a Russian warlord.
- Official Russian history is a blatant forgery concocted by a host of German scholars brought to Russia to legitimize the usurpingRomanov dynasty (1613-1917).
- Moscow was founded as late as the mid-XIV century. The battle of Kulikovo took place in Moscow.
- The tsar Ivan the Terrible represents a collation of no fewer

than four rulers, representing two rival dynasties: the legitimate Godunov rulers and the ambitious Romanov upstarts.
- English history of AD 640–1040 and Byzantine history of AD 378–830 are reflections of the same late-medieval original.

Fomenko's methods

Statistical correlation of texts

One of Fomenko's simplest methods is statistical correlation of texts. His basic assumption is that a text which describes a sequence of events will devote more space to more important events (for example, a period of war or an unrest will have much more space devoted to than a period of peaceful, non-eventful years), and that this irregularity will remain visible in other descriptions of the period. For each analysed text, a function is devised which maps each year mentioned in the text with the number of pages (lines, letters) devoted in the text to its description (which could be zero). The function of the two texts are then compared. (*Chron1*, pp. 187–194.)

For example, Fomenko compares the contemporary history of Rome written by Titus Livius with a modern history of Rome written by Russian historian V. S. Sergeev, calculating that the two have high correlation, and thus that they describe the same period of history, which is undisputed. (*Chron1*, pp. 194–196.) He also compares modern texts, which describe different periods, and calculates low correlation, as expected. (*Chron1*, pp. 194–196.) However, when he compares, for example, the ancient history of Rome and the medieval history of Rome, he calculates a high correlation, and concludes that ancient history of Rome is a copy of medieval history of Rome, thus clashing with mainstream accounts.

Statistical correlation of dynasties

In a somewhat similar manner, Fomenko compares two dynasties of rulers using statistical methods. First, he creates a database of rulers, containing relevant information on each of them. Then, he creates "survey codes" for each pair of the rulers, which contain a number which describes degree of the match of each considered property of two rulers. For example, one of the properties is the way of death: if two rulers were both poisoned, they get value of

+1 in their property of the way of death; if one ruler was poisoned and another killed in combat, they get -1; and if one was poisoned, and another died of illness, they get 0 (Fomenko claims there is possibility that chroniclers were not impartial and that different descriptions nonetheless describe the same person). An important property is the length of the rule. (*Chron1*, pp. 215–223.)

Fomenko lists a number of pairs of unrelated dynasties – for example, dynasties of kings of Israeland emperors of late Western Roman Empire (AD 300-476) – and claims that this method demonstrates correlations between their reigns. (Graphs which

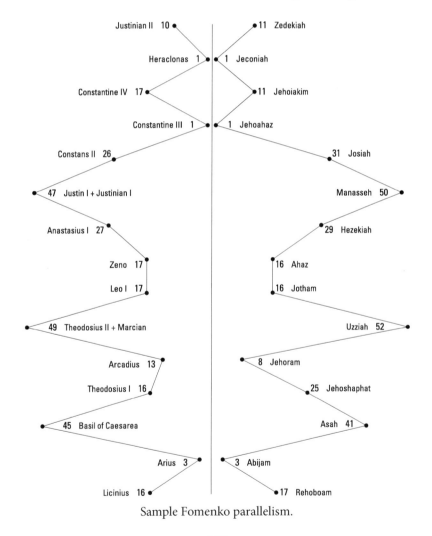

Sample Fomenko parallelism.

show just the length of the rule in the two dynasties are the most widely known; however, Fomenko's conclusions are also based on other parameters, as described above.) He also claims that the regnal history from the XVII to XX centuries never shows correlation of "dynastic flows" with each other, therefore Fomenko insists history was multiplied and outstretched into imaginary antiquity to justify this or other "royal" pretensions.

Fomenko uses for the demonstration of correlation between the reigns exclusively the data from the *Chronological Tables* of J. Blair (Moscow, 1808-1809). Fomenko says that Blair's tables are all the more valuable to us since they were compiled in an epoch adjacent to the time of Scaligerian chronology. According to Fomenko these tables contain clearer signs of "Scaligerite activity" which were subsequently buried under layers of paint and plaster by historians of the XIX and XX centuries.

Astronomical evidence

Fomenko examines astronomical events described in ancient texts and claims that the chronology is actually medieval. For example:

- He says the mysterious drop in the value of the lunar acceleration parameter D" ("a linear combination of the [angular] accelerations of the Earth and Moon") between the years AD 700–1300, which the American astronomer Robert Newton had explained in terms of "non-gravitational" (i.e., tidal) forces. By eliminating those anomalous early eclipses the New Chronology produces a constant value of D" beginning around AD 1000. (*Chron1*, pp. pp.93-94, 105-6.)
- He associates initially the Star of Bethlehem with the AD 1140 (±20) supernova (now Crab Nebula) and the Crucifixion Eclipse with the total solar eclipse of AD 1170 (±20). He also believes that Crab Nebula supernova could not have exploded in AD 1054, but probably in AD 1153. He connects it with total eclipse of AD 1186. Moreover he holds in strong doubt the veracity of ancient Chinese astronomical data.
- He argues that the star catalog in the *Almagest*, ascribed to the Hellenistic astronomer Claudius Ptolemy, was compiled in the XV to XVI centuries AD. With this objective in sight

213

he develops new methods of dating old stellar catalogues and claims that the *Almagest* is based on data collected between AD 600 and 1300, whereby the telluric obliquity is well taken into account.

- He refines and completes Morozov's analysis of some ancient horoscopes, most notably, the so-called Dendera Zodiacs—two horoscopes drawn on the ceiling of the temple of Hathor—and comes to the conclusion that they correspond to either the XI or the XIII century AD. Moreover, in his *History: Fiction or Science?* series finale, he makes computer-aided dating of all 37 Egyptian horoscopes that contain sufficient astronomical data, and claims they all fit into XI to XIX century timeframe. Traditional history usually either interprets these horoscopes as belonging to the I century BC or suggests that they weren't meant to match any date at all.

- In his final analysis of an eclipse triad described by the ancient Greek Thucydides in *History of the Peloponnesian War*, Fomenko dates the eclipses to AD 1039, 1046 and 1057. Because of the layered structure of the manuscript, he claims that Thucydides actually lived in medieval times and in describing the Peloponnesian War between the Spartans and Athenians he was actually describing the conflict between the medieval Navarrans and Catalans in Spain from AD 1374 to 1387.

- Fomenko claims that the abundance of dated astronomical records in cuneiform texts from Mesopotamia is of little use for dating of events, as the astronomical phenomena they describe recur cyclically every 30–40 years.

Rejection of common dating methods

On archaeological dating methods, Fomenko claims:

> "Archaeological, dendrochronological, paleographical and carbon methods of dating of ancient sources and artifacts are both non-exact and contradictory, therefore there is not a single piece of firm written evidence or artifact that could be reliably and independently dated earlier than the XI century." (*Chron1.*)

Dendrochronology is rejected with a claim that, for dating of objects much older than the oldest still living trees, it isn't an absolute, but arelative dating method, and thus dependent on traditional chronology. Fomenko specifically points to a break of dendrochronological scales around AD 1000.

Fomenko also cites a number of cases where carbon dating of a series of objects of known age gave significantly different dates. He also alleges undue cooperation between physicists and archaeologists in obtaining the dates, since most radiocarbon dating labs only accept samples with an age estimate suggested by historians or archaeologists. Fomenko also claims that carbon dating over the range of AD 1 to 2000 is inaccurate because it has too many sources of error that are either guessed at or completely ignored, and that calibration is done with a statistically meaningless number of samples. Consequently, Fomenko concludes that carbon dating is not accurate enough to be used on historical scale.

Fomenko rejects numismatic dating as circular, being based on the traditional chronology, and points to cases of similar coins being minted in distant periods, unexplained long periods with no coins minted and cases of mismatch of numismatic dating with historical accounts. (*Chron1*, pp. 90-92.)

He fully agrees with absolute dating methods for clay tablets or coins like thermoluminescence dating, optically stimulated luminescence dating, archaeomagnetic, metallographic dating, but claims that their precision does not allow for comprehensive pinpointing on the time axis either.

Fomenko also condemns the common archaeological practice of submitting samples for dating accompanied with an estimate of the expected age. He claims that convergence of uncertainty in archaeological dating methods proves strictly nothing per se. Even if the sum S of probabilities of the veracity of event produced by N dating methods exceeds 1.00 it does not mean that the event has taken place with 100% probability.

Reception

Fomenko's historical ideas have been universally rejected by mainstream scholars, who brand them as pseudoscience, but were popularized by former world chess champion Garry Kasparov. Billington writes that the theory "might have quietly blown away in the wind tunnels of academia" if not for Kasparov's writing in support of it in the magazine *Ogoniok*. Kasparov met Fomenko during the 1990s, and found that Fomenko's conclusions concerning certain subjects were identical to his own regarding the popular view (which is not the view of academics) that art and culture died during the Dark Ages and were not revived until the Renaissance. Kasparov also felt it illogical that the Romans and the Greeks living under the banner of Byzantium could fail to use the mounds of scientific knowledge left them by Ancient Greece and Rome, especially when it was of urgent military use. However, Kasparov does not support the reconstruction part of the New Chronology. Russian critics tended to see Fomenko's New Chronology as "an embarrassment and a potent symbol of the depths to which the Russian academy and society have generally sunk ... since the fall of Communism." Western critics see his views as part of a renewed Russian imperial ideology, "keeping alive an imperial consciousness and secular messianism in Russia."

In 2004 Anatoly Fomenko with his coauthor Gleb Nosovsky were awarded for their books on "New Chronology" the anti-prize of the Moscow International Book Fair called "Abzatz" (literally 'paragraph', a euphemism for a vulgar Russian word meaning disaster or fiasco) in the category "Esteemed nonsense" ("Pochotnaya bezgramota") awarded for the worst book published in Russia.

Critics have accused Fomenko of altering the data to improve the fit with his ideas and have noted that he violates a key rule of statistics by selecting matches from the historical record which support his chronology, while ignoring those which do not, creating artificial, better-than-chance correlations, and that these practices undermine Fomenko's statistical arguments. The new chronology was given a comprehensive critical analysis in a round table on "The 'Myths' of New Chronology" chaired by the dean of the department of history of Moscow State University in December 1999. One of the participants in that round table, the distinguished Russian archaeologist, Valentin Yanin, compared Fomenko's work to "the sleight of hand trickery of a David Copperfield." Linguist Andrey Zaliznyak argued that by using the Fomenko's approaches one can "prove" any historical correspondence, for example, between Ancient Egyptian pharaohs and French kings.

James Billington, formerly professor of Russian history at Harvard and Princeton and currently the Librarian of Congress placed Fomenko's work within the context of the political movement of Eurasianism, which sought to tie Russian history closely to that of its Asian neighbors. Billington describes Fomenko as ascribing the belief in past hostility between Russia and the Mongols to the influence of Western historians. Thus, by Fomenko's chronology, "Russia and Turkey are parts of a previously single empire." A French reviewer of Billington's book noted approvingly his concern with the phantasmagorical conceptions of Fomenko about the global "new chronology."

H. G. van Bueren, professor emeritus of astronomy at the University of Utrecht, concluded his scathing review of Fomenko's work on the application of mathematics and astronomy to historical data as follows:

> "It is surprising, to say the least, that a well-known (Dutch) publisher could produce an expensive book of such doubtful intellectual value, of which the only good word that can be said is that it contains an enormous amount of factual historical material, untidily ordered, true; badly written, yes; mixed-up with conjectural nonsense, sure; but still, much useful stuff. For the rest of the book is absolutely worthless. It reminds one of the early Soviet attempts to produce tendentious science (Lysenko!), of polywater, of cold fusion, and of modern creationism. In brief: a useless and misleading book." (H. G. van Bueren, *Mathematics and Logic*.)

Convergence of methods in archaeological dating

While Fomenko rejects commonly accepted dating methods, archaeologists, conservators and other scientists make extensive use of such techniques which have been rigorously examined and refined during decades of use.

In the specific case of dendrochronology, Fomenko claims that this fails as an absolute dating method because of gaps in the record. However, independent dendrochronological sequences beginning with living trees from various parts of North America and Europe extend back 12,400 years into the past. Furthermore, the mutual consistency of these independent dendrochronological sequences has been confirmed by comparing their radiocarbon and dendrochronological ages. These and other data have provided a calibration curve for radiocarbon dating whose internal error does not exceed ±163 years over the entire 26,000 years of the curve.

In fact, archaeologists have developed a fully anchored dendro-chronology series going back past 10,000 BCE. "The absolutely dated tree-ring chronology now extends back to 12,410 cal BP (10,461 BC)."

Misuse of historical sources and forced pattern matching

Critics of Fomenko's theory claim that his use of historical sources is highly selective and ignores the basic principles of sound historical scholarship.

"Fomenko ... provides no fair-minded review of the historical literature about a topic with which he deals, quotes only those sources that serve his purposes, uses evidence in ways that seem strange to professionally-trained historians and asserts the wildest speculation as if it has the same status as the information common to the conventional historical literature."

They also note that his method of statistically correlating of texts is very rough, because it does not take into account the many possible sources of variation in length outside of "importance." They maintain that differences in language, style, and scope, as well as the frequently differing views and focuses of historians, which are manifested in a different notion of "important events", make quantifying historical writings a dubious proposition at best. What's more, Fomenko's critics allege that the parallelisms he reports are often derived by alleged forcing by Fomenko of the data – rearranging, merging, and removing monarchs as needed to fit the pattern.

For example, on the one hand Fomenko asserts that the vast majority of ancient sources are either irreparably distorted duplicate accounts of the same events or later forgeries. In his identification of Jesus with Pope Gregory VII (*Chron2*, p. 51) he ignores the otherwise vast dissimilarities between their reported lives and focuses on the similarity of their appointment to religious office by baptism. (The evangelical Jesus is traditionally believed to have lived for 33 years, and he was an adult at the time of his encounter with John the Baptist. In contrast, according to the available primary sources, Pope Gregory VII lived for at least 60 years and was born 8 years after the death of Fomenko's John-the-Baptist equivalent John Crescentius.)

Critics allege that many of the supposed correlations of regnal durations are the product of the selective parsing and blending of the dates, events, and individuals mentioned in the original text. Another point raised by critics is that Fomenko does not explain his altering the data (changing the order of rulers, dropping rulers, combining rulers, treating interregna as rulers, switching between theologians and emperors, etc.) preventing a duplication of the effort and effectively making this whole theory an ad hoc hypothesis.

Selectivity in reference to astronomical phenomena

Critics point out that Fomenko's discussion of astronomical phenomena tends to be selective, choosing isolated examples that support the New Chronology and ignoring the large bodies of data that provide statistically supported evidence for the conventional dating. For his dating of the Almagest star catalog, Fomenko arbitrarily selected eight stars from the more than 1000 stars in the catalog, one of which (Arcturus) has a large systematic error. This star has a dominant effect on Fomenko's dating. Statistical analysis using the same method for all "fast" stars points to the antiquity of the Almagest star catalog. Rawlins points out further that Fomenko's statistical analysis got the wrong date for the Almagest because he took as constant Earth's obliquity when it is a variable that changes at a very slow, but known, rate.

Fomenko's studies ignore the abundance of dated astronomical records in cuneiform texts from Mesopotamia. Among these texts is a series of Babylonian astronomical diaries, which records precise astronomical observations of the Moon and planets, often dated in terms of the reigns of known historical figures extending back to the VI century BCE. Astronomical retrocalculations for all these moving objects allow us to date these observations, and consequently the rulers' reigns, to within a single day. The observations are sufficiently redundant that only a small portion of them are sufficient to date a text to a unique year in the period 750 BCE to 100 CE. The dates obtained agree with the accepted chronology. In addition, F. R. Stephenson has demonstrated through a systematic study of a large number of Babylonian, Ancient and Medieval European, and Chinese records of eclipse observations that they can be dated consistently with conventional chronology at least as far back as

600 BCE. In contrast to Fomenko's missing centuries, Stephenson's studies of eclipse observations find an accumulated uncertainty in the timing of the rotation of the earth of 420 seconds at 400 BCE, and only 80 seconds at 1000 CE.

Magnitude and consistency of conspiracy theory

Fomenko claims that world history prior to 1600 was deliberately falsified for political reasons. The consequences of this conspiracy theory are twofold. Documents that conflict with New Chronology are said to have been edited or fabricated by conspirators (mostly Western European historians and humanists of late XVI to XVII centuries). The lack of documents directly supporting New Chronology and conflicting traditional history is said to be thanks to the majority of such documents being destroyed by the same conspirators.

Consequently, there are many thousands of documents that are considered authentic in traditional history, but not in New Chronology. Fomenko often uses "falsified" documents, which he dismisses in other contexts, to prove a point. For example, he analyzes the Tartar Relation and arrives at the conclusion that Mongolian capital of Karakorum was located in Central Russia (equated with present-day Yaroslavl). However, the Tartar Relation makes several statements that are at odds with New Chronology (such as that Batu Khan and Russian duke Yaroslav are two distinct people). Those are said by Fomenko to have been introduced into the original text by later editors.

Many of the rulers that Fomenko claims are medieval doppelgangers moved in the imaginary past have left behind vast numbers of coins. Numismatists have made innumerable identifications of coins to rulers known from ancient sources. For instance, several Roman emperors issued coinage featuring at least three of their names, consistent with those found in written sources, and there are frequent examples of joint coinage between known royal family members, as well as overstrikes by kings who were known enemies.

Ancient coins in Greek and Latin are unearthed to this day in vast quantities from Britain to India. For Fomenko's theories to be correct, this could only be explained by counterfeit on a very grand and consistent scale, as well as a complete dismissal of all numismatic analyses of hoard findings, coin styles etc.

Popularity in forums and amongst Russian imperialists

Despite criticism, Fomenko has published and sold over one million copies of his books in his native Russia. Many internet forums have appeared which aim to supplement his work with additional amateur research. His critics have suggested that Fomenko's version of history appealed to the Russian reading public by keeping alive an imperial consciousness to replace their disillusionment with the failures of Communism and post-Communist corporate oligarchies.

Alexander Zinoviev called the New Chronology "one of the major scientific breakthroughs of the XX century."

(Wikipedia text retrieved on 2nd August, 2015)

Afterword from the publisher

Dr. Fomenko *et al* as scientists are ready to recognize their mistakes, to repent and to retract on the condition that:

- radiocarbon dating methods pass the black box tests, or
- astronomy refutes their results on ancient eclipses, or
- US astrophysicist Robert Newton was proved wrong to accuse Ptolemy of his crime.

At present, historians do not, can not, and will not comply. The radiocarbon dating labs run their very costly tests only if the sample to be dated is accompanied with an idea of age pronounced by historians on basis of … subjective … mmm … gutfeeling … and the history books they have been writing for the last 400 years. Radiocarbon labs politely bill for their fiddling and finetuning to get the dates "to order" of historians. *Circulus vitiosus* is perfect.

Bibliography

Separate books on the New Chronology

Prior to the publication of the seven-volume *Chronology,* we published a number of books on the same topic. If we are to disregard the paperbacks and the concise versions, as well as new re-editions, there are seven such books. Shortened versions of their names appear below:

1. *Introduction.*
2. *Methods 1-2.*
3. *Methods 3.*
4. *The New Chronology of Russia, Britain and Rome.*
5. *The Empire.*
6. *The Biblical Russia.*
7. *Reconstruction.*

• BOOK ONE. *Introduction.*

[*Intro*]:1. Fomenko, A. T. *New Experimental Statistical Methods of Dating Ancient Events and their Application to the Global Classical and Mediaeval Chronology.* Pre-print. Moscow, The State Television and Radio Broadcast Committee, 1981. Order #3672. Lit. 9/XI-81. No. BO7201, 100 p.

[*Intro*]:2. Fomenko, A. T. *Some New Empirico-Statistical Methods of Dating and the Analysis of Present Global Chronology.* London, The British Library, Department of Printed Books, 1981. Cup. 918/87. 100 p.

[*Intro*]3. Fomenko, A. T. *A Criticism of the Traditional Chronology of the Classical*

Age and the Middle Ages (What Century Is It Now?). Essay. Moscow, Publishing House of the Moscow State University Department of Mechanical Mathematics, 1993. 204 p.

[*Intro*]:4. 2nd edition, revised and expanded. Fomenko, A. T., and G. V. Nosovskiy. *A Criticism of the Traditional Chronology of the Classical Age and the Middle Ages (What Century Is It Now?).* Moscow, Kraft-Lean, 1999. 757 p. Kraft Publications released a concise version of this book in 2001. 487 p.

[*Intro*]:5. Another revision. Fomenko, A. T., and G. V. Nosovskiy. *What Century Is It Now?* Moscow, AIF-Print Publications, 2002. 511 p.

- **BOOK TWO, PART ONE:** *Methods-1.*

[*Meth1*]:1. Fomenko, A. T. *The Methods of Statistical Analysis of Narrative Texts and their Chronological Applications.* (The identification and dating of dependent texts, statistical chronology of the antiquity, as well as the statistics of ancient astronomical accounts.) Moscow, MSU Publishing House, 1990. 439 p.

[*Meth1*]:2. 2nd revised edition came out in 1996 as *The Methods Of Mathematical Analysis of Historical Texts. Chronological applications.* Moscow, Nauka Publications, 1996. 475 p.

[*Meth1*]:3. Several chapters of the book came out in 1996, revised and extended, as a separate book: Fomenko, A. T. *The New Chronology of Greece. Antiquity in the Middle Ages,* Vols. 1 and 2. Moscow, MSU Centre of Research and Pre-University Education, 1996. 914 p.

[*Meth1*]:4. The English translation of the book, extended and revised to a large extent, was released under the following title: Fomenko, A. T. *Empirico-Statistical Analysis of Narrative Material and its Applications to Historical Dating.* Vol. 1, *The Development of the Statistical Tools.* Vol. 2, *The Analysis of Ancient and Mediaeval Records.* The Netherlands, Kluwer Academic Publishers, 1994. Vol. 1: 211 p. Vol. 2: 462 p.

[*Meth1*]:5. A Serbian translation titled *Статистичка хронологија. Математички поглед на историју. У ком смо веку?* was published in 1997. Belgrade, Margo-Art, 1997. 450 p.

[*Meth1*]:6. The book was published in a revised and substantially extended version in 1999 as Volume 1 in a series of two: Fomenko, A. T. *The Methods of Statistical Analysis of Historical Texts. Chronological Applications.* Vol. 1. Moscow, Kraft and Lean, 1999. 801 p.

[*Meth1*]:7. A revised version of the book was published as two volumes (the first two in a series of three) in 1999 in the USA (in Russian) by the Edwin Mellen Press. Fomenko, A. T. *New Methods of Statistical Analysis of Historical Texts. Applications to Chronology,* Vols. 1 and 2. The publication is part of the series titled *Scholarly Monographs in the Russian Language,* Vols. 6-7. Lewiston, Queenston, Lampeter, Edwin Mellen Press, 1999. Vol. 1: 588 p. Vol. 2: 564 p.

- **BOOK TWO, PART TWO:** *Methods-2.*

[*Meth2*]:1. Fomenko, A. T. *Global Chronology.* (A Research of the Classical

224

and Mediaeval History. Mathematical Methods of Source Analysis. Global Chronology.) Moscow, MSU Publications, 1993. 408 p.

[*Meth2*]:2. A revised and substantially extended version of the book as the second volume in a series of two: Fomenko, A. T. *The Methods of Statistical Analysis of Historical Texts. Chronological Applications,* Vol. 2. Moscow, Kraft and Lean, 1999. 907 p.

[*Meth2*]:3. A revised version of the book was published as the last volume in a series of three in the USA (in Russian) under the title: Fomenko A. T. *Antiquity in the Middle Ages (Greek and Bible History),* the trilogy bearing the general name: Fomenko A. T. *New Methods of the Statistical Analysis of Historical Texts and their Chronological Application.* The publication is part of the series titled *Scholarly Monographs in the Russian Language.* Lewiston, Queenston, Lampeter, The Edwin Mellen Press, 1999. 578 p.

• BOOK THREE: *Methods-3.*

[*Meth3*]:1. Fomenko, A. T., V. V. Kalashnikov, and G. V. Nosovskiy. *Geometrical and Statistical Methods of Analysis of Star Configurations. Dating Ptolemy's Almagest.* USA: CRC Press, 1993. 300 p.

[*Meth3*]:2. The Russian version of the book was published in 1995 in Moscow by the Faktorial Publications under the title: Kalashnikov V. V., Nosovskiy G. V., Fomenko A. T. *The Dating of the Almagest Star Catalogue. Statistical and Geometrical Analysis.* 286 p.

[*Meth3*]:3. A substantially extended and revised version of the book: Kalashnikov, V. V., G. V. Nosovskiy, and A. T. Fomenko. *The Astronomical Analysis of Chronology. The Almagest. Zodiacs.* Moscow, The Delovoi Express Financial Publications, 2000. 895 p.

[*Meth3*]:4. Fomenko, A. T., and G. V. Nosovskiy. *The New Chronology of Egypt. The Astronomical Dating of Ancient Egyptian Monuments. Research of 2000-2002.* Moscow, Veche Press, 2002. 463 p.

• BOOK FOUR: *Russia, Britain and Rome.*

[*RBR*]:1. Fomenko, A. T., and G. V. Nosovskiy. *The New Chronology and Conception of the Ancient History of Russia, Britain, and Rome. Facts, Statistics, Hypotheses.* Vol. 1, *Russia.* Vol. 2, *Britain and Rome.* Moscow, MSU Centre of Research and Pre-University Education. Two editions, 1995 and 1996. 672 p.

[*RBR*]:2. A somewhat adapted and revised version of the book came out in 1997: Fomenko, A. T., and G. V. Nosovskiy. *Russia and Rome. How correct is our understanding of Eurasian history?* Vols. 1 and 2. Moscow, Olymp Publications, 1997. 2nd edition 1999. The next three volumes from this series of five were published in 2001. Vol. 1: 606 p. Vol. 2: 621 p. Vol. 3: 540 p. Vol. 4: 490 p. Vol. 5: 394 p.

[*RBR*]:3. A revised version of the first volume was published in 1997 as a separate book: Fomenko, A. T., and G. V. Nosovskiy. *The New Chronology of Russia.* Moscow, Faktorial Publications, 1997. Re-editions 1998 and 1999. 255 p.

[*RBR*]:4. A new, substantially extended and revised version of the first two-volume edition as a single volume: Fomenko, A. T., and G. V. Nosovskiy. *The New Chronology of Russia, Britain and Rome.* Moscow, Anvik, 1999. 540 p.

[*RBR*]:5. A new revised version of this book came out as a single volume: Fomenko A. T., and G. V. Nosovskiy. Moscow, The Delovoi Express Financial Publications, 2001. 1015 p.

- **BOOK FIVE:** *The Empire.*

[*Emp*]:1. Fomenko, A. T., and G. V. Nosovskiy. *The Empire (Russia, Turkey, China, Europe, Egypt. The New Mathematical Chronology of Antiquity).* Moscow, Faktorial, 1996. Re-editions 1997, 1998, 1999, 2001 and 2002. 752 p.

- **BOOK SIX:** *The Biblical Russia.*

[*BR*]:1. Fomenko, A. T., and G. V. Nosovskiy. *The Mathematical Chronology of the Biblical Events.* Moscow, Nauka Publications, 1997. 407 p.

[*BR*]:2. A substantially revised and extended version: Fomenko, A. T., and G. V. Nosovskiy. *The Biblical Russia. The Empire of Horde-Russia and the Bible. The New Mathematical Chronology of Antiquity.* Vols. 1 and 2. Moscow, Faktorial, 1998. Vol. 1: 687 p. Vol. 2: 582 p.

[*BR*]:3. A somewhat condensed version, which nevertheless contained some important new material: Fomenko, A. T., and G. V. Nosovskiy. *Horde-Russia on the Pages of the Biblical Books.* Moscow, Anvik Publications, 1998. 430 p.

[*BR*]:4. Fomenko, A. T., and G. V. Nosovskiy. *The Biblical Russia. Selected Chapters I (The Empire of Horde-Russia and the Bible. The New Mathematical Chronology of Antiquity. History of the Manuscripts and Editions of the Bible. The Events of the XI–XII Century A.D. in the New Testament. The Pentateuch.).* Moscow, Faktorial, 1999. 173 p.

[*BR*]:5. Fomenko, A. T., and G. V. Nosovskiy. *The Biblical Russia. Selected Chapters II (The Empire of Horde-Russia and the Bible. The New Mathematical Chronology of Antiquity. History of the XIV–XVI Century in the Last Books of the Kings. The History of the XV–XVI Century in the Last Chapters of the Books of the Kings. History of the XV–XVI Century in the Books of Esther and Judith. The Reformation Epoch of the XVI–XVII Century).* Moscow, Faktorial Press, 2000. 223 p.

- **BOOK SEVEN:** *Reconstruction.*

[*Rec*]:1. Fomenko, A. T., and G. V. Nosovskiy. *A Reconstruction of Global History (The New Chronology).* Book 1. Moscow, Delovoi Express, 1999. 735 p.

[*Rec*]:2. Fomenko, A. T., and G. V. Nosovskiy. *A Reconstruction of Global History. The Research of 1999-2000 (The New Chronology).* Moscow, Delovoi Express, 1999. 615 p.

[*Rec*]:3. Fomenko, A. T., and G. V. Nosovskiy. *A Reconstruction of Global History. Joan of Arc, Samson, and the History of Russia.* Moscow, The Delovoi Express Financial Publishers, 2002.

We have to point out that the publication of our books on the New Chronology has influenced a number of authors and their works where the new chronological concepts are discussed or developed. Some of these are: L. I. Bocharov, N. N. Yefimov, I. M. Chachukh, and I. Y. Chernyshov ([93]), Jordan Tabov ([827], [828]), A. Goutz ([220]), M. M. Postnikov ([680]), V. A. Nikerov ([579:1]), Heribert Illig ([1208]), Christian Blöss and Hans-Ulrich Niemitz ([1038], [1039]), Gunnar Heinsohn ([1185]), Gunnar Heinsohn and Heribert Illig ([1186]), Uwe Topper ([1462], [1463]).

Our research attracted sufficient attention to chronological issues for the Muscovite publishing house Kraft to print a new edition of the fundamental work of N. A. Morozov titled Christ, first published in 1924-1932.

Sources in Russian

[1]. Abalakin, V. K. *The Essential Ephemeris Astronomy.* Moscow, 1979.

[2]. Abbas, Shalabi. *The Entire Egypt, from Cairo to Abu-Simbel and Sinai.* 2nd extended Russian edition. Florence, Bonechi, 1996.

[2:1]. Avadyaeva, E., and L. Zdanovich. *The Hundred Great Afflictions.* Moscow, Veche, 1999.

[3]. Agathius. *The Reign of Justinian.* Moscow-Leningrad, USSR Academy of Sciences Publications, 1953. See also Agathius, Scholasticus. *Agathiae Myrinaei Historiarum libri quinque.* Berolini, 1967.

[4]. Mez, Adam. *The Muslim Renaissance.* Moscow, Nauka, 1966. German edition: Mez, A. *Die Renaissance des Islams.* Heidelberg, 1922.

[5]. Azarevich, D. I. *The History of the Byzantine Law.* Yaroslavl, 1876-1877.

[6]. Aydarova-Volkova, G. *The Priceless Experience. A Cultural Dialogue. Looking Across the Centuries.* The *Kazan* magazine, Issue 9-10 (1999): 13-21.

[7]. Acropolite, George. *The Chronicle of the Great Logothete George Acropolite.* St. Petersburg, 1863.

[8]. *The Historical Acts Compiled and Published by the Archaeographical Commission.* St. Petersburg, The State Document Preparation Expedition Typography. Vols. 1 and 2. 1841.

[9]. Nazarov, V. D., ed. *The Acts of the State of Russia. Archives of the Muscovite Monasteries and Cathedrals.* The XV – early XVII century. Moscow, The Ladomir Research and Publication Centre, 1998.

[10]. *Alexandria. A Novel about Alexander the Great Based on a Russian Chronicle of the XV century.* Moscow-Leningrad, Nauka, 1966.

[11]. Petrukhno, A. S., N. I. Shirinya, S. A. Gleybman, and O. V. Zavgorodniaya. *Alexander's Village (Alexandrovskaya Sloboda, or, literally, "The Freemen's Village of Alexander"). An Album.* The Russian Federation Ministry of Culture.

City of Alexandrov. The State Museum of Art, History, and Architecture of Alexander's Village. The City Council of the City of Alexandrov. 1996.

[12]. *Alexander's Village (Alexandrovskaya Sloboda).* The materials of a scientific and practical conference. Vladimir, Golden Gate Publications, 1995.

[13]. Alexandrovsky, M. I. *A Historical Reference Book for the Churches of Moscow.* Moscow, The State Museum of History, Department of Visual Arts, the Architectural Graphics Fund, 1917 (with an additional written before 1942).

[14]. Alexeyev, M. P. *On the Anglo-Russian Relations in the Time of Yaroslav the Wise.* The Scientific Bulletin of the Leningrad State University (4, 1945): 31.

[15]. Alexeyev, Y. *My Monarch Sent Me to the Sultan.* The *Rodina* magazine, No. 2 (1997): 31-36.

[16]. Alessandro, Angelini. *Piero della Francesca.* The *Great Italian Masters* series. Moscow, Slovo, 1997. The Italian edition: Italy, Scala, Instituto Fotografico Editoriale, 1995.

[16:1]. [*Altarpieces*] Caterina Limentani Virdis and Mari Pietrogiovanna. *Altarpieces. The Art of the Early Renaissance.* Translated from Italian. Byely Gorod, 2002. Arsenale editrice, Italy, 2001.

[17]. *The Alphabetic Syntagm of Matthew Vlastar.* Translated from Greek by Rev. Nikolai Ilyinsky, a teacher from the Seminary School of Tauris. Simpheropol, 1892. A new edition: Moscow, Galaxy Publications, 1996.

[18]. Alberti, L. *Leon Battista Alberti.* A collection of essays. Moscow, the USSR Academy of Sciences, Nauka, 1977. *Complete ed.* Oxford, Phaidon, 1977.

[19]. Amalrik, A. S., and A. L. Mongayt. *The Essential Archaeology.* Moscow, Prosveshchenie, 1963.

[19:0]. [Amartoles, George]. Matveyenko, V., and L. Shchegoleva. *The Chronicle of George the Monk.* Russian text, comments, indications. Moscow, Bogorodskiy Pechatnik, 2000.

[19:1]. The catalogue of the exhibition *500 Years Since the Discovery of America.* The Hermitage. Russian National Library. St. Petersburg, Slavia-Interbook, Inc., 1993.

[20]. Amousin, I. D. *The Dead Sea Scrolls.* Moscow, Nauka, 1960.

[21]. Amphitheatrov, A. *Collected Works in 8 Volumes.* Vol. 4. St. Petersburg, Prosveshchenie, 1911.

[22]. Anastasov, L. *A New Direction in Science? Be careful!* The *Science and Technology* magazine (Moscow), No. 8 (1983): 28-30.

[23]. Müller, V. K., comp. *The English-Russian Dictionary.* 70,000 words. Moscow, The State National and Foreign Dictionary Publishing House, 1961.

[24]. Andreyeva, V., V. Kuklev, and A. Rovner. *An Encyclopedia of Symbols, Signs, and Emblems.* Moscow, Lokid/Myth/Ad Marginem, 1999.

[25]. Anninskiy, S. A. *The News of the Tartars in Europe Brought by the Hungarian Missionaries.* Included in *The Historical Archive,* 71-112. Moscow-Leningrad, The RAS Institute of History, RAS Publications, 1940.

[26]. *Antwerp and its Sights.* Antwerp, Editions THILL S.A. Brussels, 1999. In Russian.

[27]. Antonov, A. V. *Genealogical Murals of Late XVII Century.* The Archaeographical Centre. The Russian State Archive of Ancient Acts. *The Russian Historical Research,* No. 6. Moscow, Archaeographical Centre Publications.

[28]. Antonova, V. I., and N. E. Mneva. *The Catalogue of Ancient Russian Art from the Tretyakov Gallery.* Moscow, 1963. Vol. 1: p. 256; Vol 2: pp. 413 and 421.

[29]. *The Apocryphal Jesus, Holy Family, and Christ Witness Legendry.* Sventsitskaya, I. S., and A. P. Skogorev, comp. Moscow, Kogelet, 1999.

[30]. Apollodorus. *The Mythological Library.* Leningrad, Nauka, 1972. English edition: Apollodorus. *The Library.* London-New York: Loeb Classical Library, 1921.

[30:1]. Arago, F. *The Biographies of the Famous Astronomers, Physicists, and Geometricians.* Books 1 and 2 (Vols. 1-3). Translated by D. Perevoshchikov. Moscow-Izhevsk, The Scientific Research Centre for Regular and Chaotic Dynamics, 2000.

[31]. Arenkova, Y. I., and G. I. Mekhova. *The Don Monastery.* Moscow, Iskusstvo, 1970.

[32]. Aristaenetus. *The Love Epistles.* Eustathius, Macrembolites. *The Story of Ismene and Istmenias.* Moscow-Leningrad, Nauka, 1965. Also see Aristaenetus. *The Love Epistles.* In W. Kelley. *Erotica.* London, Bohn's Classical Library, G. Bell & Sons, 1848. Eustathius, Macrembolites. *Ismene and Istmenias.* London, 1788.

[33]. Zdanovich, G. B., ed. *Arkaim. Research. Prospects. Findings.* A collection of essays. From the series titled *The Historical Pages of Southern Ural.* The Arkaim Reserve works, State University of Chelyabinsk, the Specialized Arkaim Nature and Landscape Centre of History and Archaeology. The State Reserve of Ilmen. Chelyabinsk, the Kamenny Poyas Creative Group, 1995.

[34]. Arnold, Y. *El Señor Kon-Tiki.* Moscow, Mysl, 1970.

[35]. Aronov, V. *The Elseviers (A History of Literary Art).* Moscow, Kniga, 1975.

[36]. *The Chronicler of Archangelsk. A complete collection of Russian chronicles,* Vol. 37. Leningrad, Nauka, 1982.

[37]. Archangelskiy, Leonid. *The Samurai Steel.* An article for the magazine called *Magnum. The New Magazine on Arms* (November-December 1998): 18-21.

[38]. Avdousina, T. D., and T. D. Panov. *Archaeological Antiquities: The Muscovite Kremlin.* The Moscow Kremlin State Museum and Reserve for History and Culture. Moscow, 1996.

[39]. Serge, Archbishop. *The Complete Oriental Menology.* Vols. 1-3. Vladimir, Typography & Lithography of V. A. Parkov in Vladimir, 1901. Reprinted Moscow, Orthodox Encyclopaedia Centre of Ecclesiastic Research, Palomnik Publications, 1997.

[40]. Archimedes. *The Works.* Moscow, Fizmatgiz, 1962. English edition: Archimedes, *The Works of Archimedes.* Cambridge, Cambridge University Press, 1912.

[40:0]. Asov, A. I. *The Book of Veles.* Moscow, Menedzher, 1995, 2nd edition.

[40:00]. Asov, A. I., Konovalov, M. Y. *The Ancient Aryans. The Slavs. Russia.* Moscow, Veche, 2002.

[40:1]. Gentili, Augusto, William Barcham, and Linda Whiteley. *The National Gallery of London.* From the *The Great Museums of the World* series. Moscow, Slovo, 2001. A translation of the Italian edition Udine: Magnus Edizioni, 2000.

[41]. Nikitin, Afanasiy. *Voyage over the Three Sees. Published in the Literary Monuments of Old Russia. 2nd Half of the XV Century.* Moscow, Khudozhestvennaya Literatura, 1982.

[42]. Nikitin, Afanasiy. *Afanasiy Nikitin's Voyage over the Three Sees. 1466-1472.* Foreword, translation, text preparation and commentary by N. I. Prokofiev. Moscow, Sovietskaya Rossiya, 1980.

[43]. Akhmanova, O. S., and others. *Precise Methods of Language Study.* Moscow, 1961.

[44]. Bayev, K. L. *Copernicus.* From the *Celebrity Biographies* series, Issue 7 (55). Moscow, The Magazine and Newspaper Consociation, 1935.

[45]. Beyer, Rolf. *The Queen of Sheba.* From the *Mark In History* series. Rostov-on-Don, Fenix Publications, 1998. A translation from the German original by Beyer, Rolf. *Die Königin von Saba.* The *Question Mark* series, Gustav Lübbe Verlag GmbH, Bergisch Gladbach. 1987.

[46]. Balandin, R. K. *A Miracle or a Scientific Enigma? Science and Religion Discussing the Shroud of Turin.* Moscow, Znaniye, 1989. The *Question Mark* series, Issue 1, 1989.

[47]. Balandin, R., and L. Bondarev. *Nature and Civilization.* Moscow, Mysl, 1988.

[48]. Baldin, V. I., and T. P. Manushkina. *The Laura of Serge and The Trinity. The Architectural Set and the Collections of Ancient Russian Art of the XIV–XVII Century.* Moscow, Nauka, 1996.

[49]. Baranov, V. *Logic Isn't Facts.* The *Science & Technology* magazine (Moscow), No. 4 (1983): 24-28.

[50]. Baronius, C. *The Ecclesial and Secular Annals from the Birth of Christ and until the Year 1198.* Typography of P. P. Ryabushinsky, from Baronius, *Annales ecclesiastici a Christo nato ad annum 1198.* Moscow, 1913.

[51]. Bartenev, S. *The Moscow Kremlin in the Antiquity and Nowadays.* Moscow, Synodal Typography, 1912.

[52]. de las Casas, Bartólome. *History of the Indias.* Leningrad, Nauka, 1968.

[53]. Baskakov, N. A. *Russian Names of Turkic Origin.* Moscow, Nauka, The Main Oriental Literature Editing Board, 1979.

[54]. Magarichev, Y. M., ed. and comp. *The Cultural and Historical Reserve of Bakhchisaray.* Simferopol, Tavria, 1995.

[55]. Bakhshi, Iman. *Jagfar Tarikhy. A Collection of Bulgarian Manuscripts from 1680.* Russian translation of the Bulgarian text by I. M. K. Nigmatoullin. Orenburg, The Orenburg Press Contact, KOPF, editorial board of the *Bulgaria Courier,* 1993.

[56]. Bashmakova, I. G., and G. S. Smirnova. *The Naissance and the Development of Algebra.* Published in the *Aperçus on the History of Mathematics* edited by B. V. Gnedenko. Moscow, MSU Publications, 1997.

[57]. Belenkiy, M. S. *Judaism.* Moscow, Gospolitizdat, 1966.

[58]. Bellosi, Luciano. *Giotto.* Moscow, Slovo Press, 1996. Translated from the 1995 Italian edition by Scala, Istituto Fotografico Editoriale.

[59]. Belova, A. G. *The Historical Morphology of the Arabic Language.* Moscow, 1994.

[59:0]. Belova G. A, Sherkova T. A. *Russians in the Land of Pyramids. Travellers, Scientists, Collectioners.* Moscow, Aleteya, 2003.

[59:1]. Belyavsky, V. A. *Legendary and Historical Babylon.* Moscow, Mysl, 1971.

[60]. Belyavsky, M. T. *M. V. Lomonosov and the Foundation of the Moscow University (1755-1955).* Edited by M. N. Tikhomirov. Moscow, MSU Publications, 1955.

[61]. Belyaev, D. V. *Byzantine. Essays, Materials and Notes concerning Byzantine Antiquity.* Book III. St. Petersburg, 1891-1906.

[62]. Belyaev, L. A. *The Ancient Monasteries of Moscow According to Archaeological Data.* Moscow, The Russian Academy of Sciences, Institute of Archaeology. Research and materials concerning the archaeology of Moscow. Vol. 6. 1995.

[63]. Belyaev, Y. *100 Monsters of Antiquity.* An illustrated encyclopaedia of mythology. Moscow, Raritet, 1997.

[64]. Bémont, C., and G. Monod. *The Mediaeval History of Europe.* Petrograd, 1915. French edition: Bémont, C., and G. Monod. *Histoire de l'Europe au Moyen Âge.* Paris, 1921.

[64:1]. Berg, L. S. *The Discovery of Kamchatka and Bering's Expedition.* Moscow-Leningrad, The USSR Academy of Sciences Press, 1946.

[64:2]. Berg, L. S. *Essays on the History of Russian Geographical Discoveries.* Moscow-Leningrad, The USSR Academy of Sciences Press, 1946.

[65]. Berry, A. *Concise History of Astronomy.* Translated by S. Zaimovskiy. Moscow-Leningrad, GITTL, 1946.

[66]. Archimandrite Nicephor. *The Biblical Encyclopedia (The Full Illustrated Biblical Encyclopedia).* Moscow, The A. I. Snegiryova Typography, 1891. A modern reprint was published by the Laura of St. Serge and the Holy Trinity in 1990.

[67]. *The Bible.* 10th edition. St. Petersburg, 1912.

[68]. *The Bible. Books from the Old and the New Covenant in Russian Translation with Anagoges and Appendices.* Moscow, Moscow Patriarchy Press, 1968. There are numerous re-editions in existence, for instance, the one published by the Russian Biblical Society in Moscow, 1995.

[69]. *The Bible. Books of the Holy Writ from the Old and the New Covenant.* Russian translation with appendices. 4th edition. Brussels, Life with God Press, 1989.

[70]. *The Bible, or the Books of the Holy Writ from the Old and the New Covenant*

with Anagoges. 2nd edition. St. Petersburg, Synodal Typography, 1900. Reprinted by the Russian Biblical Society in Moscow, 1993. (This version of the Bible dates to the 1st half of the XVIII century and is therefore occasionally called Elizabethan.)

[71]. *Scorina's Bible.* A facsimile edition of the Bible published by Francisco Scorina in 1517-1519. Volumes 1-3. Minsk, The Petrus Brovka Byelorussian Sovetskaya Encyclopaedia Press, 1990.

[72]. Bickerman, E. *Chronology of the Ancient World.* Moscow, Nauka, 1975. Translated from the English edition published in London by Thames & Hudson, 1968-1969.

[73]. Biroulia, Y. N. *Russian Naval Charts of 1701-1750. Copies from originals (Atlas).* St. Petersburg, The Military Navy Publications, 1993.

[74]. *The Book of Good Tidings. Interpretations of the Holy Gospel by St. Theophilactus, the Archbishop of Bulgaria. The Gospel According to Mark Interpreted.* St. Petersburg, P. P. Soykin's Publications. Repr. St. Petersburg, Satis Press, 1993.

[75]. Blazhko, S. N. *A Course of Practical Astronomy.* Moscow, Nauka, 1979.

[76]. Blair, G. *Chronological Tables Spanning the Entire Global History, Containing Every Year since the Genesis and until the XIX Century, Published in English by G. Blair, a Member of the Royal Society, London.* Vols. 1 and 2. Moscow University Press, 1808-1809. The English edition: *Blair's Chronological and Historical Tables, from the Creation to the Present Time, etc.* London, G. Bell & Sons, 1882.

[77]. Bobrovnitskaya, T. A. *The Royal Regalia of the Russian Rulers. The Kremlin in Moscow. Published to Commemorate the 500th Anniversary of the State Coat of Arms and the 450th Anniversary of the Inauguration of the First Russian Czar Ivan the Terrible.* Moscow, The Moscow Kremlin State Museum and Reserve for History and Culture, 1997.

[78]. Bobrovnitsky. *The Origins and the Process of the Roman Catholic Liturgy.* Kiev, 1873.

[79]. Bogdanov, Ivan. *Name Lists of the Bulgarian Khans.* Sofia, Otechestvenia Front Press, 1981.

[80]. Gousseva, E., A. Lukashov, and others. *Our Lady of Vladimir.* A collection of materials. Exhibition catalogue. The State Tretyakovskaya Gallery, The Moscow Kremlin State Museum and Reserve for History and Culture. Moscow, Avangard Press, 1995.

[80:1]. Boguslavskiy, V. V. *The Slavic Encyclopaedia.* Vols. 1 and 2. Moscow, OLMA-Press, 2001.

[81]. Bozhilov, Ivan. *The Asen Dynasty (1186-1460). Genealogy and Prosopography.* Sofia, Bulgarian Academy of Sciences Press, 1994.

[82]. Bolingbroke. *Epistles on Historical Studies and their Utility.* Moscow, Nauka, 1978.

[83]. Bolotov, V. V. *Lectures on Ancient Ecclesial History.* Vols. 1-4. Published posthumously under the editorship of Prof. A. Brilliantov. St. Petersburg, 1907. Reprinted Moscow, Spaso-Preobrazhensky Monastery of Valaam, 1994.

[84]. Bolkhovitinov, E. A. (Metropolitan Eugene). *The Concise Chronicle of Pskov.* Pskov, Otchina Press, 1993.

[85]. *The Great Soviet Encyclopaedia.* Vols. 1-51. 2nd edition. Moscow, The Soviet Encyclopaedia Press, 1949-1957.

[85:1]. *The Great Soviet Encyclopaedia.* Vols. 1-30. 3rd edition. Moscow, 1969-1978. (Electronic version on 5 CD-ROMs.)

[86]. *The Great Catechism.* Moscow, 7135 (1627 ad). Reprinted by the Royal Grodno typography in 7291 (1683 AD).

[87]. *The Great German-Russian Dictionary.* 2nd edition, Stereotyped. Moscow, Russkiy Yazyk, 1980.

[87:1]. *The Great Turkish-Russian Dictionary.* 20,000 words and word groups. The RAS Institute for Oriental Studies. 2nd edition. Moscow, Russkiy Yazyk, 1998.

[88]. *The Great Encyclopaedic Dictionary.* Moscow, The Great Russian Encyclopaedia Press, 1998.

[89]. Borisov, N. S. *Ivan Kalita.* The *Celebrity Biographies* series. Moscow, Molodaya Gvardia, 1995.

[90]. Borisovskaya, N. *Engraved Ancient Maps and Plans of the XV–XVIII century. Cosmography, Maps, Star Charts, City and Battle Plans. From the Pushkin State Museum of Art Collection.* Moscow, Galaktika Press, 1995.

[91]. *Bosch, Hieronymus.* Self-titled album of reproductions. Moscow, Uniserv, 1995.

[91:1]. *Botticelli.* An album from the *Masters of Art* series. Text by Elena Carpetti. 1997, Giunti Gruppo Editoriale, Florence, 2002. Russian edition by Byely Gorod, Moscow, 2001.

[92]. Beaufort, Louis de. *Dissertation sur l'incertitude des cinq premiers siècles de l'histoire Romaine.* Utrecht, 1738. Republished Paris, Blot, 1886.

[93]. Bocharov, L. I., N. N. Yefimov, I. M. Chachoukh, and I. Y. Chernyshev. *The Conspiracy Against Russian History. (Facts, Mysteries, Versions).* Moscow, Anvik, 1998.

[93:1]. Brant, Sebastian. *Ship of Fools.* Part of the The *World Literature Bibliothèque* series (Series 1, Vol. 33). Moscow, Khudozhestvennaya Literatura, 1971.

[94]. Brownley, C. A. *Statistical Theory and Methodology in Science and Technology.* Moscow, Nauka, 1977.

[95]. Brashinskiy, I. B. *Looking for the Scythian Treasures.* Leningrad, The USSR Academy of Sciences, Nauka, 1979.

[96]. Brodsky, B. *Kremlin – The Heart of the Fatherland.* Moscow, Izobrazitelnoye Iskusstvo, 1996.

[97]. Bronstein, I. N., and K. A. Semendyaev. *A Reference Book on Mathematics.* Moscow, Nauka, 1986.

[98]. Bronsten, V. A. *Claudius Ptolemy.* Moscow, Nauka, 1988.

[99]. Brugsch, Heinrich. *History of the Pharaohs.* Translated by G. K. Vlastov. Published in the series titled *The Chronicles and the Monuments of the*

233

Ancient Egypt. St. Petersburg, I. I. Glazounov's Typography, 1880. English edition: *Egypt under the Pharaohs. A History Derived Entirely from the Monuments.* London, J. Murray, 1891.

[99:1]. *Bruges: its Sights and Delights. City Plan.* (Russian version). E.E.C., Editions Thill S. A., Brussels, 1997.

[100]. Bryusova, V. G. *Andrei Rublev.* Moscow, Izobrazitelnoye Iskusstvo, 1995.

[101]. Bouganov, V. I. *Razin and his Followers. Documents, Accounts of the Contemporaries.* Moscow, Nauka, 1995.

[102]. Bouganov, S. I. *Native Historiography of Russian Chronicles.* Moscow, Nauka, 1975.

[103]. Bouzeskoul, V. P. *An Introduction into Greek History. Lectures.* Vol. 1. Petrograd, 1915.

[104]. Boukreyeva, T. N. *The Basel Museum of Arts.* Moscow, Izobrazitelnoye Iskusstvo, 1987.

[105]. Boulatov, A. M. *The Historical Plans of Moscow.* Release III. Moscow, Zhiraf, 2000.

[106]. Burian, Y., and B. Moukhova. *The Enigmatic Etruscans.* Moscow, Nauka, 1970.

[107]. Bouseva-Davydova, I. L. *The Temples of the Muscovite Kremlin: Holy Relics and other Antiquities.* Moscow, The Nauka Int'l Academic Publishing Co., 1997.

[108]. Boutkevich, T. I. *An Overview of Russian Sects.* Kharkov, 1910.

[109]. Boutkov, P. *Defending the Russian Chronicle of Nestor from the Vituperation of the Sceptics.* St. Petersburg, 1840.

[110]. Boutomo, S. I. *Radionuclear Datings and the Construction of an Absolute Chronological Scale of Archaeological Monuments.* In *Archaeology and Natural Sciences.* Moscow, Nauka, 1965. 35-45.

[111]. Boutromeyev, V. *Global History in Individual Personalities. Late Middle Ages.* Moscow, Olma, 1999.

[112]. Kalougin, V. I., comp. *Folk Tales and Legends.* Moscow, Sovremennik, 1991.

[113]. Bychkov, A. A., A. Y. Nizovsky, and P. Y. Chernosvitov. *The Conundrums of Ancient Russia.* Moscow, Veche, 2000.

[114]. Bychkov, V. V. *The Mediaeval Aesthetics of Russia. XI–XVII century.* Moscow, Mysl, 1992.

[114:1]. Bauval, Robert, and Adrian Gilbert. *The Orion Mystery. Unlocking the Secrets of the Pyramids.* Russian translation. Moscow, Veche, 1996.

[115]. *Bulgaria. A Traveller's Map.* Scale: 1:530000. Sofia, Datamap Revue, 1997.

[116]. Wagner, G. K. *Soviet Union and its Famous Works of Art. Old Cities of Russia. A traveller's guide.* Moscow, Iskusstvo, Edizion Leipzig, 1980.

[116:1]. Weinstein S., and M.Kryukov. *The Saddle and the Stirrup.* The *Znaniye-Sila* (Knowledge is Power) magazine (Moscow), August 1985, 24-26.

[117]. Valishevsky, K. *Ivan the Terrible.* Moscow, IKPA-press, 1989. Reprinted from Moscow, Obshchestvennaya Polza Typography, 1912.

[118]. Valishevsky, K. *Ivan the Terrible.* Moscow, Svarog, 1993.

[119]. Valishevsky, K. *The First Romanovs.* Moscow, Kvadrat, 1993.

[120]. Vasiliev, A. A. *The History of Byzantium. The Fall of Byzantium. The Palaeiologi Epoch (1261-1453).* Leningrad, Academia, 1925.

[121]. *An Introduction into Special Historical Disciplines.* Moscow, MSU Publications, 1990.

[122]. Weber, George. *Universal History.* Moscow, 1892. English edition: Weber, G. *Outline of Universal History from the Creation of the World to the Present Time.* London, 1851.

[122:1]. *Hungarian-Russian Dictionary.* 40,000 words. Moscow-Budapest, Russkiy Yazyk, The Hungarian Academy of Sciences Publishing House, 1974.

[123]. Weisman, A. D. *Greek-Russian Dictionary.* 5th edition. St. Petersburg, published by the author, 1899. Reprinted Moscow, Graeco-Latin Department of Y. A. Shichalin, 1991.

[124]. Weisman, A. D. *Latin-Russian Dictionary.* St. Petersburg: published by the author, 1899. Reprinted Moscow, Graeco-Latin Department of Y. A. Shichalin, 1991.

[125]. Venelin, Y. *News of the Varangians as Related by Arab Scribes; their Alleged Crimes as Seen by the Latter.* The Imperial Moscow University Society for History and Russian Antiquities Readings, Book IV, Section V: 1-18. 1870.

[125:1]. Vereshchagin V. V. *Vereschagin, the Artist. Napoleon I in Russia, 1812.* Tver, the Sozvezdie Agency of Tver, 1993.

[125:2]. Vermoush, G. *Diamonds in World History and Stories about Diamonds.* Moscow, Mezhdunarodnye Otnosheniya, 1988.

[126]. Veselovsky, A. N. *Russians and Veltins in the Saga of Tidrec of Berne (Verona).* St. Petersburg, Typography of the Imperial Academy of Sciences, 1906. A separate engraving from the *Russian Language and Belles Lettres Department Courier,* Vol. XI (1906), Book 3: 1-190.

[127]. Veselovsky, I. N. *Aristarchus of Samos – The Copernicus of the Antiquity.* Historical and astronomical research. Issue 7: 44. Moscow, Nauka, 1961.

[128]. Veselovsky, S. B. *A Research into the History of Oprichnina.* Moscow, 1963.

[129]. *The Russia Academy of Sciences Courier,* Vol. 68, No. 10 (October 1998). Moscow, Nauka.

[129:1]. Palaudirias, S. A., Editorial Escudo de Oro. *The Entire Antwerp.* In *The Entire Europe* Collection. Antwerp, published in Russian. Barcelona, 1998.

[129:2]. Bersnev, P. V., comp. *The Old Testament Apocrypha. The Book of the Jubilees. Testaments of the Twelve Patriarchs.* Translated by A. V. Smirnov. Published in the *Alexandrian Library* series. St. Petersburg, Amphora, 2000.

[129:3]. Vzdornov, G. I. *Book Art in Old Russia. Handwritten Books in the North-Eastern Russia in the XII – Early XV century.* Moscow, Iskusstvo, 1980.

[130]. Widukind of Corvea. *The Deeds of the Saxons.* Moscow, Nauka, 1975. See also Widukind. *Sächsische Geschichten.* Translated by R. Schottin, foreword by W. Wattenbach. GV. Leipzig, 1882. Also see: Widukind. *Sächsische Geschichten.* New revision by Paul Hirsch. GV, Bd. 33, Leipzig, 1931.

[131]. *The Byzantine Book of the Eparch.* Moscow, Oriental Literature Publications, 1962. Also see *The Book of the Eparch. Le livre du préfet,* with an introduction by Prof. Ivan Dulcev. "Reprint of … the publication (by Jules Nicole) of the *Book of the Eparch,* to which is added … a facsimile of the complete manuscript and Freshfield's English translation." 1970.

[132]. *Byzantine Historians. Dexippos, Eunapius, Olympiodorus, Malchus, Peter the Patrician, Menander, Candides, Nonnos, Theophanes the Byzantine.* St. Petersburg, 1858.

[133]. *Byzantine Legends.* Leningrad, Nauka, 1972.

[134]. Vilinbakhov, G. V. *The State Coat of Arms of Russia. 500 Years.* St. Petersburg, Slavia. The State Hermitage. The Presidential State Heraldry Commission. The Moscow Kremlin State Museum and Reserve for History and Culture, 1997.

[135]. Vilinbakhov, G., and T. Vilinbakhova. *St. George and his Image as Used in Russia.* St. Petersburg, Iskusstvo, 1995.

[136]. de Villehardouin, Geoffroy. *The Conquest of Constantinople.* Moscow, Nauka, 1993.

[137]. Vinogradov, V. K. *Theodosia. A Historical Aperçu.* Yekaterinodar, Kilius & Co Typography, 1902. (A reprint of the first part of the book is given in the historical and literary almanac titled *Okoyem [Horizon],* No. 2 for 1992, Theodosia.)

[138]. Vittorio, Serra. *The Entire Rome. (Flowers. Churches. Museums. Monuments. Fountains. The Vatican. The Sistine Chapel. Tivoli. Ostia Antica).* Bonechi Edizioni "Il Turismo." Florence, 1994.

[139]. Vladimirov, L. I. *The Omnified Literary History.* Moscow, Kniga, 1988.

[140]. Vlasov, Sergei. *The Deeds of Constantine the Great.* First Experimental Typography of the State Committee of Russian Federation, Eleemosynary Institution "The Order of Constantine the Great", 1999.

[141]. Vnouchkov, B. C. *The Prisoner of Schliesselburg.* Yaroslavl, the Upper Volga Publications, 1988.

[142]. Voyekova, I. N., and V. P. Mitrofanov. *Yaroslavl.* From the series titled *Museum Cities.* Leningrad, Avrora, 1973.

[143]. *The Military Topographic Map of Moscow and its Environs* (1860). The map was published in the *Rarities of Russian Cartography* series. Moscow, Kartair, the scientific and editorial publishing house of I. R. Anokhin, 1998.

[144]. *Around the Coliseum.* The *Izvestiya* newspaper, 18 May 1977.

[145]. *The Vologda Chronicle.* The Anthology of Ancient Russian Literature, Vol. 37. Leningrad, Nauka, 1982.

[145:1]. *The Land of Volokolamsk. Dedicated to 400 Years of Glorifying the Most Reverend Joseph of Volotsk.* Under the general editorship of Pitirim, the Metropolitan of Volokolamsk and Yurievsk. Moscow, Prosvetitel, 1994.

[146]. Volfkovich, S. I. *Nikolai Alexandrovich Morozov as a Chemist (1854-1946).* The Journal of the USSR Academy of Sciences, Department of Chemistry, No. 5 (1947).

[147]. Volfkovich, S. I. *Nikolai Alexandrovich Morozov. His Life and Works on Chemistry.* The *Priroda (Nature)* magazine, No. 11 (1947).

[148]. Voronikhina, L. N. *Edinburgh.* The *Cities and Museums of the World* series. Moscow, Iskusstvo, 1974.

[149]. Vostokov, A. *A Description of the Russian and the Slovenian Manuscripts of the Rumyantsev Museum as Compiled by Alexander Vostokov.* St. Petersburg, Typography of the Imperial Academy of Sciences, 1842.

[150]. *The Chronicle of Ivan Timofeyev.* Prepared for printing, translated and commented by O. A. Derzhavina. Moscow-Leningrad, 1951.

[151]. *Global History.* 10 volumes. Moscow, USSR Academy of Sciences, The Socio-Economic Literature Department Publications, 1958.

[152]. *The Unified Library of Russia, or the Book Catalogue for an Exhaustive and Detailed Description of our Fatherland.* 2nd extended edition. Moscow, 1845.

[153]. Maggi, G. and Valdes, G. *The Entire Turkey.* Florence, Casa Editrice Bonechi, 1995.

[154]. Wooley, L. *Ur of the Chaldees.* Moscow, Oriental Literary, 1961 (1972). English edition: Wooley, L. *Ur of the Chaldees.* London, Benn, 1950. See also: Wooley, L. *Excavations at Ur. A Record of Twelve Years.* London, Benn, 1955.

[155]. Galfridus Monmutensis. *History of the Brits. The Life of Merlin.* Moscow, Nauka, 1984. English edition: *Histories of the Kings of Britain by Geoffrey of Monmouth.* Translated by L. A. Paton. London-New York, 1912. See also: Giles, J. A., ed. *Six Old English Chronicles.* London, 1848.

[156]. Garkavi, A. Y. *The Accounts of the Slavs and the Russians as Given by Muslim Authors (from mid-VII century until the End of the X century AD).* St. Petersburg, 1870 (1872).

[157]. Genova, E., and L. Vlakhova. *24 Church Plates from the Rila Monastery.* Sofia, Bulgarsky Khudozhnik, 1988.

[158]. *GEO.* A monthly magazine. No. 1 (January, 2000). Moscow, Gruner and Yar Ltd.

[159]. *Geographical Atlas.* Moscow, The General Council of Ministers, Department of Geodetics and Cartography. 1968.

[160]. Herberstein. *Baron Sigismund Herberstein. Notes on the Affairs of the Muscovires.* St. Petersburg, A. S. Souvorin's Press, 1908. *Rerum moscoviticarum commentarii.* Wien, S. l. et d., 1549. *Rerum moscoviticarum commentarii.* Basiliae, 1551. *Rerum moscoviticarum commentarii.* Basiliae, 1556. *Moscovia, der Hauptstat in Reissen.* Wien, 1557. Major, R. H., ed. *Notes upon Russia.* 2nd edition. New York, London Hakluite Society, 1963. Vol. 10: 1-116; Vol. 12: 3-174.

[161]. Herberstein, Sigismund. *Notes on Moscovia.* Moscow, MSU Publications, 1988.

[161:1]. Herberstein. *Ziga Herberstein. Sigismund Herberstein – the Warrior, Statesman, Diplomat and Peacemaker.* An edition of the Dr. F. Preshern Society for Contact Development between Slovenia and Russia.Moscow Byelye Alvy Press, Bilio, Humar Press, 2000.

[162]. von Winkler, P. P., comp. *Coats of Arms of Cities, Provinces, Regions and Towns of the Russian Empire Included into the Complete Collection of Laws and Regulations between 1649 and 1900.* St. Petersburg: published by the book salesman Iv. Iv. Ivanov, 1899. New edition: Moscow, Planeta, 1990.

[163]. Herodotus. *History.* Leningrad, Nauka, 1972. English edition: *The History of Herodotus.* From the series *Great Books of the Western World.* Vol. 5. Chicago, Encyclopaedia Britannica, Inc., The University of Chicago, 1952 (2nd edition 1990). See also: Herodotus. *The Histories of Herodotus, etc.* London and New York, Everyman's Library, 1964.

[164]. Herzen, A. G., and Y. M. Mogarichev. *The Fortress of Gems.* Kyrk-Or, Chufut-Kale. Published as part of the series *The Archaeological Monuments of the Crimea.* Simferopol, Tavria, 1993.

[165]. Herzen, A. G., and Y. M. Mogarichev. *Salachik. The Ouspensky Monastery. Bakhchisaray.* The State Museum and Reserve for History and Culture of Bakhchisaray. 1991.

[165:1]. Hertzman, Yevgeni. *The Lost Centuries of Byzantine Music.* The XX International Congress of Byzantine Scholars. St. Petersburg, The Humanitarian Academy Publishing Centre, 2001.

[166]. Gerchouk, Y. Y. *History of Drawing and Book Art.* Moscow, Aspect, 2000.

[167]. Gililov, I. *A Passion Play of William Shakespeare, or the Mystery of the Great Phoenix.* Moscow, "Artist. Rezhissyor. Teatr" Publications, 1997.

[168]. Glazounov, I. *Russia Crucified.* The *Our Contemporary* magazine, Issues 1-5, 7-9, 11 (1996). This material was subsequently published as a book.

[169]. Gnedenko, A. M., and V. M. Gnedenko. *For One's Comrades, or Everything about the Cossacks.* Moscow, The Int'l Fund of Slavic Writing and Culture. ARP Int. Co., 1993.

[170]. The A. V. Shchusev Museum of Architecture, archive 1246/1-13.

[171]. Golenishchev-Kutuzov, I. N. *The Mediaeval Latin Literature of Italy.* Moscow, Nauka, 1972.

[172]. Golitsyn, N. S. *The Great Warlords of History.* Vol. 1. St. Petersburg, 1878.

[173]. Golovanov, Y. *Etudes on Scientists.* Moscow, Molodaya Gvardiya, 1976.

[174]. Golovin, B. N. *Language and Statistics.* Moscow, 1971.

[175]. Goloubovsky, P. V. *The Pechenegs, the Torks, and the Polovtsy before the Tartar Invasion.* Kiev, 1884.

[176]. Goloubtsov, A. P. *Selected Readings on Ecclesial Archaeology and Liturgy.* St. Petersburg, Statis, 1995.

[177]. Goloubtsova, E. S., and V. M. Smirin. *"On the Attempts of Using the 'New Methods' of Statistical Analysis to Ancient Historical Material."* The *Courier of Ancient History,* 1982, No. 1: 171-195.

[178]. Goloubtsova, E. S., and G. A. Koshelenko. *Ancient History and the "New Methods."* Historical Issues, No. 8 (1982).

[179]. Goloubtsova, E. S., and Y. A. Zavenyagin. *Another Account of the New Methods and the Chronology of Antiquity.* Historical Issues, No. 12 (1983): 68-83.

[180]. Homer. *Iliad.* Translated by N. I. Gnedich. Moscow, Khudozhestvennaya Literatura, 1969. See also: Homer, *The Iliad of Homer.* Chicago University Press, London, 1962.

[180:1]. Homer. *The Odyssey of Homer.* New York, Harper & Row, 1967.

[181]. Goneim, M. *The Lost Pyramid.* Moscow, Geographiz, 1959. English edition: Goneim, M. *The Lost Pyramid.* New York, Rinehart, 1956.

[182]. Gorbachevsky, B. *Crosses, Fires, and Books.* Moscow, Sovetskaya Rossiya, 1965.

[183]. Gordeyev, A. A. *History of the Cossacks.* Vol. 1-4. Moscow, Strastnoi Boulevard, 1992.

[184]. Gordeyev, N. V. *The Czar Cannon.* Moscow, Moskovskiy Rabochiy, 1969.

[185]. *The Towns and Cities of Russia. An Encyclopaedia.* Moscow, The Great Russian Encyclopaedia Publications, 1994.

[186]. Gorsey, Gerome. *Notes on Russia. XVI – Early XVII century.* Moscow, MSU Press, 1990.

[187]. *The State Armoury.* Album. Moscow, Sovetskiy Khudozhnik, 1988. A new edition by Galart Press, Moscow, 1990.

[188]. *The A. S. Pushkin Museum of Fine Arts.* Catalogue of paintings. Moscow, 1995, Mazzotta. Printed in Italy.

[189]. *The Ruler is a Friend of his Subjects, or Political Court Hortatives and Moralistic Speculations of Kan-Shi, Khan of Manchuria and China. Collected by his son, Khan Yun-Jin.* St. Petersburg, 1795.

[190]. Goulianitsky, N. F., ed. *The Urbanism of the Muscovite State of the XVI–XVII centuries.* Moscow, The Russian Academy of Architecture. Stroyizdat, 1994.

[191]. *The Faceted Chamber in the Moscow Kremlin.* Leningrad, Aurora, 1982.

[192]. Granovsky, T. N. *Lectures on Mediaeval History.* Moscow, Nauka, 1986.

[193]. Grebelsky, Peter K., and Alexander B. Mirvis. *The House of the Romanovs. Biographical Information about the Members of the Reigning House, their Predecessors and Relations.* St. Petersburg, LIO Redaktor, 1992.

[194]. Mina, Gregory. *Uffizi and Pitti. The Art of the Florentine Galleries.* Album. From the *Great Museums of the World* series. Moscow, Slovo, 1999. A translation of the Italian edition by Magnus Edizioni, Udine, Italy, 1994, 1996.

[195]. Gregorovius, F. *Mediaeval History of Athens.* St. Petersburg, 1900. German edition: Gregorovius, F. *Geschichte der Stadt Athen im Mittelalter.* Stuttgart, 1889.

[196]. Gregorovius, F. *Mediaeval History of Rome. The V–XVI century.* Vols. 1-5. St. Petersburg, 1902-1912. English edition: Gregorovius, F. *History of the City of Rome in the Middle Ages.* London, G. Bell & Sons, 1900-1909.

[197]. Grekov, B. D., and A. Y. Yakubovsky. *The Golden Horde and its Decline.* Moscow-Leningrad, USSR Academy of Sciences, 1950.

[198]. *Greece: Temples, Sepulchres and Treasures.* The *Lost Civilizations* Encyclopaedia. Translated from English by N. Belov. Moscow, Terra Publishing Centre, 1997. Original edition, Time-Life Books BV, 1994.

[199]. Gribanov, E. D., and D. A. Balalykin. *Medicine of Moscow on the Medals of Imperial Russia.* Moscow, Triada-X, 1999.

[200]. Nicephor, Gregoras. *Roman History, beginning from the Conquest of Constantinople by the Latins.* St. Petersburg, 1862.

[201]. Grigorovich, V. *An Account of Travelling through European Russia.* Moscow, 1877.

[202]. Grigoriev, V. V. *Saray: The Capital of the Golden Horde, and the Issue of its Location.* St. Petersburg, 1845.

[203]. Grigoriev, G. L. *Who was Ivan the Terrible Really Afraid of? On the Origins of the Oprichnina.* Moscow, Intergraph Service, 1998.

[204]. Grigoulevich, I. R. *The History of the Inquisition.* Moscow, Nauka, 1970.

[205]. Grigoulevich, I. R. *The Inquisition.* Moscow, Politizdat, 1985.

[206]. Grishin, Yakov. *The Tartars of Poland and Lithuania (the Heirs of the Golden Horde).* Kazan, The Tartar Publishing House, 1995.

[207]. Groslie, B. *Borobudur. The Greatest Collection of Buddhist Sculpture in the World is being Destroyed by Erosion.* The *UNESCO Courier,* No. 6 (1968): 23-27.

[208]. Gudzy, N. K. *History of Early Russian Literature.* Moscow, Uchpedgiz, 1938. English edition: New York, Macmillan & Co, 1949.

[209]. Gouliaev, V. I. *Pre-Columbian Voyages to America. Myths and Reality.* Moscow, Mezhdunarodnye Otnoshenia, 1991.

[210]. Gouliaev, V. I. *America and the Old World in the Pre-Columbian Epoch.* Moscow, Nauka, 1968.

[210:1]. Gouliaev, V. I. *Following the Conquistadors.* Moscow, The USSR Academy of Sciences, Nauka, 1976.

[211]. Gumilev, L. N. *Ancient Russia and the Great Steppe.* Moscow, Mysl, 1992.

[212]. Gumilev, L. N. *In Search of the Figmental Kingdom (the Legend of the Kingdom of Presbyter Johannes.* Moscow, Tanais, 1994.

[213]. Gumilev, L. N. *Hunnu.* St. Petersburg: Time-Out-Compass, 1993.

[214]. Gumilev, L. N. *The Black Legend.* Moscow, Ekopros, 1994.

[215]. Gumilev L. N. *The Huns in China.* Moscow, Nauka, 1974.

[216]. Gumilev, L. N. *From Rus' to Russia.* Moscow, Ekopros, 1992.

[217]. Gourevich, A. Y. *The Mediaeval Cultural Categories.* Moscow, Kultura, 1972.

[218]. Gourevich, V. B. *An Introduction into Spherical Astronomy.* Moscow, Nauka, 1978.

[219]. Gouter, R. S., and Y. L. Polounov. *Girolamo Cardano.* From the *Founding Fathers of Science and Technology* series. Moscow, Znaniye, 1980.

[220]. Goutz, Alexander K. *The True History of Russia.* Omsk, Omsk State University Press, 1999.

[221]. D. *The Stirrup of Quiet Don: the Enigmas of the Novel.* Paris, YMCA Press, 1974.

[222]. Davidenko, I. V. *The Word Was, The Word Is, The Word Shall Always Be... A Philological Fantasy.* Moscow, Russkiy Dvor Press, 1999.

[223]. Dal, V. *An Explanatory Dictionary of the Living Russian Language.* St. Petersburg-Moscow, The M. O. Wolf Society Press, 1912.

[224]. Dal, V. *An Explanatory Dictionary of the Living Russian Language.* St. Petersburg-Moscow, The M. O. Wolf Society Press, 1914. Reprinted Moscow, Citadel, 1998.

[225]. Dal, Vladimir. *An Explanatory Dictionary of the Living Russian Language.* Moscow, State National and Foreign Dictionary Publishing House, 1956.

[226]. Damascene, John. *Dialectic.* Moscow, 1862. See also: John of Damascus. *Dialectica.* New York, St. Bonaventure Franciscan Institute, 1953.

[227]. Damascene, John. *Three Apologies against the Detractors of the Holy Icons or Effigies.* St. Petersburg, 1893. English edition: Baker, T. *John Damascene on Holy Images Followed by Three Sermons of the Assumption.* London, 1898.

[228]. Dantas, G. *Parthenon in Peril.* The *UNESCO Courier,* No. 6 (1968): 16-18, 34.

[229]. Dante, Alighieri. *Minor Œuvres.* Moscow, Nauka, 1968. Also see: Dante, Alighieri. *Opere Minori.* Florence, 1856.

[230]. Dante, Alighieri. *The Divine Comedy.* Translated from the Italian by A. A. Ilushin. Moscow, Philological Department of the M. V. Lomonosov Moscow State University, 1995.

[231]. Darethes of Phrygia. *The History of the Destruction of Troy.* St. Petersburg, Aleteya, 1997.

[232]. Darkevich, V. P. *The Secular Art of Byzantium. Works of Byzantine Art in the Eastern Europe of the X–XIII century.* Moscow, Iskusstvo, 1975.

[233]. Darkevich, V. P. *The Argonauts of the Middle Ages.* Moscow, Nauka, 1976.

[233:1]. *The Gifts of the Magi – a Source of Bliss until Our Day.* Translated from modern Greek by M. Klimenko. The Holy Mount Athon, the Monastery of St. Paul the Apostle. Information about this book was obtained from the *Holy Lamp* newspaper published by the Preobrazhensky Temple in the Bolshie Vyazyomy village, No. 1 (1996).

[234]. *The Gifts Made by the Imperial House of Russia to the Museum of History.* Catalogue of an exhibition. Moscow, The State Museum of History, Publishing Department. 1993.

[235]. Dowley, Tim. *The Biblical Atlas.* Three's Company & Angus Hudson Ltd., 1989. Russian translation: Moscow, The Russian Biblical Society, 1994.

[236]. Cameniata, Johannes. *Two Byzantine Chronicles of the X century. The Psamathian Chronicle; The Conquest of Thessalonica.* Moscow, Oriental Literature Publications, 1962. Also see: Cameniata, Joannes. *De Exicidio Thessalonicae.* In: Clugnet, L. *Bibliothèque hagiographique orientale.* Paris, 1901-1905.

[237]. Dvoretsky, I. K. *Latin-Russian Dictionary.* 50,000 words. Moscow, Russkiy Yazyk, 1976.

[237:1]. Deveuze, Lily. *Carcassonne.* The *Golden Book* series (in Russian). Florence, Bonechi, Central Typography, 2000.

[238]. Dementyeva, V. V. *"The Roman History of Charles Rollen" as Read by a Russian Nobleman.* The *Ancient History Courier,* No. 4 (1991): 117-122.

[239]. Denisov, L. I. *The Orthodox Monasteries of the Russian Empire.* Moscow, 1908. 389-393.

[240]. Jalal, Assad. *Constantinople. From Byzantium to Istanbul.* Moscow, M. & S. Sabashnikov, 1919. French edition: Jalâl, A. *Constantinople de Byzance à Stamboul.* Paris, 1909.

[241]. Jivelegov, A. K. *Dante Alighieri.* From the *Celebrity Biographies* series. Moscow, OGIZ, The Magazine and Newspaper Trust, 1933.

[242]. Jivelegov, A. K. *Leonardo da Vinci.* From the *Celebrity Biographies* series. Moscow, OGIZ, The Magazine and Newspaper Trust, 1935.

[243]. Giovanni, Villani. *The New Chronicle, or the History of Florence.* Moscow, Nauka, 1997. Italian edition: *Cronica di Giovanni Villani a miglior lezione redotta coll'aiuto detesti a penna.* Florence, Magheri, 1823; Rome, Multigrafica, 1980. Vols. 1-8.

[244]. Giovanni, Novelli. *The Shroud of Turin: The Issue Remains Open.* Translated from Italian. Moscow, Franciscan Press, 1998.

[245]. Giua, Michele. *The History of Chemistry.* Moscow, Mir, 1975. Italian original: Giua, Michele. *Storia della chimica, dell'alchimia alle dottrine moderne.* Chiantore, Turin, 1946; Union Tipografiko-Editrice Torinese, 1962.

[246]. Digests of Justinian. Selected fragments translated by I. S. Peretersky. Moscow, Nauka, 1984.

[247]. Diehl, Ch. *History of the Byzantine Empire.* Moscow, IL, 1948. English edition: Princeton, NJ, Princeton University Press, 1925.

[248]. Diehl, Ch. *Chief Problems of the Byzantine History.* Moscow, 1947. French edition: Diehl, Ch. *Les Grands Problèmes de l'Histoire Byzantine.* Paris, Armand Diehl Library, A. Colin, 1947.

[249]. Diels, H. *Ancient Technology.* Moscow-Leningrad, ONTI-GTTI, 1934.

[250]. Diophantes. *Arithmetics.* Moscow, Nauka, 1974. See also: Diophantus, Alexandrinus. *Diophanti Alexandrini Opera Omnia, cum graecis commentaries.* Lipsiae: in aedibus B. G. Teubner, 1893-1895.

[251]. Diringer, D. *The Alphabet.* Moscow, IL, 1963. English edition: London, Hutchinson & Co., 1968.

[252]. Dietmar, A. B. *Ancient Geography.* Moscow, Nauka, 1980.

[253]. Yankov, V. P., comp. *Following the Roads of the Millennia.* A collection of historical articles and essays. Book four. Moscow, Molodaya Gvardia, 1991.

[254]. Drboglav, D. A. *Mysteries of Ancient Latin Hallmarks of IX–XIV century Swords.* Moscow, MSU Press, 1984.

[255]. *Ancient Russian Icon Art.* Moscow, Kedr, 1993. From the collection of the Tretyakovskaya Gallery.

[256]. *Ancient Russian Literature. Depictions of Society.* Moscow, Nauka, 1991.

[257]. Bonhard-Levin, G. M., ed. *Ancient Civilizations.* Moscow, Mysl, 1989.

[258]. Struve, V. V., and D. P. Kallistov., eds. *Ancient Greece.* Moscow, USSR Academy of Sciences, 1956.

[259]. Drews, Arthur. *The Christ Myth.* Vol. 2. Moscow, Krasnaya Nov', 1924. English edition by T. Fisher Unwin. London and Leipzig, 1910.

[260]. Drews, Arthur. *Did St. Peter the Apostle Really Exist?* Moscow, Atheist, 1924. See also: A. Drews. *Die Petrus-le-gende.* Jena, E. Diederichs, 1924.

[261]. Drümel, Johann Heinrich. *An Attempt of Proving the Ararat Origins of the Russians Historically as those of the First Nation after the Deluge.* St. Petersburg, 1785. A Russian translation of a German book published in Nuremberg in 1744.

[262]. Douboshin, G. N. *A Reference Book for Celestial Mechanics and Astrodynamics.* Moscow, Nauka, 1976.

[263]. Doubrovsky, A. S., N. N. Nepeyvoda, and Y. A. Chikanov. *On the Chronology of Ptolemy's Almagest. A Secondary Mathematical and Methodological Analysis.* The *Samoobrazovanie (Self-Education)* magazine (Moscow), No. 1, 1999.

[263:1]. Duby, Georges. *The Middle Ages (987-1460). From Hugo Capet to Joan of Arc.* Moscow, Mezhdunarodnye Otnosheniya, 2000. French original: Duby, Georges. *Le Moyen Âge. De Hugues Capet à Jeanne d'Arc (987-1460).* Collection *Pluriel.* Hachette, 1987.

[264]. Dupuy, R. Ernest, and Trevor N. Dupuy. *The Harper Encyclopaedia of Military History. From 3500 BC to the Present.* Commentary by the Polygon Press. Vol. 1: 3500 bc-1400 ad. Vol. 2: 1400–1800. St. Petersburg-Moscow, Polygon-AST, 1997. English original published by Harper Collins.

[265]. Dürer, Albrecht. *Tractates. Diaries. Letters.* St. Petersburg, Azbuka, 2000.

[265:1]. [Dürer] *Albrecht Dürer. Engravings.* Moscow, Magma Ltd., 2001. First published in 1980 by Hubschmidt et Bouret.

[265:2]. *The Jewish Encyclopaedia.* Vols. 1-16. A reprint of the Brockhaus-Efron edition for the Society for Scientific Judaic Publications, St. Petersburg. Moscow, Terra-Terra, 1991.

[266]. *The Hebraic Text of the Old Testament (The Tanach).* London, the British and Foreign Bible Society, 1977.

[267]. Eusebius Pamphilus. *Ecclesial History.* St. Petersburg, 1848. English edition: Eusebius Pamphilus. *History of the Church.* London, 1890.

[268]. Eusebius Pamphilus. *Eusebius Pamphilus, Bischop of the Palestinian Caesarea, on the Toponymy of the Holy Writ. St. Jerome of Strydon on the Hebraic Locations and Names.* Translated by I. Pomyalovsky. St. Petersburg, 1894. Latin edition: Eusebius Pamphilus. *Eusebii Pamphili Episcopi Caesariensis Onomasticon Urbium et Locorum Sacrae Scripturae.* Berolini, 1862.

[269]. Eutropius. *A Concise History Starting with the City's Creation.* From the *Roman Historians of the IV century* series. Moscow, Russian Political Encyclopaedia, 1997.

[270]. Yegorov, D. N. *An Introduction into the Mediaeval Studies. The Historiography and the Source Studies.* Vols. 1-2. Moscow, High Courses of Female Education, Department of History and Philosophy, Publishing Society.

[271]. Yermolayev, G. *Mystery of the "Quiet flows the Don."* Slavic and European Journal, 18, 3 (1974).

[272]. Yermolayev, G. *The True Authorship of the "Quiet flows the Don."* Slavic and European Journal, 20, 3 (1976).

[273]. Yefremov, Y. N., and E. D. Pavlovskaya. *Dating the "Almagest" by the Actual Stellar Movements.* The USSR Academy of Sciences Archive, Vol. 294, No. 2: 310-313.

[274]. Yefremov, Y. N., and E. D. Pavlovskaya. *Determining the Epoch of the Almagest Star Catalogue's Creation by the Analysis of the Actual Stellar Movements. (On the Problem of Ptolemy's Star Catalogue Authorship). The Historical and Astronomical Research.* Moscow, Nauka, 1989. 175-192.

[275]. Jambus, M. *The Hierarchical Cluster Analysis and Related Correspondences.* Moscow, Finances and Statistics, 1988. Also see: Kendall, M., and A. Stewart. *The Advanced Theory of Statistics* (4th edition). London, C. Griffin, 1977.

[275:1]. *Living History of the Orient.* Collected works. Moscow, Znanie, 1998.

[276]. Zivkovic, Branislav. *Les monuments de la Peinture Serbe Médiévale.* Zivkovic, Branislav. *Zica. Les dessins des fresques.* Belgrade, Institut pour la protection des monuments historiques de la Republique de Serbie, 1985.

[277]. *The Art of Ancient Russia. XI – early XIII century. Inlays, Frescoes, Icons.* Leningrad, Khudozhnik RSFSR, 1982.

[278]. Cellini, Benvenuto. *The Life of Benvenuto Cellini, the Son of Maestro Giovanni Cellini, a Florentine, Written in Florence by Himself.* Moscow, 1958. The English edition was published by Edito-Service in Geneva, 1968.

[278:1]. *The Hagiography of Reverend Sergiy (The Life and the Great Deeds of the Most Reverend and Blessed Father Sergiy the Thaumaturge, the Hegumen of Radonezh and the Entire Russia).* Compiled by Hieromonk Nikon (subsequently an Archimandrite). 5th edition. The Laura of Serge and The Holy Trinity. Own typography. 1904.

[279]. *The Life of Savva Storozhevsky.* Reprinted after an old XVII century edition. Published in the *Zvenigorod Region History Materials,* Issue 3. Moscow, The Archaeographical Centre, 1994.

[280]. Zhitomirsky, S. V. *The Astronomical Works of Archimedes.* Historical and Astronomical Research, Issue 13. Moscow, Nauka, 1977.

[281]. Zholkovsky, A. V. *Pasternak's Book of Books.* The *Zvezda (Star)* magazine, No. 12 (1997).

[282]. Zabelin, I. E. *Quotidian Life of Russian Czarinas in the XVI and XVII centuries.* Novosibirsk, Nauka, 1992.

[283]. Zabelin, I. E. *The History of Moscow.* Moscow, Svarog, 1996.

[284]. Zabelin, I. E. *The History of Moscow.* Moscow, Stolitsa, 1990.

[285]. Zabelin, I. E. *The Historical Description of the Stauropigial Monastery of Moscow.* 2nd edition. Moscow, 1893.

[286]. Zaborov, M. A. *History of the Crusades in Documents and Materials.* Moscow, Vyshchaya Shkola, 1977.

[287]. Zaborov, M. A. *Crusaders in the East.* Moscow, Nauka, Chief Editing Board of Oriental Literature, 1980.

[288]. Zavelskiy, F. S. *Time and its Keeping.* Moscow, Nauka, 1987.

[289]. Porfiriev, G., ed. *The Mysteries and Conundrums of the "Quiet flows the Don."* Collected works. Samara, P.S., 1996.

[290]. *The Gospel Teachings.* Jordanville, the Rev. Job. Pogayevsky Typography, 1987.

[290:1]. Zaliznyak, A. A., and V. L. Yanin. *The XI century Psalm Book of Novgorod as the Oldest Book in Russia.* The *RAS Courier,* Vol. 71, No. 3 (2001): 202-209.

[291]. Zamarovsky, V. *Mysteries of the Hittites.* Moscow, Nauka, 1968. Also see: Zamarovsky, V. *Za tajemstvism rise Chetitu.* Prague, 1964.

[291:1]. Zamkova, M. V. *Louvre. (The Masterpieces of World Art in your Home).* Album. Moscow, Olma-Obrazovanie, 2002.

[292]. *Notes of the Russian and Slavic Archaeology Department of the Russian Archaeological Society.* Vol. XII. Petrograd, Typography of Y. Bashmakov & Co, 1918.

[293]. *Star Charts of the Norhern and the Southern Hemisphere.* Edition: *Maru severni a jizni hvezdne oblohy.* Czechoslovakia, Kartografie Praha, 1971.

[294]. Kondrashina, V. A., and L. A. Timoshina, eds. *Zvenigorod Over Six Centuries.* A collection of articles. To the 600th anniversary of the Savvino-Storozhevsky monastery. The Moscow Oblast Administration Culture Committee. The Zvenigorod Museum of History, Arts, and Architecture. The Federal Archive Service of Russia. Russian State Archive of Ancient Acts. Moscow, URSS Press, 1998.

[294:1]. Zgura, V. V. *Kolomenskoye. An Aperçu of its Cultural History and Monuments.* Moscow, O.I.R.U., 1928.

[295]. Zelinskiy, A. N. *Constructive Principles of the Ancient Russian Calendar.* The *Context 1978* collection. Moscow, Nauka, 1978.

[296]. Zelinskiy, F. *Selected Biographies of Ideas.* Vols. I–IV. St. Petersburg, 1905-1922.

[297]. Zenin, D. *The Ancient Artillery: Truth and Fiction.* The *Science and Technology* magazine, No. 5 (1982): 25-29.

[298]. Zenkovsky, S. A. *Old Ritualists of Russia. The XVII century Religious Movements.* Moscow, Tserkov, 1995.

[299]. Zima, D., and N. Zima. *Nostradamus Deciphered.* Moscow, Ripol Klassik, 1998.

[299:1]. *The Banner of Reverend Serge (Sergiy) of Radonezh.* Psaltyr, 1934. Reprinted by RIO Dennitsa, Moscow, 1991.

[300]. Zoubov, V. P. *Aristotle.* Moscow, The USSR Academy of Sciences Press, 1963.

[301]. *Ivan IV The Terrible.* Essays. St. Petersburg, Azbuka, 2000.

[301:1]. Ivanov, O. *The Zamoskvorechye: Chronicle Pages.* Moscow, V. Shevchouk Publications, Inc., 2000.

[302]. Idelson, N. *History of the Calendar.* Leningrad, Scientific Publications, 1925.

[303]. Idries, Shah. *Sufism.* Moscow, 1993.

[304]. Ieger, Oscar. *Global History.* Vols. 1-4. St. Petersburg, A. F. Marx, 1894-1904.

[304:1]. Ieger, Oscar. *Global History.* Vols. 1-4. St. Petersburg, A. F. Marx, 1904. Amended and expanded. Faximile reprint: Moscow, AST, 2000.

[304:2]. Ieger, Oscar. *Global History.* Vols. 1-4. St. Petersburg, A. F. Marx, 1904. 3rd ed., amended and expanded. Faximile reprint: Moscow, AST, 2001; St Petersburg, Polygon, 2001.

[305]. *Jerusalem in Russian Culture.* Collected essays. Moscow, Nauka, 1994.

[306]. *Selected Letters of A. N. Roudnev to V. N. Leonova.* Frankfurt-am-Main, Nadezhda, 1981.

[306:1]. *A Representation of the Terrestrial Globe.* Russian map from the *Rarities of Russian Cartography* series. (There is no compilation date anywhere on the map. The publishers date it to mid-XVIII century, q.v. in the annotation). Moscow, the Kartair Cartographical Association, 1996.

[307]. Derevenskiy, B. G., comp. *Jesus Christ in Historical Documents.* From the *Ancient Christianity* series, *Sources* section. St. Petersburg, Aleteya, 1998.

[308]. Ouspensky, L. A. *Icon Art of Ancient Russia.* Album. Foreword by S. S. Averintsev, compiled by N. I. Bednik. St. Petersburg, Khudozhnik Rossii, 1993.

[309]. Ilyin, A. A. *The Classification of Russian Provincial Coins.* Issue 1. Leningrad, The State Hermitage, 1940.

[310]. Ilyin, M., and T. Moiseyeva. *Moscow and its Environs.* Moscow, 1979.

[311]. Ilyin, M. *The Ways and the Quests of an Arts Historian.* Moscow, Iskusstvo Publications, 1970.

[312]. Illarion. *On the Law and the Bliss.* Moscow, Stolitsa and Skriptoriy, 1994.

[312:1]. *The Names of Moscow Streets* (multiple authors). Under the general editorship of A. M. Pegov. Moscow, Moskovskiy Rabochiy, 1972.

[313]. de la Vega, Inca Garcilazo. *History of the State of the Incas.* Leningrad, Nauka, 1974.

[314]. *Foreigners on Ancient Moscow. Moscow of the XV–XVII centuries.* Collected texts. Moscow, Stolitsa, 1991.

[315]. of Hildesheim, Johann. *A Legend of the Three Holy Kings.* Translated from German. Moscow, Enigma-Aleteya, 1998. German edition: von Hildesheim, Johan. *Die Legende von den Heiligen Drei Königen.* Berlin, 1925.

[316]. *The Art of the Countries and the Peoples of the World. A Brief Scientific Encyclopaedia.* Vol. 1. Moscow, Soviet Encyclopaedia Publications, 1962.

[317]. *Islam: an Encyclopaedic Dictionary.* Moscow, Nauka, General Editing Board for Oriental Literature, 1991.

[318]. Martzyshevskaya, K. A., B. J. Sordo-Peña, and S. Mariñero. *Spanish-Russian and Russian-Spanish Dictionary.* Moscow, Russkiy Yazyk, 1990.

[319]. *Historical and Astronomical Research.* Moscow, Fizmatgiz, 1955.

[320]. *Historical and Astronomical Research.* Issue 8. Moscow, Fizmatgiz, 1962.

[321]. *Historical and Astronomical Research.* Issue 1. Moscow-Leningrad, 1948.

[322]. *Historical Notes of Nicephorus Vriennius.* St. Petersburg, 1858.

[323]. *History of Byzantium.* Vol. 1. Moscow, Nauka, 1967.

[324]. *History of Byzantium.* Vols. 2-3. Moscow, Nauka, 1967.

[325]. *History of the Orient. Vol. 2. Mediaeval Orient.* Russian Academy of Sciences, the Department of Oriental Sciences. Moscow, Vostochnaya Literatura, RAS, 1995.

[326]. Kouzishchin, V. I., ed. *History of the Ancient Orient.* Moscow, 1979.

[327]. Kouzishchin, V. I., and A. G. Bokshchanin., eds. *History of the Ancient Rome.* Moscow, 1971.

[328]. *History of Europe.* Published in Europe as an initiative of Frederic Delouche. A Collective of 12 European Historians. Minsk, Vysheyshaya Shkola; Moscow, Prosveshchenie, 1996. Translated from *Histoire de l'Europe.* Hachette, 1992.

[328:1]. *History of Europe. The Renaissance.* Moscow, Minsk, Harvest, AST, Inc., 2000.

[329]. Melnik, A. G., ed. *History and Culture of the Land of Rostov. 1998.* Collected essays. Rostov, The Rostov Kremlin State Museum and Reserve, 1999.

[330]. *History of the Inquisition in Three Volumes.* Vols. 1 and 2: Lee, Henry Charles. *History of the Inquisition in the Middle Ages.* A reprint of the F. A. Efron, I. A. Brockhaus edition. 1911-1912. Vol. 3: Lozinsky, S. G. *History of the Spanish Inquisition.* A reprint of the F. A. Efron, I. A. Brockhaus edition. 1914. Moscow, The Ladomir Scientific and Publishing Centre, 1994.

[330:1]. *History of Moscow in the Documents of the XII–XVIII century from the Russian State Archive of Ancient Acts.* The Russian State Archive of Ancient Acts, Moscow Municipal Archive Association. Moscow, Mosgorarkhiv, 1997.

[331]. Sakharov, A. N., ed. *History of Moscow. From the Earliest Days until Our Time.* Three volumes. Moscow, the RAS Institute of Russian History, the Moscow Municipal Association, Mosgorarkhiv Press. Vol. 1: XII–XVII century. Vol. 2: XIX century. 1997.

[332]. *Russian History. From the Ancient Slavs to Peter the Great. Encyclopaedia for Children.* Vol. 5. Moscow, Avanta, 1995.

[333]. Udaltsov, A. D., E. A. Kosminsky, O. L. Weinstein, eds. *Mediaeval History.* Moscow, OGIZ, 1941.

[334]. Skazkin, S. D., ed. *Mediaeval History.* Volumes 1-2. Moscow, 1977.

[335]. *History of French Literature.* Collected essays. St. Petersburg, 1887. English edition: Demogeot, J., *History of French Literature.* London, Rivingstons, 1884 (1883).

[336]. Helmolt, H., ed. *The History of Humanity. Global History.* Vols. 1-9. Translated from German. St. Petersburg: Prosveshchenie, 1896.

[337]. Istrin, V. M. *I–IV Editions of the Explanatory Paleya.* St. Petersburg, The Imperial Academic Typography, 1907.

[338]. Istrin, V. M. *The Chronicle of John Malalas in Slavic Translation.* A reprint of V. M. Istrin's materials. Moscow, John Wiley & Sons, 1994.

[339]. Pouchkov, P. I., ed. *Extinct Nations.* Collected essays. Moscow, Nauka, 1988.

[340]. *Itogi (The Resume).* Weekly magazine. No. 37 (223) (12 September 2000). Moscow, Sem Dney Press.

[341]. Duchich, Jovan. *Duke Sava Vladislavich. The First Serbian Diplomat at the court of Peter the Great and Catherine I.* Belgrade, Dereta, 1999.

[342]. Kazhdan, A. P. *The Origins and the Purport of Christianity.* Moscow, 1962.

[343]. Kazhdan, A. P. *The Social Compound of the Byzantine Ruling Class of the XI–XII century.* Moscow, Nauka, 1974.

[344]. Kazakova, N. A. *Western Europe in Russian Written Sources of the XV–XVI century.* Leningrad, Nauka, 1980.

[345]. Kazamanova, A. N. *An Introduction to Ancient Numismatics.* Moscow, Moscow University Press, 1969.

[346]. *The Cossack Circle.* Quiet flows the Don. Special edition 1. Moscow, Russ-koye Slovo, 1991.

[347]. Skrylov, A. I., and G. V. Gubarev. *The Cossack Dictionary and Handbook.* Cleveland, 1966. Reprinted Moscow, Sozidanie Ltd., 1992.

[348]. Fomenko, A. T., V. V. Kalashnikov, and G. V. Nosovskiy. *The Geometry of Mobile Star Configurations and the Dating of the Almagest.* Problems of stochastic model stability. Seminar works. The National System Research Institute, 1988. 59-78.

[349]. Fomenko, A. T., V. V. Kalashnikov, and G. V. Nosovskiy. *The Statistical Analysis and Dating of the Observations that the Almagest Star Catalogue is Based upon.* Report theses of the 5th Int'l Probability Theory Conference in Vilnius, the Lithuanian Academy of Sciences Institute of Mathematics and Cybernetics, Vol. 3 (1989): 271-272.

[350]. Fomenko, A. T., V. V. Kalashnikov, and G. V. Nosovskiy. *Dating the Almagest by Variable Star Configurations.* The USSR AS Reports, Vol. 307, No. 4 (1989): 829-832. English translation published in Soviet Phys. Dokl., Vol. 34, No. 8 (1989): 666-668.

[351]. Fomenko, A. T., V. V. Kalashnikov, and G. V. Nosovskiy. *A Retrospective Analysis of the Almagest Star Catalogue and the Problem of its Dating.* Pre-print. Moscow, National System Research Institute, 1990. 60 p.

[352]. Fomenko, A. T., V. V. Kalashnikov, and G. V. Nosovskiy. *A Quantitative Analysis of the Almagest Star Catalogue.* Pre-print. Moscow, National System Research Institute, 1990. 62 p.

[353]. Fomenko, A. T., V. V. Kalashnikov, and G. V. Nosovskiy. *Dating the Almagest Star Catalogue.* Preprint. Moscow, National System Research Institute, 1990. 58 p.

[354]. Fomenko, A. T., V. V. Kalashnikov, and G. V. Nosovskiy. *Ptolemy's Star Catalogue Dated by Mathematicians. Hypotheses, Predictions, and the Future of Science.* The Int'l Annual Journal. No. 23 (1990): 78-92. Moscow, Znaniye.

[355]. Fomenko, A. T., V. V. Kalashnikov, and G. V. Nosovskiy. *A Statistical Analysis of the Almagest Star Catalogue.* The USSR AS Reports. Vol. 313, No. 6 (1990): 1315-1320.

[356]. Fomenko, A. T., V. V. Kalashnikov, and G. V. Nosovskiy. *Dating the Almagest Star Catalogue. A Statistical and Geometric Analysis.* Moscow, Fak-torial, 1995.

[356:1]. Fomenko, A. T., V. V. Kalashnikov, and G. V. Nosovskiy. *An Astronomical Analysis of Chronology. The Almagest. Zodiacs.* Moscow, The Delovoi Express Financial, 2000.

[357]. Fomenko, A. T., V. V. Kalashnikov, and S. T. Rachev. *New Methods of Comparing Volume Functions of Historical Texts.* Seminar works. Moscow, National System Research Institute, 1986. 33-45.

[358]. Kaleda, G. *The Shroud of Our Lord Jesus Christ. To the Centenary of the Manifestation of the Holiest of Relics, 1898-1998.* 4th edition. Moscow, Zakatyevsky Monastery Press, 1998.

[358:1]. *Russia and the World on Russian Maps.* Moscow, published by Vneshtorgbank and the State Museum of History in 2001. Compiled by B. Sergeyev and A. Zaitsev. Maps from the collection of the State Museum of History, 16, Kuznetskiy Most, 103301, Moscow.

[359]. *The Stonework Chronicle of the old Moscow.* Moscow, Sovremennnik, 1985.

[360]. Kamensky, A. B. *The Life and the Fate of the Empress Catherine the Great.* Moscow, Znanie, 1997.

[361]. Kaneva, Katerina, Alessandro Cechi, and Antonio Natali. *Uffizi. A Guide and a Catalogue of the Art Gallery.* Scala/ Becocci, 1997. Moscow, Izobrazitelnoye Iskusstvo, 1997.

[362]. Karamzin, N. M. *History of the State of Russia.* St. Petersburg, 1842. A reprint of the fifth edition that came out as 3 books with P. M. Stroyev's *Key* attached. Books I, II, III, IV. Moscow, Kniga, 1988, 1989.

[363]. Karamzin, N. M. *History of the State of Russia* (Academic edition). Moscow, Nauka. Vol. 1: 1989. Vols. 2-3: 1991. Vol. 4: 1992. Vol. 5: 1993.

[364]. Karger, M. K. *Ancient Kiev. Essays on the History of the Material Culture of this Ancient Russian City.* Vol. 1. Moscow-Leningrad, The USSR AS Press, 1958.

[365]. Karger, M. *Novgorod the Great.* Moscow, The USSR Academy of Architecture. The Architectural History and Theory Institute. 1946.

[366]. *Karelin Andrei Osipovich. Legacy of an Artist.* Nizhni Novgorod, Arnika, 1994.

[367]. Karnovich, E. P. *Patrimonial Names and Titles in Russia.* St. Petersburg, 1886. Reprinted in Moscow, Bimpa Press, 1991.

[368]. Valcanover, Francesco. *Carpaccio.* Album. Moscow, Slovo, 1996. The Italian edition was published in the *Great Masters of Italian Art* series. Florence, Scala, Istituto Fotografico Editoriale, Antella, 1989.

[369]. Karpenko. V. V. *The Names on the Sky at Night.* Moscow, Nauka, 1981.

[370]. Carpiceci, Alberto Carlo. *The Art and History of Egypt. 5000 Years of Civilization.* Russian edition. Florence, Casa Editrice Bonechi, 1997.

[371]. Carpiceci, Alberto Carlo. *The Art and History of Egypt. 5000 Years of Civilization.* Florence, Bonechi, 1999.

[372]. Kartashev, A. V. *Essays on the History of Russian Church.* Vols. 1, 2. Moscow, Nauka, 1991.

[373]. Kartashev, A. V. *Essays on the History of Russian Church*. Moscow, Terra, 1992.

[374]. Carter, H. *The Tomb of Tutankhamen*. Moscow, Oriental Literature, 1959.

[375]. Quintus Curtius Rufus. *The Story of Alexander the Great*. Moscow, MSU Press, 1993.

[376]. Denisenko, D. V., and N. S. Kellin. *When Were the Famous Dendera Zodiacs Really Created?* An appendix to Fomenko, A. T. *Criticism of Traditional Chronology of Antiquity and the Middle Ages (What Century is it Now?)*. Moscow, MSU Publications, the MSU Department of Mechanical Mathematics, 1993. 156-166.

[377]. Fomenko, A. T., N. S. Kellin, and G. V. Nosovskiy. *The Issue of the Veracity of the "Ancient" History of Russia by M. V. Lomonosov. Lomonosov or Miller?* The Moscow University Courier, Series 9: Philology, No. 1 (1991): 116-125.

[378]. Kenderova, Stoyanka, and Beshevliev, Boyan. *The Balkan Peninsula on Alldrisi's Map. Palaeographic, Historical and Geographical Research*. Part 1. Sofia, 1990.

[379]. Ceram, C. *Gods, Graves and Scholars*. Moscow, Inostrannaya Literatura, 1960. English original: London, Victor Gollancz in association with Sidgwick & Jackson, 1971.

[380]. Ceram, C. *Gods, Graves and Scholars*. St. Petersburg, Nizhegorodskaya Yarmarka, KEM, 1994.

[381]. Kibalova, L., O. Gerbenova, and M. Lamarova. *An Illustrated Encyclopaedia of Fashion*. Prague, Artia, 1966.

[382]. Kinnam, Johann. *A Brief Review of the Reigns of John and Manuel Comneni*. St. Petersburg, 1859.

[383]. Kinzhalov, R. V. *The Ancient Mayan Culture*. Leningrad, Nauka, 1971.

[384]. Kiriaku, Georgios P. *Cyprus in Colours*. Limassol, Cyprus, K. P. Kiriaku (Books & Office Requisites) Ltd., 1987.

[385]. Kirpichnikov, A. N. *The Pages of the "Iron Book."* Nauka I Zhizn (Science and Life) magazine, No. 6 (1966): 49-55.

[385:1]. Kiselyova L. I. *What do the Mediaeval Chronicles Tell Us?* Leningrad, Nauka, 1978.

[386]. Kyetsaa, H. *The Battle for the "Quiet flows the Don."* Seanado-Statica, 22, 1976.

[387]. Kyetsaa, H. *The Battle for the "Quiet flows the Don."* USA, Pergamon Press, 1977.

[388]. Klassen, E. I. *New Materials for the Studies of the Historical Dawn of Slavs in General, and pre-Ryurik Russo-Slavs in Particular, with an Aperçu of the BC History of Russia*. Issues 1-3. With the *Descriptions of the Monuments Explaining the History of the Slavs and the Russians Compiled by Fadey Volansky and Translated by E. Klassen*. Moscow University Press, 1854. Reprinted by Andreyev i Soglasie, St. Petersburg, 1995.

[389]. Klassovsky, V. *A Systematic Description of Pompeii and the Artefacts Discovered There*. St. Petersburg, 1848.

[390]. Klein, L. S. *Archaeology Controverts Physics.* The *Priroda (Nature)* magazine, No. 2 (1966): 51-62.

[391]. Klein, L. S. *Archaeology Controverts Physics (continued).* The *Priroda (Nature)* magazine, No. 3 (1966): 94-107.

[391:1]. Klengel-Brandt, E. *A Journey into the Old Babylon.* Moscow, Nauka, General Editing Board for Oriental Literature, the USSR AS, Institute of Oriental Studies, 1979. Translated from German: Klengel-Brandt, E. *Reise in das alte Babylon.* Leipzig, 1971.

[392]. Kligene N., and L. Telxnis. *Methods of Determining Change Points in Random Processes.* Avtomatika i Telemekhanika (Automatics and Telemechanics), No. 10 (1983): 5-56.

[393]. Klimishin, I. A. *Chronology and the Calendar.* Moscow, Nauka, 2nd edition, 1985.

[394]. Klimishin, I. A. *Chronology and the Calendar.* Moscow, Nauka, 3rd edition, 1990.

[395]. Klimishin, I. A. *The Discovery of the Universe.* Moscow, Nauka, 1987.

[396]. Klyuchevsky, V. O. *Unreleased Works.* Moscow, Nauka, 1983.

[397]. *The Book of the Mormon. Another Testament of Jesus Christ.* Translated by Joseph Smith, Jun. Salt Lake City, The Church of Jesus Christ of the Latter Day Saints, 1991. (Quoting the Russian translation of 1988).

[398]. *The Book of Cosmas Indicopleustes.* Published by V. S. Golyshenko and V. F. Doubrovina. RAS, the V. V. Vinogradov Institute of the Russian Language. Moscow, Indrik, 1997.

[399]. Loparev, H. M., ed. *The Book of the Pilgrim. Holy Places in Czar-Grad Described by Anthony, the Archbishop of Novgorod in 1200.* "The Orthodox Palestinian Collection," Vol. 17, 3rd edition. St. Petersburg, 1899.

[400]. *Literary Centres of the Ancient Russia in the XI–XVI century.* St. Petersburg, Nauka, 1991.

[401]. Knorina, L. V. *Linguistic Aspects of the Hebraic Commentary Tradition. Voprosy Yazykoznania (Linguistic Issues),* No. 1 (1997): 97-108.

[402]. Kowalski, Jan Wierusz. *Papacy and the Popes.* Moscow, Political Literature Publications, 1991. A translation of the Polish book *Poczet Papiezy.* Warsaw, 1985.

[403]. Kovalchenko, I. D. *The Use of Quantitative Methods and Computers in Historical Research.* The *Voprosy Istorii (Historical Issues)* journal, No. 9 (1984): 61-73.

[404]. Kogan, V. M. *The History of the House of Ryurikovichi.* St. Petersburg, Belvedere, 1993.

[405]. Kozlov, V. *A Case of Church Robbery.* The *Moskovskiy Zhurnal (Moscow Magazine),* No. 7 (1991).

[406]. Kozlov, V. *Under the Flag of Nihilism.* The *Moskovskiy Zhurnal (Moscow Magazine),* No. 6 (1991).

[407]. Kozlov, V. P. *Falsification Mysteries. An Analysis of Historical Source Forgeries of the XVIII–XIX centuries.* Moscow, Aspekt, 1996.

[407:1]. Kozlov, V. T. *The 30-Year War. European Splendour. The Renaissance. Humanism. The Enlightenment.* Moscow, The V. T. Kozlov Regional Public Fund for the Support and Development of Arts and Culture, 2001. 44.

[408]. Kozlov, P. *Yaroslavl.* Yaroslavl, The Upper Volga Publishing House, 1972.

[409]. Kozlov, P. I., and V. F. Marov. *Yaroslavl. A Guide and a Reference Book.* Yaroslavl, The Upper Volga, 1988.

[410]. Kokkinoftas, Kostis and Theocharidis, Ioannis. *"Enkolpion." A Brief Description of St. Kykkos Monastery.* Nicosia, The St. Kykkos Monastery Research Centre, 1995.

[411]. Kolodny, L. "Turbulence over the 'Quiet flows the Don.' Fragments of the Past: the Sources used for a Certain XX century Animad version. *Moskovskaya Pravda* (5 and 7 March, 1989).

[412]. Rauschenbach, B .V., ed. *Bells. History and Contemporaneity.* Compiled by Y. V. Pukhnachev. The Scientific Counsel for World Culture History, the USSR AS. Moscow, Nauka, 1985.

[413]. Kolosov, Vassily. *Perambulations in the Environs of the Simonov Monastery.* Moscow, 1806.

[414]. Kolchin, B. A., and Y. A. Sher. *Absolute Archaeological Datings and their Problems.* Moscow, Nauka, 1972.

[415]. Kohlrausch, F. *History of Germany.* Vols. I, II. Moscow, 1860. English edition: Kohlrausch, F. *A History of Germany, from the Earliest Period to the Present Time.* New York, D. Appelton & Co, 1896.

[415:1]. Kolyazin, V. F. *From The Passion Play Mystery to the Carnival. The Histrionics of the German Religious and Popular Stage of the Early and the Late Middle Ages.* Moscow, Nauka, 2002.

[416]. *Archimandrite Palladius Kafarov Commentary on Marco Polo's Voyage through Northern China.* St. Petersburg, 1902.

[417]. Comnena, Anna. *The Alexiad.* Moscow, Nauka, 1965. English edition: Harmondsworth, Penguin, 1969.

[418]. Comnena, Anna. *The Alexiad.* St. Petersburg. Aleteya, 1996.

[419]. Comnena, Anna. *A Brief Account of the Deeds of King Alexis Comnenus.* St. Petersburg, 1859.

[420]. Kondakov, N. P. *The Iconography of Our Lady.* 3 volumes. Moscow, Palomnik. Vols. 1 and 2, 1998. Vol. 3, 1999.

[420:1]. Kondratov, Alexander. *The Mysteries of the Three Oceans.* Leningrad, Gidrometeoizdat, 1971.

[421]. Kondratyev, I. K. *The Ancient Moscow. A Historical Review and a Full List of the City's Monuments.* Moscow, Voyenizdat, 1996.

[422]. Kondrashina, V. A. *The Savvino-Storozhevsky Monastery. 600 Years since the Foundation of the Coenoby of Rev. Savva.* An album of photographs. Moscow, Leto, 1998.

[423]. Koniskiy, G. (The Archbishop of Byelorussia). *The History of Russians, or the Lesser Russia.* The Moscow University Typography, 1846.

[424]. *Konstantin Mikhailovich from Ostrovitsa. The Notes of a Janissary.* In-

troduction, translation, and commentary by A. I. Rogov. Published in the *Monuments of Mediaeval History of the Nations of Central and Eastern Europe* series. The USSR AS, Institute of Slavic and Balkan Studies. Moscow, Nauka, 1978.

[425]. Konstantinov, N. *The Secret Alphabet of Stolnik Baryatinsky.* The *Nauka i Zhizn (Science and Life)* magazine, No. 10 (1972): 118-119.

[426]. *Context 1978.* Collected works. Moscow, Nauka, 1978.

[427]. *The Koran.* Moscow, Oriental Literature, 1963.

[428]. *The Koran.* Translated by I. Y. Krachkovsky. Moscow, Raritet, 1990.

[429]. Al Rosha, Dr. Mohammed Said., ed. *The Koran.* 2nd edition, revised and enlarged by Valeria Prokhorova. Damascus-Moscow, The Al-Furkan Centre and Mikhar Corp., 2553, 10.2.95, 1996.

[430]. *The Ecclesial Law Book (Kormchaya) of 1620.* 256/238, The Manuscript Fund of the Russian National Library (Moscow).

[430:1]. Kornilov N. I., Solodova Y. P. *Jewels and gems.* Moscow, Nedra, 1983.

[431]. Korkh, A. S. *Mikhail Illarionovich Koutouzov.* The Moscow State Museum of History. n.d.

[432]. Korsh, M. *A Brief Dictionary of Mythology and Antiquities.* St. Petersburg, A. S. Souvorin, 1894. Reprinted: Kaluga, Amata, Golden Alley, 1993.

[433]. Kosambi, D. *The Culture and Civilization of Ancient India.* Moscow, Progress, 1968. English edition: Kosambi D. *The Culture and Civilization of Ancient India in Historical Outline.* London, Routledge & Kegan Paul, 1965.

[434]. Kosidowski, Z. *When the Sun was God.* Moscow, Nauka, 1968. Polish edition: Kosidowsky Z. *Gdy Slonce Bylo Bogiem.* Warsaw, 1962.

[435]. Kostomarov, N. I. *The Reign of the House of St. Vladimir.* Moscow, Voyenizdat, 1993.

[436]. Kostomarov, N. I. *The Age of Turmoil in Early XVII century Moscovia (1604-1613).* Moscow, Charli, 1994.

[437]. Kostomarov, N. I. *Bogdan Khmelnitsky.* Moscow, Charlie, 1994.

[437:1]. Kochergina, V. A. *Sanskrit-Russian Dictionary.* About 30.000 words. Moscow, Filologia, 1996.

[438]. Golubev, A. A., comp. *The Kostroma Region.* Moscow, Planeta, 1988.

[439]. Cramer, C. *Mathematical Methods of Statistics.* Moscow, Mir, 1975. English original: Princeton, NJ, Princeton University Press, 1958.

[440]. *The Concise Geographical Encyclopaedia.* Vol. 1, Moscow, State Academic Soviet Encyclopaedia Publications, 1960.

[440:1]. Krekshin, P. N. *A Criticism of the Freshly-Printed Book of 1761 about the Origins of Rome and the Actions of its People and Monarchs.* The reverse of the last sheet says: "Criticism by the Nobleman of the Great New Town Peter of Nicephor, son of Kreksha, in 1762, on the 30th day of September, St. Petersburg." The manuscript is kept in the State Archive of the Yaroslavl Oblast as Manuscript #43 (431).

[441]. *The Peasant War in Russia Led by Stepan Razin.* Collected documents. Vols. 1-4. Moscow, Academy of Sciences, 1954-1970.

[442]. Luchinat, Christina Acidini. *Benozzo Gozzoli*. Published in the *Great Masters of Italian Art* series. Moscow, Slovo, 1996. Italian edition: Scala, Istituto Fotografico Editoriale, 1995.

[443]. Kriesh, Elli G. *The Treasure of Troy and its History*. Moscow, Raduga, 1996. German original: Kriesh, Elli G. *Der Schatz von Troja und seine Geschichte*. Carlsen, 1994.

[444]. Kryvelev, I. A. *The Excavations in the "Biblical" Countries*. Moscow, Sovietskaya Rossia, 1965.

[445]. Kryvelev, I. A. *A Book about the Bible*. Moscow, Sotsekgiz, 1958.

[446]. Krylov, A. N. *Newton and his Role in Global Science. 1643-1943*. The USSR Academy of Sciences. Moscow-Leningrad, USSR AS Publications, 1943.

[447]. Xenophon. *History of the Hellenes*. Leningrad, Ogiz, 1935. English edition: Xenophon. *Hellenica*. In: W. Briggs, Tutorial Series, Books III, IV. London, 1894.

[448]. Koublanov, M. M. *The New Testament. Research and Discoveries*. Moscow, Nauka, 1968.

[449]. Koudriavtsev, M. P. *Moscow the Third Rome. A Historical and Urbanistic Research*. Moscow, Sol System, 1994.

[450]. Koudriavtsev, O. F., comp. *Russia in the First Half of the XVI century. A European View*. The Russian AS, Global History Institute. Moscow, Russkiy Mir, 1997.

[451]. Kouznetsov, V. G. *Newton*. Moscow, Mysl, 1982.

[452]. Koulakovsky, Y. A. *Byzantine History*. Vols. 1, 2. St. Petersburg, Aleteya, 1996.

[453]. Koulikovsky, P. G. *Stellar Astronomy*. Moscow, Nauka, 1978.

[454]. Koun, N. A. *The Predecessors of Christianity*. Moscow, 1922.

[455]. Kourbatov, L. G. *Byzantine History*. Moscow, Vyshaya Shkola, 1984.

[456]. *The UNESCO Courier* magazine, No. 12 (1968).

[457]. Koutouzov, B. *The Church Reform of the XVII century*. The *Tserkov (Church)* magazine (Moscow), Issue 1 (1992).

[457:1]. Koutsenko, G., and Y. Novikov. *Make Yourself A Present of Health*. Moscow, Moskovskiy Rabochiy, 1988.

[458]. Cimpan, F. *The History of the Pi Number*. Moscow, Nauka, 1971 (1984). Romanian original: Cipman, F. *Istoria Numarului pi*. Bucharest, Tineret Press, 1965.

[458:1]. Cumont, Franz. *The Mysteries of Mithras. Magicum*. St. Petersburg, Eurasia, 2000. Original edition: Franz Cumont. *Les Mystères de Mithra. Magicum*. Brussels, H. Lamertin, 1913.

[459]. Lavisse, E., and A. Rambaud. *History of the Crusades*. Vols. I and II. Moscow, 1914. French original: *Histoire générale du IVe siècle à nos jours. L'Europe féodale, les croisades, 1095-1270*. Paris, A. Colin & Cie, 1893-1901.

[460]. *The Lavrenty Chronicle*. (A complete compilation of Russian chronicles). V. 1. Moscow, Yazyki Russkoi Kulturi, 1997.

[461]. Lavrov, N. F. *A Guide to the Churches of Uglich*. Uglich, the Municipal Mu-

seum of Arts and History, 1994. A re-print from an 1869 original, Yaroslavl, the Province Typography.

[462]. Lazarev, V. N. *The Icon Art of Novgorod.* Moscow, Iskusstvo, 1969.

[462:1]. Lombroso. C. *Genius and Madness.* Moscow, Respublika, 1995.

[463]. Lann, E. *A Literary Mystification.* Moscow, 1930.

[464]. Lauer, Jean-Philippe. *The Mystery of the Egyptian Pyramids.* Moscow, Nauka, 1966. French edition: *Le Mystère des Pyramides.* Paris, Presses de la Cité, 1974.

[465]. Deacon, Leon. *History.* Moscow, Nauka, 1988. See also: *Leonis Diaconi Caloensis Historiae libri decem.* E recensione C. B. Hasii. Bonnae, 1828.

[466]. Levandovsky, A. P. *Charlemagne. From the Empire towards Europe.* Moscow, Soratnik, 1995.

[467]. Levitan, E., and N. Mamouna. *The Star of Bethlehem.* The *Nauka i Zhizn (Science and Life)* magazine, No. 11 (1989).

[468]. Levchenko, M. V. *Byzantine History.* Moscow-Leningrad, Ogiz, Sotsekgiz, 1940.

[469]. *The Legend of Dr. Faustus.* Moscow, Nauka, 1978. Also see: *The History of the Damnable Life and Deserved Death of Doctor John Faustus.* London, G. Routledge; New York, E. P. Duttom, 1925.

[470]. Lehmann. *An Illustrated History of Superstition and Sorcery from the Antiquity to Our Days.* Moscow, Knizhnoe Delo, 1900. Also see: Lehmann, A. *Overto og trolddom fra de aeldste til vore dage.* Copenhagen, J. Frimodt, 1893-1896.

[471]. Lentsman, Y. A. *The Origins of Christianity.* Moscow, USSR AS Press, 1958.

[471:1]. *The Life and Art of Leonardo.* Moscow, Byely Gorod, 2001. Giunti Gruppo Editoriale, Florence, 2000.

[472]. Leonid. *A Systematic Description of A. S. Ouvarov's Russo-Slavic Manuscripts.* Moscow, 1894.

[473]. Leontyeva, G. A., Shorin, P. A. and Kobrin, V. B. *The Keys to the Mysteries of Clio. Palaeography, Metrology, Chronology, Heraldic Studies, Numismatics, Onomatology and Genealogy.* Moscow, Prosveshchenie, 1994.

[473:1]. Leskov, A. M. *Burial Mounds: Findings and Problems.* Leningrad, Nauka, 1981.

[474]. Lesna, Ivan. *On the Ails of the Great.* Prague, Grafit, 1990.

[475]. Lesnoy, Sergei. *History of the Slavs Revised.* Melbourne, 1956.

[476]. Lesnoy, Sergei. *A Non-Distorted History of the Russians.* Vols. 1-10. Paris, 1957.

[477]. Lesnoy, Sergei. *Russia, where are you from?* Winnipeg, 1964.

[477:0]. Lesnoy, Sergei. *The Book of Veles.* Moscow, Zakharov, 2002.

[477:1]. *A Chronicler of Hellas and Rome.* Vol. 1. The RAS Institute of Russian Literature (The House of Pushkin). St. Petersburg, Dmitry Boulanin, 1999.

[478]. Libby, W. F. *Carbon-14: a Nuclear Chronometer of Archaeology.* The *UNESCO Courier,* No. 7 (No. 139)(1968).

[479]. Libby, W. F. *The Radiocarbon Dating Method.* The International Peaceful Nuclear Energy Conference materials (Geneva), Vol. 16 (1987): 41-64.

[480]. Libby, W. F. *Radiocarbon: an Atomic Clock.* The annual *Nauka i Chelovechestvo (Science and Humanity)* journal (1962): 190-200. Moscow, Znaniye.

[481]. Libman, M., and G. Ostrovskiy. *Counterfeit Masterpieces.* Moscow, Sovetskiy Khudozhnik, 1966.

[482]. Livy, Titus. *Roman History since the Foundation of the City.* 6 volumes. Translation and general editorship by P. Adrianov. Moscow, E. Herbeck Typography, 1897-1899.

[483]. Livy, Titus. *Roman History since the Foundation of the City.* Vols. 1, 2 and 3. Moscow, Nauka, Vol. 1 (1989), Vol. 2 (1991), Vol. 3 (1993). English edition: Livy, Titus. *Works.* Cambridge, Mass; London, Heinemann, 1914.

[484]. Livraga, Jorge A. *Thebe.* Moscow, New Acropolis, 1995.

[485]. *Linguistic Encyclopedic Dictionary.* Moscow, Soviet Encyclopedia Publications, 1990.

[486]. Lipinskaya, Y., and M. Martsinyak. *Ancient Egyptian Mythology.* Moscow, Iskusstvo, 1983.

[487]. Lituanus, Michalonis. *On the Customs of the Tartars, the Lithuanians and the Muscovites.* Moscow, MSU Publications, 1994. See also: Michalonis Lituani. *De moribus tartarorum, lituanorum et moschorum fragmina X, multiplici historia referta et Johannis Lascii poloni De diis samagitarum, caeterorumque sarmatarum et falsorum christianorum. Item de religione armeniorum et de initio regiminus Stephani Batori.* Nunc primum per J. Jac. Grasserum, C. P. ex manuscriptio authentico edita. Basileae, apud Conradum Waldkirchium, MDCXV, 1-41.

[488]. *Literary legacy. V. I. Lenin and A. V. Lunacharsky. Correspondence, Reports, Documents.* Moscow, Nauka, 1971.

[489]. Lifshitz, G. M. *Essays on Early Christianity and Biblical Historiography.* Minsk: Vysheyshaya Shkola, 1970.

[490]. Likhachev, N. P. *The Artistic Manner of Andrei Rublev.* St. Petersburg, 1907.

[490:1]. Likhacheva, E. A. *The Seven Hills of Moscow.* Moscow, Nauka, 1990.

[491]. Lozinsky, S. G. *History of the Spanish Inquisition.* St. Petersburg, Brockhaus and Efron, 1914.

[492]. Lozinsky, S. G. *History of the Papacy.* Vols. I and II. Moscow, The Central TsS SWB Publications of USSR, 1934.

[493]. Lomonosov, M. V. *Selected Works.* Vol. 2. History, philology, poetry. Moscow, Nauka, 1986.

[493:1]. Gowing, Sir Lawrence. *Paintings in the Louvre.* Introduction by Michel Laclotte. Russian Translation by MK-Import, Ltd., Moscow, Mezhdunarodnaya Kniga, 1987. English edition: Stewart, Tabori & Chang, Inc., 1987.

[493:2]. Loades, D. *Henry VIII and his Queens.* The *Mark in History* series. Moscow, Feniks.

[494]. Pardi, J., comp. *The Pilot Chart of the Gibraltar and the Mediterranean.* Translated by I. Shestakov. Moscow, 1846.

[495]. Lourie, F. M. *Russian and Global History in Tables. Synchrony tables (XXX century BC – XIX Century). World Governors. Genealogical Tables. Glossary.* St. Petersburg, Karavella, 1995.

[496]. Louchin, A. A. *The Slavs and History.* An appendix to the *Molodaya Gvardia (Young Guard)* magazine, No. 9 (1997): 260-351.

[497]. Lyzlov, Andrei. *History of the Scythians.* Moscow, Nauka, 1990.

[497:1]. Liozzi, Mario. *History of Physics.* Moscow, Mir, 1970.

[498]. Lewis, G. C. *A Research of Ancient Roman History and its Veracity.* Hannover, 1852. German edition: *Untersuchungen über die Glaubwürdigkeit der altrömischen Geschichte,* Hannover, 1858.

[499]. Magi, Giovanna. *Luxor. The Valleys of the Kings, Queens, Noblemen and Craftsmen. Memnon's colossi. Deir-el-Bakhari – Medinet-Abu – Ramesseum.* Florence, Casa Editrice Bonechi via Cairoli, 1999.

[500]. Makariy (Boulgakov), the Metropolitan of Moscow and Kolomna. *History of the Russian Church.* Books 1-7. Moscow, The Spaso-Preobrazhensky Monastery of Valaam Publications, 1994-1996.

[500:1]. Makariy, Archimandrite. *Ancient Ecclesial Monuments. History of the Hierarchy of Nizhniy Novgorod.* The *True Tales of Nizhniy Novgorod* series. Nizhniy Novgorod, Nizhegorodskaya Yarmarka, 1999.

[501]. Makarov, A. G., and S. E. Makarova. *The Scotch Thistle Blossom. Towards the Sources of the "Quiet flows the Don."* Moscow, Photocopied by the General Research Institute of Gas Industry, 1991.

[502]. Makarov, A. G., and S. E. Makarova. *Around the "Quiet flows the Don." From Myth Creation to a Search for Truth.* Moscow, Probel, 2000.

[502:1]. Machiavelli, Niccolo. *The Prince. Ruminations in re the First Decade of Titus Livy.* – St. Petersburg, Azbuka, 2002.

[502:2]. Machiavelli, Niccolo. *The History of Florence.* – Leningrad, Nauka, 1973.

[503]. Malalas, John. *The Chronicle.* Published by O. V. Tvorogov according to *The Chronographer of Sofia* in the *Works of the Ancient Russian Literature Department,* Vol. 37, pp. 192-221. Moscow, Nauka. English edition: *The Chronicle of John Malalas.* Chicago, Chicago University Press, 1940.

[504]. Kantor, A. M., ed. *A Concise History of Fine Arts.* Moscow, Iskusstvo, 1981; Dresden, VEB Verlag der Kunst, 1981.

[504:1]. *The Compact Soviet Encyclopaedia.* Vols. 1-10. Moscow, Sovetskaya Encyclopaedia, Inc., 1928.

[505]. Malinovskaya, L. N. *The Graveyard of the Khans (Mezarlyk).* Bakhchisaray, the State Historical and Cultural Reserve, 1991.

[506]. Malinovskiy, A. F. *A Review of Moscow.* Moscow, Moskovskiy Rabochiy, 1992.

[507]. *A Concise Atlas of the World.* Moscow, General Department of Geodetics and Cartography of the USSR Council of Ministers. 1979.

[508]. Malver, A. *Science and Religion.* Russian translation by L. and E. Kroukovsky. N.p., 1925.

[509]. Marijnissen, R. H., and P. Ruyffelaere. *Hieronymus Bosch.* Commentated album. Antwerp, Mercatorfonds, 1987, 1995. Russian translation by Mezhdunarodnaya Kniga. Moscow, 1998.

[510]. Marco Polo. *A Book on the Diversity of the World.* The Personal Library of Borges. St. Petersburg, Amphora, 1999.

[511]. Markov, A. A. *One of the Uses of the Statistical Method. The Academy of Sciences News,* Series 6, Vol. X, Issue 4 (1916).

[512]. Martynov, G. *On the Origins of Roman Chronicles.* Moscow University Press, 1903.

[513]. Massa, Isaac. *A Brief Report of the Beginning and the Origins of Modern Muscovite Wars and Unrest that Occurred Before 1610 in the Brief Time when Several Rulers Reigned.* Moscow, The Sergei Doubnov Fund, Rita-Print, 1997.

[514]. Massa, Isaac. *A Brief Report on Moscovia.* Moscow, 1937.

[514:1]. Matveyenko, V. A., and L. I. Shchegoleva. *The Chronicle of George the Coenobite.* Russian text, comments, indications. Moscow, Bogorodskiy Pechatnik, 2000.

[515]. Matvievskaya, G. P. *Albrecht Dürer the Scientist. 1471-1528.* A series of scientist biographies. Moscow, The USSR AS, Nauka, 1987.

[516]. Matvievskaya, G. P. *As-Sufi.* In *Historical and Astronomical Research* (Moscow, Nauka), Issue 16 (1983): 93-138.

[517]. Matuzova, V. I. *Mediaeval English Sources.* Moscow, Nauka, 1979.

[518]. Vlastar, Matthew. *Collection of Rules Devised by Holy Fathers.* Balakhna, P. A. Ovchinnikov, The F. P. Volkov typography, 1908.

[519]. Smirnov B. L., editor and translator. *The Mahabharata.* Vols. 1-8. Tashkent, the Turkmenian SSR Academy of Sciences, 1955-1972. Vol. 1: two poems from the III book – *Nala* and *Savitri* (*The Greatness of Marital Virtue*) (2nd edition 1959); Vol. 2 – *The Bhagavad Gita* (1956); Vol. 3: *The Highlander* (1957); Vol. 4: *The Conversation of Markandhea* (1958); Vol. 5: *Mokshadharma* (1961); Vol. 6: *A Journey Through the Treasuries* (1962); Vol. 7: *The Book of Bheeshma and the Book of the Battle of Maces* (1963); Vol. 8: *Attacking the Sleeping Ones* (1972). English edition: Chicago-London, Chicago University Press, 1973. Also see the edition by the Jaico Publishing House, Bombay, 1976.

[519:1]. *The Mahabharata. Narayana.* Issue V, book 2. 2nd edition. Translated and edited by Academician B. L. Smirnov of the Turkmenian SSR Academy of Sciences. The TSSR AS, Ashkhabad, Ylym, 1984.

[519:2]. *The Mahabharata. The Four Tales.* Translated from Sanskrit by S. Lipkin. Interlineary by O. Volkova. Moscow, Khudozhestvennaya Literatura, 1969.

[520]. *The Mahabharata. The Ramayana.* Moscow, Khudozhestvennaya Literatura, 1974. Also see: *The Ramayana.* Madras, Periyar Self-Respect Propaganda Institution, 1972.

[520:1]. *The Mahabharata. Book 2. Sabhaparva, or the Book of the Congregation.* Translated from Sanskrit by V. I. Kalyanov. The *Literary Monuments* series. Moscow-Leningrad, Nauka, 1962.

[520:2]. *The Mahabharata. Book 4. Virataparva, or the Book of Virata.* Translated from Sanskrit by V. I. Kalyanov. The *Literary Monuments* series. Leningrad, Nauka, 1967.

[520:3]. *The Mahabharata. Book 5. Udhiyogaparva, or the Book of Diligence.* Translated from Sanskrit by V. I. Kalyanov. The *Literary Monuments* series. Leningrad, Nauka, 1976.

[520:4]. *The Bhagavad Gita as it is.* Complete edition with authentic Sanskrit texts, Russian transliteration, word-for-word and literary translation, and extensive commentaries. The Bhaktivedanta Book Trust. Moscow-Leningrad-Calcutta-Bombay-New Delhi, 1984. The first English edition of the Bhagavad Gita: Wilkins. *The Bhagavad Gita, or dialogs of Kreeshna and Arjoon.* London, 1785. See also: Etgerton, F. *Bhagavad Gita,* Vols. 1-2. Harvard University Press, 1946 (with transcr. of the text).

[520:5]. *The Mahabharata. Book 7. Dronaparva, or the Book of Drona.* Translated from Sanskrit by V. I. Kalyanov. The *Literary Monuments* series. St. Petersburg, Nauka, 1993.

[520:6]. *The Mahabharata. Book 3. The Book of the Woods (Aryanyakaparva).* Translated from Sanskrit by A. V. Vasilkov and S. L. Neveleva. The *Monuments of Oriental Literature* series. LXXX, 1987.

[520:7]. *The Burning of the Snakes. A Tale from the Indian Epic, the Mahabharata.* Translated by V. I. Kalyanov. Moscow, Goslitizdat, 1958.

[521]. Mezentsev, M. T. *The Fate of Novels (Concerning the Discussion on the "Quiet flows the Don" Authorship Problem).* Samara, P. S. Press, 1994.

[522]. Medvedev, R. *Who Wrote the "Quiet flows the Don"?* Paris, Christian Bourg, 1975.

[522:1]. Meyer, M. S., A. F. Deribas, and N. B. Shuvalova. *Turkey. The Book of Wanderings.* A historical guidebook. Project author S. M. Bourygin. Moscow, Veche, Khartia, 2000.

[523]. Melnikova, E. A. *Ancient Scandinavian Geographical Works.* Moscow, Nauka, 1986.

[524]. *Memoirs of Margaret de Valois.* Translated by I. V. Shevlyagina. Introduction and comments by S. L. Pleshkova. French original: *Mémoires de Marguerite de Valois.* Paris, The Library of P. Jannet, MDCCCLVIII. Moscow University Press, 1995.

[525]. *Methods of Studying the Oldest Sources on the History of the USSR Nations.* Collected articles. Moscow, Nauka, 1978.

[526]. *Methodical Research of Absolute Geochronology. Report Theses of the 3rd Methodical Symposium of 1976.* Moscow, USSR AS Press, 1976.

[527]. Meshchersky, N. A. *History of the Literary Russian Language.* Leningrad, 1981.

[528]. Miceletti, Emma. *Domenico Ghirlandio.* Moscow, Slovo, 1996. Italian original: Italy, Scala, Istituto Fotografico Editoriale, 1995.

[529]. Miller, G. F. *Selected Oeuvres on Russian History.* The *Monuments of Historical Thought* series. Moscow, Nauka, RAS, 1996.

[530]. *The World of the Bible.* Magazine. 1993/1(1). Published by the Russian Society of Bible Studies.

[531]. *The World of Geography. Geography and the Geographers. The Environment.* Moscow, Mysl, 1984.

[532]. Meletinsky, E. M., ed. *Dictionary of Mythology.* Moscow, Sovetskaya Encyclopaedia, 1991.

[533]. *Myths of the World. An Encyclopaedia.* Vols. 1 and 2. Moscow, Sovetskaya Encyclopaedia, 1980 (Vol. 1) and 1981 (Vol. 2).

[534]. Mikhailov, A. A. *The Eclipse Theory.* Moscow, Gostekhteoretizdat, 1954.

[535]. Mikhailov, A. A. *This Peculiar Radiocarbon Method.* In *Science and Technology,* No. 8 (1983): 31-32.

[536]. Mokeyev, G. A. *Mozhaysk – A Holy Town for the Russians.* Moscow, Kedr, 1992.

[537]. Mokretsova, I. P., and V. L. Romanova. *French Miniature Illustrations of the XIII century in Soviet Publications. 1270-1300.* Moscow, Iskusstvo, 1984.

[537:1]. Moleva, N. M. *True Muscovite Stories. A Hundred Addresses of Russian History and Culture.* To the 850-year anniversary of Moscow. Moscow, Znaniye, 1997.

[538]. Mommsen, T. *The History of Rome.* Moscow, 1936.

[539]. Mommsen, T. *The History of Rome.* Vol. 3. Moscow, Ogiz, 1941. English edition: London, Macmillan & Co, 1913.

[540]. Mongayt, A. L. *The Writing upon the Stone.* Moscow, Znanie, 1969.

[541]. *Mongolian Sources Related to Dayan-Khan.* A compilation. Moscow, Nauka, 1986

[541:1]. Mordovtsev, D. L. *Collected works.* Vols. 1-14. Moscow, Terra, 1995.

[542]. Morozov, N. A. *The Revelation in Thunder and Storm. History of the Apocalypse.* Moscow, 1907. 2nd edition Moscow, 1910. English translation: Northfield, Minnesota, 1941.

[543]. Morozov, N. A. *The History of the Biblical Prophecies and their Literary Characteristics. The Prophets.* Moscow, the I. D. Sytin Society Typography, 1914.

[544]. Morozov, N. A. *Christ. History of Humanity in the Light of Natural Scientific Studies.* Vols. 1-7. Moscow-Leningrad, Gosizdat, 1924-1932. Vol. 1: 1924 (2nd edition 1927), Vol. 2: 1926, Vol. 3: 1927, Vol. 4: 1928, Vol. 5: 1929, Vol. 6: 1930, Vol. 7: 1932. The first volume was published twice: in 1924 and 1927. Kraft Publications in Moscow made a reprint of all seven volumes in 1998.

[545]. Morozov, N. A. *An Astronomical Revolution in Historical Science.* The *Novy Mir (New World)* magazine, No. 4 (1925): 133-143. In reference to the article by Prof. N. M. Nikolsky.

[546]. Morozov, N. A. *Linguistic Ranges.* The AS Newsletter, Department of Russian Language and Literature. Books 1-4, Vol. XX, 1915.

[547]. Morozov, N. A. *On Russian History.* The manuscript of the 8th volume of the work *Christ.* Moscow, the RAS Archive. Published in Moscow by Kraft and Lean in the end of the year 2000, as *A New Point of View on Russian History.*

[547:1]. Morozov, N.A. *The Asian Christs. (History of Humanity in the Light of Natural Scientific Studies).* Vol. 9 of the work titled *Christ.* Moscow, Kraft+ Ltd., 2003.

[547:2]. Morozov, N.A. *The Mirages of Historical Wastelands between Tigris and Euphrates. (History of Humanity in the Light of Natural Scientific Studies).* Vol. 10 of the work titled *Christ.* Moscow, Kraft+ Ltd., 2002.

[548]. Fomenko A. T., and L. E. Morozova. *Quantitative Methods in Macro-Textology (with Artefacts of the XVI–XVII "Age of Troubles" Used as Examples).* Complex methods in the study of historical processes. Moscow, the USSR Institute of History, Academy of Sciences, 1987. 163-181.

[549]. *Moscow.* An album. Moscow, Avrora Press; St. Petersburg, 1996.

[550]. *Illustrated History of Moscow.* Vol. 1. From the dawn of time until 1917. Moscow, Mysl, 1985.

[551]. *Moscow and the Moscow Oblast. City Plan. Topographical Map. 1:200000.* 3rd edition. Moscow, The Military Typography Headquarters Department, 1998.

[552]. *The Moscow Kremlin. Arkhangelsky Cathedral.* Moscow, The Moscow Kremlin State Museum and Reserve for History and Culture, 1995.

[553]. *The Moscow Kremlin. Ouspensky Cathedral.* Moscow, The Moscow Kremlin State Museum and Reserve for History and Culture, 1995.

[554]. *The Moscow Chronicler.* Compilation. Issue 1. Moscow, Moskovskiy Rabochiy, 1988.

[555]. *The Moscow Oblast Museum of History in Istra. A Guide-book.* Moscow, Moskovskiy Rabochiy, 1989.

[556]. *The Andrei Rublev Museum.* A brochure. Published by the Central Andrei Rublev Museum of Ancient Russian Culture and Art in Moscow, 10, Andronyevskaya Square. n.d.

[557]. Mouravyev, M. V. *Novgorod the Great. A Historical Account and Guidebook.* Leningrad: The State Historical Material Culture Academy Art Edition Popularization Committee, n.d.

[558]. Mouravyev, S. *History of the First Four Centuries of Christianity.* St. Petersburg, 1866.

[559]. Murad, Aji. *The Polovtsy Field Wormwood.* Moscow, Pik-Kontekst, 1994

[560]. Murad, Aji. *Europe, the Turkomans and the Great Steppe.* Moscow, Mysl, 1998

[561]. Mouratov, K. I. *Peasant War Led by E. I. Pougachev.* Moscow, Prosveshchenie, 1980.

[562]. Mylnikov, A. S. *A Picture of a Slavic World as Viewed from the Eastern Europe. Ethnogenetic Legends, Conjectures, and Proto-Hypotheses of the XVI – Early XVIII century.* St. Petersburg, The Petersburg Oriental Studies Centre, 1996.

[563]. Mylnikov, A. S. *The Legend of the Russian Prince (Russo-Slavic Relations of the XVIII century in the World of Folk Culture).* Leningrad, Nauka, 1987.

[564]. Malory, Thomas. *Le Morte d'Arthure.* Moscow, Nauka, 1974. English

original taken from *The Works of Sir Thomas Malory* edited by E. Vinaver, Oxford, 1947.

[565]. Najip, E. N. *A Comparative Historical Dictionary of the XIV century Turkic Languages*. Book I. Moscow, 1979.

[566]. *The Land of Smolensk*. Moscow, Moskovskiy Rabochiy, 1971.

[567]. Takeshi, Nagata. *The Magnetic Field of the Earth in the Past*. In *Nauka i Chelovechestvo (Science and Humanity)*. 1965 annual edition. Moscow, Znani-ye. 169-175.

[568]. Nazarevskiy, V. V. *Selected Fragments of Muscovite History. 1147-1913*. Moscow, Svarog, 1996.

[569]. Vyacheslav (Savinykh). *Concise History of the Andronicus Monastery*. Moscow, The Sudarium Temple of the Andronicus Monastery, 1999.

[570]. *The Scientific Research Museum of Architecture*. Moscow, 1962.

[571]. Neugebauer, O. *The Exact Sciences in Antiquity*. Moscow, Nauka, 1968. English edition in the series *Acta Historica Scientiarum Naturalism et Medicinalium*. Vol. 9. Copenhagen, 1957. New York, Harper & Bros., 1962.

[572]. Neuhardt, A. A., and I. A. Shishova. *The Seven Wonders of the Ancient World*. The USSR AS, the Leningrad Department of the History Institute. Moscow-Leningrad, Nauka, 1966.

[573]. Leping, A. A., and N. P. Strakhova, eds. *German-Russian Dictionary*. 80,000 words. Moscow, The State National and International Dictionary Publications, 1958.

[574]. Nemirovskiy, A. I. *The Etruscans. From Myth to History*. Moscow, Nauka, 1983.

[575]. Nemirovskiy, E. L. *The Literary World from the Dawn of History until the Early XX century*. Moscow, Kniga, 1986.

[576]. Nemoyevskiy, Andrei. *Jesus the God*. Petersburg, State Publishing House, 1920.

[577]. Nennius. *History of the Brits*. From: Geoffrey of Monmouth. *History of the Brits. The Life of Merlin*. Moscow, Nauka, 1984. English edition: Nennius. *Historia Brittonum*. Galfridus Monemutensis (Geoffrey of Monmouth). *Historia Britonum. Vita Merlini. Six old English Chronicles*. Edited by J.A.Giles. London, 1848.

[577:1]. Nersesyan, L. V. *Dionysius the Icon Master and the Murals of the Feropontov Monastery*. Moscow, Severniy Palomnik, 2002.

[578]. Nechvolodov, A. *Tales of the Russian Land*. Books 1 and 2. Moscow, Svarog, 1997. A new edition of the books published by the State Typography of St. Petersburg in 1913.

[579]. Niese, B. *A Description of the Roman History and Source Studies*. German edition: *Grundriss der römischen Geschichte nebst Quellenkunde*. St. Petersburg, 1908. German edition: Munich, 1923.

[579:1]. Nikerov, V. A. *History as an Exact Science*. (Based on the materials of A. T. Fomenko and G. V. Nosovskiy. *The New Chronology*). Moscow, Ecmo-Press, Yauza, 2002.

[580]. Nikolayev, D. *The Weapon that Failed to Save Byzantium.* In *Tekhnika i Nauka (Science and Technology),* No. 9 (1983): 29-36.

[581]. Nikolayeva, T. V. *The Ancient Zvenigorod.* Moscow, Iskusstvo, 1978.

[582]. *Nikolai Aleksandrovich Morozov.* In *Bibliography of the Scientists of the USSR.* Moscow, Nauka, 1981.

[583]. *Nikolai Aleksandrovich Morozov, the Encyclopaedist Scientist.* A collection of articles. Moscow, Nauka, 1982.

[584]. *Nikolai Aleksandrovich Morozov. Biographical Stages and Activities.* The *USSR AS Courier,* Nos. 7 and 8 (1944).

[585]. Nikolskiy, N. M. *An Astronomical Revolution in Historical Science.* The *Novy Mir (New World)* magazine, Vol. 1 (1925): 157-175. (In re. N. Morozov's œuvre *Christ.* Leningrad, 1924.)

[586]. Nikonov, V. A. *Name and Society.* Moscow, Nauka, 1974.

[586:1]. *A Collection of Chronicles titled the Patriarchal, or the Nikon Chronicle.* The Complete Collection of Russian Chronicles (CCRC), Vols. IX–XIV. Moscow, Yazyki Russkoi Kultury, 2000.

[587]. *Novellino.* Literary monuments. Moscow, Nauka, 1984.

[588]. Novozhilov, N. I. *The Meteorological Works of N. A. Morozov.* The *Priroda (Nature)* magazine, No. 10 (1954).

[589]. *The New Testament of Our Lord Jesus Christ.* Brussels, Life with God, 1965.

[590]. Nosovskiy, G. V. *Certain Statistical Methods of Researching Historical Sources, and Examples of their Application.* Source study methods of Russian social thinking; historical studies of the feudal epoch. A collection of academic publications. Moscow, The USSR History Institute, AS, 1989. 181-196.

[591]. Nosovskiy, G. V. *The Beginning of Our Era and the Julian Calendar.* Information processes and systems. Scientific and technological information, Series 2. Moscow, the National Science and Technology Information Institute, No. 5 (1992): 7-18.

[592]. Nosovskiy, G. V. *The True Dating of the Famous First Oecumenical Counsel and the Real Beginning of the AD Era.* An appendix of A. T. Fomenko's *Global Chronology.* Moscow, The MSU Mathematical Mechanics Department, 1993. 288-394.

[593]. Fomenko, A. T., and G. V. Nosovskiy. *The Determination of Original Structures in Intermixed Sequences.* Works of a vector and tensor analysis seminar. Moscow, MSU Press, Issue 22 (1985): 119-131.

[594]. Fomenko, A. T., and G. V. Nosovskiy. *Some Methods and Results of Intermixed Sequence Analysis.* Works of a vector and tensor analysis seminar. Moscow, MSU Press, Issue 23 (1988): 104-121.

[595]. Fomenko, A. T., and G. V. Nosovskiy. *Determining the Propinquity Quotient and Duplicate Identification in Chronological Lists.* Report theses of the 5th International Probability Theory and Mathematical Statistics Conference. Vilnius, The Lithuanian AS Institute of Mathematics and Cybernetics, Vol. 4 (1989): 111-112.

[596]. Fomenko, A. T., and G. V. Nosovskiy. *Statistical Duplicates in Ordered Lists with Subdivisions. Cybernetic Issues.* Semiotic research. Moscow, Scientific Counsel for the Study of the General Problem of Cybernetics. The USSR AS, 1989. 138-148.

[597]. Fomenko, A. T., and G. V. Nosovskiy. *Duplicate Identification in Chronological Lists (The Histogram Method of Related Name Distribution Frequencies).* Problems of stochastic model stability. Seminar works. Moscow, The National System Research Institute, 1989. 112-125.

[598]. Fomenko, A. T., and G. V. Nosovskiy. *Statistical Research of Parallel Occurrences and Biographies in British Chronological and Historical Materials.* Semiotics and Informatics. Moscow, The National System Research Institute, Issue 34 (1994): 205-233.

[599]. Fomenko, A. T., and G. V. Nosovskiy. *The New Chronology and the Concept of the Ancient History of Russia, Britain and Rome. (Facts. Statistics. Hypotheses.)* Vol. 1: *Russia.* Vol. 2: *England, Rome.* Moscow, the MSU Centre of Research and Pre-University Education, 1995. 2nd edition: 1996.

[600]. Fomenko, A. T., and G. V. Nosovskiy. *Mathematical and Statistical Models of Information Distribution in Historical Chronicles.* The Mathematical Issues of Cybernetics. Physical and Mathematical Literature (Moscow, Nauka), Issue 6 (1996): 71-116.

[601]. Fomenko, A. T., and G. V. Nosovskiy. *The Empire (Russia, Turkey, China, Europe and Egypt. New Mathematical Chronology of Antiquity).* Moscow, Faktorial, 1996. Re-editions: 1997, 1998 and 1999.

[602]. Fomenko, A. T., and G. V. Nosovskiy. *Russia and Rome. The Correctness of Our Understanding of Eurasian History.* Vols. 1 and 2. Moscow, Olimp, 1997. 2nd edition: 1999.

[603]. Fomenko, A. T., and G. V. Nosovskiy. *The New Chronology of Russia.* Moscow, Faktorial, 1997. Re-editions: 1998 and 1999.

[604]. Fomenko, A. T., and G. V. Nosovskiy. *The Mathematical Chronology of Biblical Events.* Moscow, Nauka, 1997.

[605]. Fomenko, A. T., and G. V. Nosovskiy. *The Biblical Russia.* Vols. 1 and 2. Moscow, Faktorial, 1998.

[606]. Fomenko, A. T., and G. V. Nosovskiy. *Horde-Russia as Reflected in Biblical Books.* Moscow, Anvik, 1998.

[607]. Fomenko, A. T., and G. V. Nosovskiy. *An Introduction to the New Chronology (Which Century is it Now?).* Moscow, Kraft and Lean, 1999.

[608]. Fomenko, A. T., and G. V. Nosovskiy. *The New Chronology of Russia, Britain and Rome.* Moscow, Anvik, 1999. A substantially revised and enlarged single-volume edition.

[608:1]. Fomenko, A. T., and G. V. Nosovskiy. *The New Chronology of Russia, Britain and Rome.* Moscow, Delovoi Express Financial, 2001.

[609]. Fomenko, A. T., and G. V. Nosovskiy. *The Biblical Russia. Selected Chapters I. (The Empire of Horde-Russia and the Bible. The New Mathematical Chronology of Antiquity. A History of Biblical Editions and Manuscripts. XI–*

XII century Events in the New Testament. The Pentateuch). Moscow, Faktorial, 1999.

[610]. Fomenko, A. T., and G. V. Nosovskiy. *A Reconstruction of Global History (The New Chronology)*. Moscow, Delovoi Express Financial, 1999.

[611]. Fomenko, A. T., and G. V. Nosovskiy. *Old Criticisms and the New Chronology*. The *Neva* magazine (St. Petersburg), No. 2 (1999): 143158.

[612]. Fomenko, A. T., and G. V. Nosovskiy. *The Biblical Russia. Selected Chapters II. (The Empire of Horde-Russia and the Bible. History of the XIV–XVI century in the Final Chapters of the Books of Kings. XV–XVI century History of the Pages of the Books of Esther and Judith. Reformation Epoch of the XVI–XVII century)*. Moscow, Faktorial, 2000.

[613]. Fomenko, A. T., and G. V. Nosovskiy. *A Reconstruction of Global History. The Research of 1999-2000 (The New Chronology)*. Moscow, Delovoi Express Financial, 2000.

[613:1]. Fomenko, A. T., and G. V. Nosovskiy. *The New Chronology of Egypt. The Astronomical Dating of the Ancient Egyptian Monuments. The Research of 2000-2002*. Moscow, Veche, 2002.

[613:2]. Fomenko, A. T., and Nosovskiy, G. V. *The New Chronology of Egypt. The Astronomical Dating of the Ancient Egyptian Monuments*. 2nd edition, re-worked and expanded. Moscow, Veche, 2003.

[614]. Newton, Robert. *The Crime of Claudius Ptolemy*. Moscow, Nauka, 1985. English original: Baltimore-London, John Hopkins University Press, 1977.

[615]. Olearius, Adam. *A Detailed Account of the Moscovian and Persian Journey of the Holstein Ambassadors in 1633, 1636 and 1639*. Translated from German by P. Barsov. Moscow, 1870.

[616]. Oleynikov, A. *The Geological Clock*. Leningrad, Nedra, 1975.

[617]. Orbini, Mavro. *A Historiographical Book on the Origins of the Names, the Glory and the Expansion of the Slavs. Compiled from many Historical Books through the Office of Marourbin, the Archimandrite of Raguzha*. Translated into Russian from Italian. Typography of St. Petersburg, 1722.

[618]. Orbini, Mavro. *Kingdom of the Slavs*. Sofia, Nauka i Izkustvo, 1983.

[618:1]. Oreshnikov, A. V. *Pre-1547 Russian Coins*. A reprint of the 1896 edition by the State Museum of History. Russian State Archive of Ancient Acts. Moscow, The Archaeographical Centre, 1996.

[619]. Orlenko, M. I. *Sir Isaac Newton. A Biographical Aperçu*. Donetsk, 1927.

[620]. Orlov, A. S. *Certain Style Characteristics of Russian History Fiction of the XVI–XVII century*. In *Russian Philological News*, Vol. 13, Book 4 (1908): 344-379.

[621]. *The Ostrog Bible (The Bible, or the Books of the Old and the New Covenant, in the Language of the Slavs)*. Ostrog, 1581. Reprinted as *The Ostrog Bible*. The Soviet Culture Fund Commission for the Publication of Literary Artefacts. Moscow-Leningrad, Slovo-Art, 1988. "The phototypic copy of the 1581 text was supervised by I. V. Dergacheva with references to the copies from the Scientific Library of A. M. Gorky Moscow State University."

[622]. *National History from the Earliest Days and until 1917*. Encyclopaedia, Vol. 1. Moscow, The Great Russian Encyclopaedia Publications, 1994.

[623]. Bavin, S. P., and G. V. Popov. *The Revelation of St. John as Reflected in the Global Literary Tradition*. The catalogue of an exhibition organized in Moscow by the Greek Embassy in 1994. A joint publication of the Greek Embassy and the State Library of Russia. Moscow, Indrik, 1995.

[623:1]. A postcard with an Egyptian zodiac. *The Creation Scene*. Egypt, El-Faraana Advertising & Printing, 2000.

[624]. *Historical and Folk Tale Aperçus. From Cheops to Christ*. A compilation. Translated from German. Moscow, 1890. Reprinted by the Moscow Int'l Translator School in 1993.

[625]. Pausanius. *A Description of Hellas, or a Voyage through Greece in II century AD*. Moscow, 1880. English edition: Pausanius. *Guide to Greece*. Harmondsworth, Penguin, 1979.

[626]. Makarevich, G. V., ed. *The Architectural Monuments of Moscow. The Earthenware Town*. Moscow, Iskusstvo, 1989-1990.

[627]. Posokhin, M. V., ed. *The Architectural Monuments of Moscow. KitaiGorod*. Moscow, Iskusstvo, 1982.

[628]. Makarevich, G. V., ed. *The Architectural Monuments of Moscow. White Town*. Moscow, Iskusstvo, 1989.

[629]. Makarevich, G. V., ed. *The Architectural Monuments of Moscow. Zamoskvorechye*. Moscow, Iskusstvo, 1994.

[630]. *Artefacts of Diplomatic Relations with the Roman Empire*. Vol. 1. St Petersburg, 1851.

[631]. Rybakov, B. A., ed. *Artefacts of the Kulikovo Cycle*. St. Petersburg, RAS, The Institute of Russian History. Blitz, the Russo-Baltic Information Centre, 1998.

[632]. *Literary Artefacts of Ancient Russia. The XI – Early XII century*. Moscow, Khudozhestvennaya Literatura, 1978.

[633]. *Literary Artefacts of Ancient Russia. The XII century*. Moscow, Khudozhestvennaya Literatura, 1980.

[634]. *Literary Artefacts of Ancient Russia. The XIII century*. Moscow, Khudozhestvennaya Literatura, 1981.

[635]. *Literary Artefacts of Ancient Russia. The XIV – mid-XV century*. Moscow, Khudozhestvennaya Literatura, 1981.

[636]. *Literary Artefacts of Ancient Russia. Second Half of the XV century*. Moscow, Khudozhestvennaya Literatura, 1982.

[637]. *Literary Artefacts of Ancient Russia. Late XV – Early XVI century*. Moscow, Khudozhestvennaya Literatura, 1984.

[638]. *Literary Artefacts of Ancient Russia. Mid-XVI century*. Moscow, Khudozhestvennaya Literatura, 1985.

[639]. *Literary Artefacts of Ancient Russia. Second Half of the XVI century*. Moscow, Khudozhestvennaya Literatura, 1986.

[640]. *Literary Artefacts of Ancient Russia. Late XVI – Early XVII century*. Moscow, Khudozhestvennaya Literatura, 1987.

[641]. *Significant Works in Russian Law.* Issue 2. Moscow, 1954.

[642]. *Significant Works in Russian Law.* Issue 3. Moscow, 1955.

[643]. Pannekuk, A. *The History of Astronomy.* Moscow, Nauka, 1966.

[644]. Parandowski, J. *Petrarch.* The *Inostrannaya Literatura (Foreign Literature)* magazine, No. 6 (1974). Also see: Parandowski, J. *Petrarca.* Warsaw, 1957.

[645]. Paradisis, Alexander. *The Life and Labours of Balthazar Cossas (Pope John XXIII).* Minsk, Belarus, 1980.

[646]. Pasek. *A Historical Description of Simon's Monastery in Moscow.* Moscow, 1843.

[647]. Romanenko, A. *The Patriarch Chambers of the Moscow Kremlin.* Moscow, The Moscow Kremlin State Museum and Reserve for History and Culture, 1994.

[648]. Pahimer, George. *The Story of Michael and Andronicus Palaeologi. The Reign of Michael Palaiologos.* St. Petersburg, 1862.

[648:1]. Pashkov, B. G. *Holy Russia – Russia – The Russian Empire. The Genealogical Tree of the Principal Russian Clans (862-1917).* Moscow, TsentrKom, 1996.

[649]. *The First Muscovite Princes.* In *Historical Portraits* series. Moscow, Ganna, 1992.

[650]. Perepyolkin, Y. A. *The Coup of Amenkhotep IV.* Part 1. Books 1 and 2. Moscow, Nauka, 1967.

[651]. *The Correspondence of Ivan the Terrible and Andrei Kurbskiy.* In *Literary Landmarks* series. Leningrad, Nauka, 1979. 2nd edition: Moscow, Nauka, 1993.

[652]. *The Song of Roland.* International Literature Collection. Moscow, Khudozhestvennaya Literatura, 1976. English edition by J. M. Dent & Sons, 1972.

[653]. Petrov, A. M. *The Great Silk Route. The Simplest, but Largely Unknown Facts.* Moscow, Vostochnaya Literatura, RAS, 1995.

[654]. Petruchenko, O. *Latin-Russian Dictionary.* Moscow, published by the V. V. Dumnov and the Heirs of Silayev Brothers, 1914. Reprinted by the Graeco-Latin Department of Y. A. Shichalin, 1994.

[654:1]. *The Maritime Voyage of St. Brendan (Navigation Sancti Brendani Abbatis saec X AD).* St. Petersburg, Azbuka-Klassika, 2002. English translation: *Navigatio Sancti Brendani Abbatis from Early Latin Manuscripts.* Ed., introd. and notes: C. Selmer, Notre Dame, 1959.

[655]. *Plan of the Imperial Capital City of Moscow, Created under the Supervision of Ivan Michurin, the Architect, in 1739. The First Geodetic Plan of Moscow.* The General Council of Ministers, Department of Geodetics and Cartography (the Cartographer Cooperative). Published together with a calendar for 1989.

[656]. Plano Carpini, G. del. *History of the Mongols.* William of Rubruck. *The Journey to the Oriental Countries. The Book of Marco Polo.* Moscow, Mysl, 1997. See also: *The Journey of William of Rubruck to the Eastern Parts of the World, 1253-55.* Prepared by W. W. Rockhill. 1900.

[657]. Plato. *Collected Works.* Vol. 3. Moscow, Mysl, 1972. English edition: *The Works of Plato.* Bohn's Classical Library, 1848.

[658]. Pletnyova, S. A. *The Khazars.* Moscow, Nauka, 1976.

[659]. Pleshkova, S. L. *Catherine of Medici. The Black Queen.* Moscow, Moscow University Press, 1994.

[660]. Plutarch. *Comparative Biographies.* Vol. 1: Moscow, USSR AN Press, 1961; Vol. 2: Moscow, USSR AN Press, 1963; Vol. 3: Moscow, Nauka, 1964. English edition: Plutarch. *The Lives of the Noble Graecians and Romans.* In *Great Books of the Western World* series. Vol. 13. Encyclopaedia Britannica, Inc. Chicago, University of Chicago, 1952 (2nd edition 1990). See also: Plutarch. *Plutarch's Lives.* London, Dilly, 1792.

[661]. Plyukhanova, M. B. *Subjects and Symbols of the Muscovite Kingdom.* St. Petersburg, Akropol, 1995.

[662]. *Kremlin. A Brief Guide.* Moscow, Moskovskiy Rabochiy, 1960.

[663]. *The Yearly Chronicle.* Part 1. Text and translation. Moscow-Leningrad, The USSR AN Press, 1950.

[664]. *The Yearly Chronicle.* Published in the *Dawn of the Russian Literature* series (XI – early XII century). Moscow, Khudozhestvennaya Literatura, 1978. 23-277.

[665]. *The Tale of Varlaam and Ioasaph.* Leningrad, Nauka, 1985.

[666]. Likhachev, D. S., ed. *The Tale of the Kulikovo Battle. The Text and the Miniatures of the Authorized Compilation of the XVI century.* Published by the XVI century manuscript kept in the USSR Academy of Sciences Library (The Authorized Compilation of Chronicles, Osterman's Vol. II, sheet 3 – 126 reverse). Leningrad, Aurora, 1984.

[666:1]. Podosinov, A. V., and A. M. Belov. *Lingua Latina. Latin-Russian Dictionary.* About 15,000 words. Moscow, Flinta, Nauka, 2000.

[667]. Pokrovskiy, N. N. *A Voyage in Search of Rare Books.* Moscow, Kniga. 2nd edition, 1988.

[668]. Polak, I. F. *A Course of General Astronomy.* Moscow, Gonti, 1938.

[669]. Polybius. *History in 40 Volumes.* Moscow, 1899.

[670]. *The Complete Symphony of the Canonical Books of the Holy Writ.* St. Petersburg, The Bible For Everybody, 1996.

[671]. *The Complete Collection of Russian Chonicles.* Vol. 33. Leningrad, Nauka, 1977.

[672]. *The Complete Collection of Russian Chonicles.* Vol. 35. Moscow, Nauka, 1980.

[673]. Polo, M. *The Journey.* Translated from French. Leningrad, 1940.

[674]. Poluboyarinova, M. D. *Russians in the Golden Horde.* Moscow, Nauka, 1978.

[674:1]. [*Pompeii*]. *Pompeii.* Album. Authors: Filippo Coarelli, Emilio de Albentiis, Maria Paola Guidobaldi, Fabricio Pesando, and Antonio Varone. Moscow, Slovo, 2002. Printed in Italy.

[674:2]. [*Pompeii*]. Nappo, Salvatore. *Pompeii.* Album. From the *World Wonder*

Atlas series. Moscow, Bertelsmann Media Moskau, 2001. English original: Salvatore Ciro Nappo. *Pompeii*. White Star, 1998, Vercelli, Italy.

[675]. Popovskiy, M. A. *Time Conquered. A Tale of Nikolai Morozov*. Moscow, Political Literature, 1975.

[676]. *The Portuguese-Russian and Russian-Portuguese Dictionary*. Kiev, Perun, 1999.

[677]. *The Successors of Marco Polo. Voyages of the Westerners into the Countries of the Three Indias*. Moscow, Nauka, 1968.

[678]. Pospelov, M. *The Benediction of Reverend Sergei*. *Moskva* magazine, 1990

[679]. Postnikov, A. V. *Maps of the Russian Lands: A Brief Review of the History of Geographical Studies and Cartography of Our Fatherland*. Moscow, Nash Dom – L'Age d'Homme, 1996.

[680]. Postnikov, M. M. *A Critical Research of the Chronology of the Ancient World*. Vols. 1-3. Moscow, Kraft and Lean, 2000. [A. T. Fomenko's remark: This book is a publication of a manuscript of more than 1000 pages written by Doctors of Physics and Mathematics A. S. Mishchenko and A. T. Fomenko. It was edited by M. M. Postnikov, and came out signed with his name. He acknowledges this fact in the preface to Vol. 1, on page 6, albeit cagily.]

[681]. Fomenko A. T., and M. M. Postnikov. *New Methods of Statistical Analysis of the Narrative and Digital Material of Ancient History*. Moscow, Scientific Counsel for the Study of the General Problem of Cybernetics, USSR AS, 1980. 1-36.

[682]. Fomenko A. T., and M. M. Postnikov. *New Methods of Statistical Analysis of the Narrative and Digital Material of Ancient History*. Scientific note of the Tartu University, works related to sign symbols. XV, Cultural Typology, Cultural Influence Feedback. Tartu University Press, Release 576 (1982): 24-43.

[683]. Postnikov, M. M. *The Greatest Mystification in the World?* In *Tekhnika i Nauka (Science & Technology)*, 1982, No. 7, pp. 28-33.

[684]. Potin, V. M. *Coins. Treasures. Collections. Numismatic essays*. St. Petersburg, Iskusstvo-SPb, 1993.

[685]. Potin, V. M. *Ancient Russia and the European States of the X–XIII century*. Leningrad, Sovetskiy Khudozhnik, 1968.

[685:1]. Pope-Hennessy, John. *Fra Angelico*. Album. Moscow, Slovo, 1996. Scala, 1995, Istituto Fotografico Editoriale.

[686]. Pokhlyobkin, V. V. *The Foreign Affairs of the Holy Russia, Russia and the USSR over the 1000 Years in Names, Dates and Facts. A Reference Book*. Moscow, Mezhdunarodnye Otnoshenya, 1992.

[687]. *Merited Academician N. A. Morozov. Memoirs*. Vols. 1 and 2. The USSR Academy of Sciences. Moscow, USSR AS Press, 1962.

[688]. *Orthodox Art and the Savvino-Storozhevsky Monastery*. Materials of scientific conferences dedicated to the 600th anniversary of the Savvino-Storozhevsky Monastery, 17 December 1997 and 22 September 1998. The Zvenigorod Museum of Architecture, History, and Arts. Zvenigorod, Savva Plus M, 1998.

[689]. Malinovskaya, N., ed. *Prado. Paintings.* Album. Translated from Spanish. Lunwerg Editores. Barcelona-Madrid, 1994. Russian translation: Moscow, MK-Import, 1999.

[690]. *Reverend Joseph Volotsky. The Illuminator.* Published by the Spaso-Preobrazhensky Monastery of Valaam. Blessed by the Holiest Patriarch of Moscow and the Entire Russia, Alexiy II. Moscow, 1993.

[691]. Priester, E. *A Brief History of Austria.* Moscow, IL, 1952. German edition: *Kurze Geschichte Österreichs.* Vienna, Globus, 1946.

[692]. Prishchepenko, V. N. *The Pages of Russian History.* Vol. 1: 1988. Vol. 2: 2000. Moscow, Profizdat.

[693]. *Problems of Museum Collection Formation and Studies of the State Museum of Religious History.* Leningrad, The RSFSR Ministry of Culture, publised by the State Museum of History of Religions, 1990.

[694]. Procopius of Caesarea. *On the Buildings.* The *Vestnik Drevnei Istorii (Courier of Ancient History)* magazine, No. 4 (1939): 201-298. See also: Procopius of Caesarea. *On the Buildings of Justinian.* London, Palestine Piligrim Society, 1888.

[695]. Procopius. *The Gothic War.* Moscow, The USSR AS Press, 1950.

[696]. Procopius. *The Gothic War. On the Buildings.* Moscow, Arktos, Vika-Press, 1996. See also: Procopius of Caesarea. *Procopius.* Vol. 7. London, William Heinemann; New York, Macmillan & Co. 1914-1940.

[697]. Procopius of Caesarea. *The Persian War. The War with the Vandals. Arcane History.* St. Petersburg, Aleteya, 1998.

[698]. Proskouriakov, V. M. *Johannes Gutenberg.* The *Celebrity Biographies* series. Moscow, the Literary Magazine Union, 1933.

[699]. Prokhorov, G. M. *The Tale of Batu-Khan's Invasion in Lavrenty's Chronicle.* Published as part of *The Russian Literary History Research. XI–XVII centuries.* Leningrad, Nauka, 1974.

[700]. *Book of Psalms.* Moscow, 1657. (Private collection.)

[701]. *The book of Psalms with Appendices.* Published in the *Great City of Moscow in the Year 7160 [1652 AD], in the Month of October, on the 1st Day.* New edition: Moscow, The Vvedenskaya Church of St. Trinity Coreligionist Typography, 1867.

[702]. Psellus, Michael. *Chronography.* Moscow, Nauka, 1978. English edition: *The Chronographia of Michael Psellus.* London, Routledge & Kegan Paul, 1953.

[703]. Pskovskiy, Y. P. *Novae and Supernovae.* Moscow, Nauka, 1974.

[704]. Ptolemy, Claudius. *Almagest, or the Mathematical Tractate in Thirteen Volumes.* Translated by I. N. Veselovskiy. Moscow, Nauka, Fizmatlit, 1998.

[705]. Poisson, A., N. A. Morozov, F. Schwarz, M. Eliade, and K. G. Jung. *The Theory and Symbols of Alchemy. The Great Work.* Kiev, Novy Akropol, Bront Ltd., 1995.

[706]. Mashkov, I. P., ed. *A Guide to Moscow.* Moscow, Muscovite Architectural Society for the Members of the V Convention of Architects in Moscow, 1913.

[707]. *The Voyage of Columbus. Diaries, Letters, Documents.* Moscow, The State Geographical Literature Press, 1952.

[708]. Putilov, Boris. *Ancient Russia in Personae. Gods, Heroes, People.* St. Petersburg, Azbuka, 1999.

[709]. Pushkin, A. *Collected Works.* Leningrad, The State Fiction Publishers, 1935.

[710]. *Pushkin A. in the Recollections of Contemporaries.* Two volumes. Moscow, Khudozhestvennaya Literatura, 1974.

[711]. *Pushkin's Memorial Places in Russia. A Guidebook.* Moscow, Profizdat, 1894.

[711:1]. Pylyaev, M. I. *The Old Petersburg. Accounts of the Capital's Past.* A reprint of A. S. Souvorov's 1889 St. Petersburg edition. Moscow, IKPA, 1990.

[712]. Lukovich-Pyanovich, Olga. *The Serbs . . . The Oldest of Nations.* Vols. 1-3. Belgrade, Miroslav, 1993-1994.

[713]. Pietrangeli, Carlo. *Vatican.* From the *Great Museums of the World* series. Moscow, Slovo, 1998. A translation of the Italian edition by Magnus Editioni, Udine, 1996.

[714]. *Five Centuries of European Drawings.* The drawings of old masters from the former collection of Franz König. The 1.10.1995-21.01.1996 exhibition catalogue. The Russian Federation Ministry of Culture, The State A. S. Pushkin Museum of Fine Art. Moscow-Milan, Leonardo Arte (versions in Russian and in English).

[715]. *The Radzivillovskaya Chronicle.* The text. The research. A description of the miniatures. St. Petersburg, Glagol; Moscow, Iskusstvo, 1994.

[716]. *The Radzivillovskaya Chronicle.* The Complete Collection of Russian Chronicles, Vol. 38. Leningrad, Nauka, 1989.

[717]. *Radiocarbon.* Collected articles. Vilnius, 1971.

[718]. *The Imprecision of Radiocarbon Datings.* The *Priroda (Nature)* magazine, No. 3 (1990): 117. (*New Scientist,* Vol. 123, No. 1684 (1989): 26).

[719]. Radzig, N. *The Origins of Roman Chronicles.* Moscow University Press, 1903.

[720]. *The Book of Rank. 1457-1598.* Moscow, Nauka, 1966.

[721]. Razoumov, G. A., and M. F. Khasin. *The Drowning cities.* Moscow, Nauka, 1978.

[722]. Wright, J. K. *The Geographical Lore of the Time of the Crusades. A Study in the History of Medieval Science and Tradition in Western Europe.* Moscow, Nauka, 1988. English original published in New York in 1925.

[722:1]. Reizer, V. I. *The Process of Joan of Arc.* Moscow-Leningrad, Nauka, 1964.

[723]. Fomenko, A. T., and S. T. Rachev. *Volume Functions of Historical Texts and the Amplitude Correlation Principle.* Source study methods of Russian social thinking historical studies of the feudal epoch. A collection of academic publications. Moscow, The USSR History Institute, AS, 1989. 161-180.

[724]. Rashid ad-Din. *History of the Mongols.* St. Petersburg, 1858.

[725]. Renan, J. *The Antichrist.* St. Petersburg, 1907. English edition: *Renan's Antichrist.* The Scott Library, 1899.

[726]. *Rome: Echoes of the Imperial Glory.* Translated from English by T. Azarkovich. The *Extinct Civilizations* series. Moscow, Terra, 1997. Original by Time-Life Books, 1994.

[727]. Rich, V. *Was there a Dark Age?* The *Khimia i Zhizn (Chemistry and Life)* magazine, No. 9 (1983): 84.

[728]. Riesterer, Peter P., and Roswitha Lambelet. *The Egyptian Museum in Cairo.* Cairo, Lehnert & Landrock, Orient Art Publishers, 1980. Russian edition, 1996.

[729]. Robert of Clari. *The Conquest of Constantinople.* Moscow, Nauka, 1986. English edition: McNeal, E. H. *The Conquest of Constantinople of Robert of Clari.* Translated with introduction and notes by E. Holmes McNeal. New York, 1936. Records of Civilization: Sources and Studies. Vol. XXIII. Reprint: New York, 1964, 1969.

[730]. Rogozina, Z. A. *The Earliest Days of Egyptian History.* Issue 2. Petrograd, A. F. Marx Typography, n.d.

[731]. Rozhdestvenskaya, L. A. *The Novgorod Kremlin. A Guide-book.* Lenizdat, 1980.

[732]. Rozhitsyn, V. S., and M. P. Zhakov. *The Origins of the Holy Books.* Leningrad, 1925.

[733]. Rozhkov, M. *N. A. Morozov – The Founding Father of the Dimension Number Analysis.* The *Successes of the Physical Sciences,* Vol. 49, Issue 1 (1953).

[734]. Rozanov, N. *History of the Temple of Our Lady's Birth in Staroye Simonovo, Moscow, Dedicated to its 500th Anniversary (1370-1870).* Moscow, Synodal Typography on Nikolskaya Street, 1870.

[735]. Romanyuk, S. *From the History of Small Muscovite Streets.* Moscow, 1988.

[735:1]. Romanyuk, S. *From the History of Small Muscovite Streets.* Moscow, Svarog, 2000.

[735:2]. Romanyuk, S. *The Lands of the Muscovite Villages.* Part I. Moscow, Svarog, 2001.

[735:3]. Romanyuk, S. *The Lands of the Muscovite Villages.* Part II. Moscow, Svarog, 1999.

[736]. *The Russian Academy of Sciences. Personae.* Three books. Book 1: 1724-1917. Book 2: 1918-1973. Book 3: 1974-1999. Moscow, Nauka, 1999.

[737]. Rossovskaya, V. A. *The Calendarian Distance of Ages.* Moscow, Ogiz, 1930.

[738]. *A Guide to the Paschalia for the Seminary Schools.* Moscow, The V. Gautier Typography, 1853. Reprinted in Moscow by Grad Kitezh in 1991.

[739]. Bleskina, O. N., comp. *An Illustrated book of Manuscripts of the USSR AS Library.* Catalogue for an exhibition of illustrated chronicles of the XI–XIX century written with roman letters. Leningrad, The USSR AS Library, 1991.

[740]. *Handwritten and Typeset Books. Collected Articles.* Moscow, Nauka, 1975.

[741]. *Manuscripts of the Late XV – early XVI century.* The Kirillo-Belozersk Collection, 275/532. The M. E. Saltykov-Shchedrin Public Library, St. Petersburg.

[742]. Roumyantsev, A. A. *Methods of Historical Analysis in the Works of Nikolai Aleksandrovich Morozov.* The Scientific Institute of P. F. Lesgaft Notes, Vol. 10. Leningrad, 1924.

[743]. Roumyantsev, A. A. *The Death and the Resurrection of the Saviour.* Moscow, Atheist, 1930.

[744]. Roumyantsev, N. V. *Orthodox Feasts.* Moscow, Ogiz, 1936.

[745]. *The Russian Bible. The Bible of 1499 and the Synodal Translation of the Bible.* Illustrated. 10 Vols. The Biblical Museum, 1992. Publishing department of the Muscovite Patriarchy, Moscow, 1992 (The Gennadievskaya Bible). Only the following volumes came out before the beginning of 2002: Vol. 4 (Book of Psalms), Vols. 7 and 8 (The New Testament), and Vol. 9 (Appendices, scientific descriptions). Vols. 7 and 8 were published by the Moscow Patriarchy in 1992; Vols. 4 and 9 published by the Novospassky Monastery, Moscow, 1997 (Vol. 4), 1998 (Vol. 9).

[746]. *The Pioneer of Russian Printing. A Brief Biography. Ivan Fedorov's "Alphabet" Published in 1578.* In collaboration with Translesizdat Ltd. Blessed by the Editing Board of the Muscovite Patriarchy. Moscow, Spolokhi, 2000.

[747]. *Russian Chronographer of 1512.* The Complete Collection of Russian Chronicles, Vol. 22. St. Petersburg, 1911.

[748]. Knyazevskaya, T. B., comp. *Russian Spiritual Chivalry.* Collected articles. Moscow, Nauka, 1996.

[749]. Leyn, K., ed. *Russian-German Dictionary.* 11th stereotype edition. Moscow, Russkiy Yazyk, 1991.

[750]. Dmitriev, N. K., ed. *Russian-Tartarian Dictionary.* The USSR AS, Kazan Affiliate of the Language, Literature and History Institute. Kazan, Tatknigoizdat, 1955.

[750:1]. Mustaioki, A., and E. Nikkilä. *Russian-Finnish Didactic Dictionary.* Abt. 12,500 words. Moscow, Russkiy Yazyk, 1982.

[751]. Shcherba, L. V., and M. R. Matousevich. *Russian-French Dictionary.* 9th stereotype edition. Moscow, Sovetskaya Encyclopaedia, 1969.

[752]. Rybakov, B. A. *From the History of Ancient Russia and Its Culture.* Moscow, MSU Press, 1984.

[753]. Rybakov, B. A. *The Kiev Russia and Russian Principalities. The XII–XIII century.* Moscow, Nauka, 1982, 1988.

[754]. Rybakov, B. A. *The Kiev Russia and Russian Principalities.* Moscow, Nauka, 1986.

[755]. Rybnikov, K. A. *History of Mathematics.* Moscow, MSU Press, 1974.

[756]. Ryabtsevitch, V. N. *What the Coins Tell Us.* Minsk, Narodnaya Asveta, 1977.

[757]. Savelyev, E. P. *Cossacks and their History.* Vols. 1 and 2. Vladikavkaz, 1991. A reprint of E. Savelyev's *Ancient History of the Cossacks.* Novocherkassk, 1915.

[758]. Savelyeva, E. A. *Olaus Magnus and his "History of the Northern Peoples."* Leningrad, Nauka, 1983. [Olaus Magnus. *Historia de gentibus septentrionalibus,* 1555].

[759]. *Prince Obolensky's Almanach.* Part 1, Sections 1-7. N.p., 1866.

[760]. Suetonius Caius Tranquillius. *History of the Twelve Caesars.* Moscow, Nau-

ka, 1966. See also the English edition: New York, AMS Press, 1967; as well as the one titled *The Twelve Caesars.* London, Folio Society, 1964.

[760:1]. *Collected Historical and Cultural Monuments of the Tatarstan Republic. Vol. 1. Administrative regions.* Kazan, Master Line, 1999.

[761]. *The General Catalogue of Slavic and Russian Handwritten Books Kept in USSR: The XI–XIII century.* Moscow, 1984.

[762]. *St. Stephen of Perm.* The *Old Russian Tales of Famous People, Places and Events* series. Article, text, translation from Old Russian, commentary. St. Petersburg, Glagol, 1995.

[763]. *Holy Relics of Old Moscow.* Russian National Art Library. Moscow, Nikos, Kontakt, 1993.

[763:1]. Stogov, Ilya, comp. *Holy Writings of the Mayans: Popol-Vukh, Rabinal-Achi.* Translated by R. V. Kinzhalov. With *The Report of Yucatan Affairs* by Brother Diego de Landa attached, translated by Y. V. Knorozov. The *Alexandrian Library* series. St. Petersburg, Amphora, 2000.

[764]. Semashko, I. I. *100 Great Women.* Moscow, Veche, 1999.

[765]. Sunderland, I. T. *Holy Books as Regarded by Science.* Gomel, Gomelskiy Rabochiy Western Regional, 1925.

[766]. Sergeyev, V. S. *The History of Ancient Greece.* Moscow-Leningrad, Ogiz, 1934.

[767]. Sergeyev, V. S. *Essays on the History of the Ancient Rome.* Vols. 1 and 2. Moscow, Ogiz, 1938.

[768]. Sizov, S. *Another Account of the Three "Unidentified" Sepulchres of the Arkhangelsky Cathedral of the Moscow Kremlin. Materials and Research.* Iskusstvo (Moscow), No. 1 (1973).

[768:1]. Shevchenko, V. F., ed. *Simbirsk and its Past. An Anthology of Texts on Local History.* Oulianovsk, Culture Studies Lab, 1993. The compilation includes the book by M. F. Superanskiy titled *Simbirsk and its Past (1648-1898). A Historical Account,* among others. Simbirsk, The Simbirsk Regional Scientific Archive Commission, The O. V. Mourakhovskaya Typography, 1899.

[769]. Sinelnikov, Vyacheslav (Rev. V. Sinelnikov). *The Shroud of Turin at Dawn of the New Era.* Moscow, Sretensky Friary, 2000.

[769:1]. Sinha, N. K., Banerjee, A. C. *History of India.* Moscow, Inostrannaya Literatura, 1954. English original: Calcutta, 1952.

[770]. Sipovskiy, V. D. *Native Antiquity: History of Russia in Accounts and Pictures.* Vol. 1: IX–XVI century. St. Petersburg, The V. F. Demakov Typography, 1879, 1888. Vol. 2: XIV–XVII century. St. Petersburg, D. D. Poluboyarinov Publishing House, 1904. Reprinted: Moscow, Sovremennik, 1993.

[771]. *The Tale of the Mamay Battle.* Facsimile edition. Moscow, Sovetskaya Rossiya, 1980.

[772]. *A Tale of the Lord's Passion.* Part of the Russian handwritten collection of Christian works in Church Slavonic. Private collection. The XVIII–XIX century.

[772:1]. *The Scythians, the Khazars and the Slavs. Ancient Russia. To the Centen-*

nary since the Birth of M. I. Artamonov. Report theses for the international scientific conference. St. Petersburg, State Hermitage, the State University of St. Petersburg, the RAS Institute of Material Culture History.

[773]. Skornyakova, Natalya. *Old Moscow. Engravings and Lithographs of the XVI–XIX Century from the Collection of the State Museum of History.* Moscow, Galart, 1996.

[774]. Skromnenko, S. (Stroev, S. M.) *The Inveracity of the Ancient Russian History and the Error of the Opinions Deeming Russian Chronicles Ancient.* St. Petersburg, 1834.

[775]. Skrynnikov, R. G. *The Reign of Terror.* St. Petersburg, Nauka, 1992.

[776]. Skrynnikov, R. G. *Ivan the Terrible.* Moscow, Nauka, 1975. The 2nd edition came out in 1983.

[777]. Skrynnikov, R. G. *Boris Godunov.* Moscow, Nauka, 1983.

[778]. Skrynnikov, R. G. *The State and the Church in Russia. The XIV–XVI Century. Eminent Figures in the Russian Church.* Novosibirsk, Nauka, Siberian Affiliate, 1991.

[779]. Skrynnikov, R. G. *The Tragedy of Novgorod.* Moscow, Sabashnikov, 1994.

[780]. Skrynnikov, R. G. *Russia before the "Age of Turmoil."* Moscow, Mysl, 1981.

[781]. *The Slavic Mythology. An Encyclopaedic Dictionary.* Moscow, Ellis Luck, 1995.

[781:0]. Tsepkov, A., comp. *The Slavic Chronicles.* St. Petersburg, Glagol,1996.

[781:1]. *A Dictionary of Russian Don Dialects,* Vols. 1 and 2. Rostov-on-Don, Rostov University Press, 1991.

[782]. *Dictionary of the Russian Language in the XI–XVII centuries.* Edition 1. Moscow, Nauka, 1975.

[783]. *Dictionary of the Russian Language in the XI–XVII centuries.* Edition 2. Moscow, Nauka.

[784]. *Dictionary of the Russian Language in the XI–XVII centuries.* Edition 3. Moscow, Nauka.

[785]. *Dictionary of the Russian Language in the XI–XVII centuries.* Edition 5. Moscow, Nauka.

[786]. *Dictionary of the Russian Language in the XI–XVII centuries.* Edition 6. Moscow, Nauka, 1979.

[787]. *Dictionary of the Russian Language in the XI–XVII centuries.* Edition 7. Moscow, Nauka, 1980.

[788]. *Dictionary of the Russian Language in the XI–XVII centuries.* Edition 8. Moscow, Nauka.

[789]. *Dictionary of the Russian Language in the XI–XVII centuries.* Edition 11. Moscow, Nauka, 1986.

[790]. *Dictionary of the Russian Language in the XI–XVII centuries.* Edition 13. Moscow, Nauka, 1987.

[791]. *Dictionary of the Russian Language in the XI–XVII centuries.* Edition 19. Moscow, Nauka.

[792]. Smirnov, A. P. *The Scythians.* The USSR AS Institute of Archaeology. Moscow, Nauka, 1966.

[793]. Smirnov, F. *Christian Liturgy in the First Three Centuries.* Kiev, 1874.

[794]. Soboleva, N. A. *Russian Seals.* Moscow, Nauka, 1991.

[795]. *A Collection of State Edicts and Covenants.* Moscow, 1894.

[796]. *The Soviet Encyclopaedic Dictionary.* Moscow, Sovetskaya Encyclopaedia, 1979.

[797]. *The Soviet Encyclopaedic Dictionary.* Moscow, Sovetskaya Encyclopaedia, 1984.

[797:1]. *The Great Treasures of the World.* Gianni Guadalupi, ed. Moscow, Astrel, AST, 2001. Italian original: *I grandi tresori – l'arte orafa dall' antico egitto all XX secolo.* Edizioni White Star, 1998.

[798]. Solovyov, V. *Collected Works.* Vol. 6. St. Petersburg, 1898.

[799]. Solovyov, S. M. *Collected Works.* Book 4, Vols. 7-8. Moscow, Mysl, 1989.

[800]. Solovyov, S. M. *Collected Works.* Book 6. Moscow, Mysl, 1991.

[800:1]. Solovyov, S. M. *The History of the Ancient Russia.* Moscow, Prosveshche-nie, 1992.

[801]. Solonar, P. *Most Probably Fiction...* The *Tekhnika i Nauka* magazine, No. 4 (1983): 28-32.

[802]. *The Reports of the Imperial Orthodox Society of Palestine.* April 1894. St. Petersburg, 1894.

[803]. Palamarchuk, Pyotr, comp. *Fourty Times Fourty. A Concise Illustrated History of All the Churches in Moscow.* 4 volumes. Moscow, Kniga i Biznes Ltd., Krom Ltd., 1995.

[804]. Sotnikova, M. P. *The Oldest Russian Coins of the X–XI century. Catalogue and Study.* Moscow, Banki i Birzhi, 1995.

[805]. *The Spaso-Andronikov Monastery. A scheme. The Central Andrey Roublyov Museum of Ancient Russian Culture and Art.* Moscow, MO Sintez, 1989.

[806]. Spasskiy, I. G. *The Russian Monetary System.* Leningrad, Avrora, 1970.

[807]. Spasskiy, I. G. *The Russian "Yefimki." A Study and a Catalogue.* Novosibirsk, Nauka, Siberian Affiliation, 1988.

[808]. Speranskiy, M. N. *Cryptography in Southern Slavic and Russian Literary Artefacts.* Published in the *Encyclopaedia of Slavic Philology* series. Leningrad, 1929.

[808:1]. Spiridonov, A. M., and O. A. Yarovoy. *The Valaam Monastery: from Apostle Andrew to Hegumen Innocent (Historical Essays of the Valaam Monastery).* Moscow, Prometei, 1991.

[809]. Spirina, L. M. *The Treasures of the Sergiev Posad State Reserve Museum of Art and History. Ancient Russian Arts and Crafts.* Nizhny Novgorod, Nizh-poligraf, n.d.

[810]. *Contentious Issues of Native History of the XI–XVIII century.* Report theses and speeches of the first readings dedicated to the memory of A. A. Zimin. 13-18 May, 1990. Moscow, The USSR AS, Moscow State Institute of Historical and Archival Science, 1990.

[811]. Brouyevich, N. G., ed. *220 Years of the USSR Academy of Sciences. 1725-1945.* Moscow-Leningrad, The USSR AS Press, 1945.

[812]. *Mediaeval Decorative Stitching. Byzantium, the Balkans, Russia.* Catalogue of an exhibition. The XVIII Int'l Congress of Byzantine Scholars. Moscow, 8-15 August, 1991. Moscow, The USSR Ministry of Culture. State Museums of the Moscow Kremlin, 1991.

[813]. Sobolev, N. N., ed. *The Old Moscow.* Published by the Commission for the Studies of Old Moscow of the Imperial Archaeological Society of Russia. Issues 1, 2. Moscow, 1914 (Reprinted: Moscow, Stolitsa, 1993).

[814]. *A Dictionary of Old Slavic (by the X–XI century Manuscripts).* Moscow, Russkiy Yazyk, 1994.

[815]. Starostin, E. V. *Russian History in Foreign Archives.* Moscow, Vysshaya Shkola, 1994.

[815:1]. Stelletsky, I. Y. *In Search of the Library of Ivan the Terrible.* The *Mysteries of Russian History* series. Moscow, Sampo, 1999.

[816]. Stepanov, N. V. *The New Style and the Orthodox Paschalia.* Moscow, 1907.

[817]. Stepanov, N. V. *The Calendarian and Chronological Reference Book (for the Solution of Chronographical Time Problems).* Moscow, Synodal typography, 1915.

[817:1]. Pletneva, S. A., volume ed. *The Eurasian Steppes in the Middle Ages.* Collected works. In the *USSR Archaeology* series. B. A. Rybakov, general ed. Moscow, Nauka, 1981.

[818]. Stingl, Miloslav. *Mysteries of the Indian Pyramids.* Transl. from Czech by I. O. Malevich. Moscow, Progress, 1982.

[819]. Strabo. *Geography.* Moscow, Ladomir, 1994. English edition: Jones, H.L. *The Geography of Strabo. With an English translation. I–VIII.* London, 1917-1932.

[820]. *Builders of the Burial Mounds and Dwellers of the Caves.* The *Extinct Civilizations* encyclopaedia. Moscow, Terra, 1998. Translated from English by E. Krasoulin. Original edition: Time-Life Books BV, 1992.

[821]. Struyck, D. J. *A Brief Account of the History of Mathematics.* Moscow, Nauka, 1969.

[821:1]. Suzdalev, V. E. *Kolomenskoye – "Memory for Ages."* Moscow, Praktik-A, 1993.

[822]. Sukina, L. B. *History of Esther in the Russian Cultrure of the Second Half of the XVII century.* Part of the compilation: Melnik, A. G., ed. *History and Culture of the land of Rostov.* 1998. Collected essays. Rostov, The Rostov Kremlin State Museum and Reserve, 1999.

[823]. Suleimanov, Olzhas. *Az and Ya.* Alma-Ata, Zhazushy, 1975.

[823:1]. Sukhoroukov, Alexander. *From the History of Cards. The Cards Don't Lie!* The *Bridge in Russia* magazine, No. 1 (18) (2002), pp. 78-80. Moscow, Minuvsheye.

[824]. Sytin, P. V. *From the History of Russian Streets.* Moscow, Moskovskiy Rabochiy, 1958.

[825]. Sytin, P. V. *The Toponymy of Russian Streets.* Moscow, 1959.

[826]. Samuels, Ruth. *Following the Paths of Hebraic History.* Moscow, Art-Business-Centre, 1993.

[827]. Tabov, Jordan. *The Decline of Old Bulgaria.* Sofia, Morang, 1997. Russian transl.: Moscow, Kraft and Lean, 2000.

[828]. Tabov, Jordan. *The New Chronology of the Balkans. The Old Bulgaria.* Sofia, PCM-1, 2000.

[828:1]. Tabov, Jordan. *When did the Kiev Russia Become Baptized?* St. Petersburg, Neva. Moscow, Olma, 2003.

[829]. Rakhmanliev, R., comp. *Tamerlane. The Epoch. The Person. The Actions.* Collected works. Moscow, Gourash, 1992.

[830]. Tantlevskiy, I. R. *History and Ideology of the Qumran Community.* St. Petersburg, the RAS Institute of Oriental Studies, 1994.

[830:1]. Tate, Georges. *The Crusades.* Moscow, Olimp, Astrel, Ast, 2003.

[831]. *Tartarian-Russian Didactic Dictionary.* Moscow, Russkiy Yazyk, 1992.

[832]. Tatishchev, V. N. *Collected Works in Eight Volumes.* Moscow, Ladomir, 1994-1996.

[833]. Tacitus, Cornelius. *Collected Works.* Vols. I, II. Leningrad, Nauka, 1969. English ed.: *The Works of Tacitus.* London, Cornelii Taciti Historiarum libri qui supersunt. Published by Dr. Carl Heraeus. 4th ed.: Leipzig, G. Teubner, 1885.

[834]. *The Works of Maxim the Confessor.* The œuvres of the Holy Fathers in Russian translation. Vol. 69. The Moscow Seminary Academy, 1915.

[835]. *The Works of Nicephor, the Archbischop of Constantinople.* Moscow, 1904.

[836]. *The Works of Nile, the Holy Pilgrim of Sinai.* The œuvres of the Holy Fathers in Russian translation. Vols. 31-33. The Moscow Seminary Academy, 1858-1859.

[837]. *The Works of St. Isidore the Pelusiote.* The œuvres of the Holy Fathers in Russian translation. Vols. 34-36. The Moscow Seminary Academy, 1859-1860.

[838]. Tvorogov, O. V. *Ancient Russia: Events and People.* St. Petersburg, Nauka, 1994.

[839]. Tvorogov, O. V. *The Ryurikovichi Princes. Short Biographies.* Moscow, Russkiy Mir, 1992.

[840]. Tereshchenko, Alexander. *A Final Study of the Saray Region, with a Description of the Relics of the Desht-Kipchak Kingdom.* Scientific Notes of the Imperial Academy of Sciences, the 1st and 3rd Department. Vol. 2. St. Petersburg, 1854. 89-105.

[841]. Tikhomirov, M. N. *Old Moscow. The XII–XV century. Mediaeval Russia as the International Crossroads. XIV–XV century.* Moscow, Moskovskiy Rabochiy, 1992.

[842]. Tikhomirov, M. N. *Russian Culture of the X–XIII century.* Moscow, 1968.

[843]. Tikhomirov, M. N. *Mediaeval Moscow in the XIV–XV century.* Moscow, 1957.

[844]. Tokmakov, I. F. *A Historical and Archaeological Description of the Moscow Stauropigial Monastery of St. Simon.* Issues 1 and 2, Moscow, 1892-1896.

[845]. Lopukhin, A. P., ed. *Explanatory Bible, or the Commentary to all of the*

Books of the Holy Writ, from both the Old and the New Covenant. Vols. 1-12. Petersburg, published by the heirs of A. P. Lopukhin, 1904-1913. (2nd edition: Stockholm, the Bible Translation Institute, 1987).

[846]. Toll, N. P. *The Saviour's Icon from K. T. Soldatenkov's Collection.* Moscow, 1933.

[847]. Tolochko, P. P. *The Ancient Kiev.* Kiev, Naukova Dumka, 1976.

[848]. Tolstaya, Tatyana. *The River Okkerville. Short Stories.* Moscow, Podkova, 1999.

[849]. Troels-Lund, T. *The Sky and the Weltanschauung in the Flux of Time.* Odessa, 1912. German edition: Troels-Lund, T. *Himmelsbild und Weltanschauung im Wandel der Zeiten.* Leipzig, B. G. Teubner, 1929.

[850]. Tronskiy, I. M. *The History of Ancient Literature.* Leningrad, Uchpedgiz, 1947.

[850:1]. Trofimov, Zhores. *The N. M. Karamzin Memorial in Simbirsk. Known and Unknown Facts.* Moscow, Rossia Molodaya, 1992.

[851]. *Trojan Tales. Mediaeval Courteous Novels on the Trojan War by the Russian Chronicles of the XVI and XVII century.* Leningrad: Nauka, 1972.

[851:1]. Thulsi Das. *The Ramayana, or Ramacharitamanasa. The Multitude of Rama's Heroic Deeds.* Translated from Hindi by Academician A. P. Barannikov. Moscow-Leningrad, The USSR AS, Institute of Oriental Studies. Published by the USSR Academy of Sciences in 1948.

[852]. Tunmann. *The Khans of Crimea.* Simferopol, Tavria, 1991.

[853]. Turaev, B. A. *The History of the Ancient Orient.* Moscow, Ogiz, 1936.

[854]. Shcheka, Y. V. *The Turkish-Russian Dictionary.* Abt. 18,000 words. 3rd stereotype edition. Moscow, Citadel, 2000.

[855]. Turkhan, Gian. Istanbul. Gate to the Orient. Istanbul, Orient, 1996 (in Russian).

[855:1]. *Turkey. The Book of Wanderings. A Historical Guide-book.* Moscow, Veche, Khartia, 2000.

[856]. *A Millennium since the Baptism of Russia.* The materials of the International Ecclesian and Historical Conference (Kiev, 21-28 July, 1986). Moscow, Moscow Patriarchy, 1988.

[857]. Ouzdennikov, V. V. *Russian Coins. 1700-1917.* Moscow, Finances and Statistics, 1986.

[857:1]. *The Ukrainian Books Printed in Cyrillics in the XVI–XVII century.* A catalogue of editions kept in the V. I. Lenin State Library of USSR. Issue I. 1574 – 2nd half of the XVII century. Moscow, The State V. I. Lenin Library of the Lenin Order. Rare books department. 1976.

[858]. *The Streets of Moscow. A Reference Book.* Moscow, Moskovskiy Rabochiy, 1980.

[859]. *The Ural Meridian. Topical Itineraries. A Reference Guide-book.* Chelyabinsk, The Southern Ural Press, 1986.

[860]. Ousanovich, M. I. *The Scientific Foresight of N. A. Morozov. The Successes of Chemistry,* Vol. 16, Issue 3 (1947).

[861]. Ouspensky, D. N. *Modern Problems of Orthodox Theology.* The *Moscow Patriarchy* magazine, No. 9 (1962): 64-70.

[862]. *The Writ. The Pentateuch of Moses (from the Genesis to the Revelation).* Translation, introduction, and comments by I. S. Shifman. Moscow, Respublika, 1993.

[863]. Fyson, Nance. *The Greatest Treasures of the World. An Atlas of the World's Wonders.* Moscow, Bertelsmann Media Moskau, 1996. Mondruck Graphische Betriebe GmbH, Güntherslau (Germany), 1996. Translated from the English edition published by AA Publishing (a trading name of Automobile Association Development Limited, whose registred office is Norfolk House, Priestly Road, Basing-stoke, Hampshire RG24 9NY).

[864]. Falkovich, S. I. *Nikolai Alexandrovich Morozov, His Life and Works on Chemistry.* The *Priroda (Nature)* magazine, No. 11 (1947).

[865]. Falkovich, S. I. *Nikolai Alexandrovich Morozov as a Chemist (1854-1946).* The *USSR AS Courier,* Chemical Studies Department, No. 5 (1947).

[866]. Fasmer, M. *An Etymological Dictionary of the Russian Language.* Vols. 1-4. Translated from German. Moscow, Progress, 1986-1987.

[867]. [Fedorov]. *Ivan Fedorov [The Alphabet].* A facsimile edition. Moscow, Prosveshchenie, 1974.

[868]. Fedorov, V. V., and A. T. Fomenko. *Statistical Estimation of Chronological Nearness of Historical Texts.* A collection of articles for the *Problems of stochastic model stability* magazine. Seminar works. The National System Research Institute, 1983. 101-107. English translation published in the *Journal of Soviet Mathematics,* Vol. 32, No. 6 (1986): 668-675.

[869]. Fedorov-Davydov, G. A. *The Coins of the Muscovite Russia.* Moscow, MSU Press, 1981.

[870]. Fedorov-Davydov, G. A. *The Coins of the Nizhny Novgorod Principality.* Moscow, MSU Press, 1989.

[870:1]. Fedorov-Davydov, G. A. *Burial Mounds, Idols and Coins.* Moscow, Nauka, 1968.

[871]. Fedorov-Davydov, G. A. *Eight Centuries of Taciturnity.* The *Nauka i Zhizn (Science and Life)* magazine, No. 9 (1966): 74-76.

[872]. Fedorova, E. V. *Latin Epigraphics.* Moscow University Press, 1969.

[873]. Fedorova, E. V. *Latin Graffiti.* Moscow University Press, 1976.

[874]. Fedorova, E. V. *Imperial Rome in Faces.* Moscow University Press, 1979.

[875]. Fedorova, E. V. *Rome, Florence, Venice. Historical and Cultural Monuments.* Moscow University Press, 1985.

[876]. Theophilactus Simocattas. *History.* Moscow, Arktos, 1996.

[876:1]. Fersman, A. E. *Tales of Gemstones.* Moscow, Nauka, 1974.

[877]. Flavius, Joseph. *The Judean War.* Minsk, Belarus, 1991.

[878]. Flavius, Joseph. *Judean Antiquities.* Vols. 1, 2. Minsk, Belarus, 1994.

[879]. *Florentine Readings: The Life and Culture of Italy. Summer Lightnings.* Collected essays, translated by I. A. Mayevsky. Moscow, 1914.

[880]. Florinsky, V. M. *Primeval Slavs according to the Monuments of their Pre-Historic Life.* Tomsk, 1894.

[881]. Voigt, G. *The Renaissance of the Classical Literature.* Vols. I and II. Moscow, 1885. German edition: *Die Wiederbelebung des classischen Altertums oder das erste Jahrhundert des Humanismus.* Berlin, G. Reimer, 1893.

[882]. Foley, John. *The Guinness Encyclopaedia of Signs and Symbols.* Moscow, Veche, 1996. Original by Guinness Publishing Ltd., 1993.

[883]. Fomenko, A. T. "On the Calculations of the Second Derivative of Lunar Elongation." The problems of the mechanics of navigated movement. *Hierarchic systems.* The Inter-University Collection of Scientific Works. Perm, 1980. 161-166.

[884]. Fomenko, A. T. "Several Statistical Regularities of Information Density Disribution in Texts with Scales." *Semiotics and Informatics.* Moscow, The National Scientific and Technical Information Institute Publication, Issue 15 (1980): 99-124.

[885]. Fomenko, A. T. *Informative Functions and Related Statistical Regularities.* Report theses of the 3rd International Probability Theory and Mathematical Statistics Conference in Vilnius, the Lithuanian Academy of Sciences Institute of Mathematics and Cybernetics, 1981, Volume 2, pages 211-212.

[886]. Fomenko, A. T. *Duplicate Identification Methods and some of their Applications.* In *Doklady AN SSSR* (The USSR Academy of Sciences), Vol. 256, No. 6 (1981): 1326-1330.

[887]. Fomenko, A. T. *On the Qualities of the Second Derivative of Lunar Elongation and Related Statistical Regularities.* The Issues of Computational and Applied Mathematics. A collection of academic works. The Academy of Sciences of the Soviet Republic of Uzbekistan. Tashkent, Issue 63 (1981): 136-150.

[888]. Fomenko, A. T. *New Experimental Statistical Methods of Dating the Ancient Events and their Applications to the Global Chronology of the Ancient and Mediaeval World.* Pre-print. Order No. 3672, No. BO7201. Moscow, State Committee for Radio and TV Broadcasting, 1981. 1-100. English translation: Fomenko, A. T. *Some new empirical-statistical methods of dating and the analysis of present global chronology.* London, The British Library, Department of Printed Books. 1981. Cup. 918/87.

[889]. Fomenko, A. T. *Calculating the Second Derivative of Lunar Elongation and Related Statistical Regularities in the Distribution of Some Astronomical Data.* In *Operational and Automatic System Research,* Issue 20 (1982): 98-113. Kiev University Press.

[890]. Fomenko, A. T. *Concerning the Mystification Issue.* In *Science and Technology,* No. 11 (1982): 26-29.

[891]. Fomenko, A. T. *New Empirico-Statistical Method of Ordering Texts and Applications to Dating Problems.* In *Doklady AN SSSR* (The USSR Academy of Sciences Publications), Vol. 268, No. 6 (1983): 1322-1327.

[892]. Fomenko, A. T. *Distribution Geometry for Entire Points in Hyperregions.* The Vector and Tensor Analysis Seminar works (Moscow, MSU Press), Issue 21 (1983): 106-152.

[893]. Fomenko, A. T. *The Author's Invariant of Russian Literary Texts.* Methods

of Qualitative Analysis of Narrative Source Texts. Moscow, The USSR History Institute (The USSR Academy of Sciences), 1983. 86-109.

[894]. Fomenko, A. T. *The Global Chronological Map*. In *Chemistry and Life*, No. 11 (1983): 85-92.

[895]. Fomenko, A. T. *New Methods of the Chronologically Correct Ordering of Texts and their Applications to the Problems of Dating the Ancient Events.* Operational and Automatic System Research (Kiev University Press), Issue 21 (1983): 40-59.

[896]. Fomenko, A. T. *Methods of Statistical Processing of Parallels in Chronological Text and the Global Chronological Map.* Operational and Automatic System Research (Kiev University Press), Issue 22 (1983): 40-55.

[897]. Fomenko, A. T. *Statistical Frequency Damping Analysis of Chronological Texts and Global Chronological Applications.* Operational and Automatic System Research (Kiev University Press), Issue 24 (1984): 49-66.

[898]. Fomenko, A. T. *New Empirico-Statistical Method of Parallelism Determination and Duplicate Dating.* Problems of stochastic model stability. Seminar works. The National System Research Institute, Moscow, 1984. 154-177.

[899]. Fomenko, A. T. *Frequency Matrices and their Applications to Statistical Processing of Narrative Sources.* Report theses of the "Complex Methods of Historical Studies from Antiquity to Contemporaneity" conference. The Commission for Applying Natural Scientific Methods to Archaeology. Moscow, The USSR History Institute (The USSR Academy of Sciences), 1984. 135-136.

[900]. Fomenko, A. T. *Informative Functions and Related Statistical Regularities.* Statistics. Probability. Economics. The *Academic Statistical Notes* series. Vol. 49. Moscow, Nauka, 1985. 335-342.

[901]. Fomenko, A. T. *Duplicates in Mixed Sequences and the Frequency Damping Principle.* Report theses of the 4th Int'l Probability Theory and Mathematical Statistics Conference in Vilnius, the Lithuanian Academy of Sciences Institute of Mathematics and Cybernetics, Vol. 3. 1985. 246-248.

[902]. Fomenko, A. T., and L. E. Morozova. *Several Issues of Statistical Annual Account Source Processing Methods.* Mathematics in mediaeval narrative source studies. Moscow, Nauka, 1986. 107-129.

[903]. Fomenko, A. T. *Identifying Dependencies and Layered Structures in Narrative Texts.* Problems of stochastic model stability. Seminar works. The National System Research Institute, 1987. 33-45.

[904]. Fomenko, A. T. *Methods of Statistical Analysis of Narrative Texts and Chronological Applications. (The Identification and the Dating of Derivative Texts, Statistical Ancient Chronology, Statistics of the Ancient Astronomical Reports).* Moscow, Moscow University Press, 1990.

[905]. Fomenko, A. T. *Statistical Chronology.* New facts in life, science and technology. The *Mathematics and Cybernetics"* series, No. 7. Moscow, Znanie, 1990.

[906]. Fomenko, A. T. *Global Chronology. (A Research of Classical and Mediaeval*

History. Mathematical Methods of Source Analysis.) Moscow, MSU Department of Mathematics and Mechanics, 1993.

[907]. Fomenko, A. T. *A Criticism of the Traditional Chronology of Antiquity and the Middle Ages (What Century is it Now?).* A précis. Moscow, MSU Department of Mathematics and Mechanics, 1993.

[908]. Fomenko, A. T. *Methods of Mathematical Analysis of Historical Texts. Chronological Applications.* Moscow, Nauka, 1996.

[909]. Fomenko, A. T. *The New Chronology of Greece. Antiquity in the Middle Ages.* Vols. 1 and 2. Moscow, MSU Centre of Research and Pre-University Education, 1996.

[910]. Fomenko, A. T. *Statistical Chronology. A Mathematical View of History. What Century is it Now?* Belgrade, Margo-Art, 1997.

[911]. Fomenko, A. T. *Methods of Statistical Analysis of Historical Texts. Chronological Applications.* Vols. 1 and 2. Moscow, Kraft and Lean, 1999.

[912]. Fomenko, A. T. *New Methods of Statistical Analysis of Historical Texts. Applications to Chronology.* Vol. 1, Vol. 2. Vol. 3: Fomenko, A. T. *Antiquity in the Middle Ages. (Greek and Bible History).* Published in the series *Russian Studies in Mathematics and Sciences.* Scholary Monographs in Russian. Vol. 6-7. Lewiston-Queenston-Lampeter, The Edwin Mellen Press, 1999.

[912:1]. Fomenko, A. T., and G. V. Nosovskiy. *Demagogism instead of Scientific Analysis.* The RAS Courier, Vol. 9, No. 9 (2000): 797-800.

[912:2]. Fomenko, A. T., and G. V. Nosovskiy. *In Re the "Novgorod Datings" of A. A. Zaliznyak and V. L. Yanin.* The RAS Courier, Vol. 72, No. 2 (2002): 134-140.

[912:3]. Fomenko, T. N. *The Astronomical Datings of the "Ancient" Egyptian Zodiacs of Dendera and Esne (Latopolis).* In: Kalashnikov, V. V., G. V. Nosovskiy, and A. T. Fomenko. *The Astronomical Analysis of Chronology. The Almagest. Zodiacs.* Moscow, The Delovoi Express Financial, 2000. 635-810.

[913]. *The Epistle of Photius, the Holy Patriarch of Constantinople, to Michael, Prince of Bulgaria, on the Princely Incumbencies.* Moscow, 1779. See also: Photius. *Patriarch of Constantinople, Epistola ad Michaelem Bulgarorum Regem.* In: *Roman Spicilegium.* Rome, 1839-1844.

[914]. Cardini, Franco. *Origins of the Mediaeval Knightage.* A condensed translation from Italian by V. P. Gaiduk. La Nuova Italia, 1982. Moscow, Progress Publications, 1987.

[914:1]. France, Anatole. *Selected Short Stories.* Leningrad, Lenizdat, 1959.

[915]. Pototskaya, V. V., and N. P. Pototskaya. *French-Russian Dictionary.* 12th stereotype edition. Moscow, Sovetskaya Encyclopaedia. 1967.

[916]. Godfrey, Fr. O. F. M. *Following Christ.* Israel, Palphot Ltd., Millennium 2000, 2000.

[917]. Frazer, J. *Attis.* Moscow, Novaya Moskva, 1924. English ed.: *Adonis, Attis, Osiris.* London, Macmillan & Co, 1907.

[918]. Frazer, J. *Golden Bough.* Release 1. Moscow-Leningrad, Ogiz, 1931.

[919]. Frazer, J. *Golden Bough.* Releases 3, 4. Moscow, Atheist, 1928.

[920]. Frazer, J. *The Folklore in the Old Testament. Studies in Comparative Religion.* Moscow-Leningrad, Ogiz, The State Social Economics, 1931. English original: London, Macmillan & Co., 1918.

[921]. Fren, H. M. *Coins of the Khans of Juchiev Ulus of the Golden Horde.* St. Petersburg, 1832.

[922]. Frumkina, R. M. *Statistical Methods of Lexical Studies.* Moscow, 1964.

[923]. Thucydides. *The History of the Peloponnesian War.* Eight books. Translated by F. G. Mishchenko. Vols. 1, 2. Vol. 1: books 1-4. Vol. 2: books 5-8. Moscow, 1887-1888. English edition published in the series *"Great Books of the Western World.* Vol. 5. Encyclopaedia Britannica, Inc. Chicago, The University of Chicago, 1952 (2nd edition 1990). See also the Penguin Books edition. London, 1954.

[924]. Thucydides. *History.* Leningrad, Nauka, 1981.

[925]. von Senger, Harro. *Stratagems. On the Chinese Art of Life and Survival.* Moscow, Progress, 1995.

[926]. Herrmann, D. *The Pioneers of the Skies.* Translated from German by K. B. Shingareva and A. A. Konopikhin. Moscow, Mir, 1981. German edition: Herrmann, Dieter B. *Entdecker des Himmels.* Leipzig-Jena-Berlin, Urania-Verlag, 1979.

[927]. Chlodowski, R. I. *Francesco Petrarch.* Moscow, Nauka, 1974.

[928]. *The Pilgrimage of Hegumen Daniel.* Literary Monuments of Ancient Russia. XII Century. Moscow, Khudozhestvennaya Literatura, 1980. 25-115.

[929]. *Afanasy Nikitin's Voyage over the Three Seas. 1466-1472.* Moscow-Leningrad, the Academy of Sciences, Literary Masterpieces, The USSR AS Publications, 1948.

[930]. Hollingsworth, Mary. *Art in the History of Humanity.* Moscow, Iskusstvo, 1989. Russian translation of the edition titled *L'Arte Nella Storia Dell'Uomo.* Saggio introduttivo di Giulio Carlo Argan. Firenze, Giunti Gruppo Editoriale, 1989.

[931]. *The Kholmogory Chronicle. The Dvina Chronicler.* The Complete Collection of Russian Chronicles, Vol. 33. Leningrad, Nauka, 1977.

[932]. Khomyakov, A. S. *Collected Works in Two Volumes.* A supplement to the *Issues of Philosophy.* Vol. 1. Works on historiosophy. Moscow, the Moscow Fund of Philosophy, Medium Press, 1994.

[933]. Aconiatus, Nicetas. *History Beginning with the Reign of John Comnenus.* St. Petersburg, 1860. Also see the *Historia* by Nicetas Aconiatus in J. P. Migne's *Patrologiae cursus completes. Series graeca.* Vol. 140. Paris, 1857-1886.

[934]. Aconiatus, Nicetas. *History Beginning with the Reign of John Comnenus (1186-1206).* The *Byzantine Historians* series, Vol. 5. St. Petersburg, 1862. Also see the *Historia* by Nicetas Aconiatus in J. P. Migne's *Patrologiae cursus completes. Series graeca.* Vol. 140. Paris, 1857-1886

[935]. Hogue, John. *Nostradamus. The Complete Prophecies.* First published in Great Britain in 1996 by Element Books Ltd., Shaftesbury, Dorset. Moscow, Fair-Press, The Grand Publishing and Trading House, 1999.

[935:1]. Boutenev, Khreptovich. *Florence and Rome in Relation to Two XV-century Events in Russian History. A Concise Illustrated Account Compiled by Khreptovich Boutenev, Esq.* Moscow, 1909.

[936]. *Christianity. An Encyclopaedic Dictionary.* The Encyclopaedic Dictionary of Brockhaus and Efron. New Encyclopaedic Dictionary of Brockhaus and Efron. The Orthodox Encyclopaedia of Theology. Vols. 1-3. Moscow, The Great Russian Encyclopaedia, 1993.

[937]. Pokrovskiy, N. N., ed. *Christianity and the Russian Church of the Feudal Period (Materials).* Novosibirsk, Nauka, Siberian Affiliation, 1989.

[938]. Istrin, V. M., ed. *The Chronicle of John Malalas (A Slavic Translation).* St. Petersburg, 1911.

[939]. *The Chronographer.* Russian National Library, the Manuscript Section. Rumyantsevsky Fund, 457.

[940]. *The Lutheran Chronographer.* Private collection, 1680.

[941]. Rantsov, V. L., comp. *The Chronology of Global and Russian History.* St. Petersburg, Brockhaus-Efron, 1905. Reprinted in Kaliningrad: Argument, Yantarny Skaz, 1995.

[942]. *The Chronology of Russian History. An Encyclopaedic Reference Book.* Moscow, Mezhdunarodnye Otnosheniya, 1994.

[943]. Prakhov, Adrian, ed. *The Treasures of Russian Art.* A Monthly Almanac of the Imperial Society for Supporting Fine Arts. Year IV, No. 2-4, No. 5 (1904). Issue 5: The Relics of the Savvino-Storozhevsky monastery. Historical review by Alexander Ouspensky. Reprinted in Moscow, Severo-Print Typography, 1998. To the 600th anniversary of the Savvino-Storozhevsky stauropigial friary.

[944]. Khoudyakov, M. G. *Accounts of the History of the Kazan Khanate.* Kazan, State Publishing House, 1923. Reprinted in: *On the Junction of Continents and Civilizations.* Moscow, Insan, 1996. Published separately: Moscow, Insan, SFK, 1991.

[945]. Kjetsaa, G., S. Gustavsson, B. Beckman, and S. Gil. *The Problems of the "Quiet flows the Don's" Authorship. Who Wrote the "Quiet flows the Don"?* Moscow, Kniga, 1989. Translated from the Solum Forlag edition. Oslo-New Jersey, Humanities Press.

[946]. Zeitlin, Z. *Galileo.* The *Celebrity Biographies* series, Issue 5-6. The Literary Magazine Association, Moscow, 1935.

[947]. Petrov, Leonid, comp. *The Dictionary of Ecclesial History. (A Referential Theological Dictionary, Predominantly Oriented At Ecclesial History).* St. Petersburg, the Province Department Typography, 1889. Reprinted: the Sretenskiy Monastery, 1996.

[948]. Cicero, Marcus Tullius. *Dialogues. On the State. On the Laws.* Moscow, Nauka, 1966. English edition: Cicero, Marcus Tullius. *Works.* Cambridge, Mass; Harvard University Press; London, Heinemann, 1977.

[949]. Cicero, Marcus Tullius. *Three Tractates on the Art of Rhetoric.* Moscow, Nauka, 1972. English edition: Cicero, Marcus Tullius. *Works.* Cambridge, Mass; Harvard University Press; London, Heinemann, 1977.

[950]. Cicero, Marcus Tullius. *On the Old Age. On Friendship. On Responsibilities.* Moscow, Nauka, 1972. English edition: Cicero, Marcus Tullius. *Old Age and Friendship...* London, Cassel's National Library, 1889.

[951]. Cicero, Marcus Tullius. *Philosophical Tractates.* Moscow, Nauka, 1985. English edition: Cicero, Marcus Tullius. *Works.* Cambridge, Mass; Harvard University Press; London, Heinemann, 1977.

[952]. Chagin, G. N. *The Ancient Land of Perm.* Moscow, Iskusstvo, 1988.

[953]. Chekin, L. S. *The Cartography of the Christian Middle Ages in the VIII–XIII century.* Moscow, Oriental Literature, RAS, 1999.

[953:1]. Chernetsov, A. V. *The Gilded Doors of the XVI century. The Cathedrals of the Moscow Kremlin and the Trinity Cathedral of the Ipatyevsky Monastery in Kostroma.* Moscow, The RAS, Nauka, 1992.

[954]. Chernin, A. D. *The Physics of Time.* Moscow, Nauka, 1987.

[955]. Chernykh, P. Y. *A Historical and Etymological Dictionary of the Modern Russian Language.* Vols. 1, 2. Moscow, Russkiy Yazyk, 1993.

[955:1]. Chernyak, E. B. *The Mysteries of France. Conspiracy, Intrigue, Mystification.* Moscow, Ostozhye Press, 1996.

[955:2]. Chernyak, E. B. *The Time of the Conspiracies Long Forgotten.* Moscow, Mezhdunarodnye Otnosheniya, 1994.

[956]. Chertkov, A. D. *On the Language of the Pelasgians that used to Inhabit Italy, and its Comparison to Ancient Slavic.* The periodical edition of the Moscow Society for the Historical Studies of Russian Antiquities, Book 23. Moscow, 1855.

[957]. Chertkov, A. D. *A Description of Ancient Russian Coins.* Moscow, Selivanovsky Typography, 1834.

[958]. Cinzia, Valigi. *Rome and the Vatican.* Narni-Terni, Italy, Plurigraf, 1995.

[959]. Chistovich, I. *Textual Corrections of the Slavic Bible Before the 1751 Edition.* (Article 2). The Orthodox Review, Vol. 2 (May Book, 1860): 41-72.

[960]. Chistyakov, A. S. *The Story of Peter the Great.* Reprint. Moscow, Buklet, Dvoinaya Raduga, 1992.

[961]. Chistyakova, N. A., and N. V. Voulikh. *The History of Ancient Literature.* Moscow, Vyshaya Shkola, 1972.

[962]. *Imperial Society for History and Russian Antiquities Readings.* Book I, Part 5. 1858.

[963]. *The Miraculous Icons of Our Lady.* Sisterhood of the Holy Martyr Elizabeth, the Great Princess. 103287. Moscow, 40, 2nd Khutorskaya St., 1998.

[964]. [Champollion] *J. F. Champollion and Egyptian Hieroglyphs Deciphered.* Collected works under the general editorship of I. S. Katznelson. Moscow, Nauka, 1979.

[965]. Chantepie de la Saussaye, D. P. *Illustrated History of Religions.* Moscow, 1899. English edition: *Manual of the Science of Religion.* London-New York, Longmans, Green and Co., 1891.

[966]. Chantepie de la Saussaye, D. P. *Illustrated History of Religions.* Vols. 1 and 2. Moscow, Spaso-Preobrazhensky Stauropigial Monastery of Valaam, reprinted in 1992.

[967]. Shakhmatov, A. A. *Manuscript Description. The Radzivilovskaya Chronicle, or the Chronicle of Königsberg.* Vol. 2. Articles on the text and the miniatures of the manuscript. St. Petersburg, Imperial Antiquarian Bibliophile Society, CXVIII, 1902.

[968]. Shevchenko, M. Y. *The Star Catalogue of Claudius Ptolemy: Special Characteristics of Ancient Astronomical Observations.* Historico-Astronomical Research. Issue 17. Moscow, Nauka, 1988. 167-186.

[969]. *Masterpieces among the Paintings in the Museums of the USSR. The Art of Ancient Russia. The Renaissance Art.* Issue 1. Moscow, Goznak, 1974.

[970]. Sheynman, M. M. *Belief in the Devil in the History of Religion.* Moscow, Nauka, 1977.

[971]. Shakespeare. *Collected Works in Five Volumes.* From the *Library of Great Writers* series under the editorship of S. A. Vengerov. St. Petersburg, Brockhaus-Efron, 1902-1904.

[972]. Shakespeare, William. *The Complete Works in Eight Volumes.* Under the editorship of A. Smirnov and A. Anixt. Moscow, Iskusstvo, 1960.

[973]. Shakespeare, William. *King Richard III. Tragedy in Five Acts.* Translated by Georgy Ben. St. Petersburg, Zvezda, 1997.

[974]. *600th Anniversary of the Kulikovo Battle.* Brochure. Vneshtorgizdat, Moscow State Museum of History. 1980.

[975]. Shilov, Y. A. *The Proto-Homeland of the Aryans. History, Tradition, Mythology.* Kiev, Sinto, 1995.

[976]. Shiryaev, A. N. *Consecutive Statistical Analysis.* Moscow, Nauka, 1976.

[977]. Shiryaev, E. E. *Belarus: White Russia, Black Russia and Lithuania on the Maps.* Minsk, Science & Technology, 1991.

[978]. Shklovsky, I. S. *Supernovae.* Moscow, 1968 (1st edition). Moscow, Nauka, 1976 (2nd edition). English edition: London-New York, Wiley, 1968.

[979]. Schlezer, A. L. *Public and Private Life of Augustus Ludwig Schlezer as Related by Himself.* In the *Imperial Academy of Sciences, Russian Language and Literature Department* series, Vol. 13. St. Petersburg, 1875.

[980]. Shlyapkin I. A. *Description of the Manuscripts of the Spaso-Yefimiev Monastery in Suzdal.* The Masterpieces of Ancient Literature, Issue 4, No. 16. St. Petersburg, 1881.

[981]. Spilevskiy A. V. *The Almagest and Chronology.* The Ancient History Courier, No. 3 (1988): 134-160.

[982]. Schulmann, Eliezer. *The Sequence of Biblical Events.* Translated from Hebrew. Moscow, the Ministry of Defence Publications, 1990.

[983]. Shchepkin, V. N. *Russian Palaeography.* Moscow, Nauka, 1967.

[984]. Shcherbatov, M. M. *Russian History from the Dawn of Time.* St. Petersburg, 1901.

[985]. Eulia, Chelebi. *The Book of Travels. Campaigns of the Tatars and Voyages through the Crimea (1641-1667).* Simferopol, Tavria, 1996.

[985:1]. Eisler, Colin (Leman, Robert). *The Museums of Berlin.* Moscow, Colin Eisler and Little, Brown and Company, Inc. Compilation. Slovo, the *World's Greatest Museums* series, 2002 (1996).

[985:2]. Eisler, Colin. *The Art of the Hermitage.* Moscow, Biblion, 2001.

[986]. Aitken, M. J. *Physics and Archaeology.* Moscow, IL, 1964. English original: New York, Interscience Publishers, 1961.

[987]. Ehlebracht, Peter. *Tragedy of the Pyramids. Egyptian Shrines Plundered for 5000 Years.* Moscow, Progress, 1984. German original: *Haltet die Pyramiden Fest! 5000 Jahre Grabraub in Ägypten.* Düsseldorf-Vienna, Econ, 1980.

[987:1]. Englund, Peter. *Poltava. How an Army Perished.* Moscow, Novoye Literaturnoye Obozrenie, 1995. Original: Stockholm, Bokförgalet Atlantis, 1988.

[988]. *The Encyclopaedic Dictionary.* Vols. 1-82; supplementary volumes 1-4. St. Petersburg, Brockhaus and Efron, 1890-1907.

[988:0]. Brockhaus, F. A., and I. A. Efron. *The Encyclopaedic Dictionary.* St. Petersburg, 1898. Reprinted: St. Petersburg, Polradis, 1994.

[988:1]. *Encyclopaedia for Children.* Vol. 7: Art. Moscow, Avanta-plus, 1997.

[989]. *The Encyclopaedia of Elementary Mathematics. Book 1. Arithmetics.* Moscow-Leningrad, the State Publishing House of Theoretical Technical Literature, 1951.

[990]. Artamonov, M. I., ed. *The Hermitage.* Album. Leningrad, Sovetskiy Khudozhnik, 1964.

[991]. Ern, V. *The Revelation in Thunder and Storm. Anatomy of N. A. Morozov's Book.* Moscow, 1907.

[991:1]. *The Art of Goldsmithery in Russia.* Album. Moscow, Interbook-Business, Yural Ltd, 2002.

[992]. Yuvalova, E. P. *German Sculpture of 1200-1270.* Moscow, Iskusstvo, 1983.

[993]. Yanin, V. L. *I Sent You a Birch-Rind Epistle.* Moscow, MSU Press, 1965. A revised edition: Moscow, 1998.

[993:1]. Jannella, Cecilia. *Simone Martini.* Album. Moscow, Slovo, 1996. Scala, 1995, Istituto Forografico Editoriale.

[994]. Ponomaryov, A. M., ed. *Yaroslavl. History of the City in Documents and First-Hand Materials from First References to 1917.* Yaroslavl, Upper Volga Publications, 1990.

[995]. *Yaroslavl. Map 0-37 (1:1,000,000).* The General Council of Ministers, Department of Geodetics and Cartography, 1980.

[996]. *Yaroslavl. Monuments of Art and Architecture.* Yaroslavl: Upper Volga Publications, 1994.

Sources in foriegn languages

[997]. Chrysostomos, Abbot. *The Holy Royal Monastery of Kykko Founded with a Cross.* Limassol, Cyprus, Kykko Monastery, printed by D. Couvas & Sons, Ltd., 1969.

[998]. *ABC kulturnich pamatek Ceskoslovenska.* Prague, Panorama, 1985.

[999]. Abulafia, David. *Frederick II. A Medieval Emperor.* New York-Oxford, Oxford University Press, 1988.

[1000]. Abu Mashar. *De magnis coinctiombus.* Augsburg, Erhard Ratdolt (The Pulkovo Observatory Library), 1489.

[1001]. Adam, L. *North-West American Indian Art and its Early Chinese Parallels.* Man, Volume 36, No. 2-3 (1936): 45.

[1002]. Puech, Aime. *St. Jean Chrisostome et les mœurs de son temps.* Paris, 1891.

[1003]. Albright, W. F. *From the Stone Age to Christianity.* 7th edition. New York, 1957.

[1004]. Albumasar. *De Astrú Scientia.* 1515. (The Pulkovo Observatory Library.)

[1005]. Alibert, Louis. *Dictionnaire Occitan-Francais. Selon les parles languedociens.* Toulouse, Institut d'études Occitanes, 1996.

[1006]. *A List of Books on the History of Science.* 2nd supplement, Part 3. Astronomy. Chicago, The J. Crerar Library, 1944.

[1007]. Allen, Phillip. *L'Atlas des Atlas. Le monde vu par les cartographes.* Brepols, 1993.

[1008]. *Almagestu Cl. Ptolemaei Phelusiensis Alexandrini.* Anno Virginei Partus, 1515.

[1009]. *America. Das frühe Bild der Neuen Welt. Ausstellung der Bayerischen Staatsbibliothek München.* Munich, Prestel Verlag, 1992.

[1009:1]. Silverman, David P., ed. *Ancient Egypt.* New York, Oxford University Press, 1977.

[1010]. Thorpe, B., ed. *Ancient Laws and Institutes of England...* Volume 1. London, 1840. 198.

[1011]. Anke, Victor. *The Life of Charlemagne.* Aachen, Einhard Verlag, 1995.

[1012]. *Annales de la Société Royale d'Archéologie de Bruxelles. Fondée a Bruxelles en 1887. Mémoires, rapports et documents.* Publication périodique. Tome 41e. Secrétariat Général. Musée de la Porte de Hal Bruxelles. 1937.

[1013]. Apianus, P. *Cosmographicus Liber Petri Apiani mathematici studiose collectus.* (The Pulkovo Observatory Library). Landshutae, impensis P. Apiani, 1524.

[1013:1]. Arellano, Alexandra. *All Cuzco. Peru.* Fisa Escudo de Oro. Centre of Regional Studies of the Andes Bartolomé de las Casas, Lima, Peru. Instituto de Investigacion de la Facultad de Turismo y Hotelria, Universidad San Martin de Porres. 1999.

[1014]. Arnim, H. *Sprachliche Forschungen zur Chronologie der platonischen Dialoge.* Volume 269. Appendix 3. Sitzungen Wiener Akademie, 1912.

[1015]. Wolff, Arnold. *Cologne Cathedral. Its history – Its Works of Art.* Greven Verlag Köln GmbH, 1995.

[1016]. Wolff, Arnold, Rainer Gaertner, and Karl-Heinz Schmitz. *Cologne on the Rhine with City Map.* Cologne, Verlagsgesellschaft GmbH, 1995.

[1017]. Wolff, Arnold. *The Cologne Cathedral.* Cologne, Vista Point Verlag, 1990.

[1017:0]. Sachs, Abraham J. *Astronomical Diaries and Related Texts from Babylonia.* Compiled and edited by Hermann Hunger. Volume 1: Diaries from 652 BC to 262 BC. Volume 2: Diaries from 261 BC to 165 BC. Österreichische Akademie der Wissenschaften Philosophisch-Historische Klasse Denkschriften, 195. Bad. Verlag der Österreichischen Akademie der Wissenschaften. Vienna, 1988.

[1017:1]. Walker, Christopher, ed. *Astronomy before the Telescope*. Foreword by P. Moore. British Museum Press, 1996.

[1018]. Palairet, Jean. *Atlas Méthodique, Composé pour l'usage de son altesse sérénissime monseigneur le prince d'Orange et de Nassau stadhouder des sept provinces unies, etc. etc. etc.* Se trouve à Londres, chez Mess. J. Nourse & P. Vaillant dans le Strand; J. Neaulme à Amsterdam & à Berlin; & P. Gosse à La Haye. 1755.

[1019]. *Atlas Minor sive Geographia compendiosa in q.v. a Orbis Terrarum pavcis attamen novissimis Tabvlis ostenditvr.* // *Atlas Nouveau, contenant toutes les parties du monde, Où font Exactement Remarquees les Empires Monarchies, Royaumes, Etats, Republiques, &c, &c, &c. Receuillies des Meilleurs Auteurs.* Amsterdam: Regner & Josue Ottens, n.d.

[1020]. Auè, Michèlé. *Discover Cathar country. Le Pays Cathare.* Toulouse, MSM, 1992.

[1021]. Bacharach. *Astronomia.* (The Pulkovo Observatory Library), 1545.

[1022]. Bailly, J. S. *Histoire de l'astronomie ancienne depuis son origine jusqu'à l'établissement de l'école d'Alexandrie.* Paris, 1st edition 1775, 2nd edition 1781.

[1023]. Baily, F. *An account of the life of Sir John Flaemsteed.* London, 1835.

[1024]. Baily, F. *The Catalogues of Ptolemy, Ulugh Beigh, Tycho Brahe, Halley and Hevelins, deduced from the best authorities.* Royal Astr. Soc. Memoirs, XIII (1843): 1-248.

[1025]. Bakker, I., I. Vogel, and T. Wislanski. *TRB and other C-14 Dates from Poland. Helinium*, IX, 1969.

[1025:1]. Baldauf, Robert. *Historie und Kritik. (Einige kritische Bemerkungen.).* Basel: Friedrich Reinhardt, Universitäts-buchdruckerei, 1902.

[1026]. Bartholomaeus, Angicus. *De proprietatibus rerum.* lib. XV, cap. CXXXI. Apud A. Koburger. Nurenbergi, 1492,

[1027]. Barron, Roderick. *Decorative Maps. With Forty Full Colour Plates.* London, Bracken Books, 1989.

[1028]. Basilica, Sainte Cécile. *Albi. As de Cœur Collection. Guided Visit.* Albi, France: Apa-Poux S. A. Albi, 1992.

[1028:1]. Bély, Lucien. *Discovering the Cathars.* France, Éditions Sud Ouest, 2001.

[1029]. Bennet, J.A. *The Divided Circle. A History of Instruments for Astronomy Navigation and Surveying.* Christie's, Oxford, Phaidon, 1987.

[1030]. de Sainte-Maure, Benoit. *Chronique des ducs de Normandie par Benoit.* Publee... par C. Fahlin, t. I. In: Bibliotheca Ekmaniana universitatis regiae Upsaliensis, Uppsala, 1951. 8-11.

[1031]. del Castillo, Conquistador Bernal Días. *The Discovery and Conquest of Mexico.* New Introduction by Hugh Thomas. New York, Da Capo Press. 1996.

[1032]. Bernard, Lewis. *The Middle East. A brief History of the Last 2000 Years.* New York, Simon & Schuster, 1997.

[1033]. *Bibliography of books and papers published in 1963 on the History of Astronomy.* Moscow: Nauka, 1964.

[1034]. Binding, Rudolf G. *Der Goldene Schrein. Bilder deutschen Meister auf Goldgrund.* Leipzig, 1934.

[1035]. Blaeu, Joan. *Novus Atlas Sinensis,* 1655. Faksimiles nach der Prachtausgabe der Herzog von der August Bibliothek Wolfenbüttel. Herausgegeben von der Stiftung Volkswagenwerk Hannover. Mit Beiträgen von Hans Kauffmann und Yorck Alexander Haase, und einem Geleitwort von Gotthard Gambke. Verlag Müller und Schindler, 1973.

[1036]. *Le Grand Atlas de Blaeu. Le Monde au XVIIe siècle.* Introduction, descriptions et choix des cartes par John Goss. Ancient conseiller-expert cartographe chez Sotheby's. Avant-propos de Peter Clark. Conservateur à la Royal Geographical Society. Adaptation Française de Irmina Spinner. Publié avec le concours de la Royal Geographical Society. Paris: Gründ, 1992. Les cartes originales de *Grand Atlas de Blaeu. Le monde au XVIIe siècle* ont été publiées par Blaeu dans son *Atlas Major* publié à Amsterdam en 1662. L'édition originale 1990 par Studio Editions sous le titre original *Blaeu's Grand Atlas of the 17th Century World.* Première édition francaise 1992 par Librairie Gründ, Paris.

[1037]. Bloch, M. *La societe féodale.* Paris, 1968.

[1038]. Blöss, Christian, and Hans-Ulrich Niemitz. *C14-Crash. (Das Ende der Illusion mit Radiokarbonmethode und Dendrochronologie datieren zu können).* Gräfelfing, Mantis Verlag, 1997.

[1039]. Blöss, Christian, and Hans-Ulrich Niemitz. *The Self-Deception of the C14 Method and Dendrochronology.* Zeitensprünge 8 (1996) 3 361-389. Mantis Verlag, January 1997.

[1040]. Bode, J.E. *Claudius Ptolemäeus, Astronom zu Alexandrien im zweyten Jahrhundert. Beobachtung und Beschreibung der Gestirne und der Bewegung. Vergleichnungen der neuern Beobachtungen von J.E.Bode.* With a historical review and commentary. Berlin und Stettin, 1795.

[1041]. Boll, F. *Studien über Claudius Ptolemäus.* Leipzig, 1894.

[1042]. Bonhoeffer, Dietrich. *Das Geheimnis der Heiligen Nacht.* Kiefel Verlag, Wuppertal/Gütersloh, Germany, 1995.

[1043]. Bonnet, C. *Geneva in Early Christian times.* Geneva, Foundation des Clefs de Saint-Pierre, 1986.

[1044]. Boquet, F. J. C. J. *Historie de l'Astronomie.* Paris, Payot, 1925.

[1045]. Borman, Z. *Astra.* (The Pulkovo Observatory Library). 1596.

[1045:1]. [Bosch] *Tout l'œuvre peint de Jerôme Bosch.* Introduction par Max J.Friedländer. Documentation par Mia Cinotti. Paris, Flammarion, 1967.

1045:2 [Bosch] Fraenger, Wilhelm. *Hieronymus Bosch.* VEB Verlag der Kunst Dresden, 1975.

[1046]. Boszkowska, Anna. *Tryumf Luni i Wenus. Pasja Hieronima Boscha.* Wydawnictwo Literacklie, Krakow, 1980.

[1047]. Bourbon, Fabio. *Lithographien von Frederick Catherwood. Die Mayas. Auf den Spuren einer versunkenen Kultur.* White Star, Via Candido Sassone, 22/24 13100, Vercelli, Italien, 1999. Deutschsprachige Ausgabe: Karl Mükker Verlag, Danziger Strasse 6, 91052 Erlangen.

291

[1048]. Brahe, T. *Tychonis Brahe Dani Opera omnia*. Ed. J. L. E. Dreyer. 15 Volumes. Copenhagen, 1913-1929.

[1049]. Brahe, T. *Equitis Dani Astronomorum Coryhaei Vita*. Authore Petro Gassendo. Regio ex Typographia Adriani Vlac. MDCLV.

[1049:1]. Lehane, Brendan (texte), Richard Novitz (photographies). *Irlande*. London, Flint River, 1997; Paris, Booking Int'l, 1997.

[1050]. Brenon, Anne. *Le vrai visage du Catharisme*. Toulouse, Ed. Loubatières, 1988.

[1050:1]. *British Museum. A Guide to the First, Second and Third Egyptian Rooms. Predynastic Human Remains, Mummies, Wooden Sarcophagi, Coffins and Cartonnage Mummy Cases, Chests and Coffers, and other Objects connected with the Funerary Rites of the Ancient Egyptians.* Third Edition, Revised and Enlarged. With 3 coloured and 32 half-tone plates. British Museum, 1924.

[1050:2]. *British Museum. A Guide to the Fourth, Fifth and Sixth Egyptian Rooms and the Coptic Room. A series of Collections of Small Egyptian Antiquities, which illustrate the Manners and Customs, the Arts and Crafts, the Religion and Literature, and the Funeral Rites and Ceremonies of the Ancient Egyptians and their Descendants, the Copts, from about B.C. 4500 to A.D. 1000.* With 7 plates and 157 illustrations in the text. British Museum, 1922.

[1050:3]. *British Museum. A Guide to the Egyptian Collections in the British Museum.* With 53 plates and 180 illustrations in the text. British Museum, 1909.

[1051]. Brodsky, B. E., and B. S. Darkhovsky. *Nonparametric Methods in Change-Point Problems*. The Netherlands, Kluwer Academic Publishers, 1993.

[1051:1]. Brodrick, M., and A. A. Morton. *A Concise Dictionary of Egyptian Archaeology. A handbook for students and travellers*. London, 1902. 2nd edition 1923, 3rd edition 1924. Reprint: Chicago, Aries, 1980.

[1052]. Brooke, Christopher. *From Alfred to Henry III. 871-1272*. The Norton Library History of England. New York, London, W. W. Norton & Company, 1961, 1968, 1969.

[1053]. Broughton, T. R. S. *The Magistrates of the Roman Republic*. Volumes 1, 2. London, 1951-1960.

[1053:1]. [Bruegel] Gerhard W. Menzel. *Pieter Bruegel der Ältere*. Leipzig, VEB E. A. Seemann, Buch- und Kunstverlag, 1966; 2 Auflage, 1974.

[1053:2]. Bovi, Arturo. *Bruegel. The life and work of the artist illustrated with 80 colour plates*. A Dolphin Art Book. London, Thames and Hudson, 1971. Reprinted 1974.

[1054]. Brugsch, H. *Recueil de Monuments Egyptiens, dessinés sur lieux*. Leipzig, 1862-1865.

[1055]. Buck, C. E., W. G. Gavanagh, and C. D. Litton. *Bayesian Approach to Interpreting Archaeological Data*. Series: Statistics in Practice. John Wiley & Sons, 1996.

[1056]. Bustos, Gerardo. *Yucatan and its Archaeological Sites*. Mexico, Monclem; Florence, Casa Editrice Bonechi, 1992.

[1057]. Cagnat, R. *Cours d'épigraphie latine.* 4e éd. Paris, 1914.

[1058]. Campbell, Tony. *Early Maps.* New York, Abbeville Press Publishers, 1981.

[1059]. Campos, José Guerra, and Jesús Precedo Lafuente. *Guide to the Cathedral of Santiago de Compostela.* Spain, Aldeasa, División Palacios y Museos, 1993.

[1060]. Cantacuzeny, Ioannis. *Opera Omnia. Patrologiae curcus completus. Series graeca.* T. CLIII, CLIV. J.-P. Migne, 1866.

[1060:1]. *Carcassonne (The City of Carcassonne. Cathar Castles).* Production Leconte. Editions Estel-Blois. B. P. 45 - 41260 La Chaussée-Saint-Victor. Printed in E.E.C.

[1060:2]. *Cathares. Les ombres de l'Histoire. Carcassone: Histoire d'une Cité unique.* In: Pyrénées (Magazine). Une publication de Milan Presse. 2001. Éditions Milan et les auteurs. Ariège Pyrenées. (A special edition of the magazine dedicated to Cathar history).

[1061]. *Cathedral and Metropolitan Church of St. Stephen in Vienna.* Germany, Verlag Schnell & Steiner Regensburg, 1995.

[1061:1]. *Cathédrale de l'Annonciation. Le Kremlin de Moscou.* Les Musées d'Etat du Kremlin de Moscou, 1990.

[1062]. Cauville, S. *Le Zodiaque d'Osiris.* Peeters, Uitgeverij Peeters, Bondgenotenlaan 153, B-3000 Leuven.

[1062:1]. Cauville, S. *Dendara. Les chapelles osiriennes.* (5 vols.) Institut francais d'archeologie orientale du Caire, 1977.

[1063]. Chabas, F. *Mélanges égyptologiques. Deuxième série.* Ägyptolog. Zeitschrift. 1868. S. 49.

[1064]. Champfleury. *Historie de la Caricature au Moyen Age.* Paris, 1867-1871.

[1064:0]. Chapront-Touze, M., and J. Chapront. Lunar ephemere des computation software. (Program ELP2000-85, version 1.0, Fortran 77). Bureau des Longitudes, URA 707. 1988. Available online.

[1064:1]. *Château de Chillon.* Booklet. Château de Chillon, Veytaux (www.chillon.ch), 2000.

[1065]. Childress, David Hatcher. *Lost Cities of Atlantis, Ancient Europe & the Mediterranean.* Stelle, Illinois 60919 USA, Adventures Unlimited Press, 1996.

[1066]. Chirikov, B. V., and V. V. Vecheslavov. *Chaotic dynamics of comet Halley.* Astronomy and Astrophysics, Volume 221, No. 1 (1989): 146-154.

[1067]. Chmelarz, Eduard. *Die Ehrepforte des Kaisers Maximilian I.* Unterscheidheim 1972. Verlag Walter Uhl. Jahrbuch der Kunsthistorischen Sammlungen des Allerhöchsten Kaiserhauses. Herausgegeben unter Leitung des Oberstakämmerers seiner Kaiserlichen und Königlichen Apostolischen Majestät. Ferdinand Grafen zu Trauttmansdorff-Weinsberg vom K. K. Oberstkämmerer-Amte. Vierter Band. Mit 39 Kupfertafeln in Heliogravure und Radierung, 100 Holzschnittafeln und 56 Text-Illustrationen in Heliogravure, Holzschnitt und Zinkographie. Als Beilage: 16 Holzschnitte der Ehrenpforte des Kaisers Maximilian I. Wien, Druck und Verlag von Adolf Holzhausen, K. K. Hofbuchdrucker, 1886.

[1068]. Stubbs, W., ed. *Chronica magistri Rogeri de Houedone*. RS, N 51, Volume II. London, 1869, page 236. English translation: *The Annals of Roger de Hoveden, comprising the history of England and of other countries of Europe from A.D. 732 to A.D. 1201*. Tr. H. T. Riley, Volumes 1-2. London, Bohn's Antiquarian Library, 1853.

[1069]. Pestman, P.W. *Chronologie égyptienne d'après les textes démotiques*. Papyrologia Lugduno-Batava edidit Institutum Papyrologicum Universitatis Lugduno-Batavae Moderantibus M.David et B. A. von Groningen. Volume 15. Lugdunum Batavorum, 1967.

[1070]. Cipolla, Carlo M. *Money, Prices and Civilization in the Mediterranean World. 5-17 century*. Princeton University Press, 1956.

[1071]. *Claudii Ptolemaei Magnae Constructionis, id est perfectae coelestium motuum pertractationis. Lib. XIII. Theonis Alexanrini in eosdem Commentariorum Libri XI*; Basileal apud Ioannem Waledrum. C. priv. Caes. ad Quinquennium. 1538.

[1072]. *Claudii Ptolemaei Phelusiensis Alexandrini*. Anno Salutis, 1528.

[1073]. *Claudii Ptolemaei Pelusiensis Alexandrini omnia quac extant opera*. 1551.

[1074]. Clemens, Jöcle. *Speyer Cathedral*. Regensburg, Scgnell & Steiner, 1997.

[1075]. Clinton, H.F. *Fasti Hellenici, a Civil and Literary Chronology from the Earliest Times to the Death of Augustus*. Oxford, 1830-1841.

[1076]. Copernici, N. *Revolutionibus Orbium Caelestium. Lib. VI*. Ed. by G. Loachimi. Thoruni, 1873.

[1077]. Corbinianus. *Firmamentum Firmianum*. (Pulkovo Observatory Library). 1731.

[1078]. Cordier, H. *Marco Polo and His Book*. Introductory notices. In: *The Travels of Marco Polo*. The complete Yule-Cordier. Volumes 1 and 2. New York, Dover, 1993.

[1078:1]. Wytfliet, Cornelius. *Descriptionis Ptolemaicae Augmentum sive Occidentis notitia brevis commentario*. Louvain 1597. With an introduction by R. A. Skelton. Theatrvm Orbis Terrarvm. A Series of Atlases in Facsimile. 1st Series, Vol. V. Amsterdam, N. Israel, Meridian, 1964.

[1079]. Costard, G. *The History of Astronomy with its Application to Geography, History and Chronology*. London, J. Lister, 1967.

[1080]. Harmon, Craig. *The Natural Distribution of Radiocarbon and the Exchange Time of Carbon Dioxides between Atmosphere and Sea*. Volume 9. Tellus. 1957. 1-17.

[1081]. Harmon, Craig. *Carbon-13 in Plants and the Relationships between Carbon-13 and Carbon-14 Variations in Nature*. J. Geol., 62 (1954): 115-149.

[1081:1]. El Mahdy, Christine. *Mummies, Myths and Magic in Ancient Egypt*. Thames and Hudson, 1989.

[1082]. Crowe, C. *Carbon-14 activity during the past 5000 years*. Nature, Volume 182 (1958): 470.

[1083]. Danit Hadary-Salomon, ed. *2000 Years of Pilgrimage to the Holy Land*. Israel, AC Alfa Communication Ltd., 1999.

[1084]. *Das Münster zu Bonn. The Bonn Minster.* Former Collegiate Church of SS. Cassius and Florentius. Series: Kleine Kunstfürer. Achnell, Art Guide No. 593 (of 1954). Second English edition 1997. Regensburg, Germany, Verlag Schnell & Steiner GmbH Regensburg, 1997.

[1085]. David, Daniel. *Let There be Light. William Tyndale and the Making of the English Bible.* A British Library Exhibition at The Huntington. 19 November, 1996 – 7 February, 1997. London, The British Library, 1994.

[1086]. Davidovits, Joseph. *Alchemy and Pyramids. The Book of Stone.* Vol. 1. France-USA, Geopolymer Institute, 1983.

[1087]. Davidovits, Joseph. *Alchemy and Pyramids.* Translated from French by A. C. James and J. James. Rev. ed. *Que le Khnoum protège Khéops constructeur de pyramide.* Saint Quentin, France, 1983; Miami Shores, Fla., USA, Institute for Applied Archaeological Science, Barry University, 1984.

[1088]. Davidovits, Joseph. *Amenhotep, Joseph and Solomon.* 1st ed. Miami Shores, Fla., U.S.A., Geopolymer Institute, Institute for Applied Archaeological Science, Barry University, 1984.

[1089]. Davidovits, Joseph. *Que le dieu Khnoum protège Khéops constructeur de pyramide: histoire de la civilisation Égyptienne de 3500 é 1500 ans avant J.-C.* Saint-Quentin, 1978.

[1090]. Davidovits, Joseph. *Le calcaire des pierres des Grandes Pyramides d'Égypte serait un béton géopolymére vieux de 4.600 ans.* Résumé des cours-conférences tenus en 1983 et 1984. *Revue des Questions Scientifiques,* Volume 156(2) (1986): 199-225.

[1091]. Davidovits, Joseph. *No more than 1,400 workers to build the Pyramid of Cheops with manmade stone.* 3rd Int. Congress of Egyptologists. Toronto, Canada: paper AA-126, publié dans Appendix 3 de Davidovits, 1983.

[1092]. Davidovits, Joseph, and Margie Morris. *The Pyramids: an Enigma Solved.* New York, Hippocrene Books, 1988. New York, Dorset Press, 1989, 1990.

[1093]. Davidovits J., J. Thodez, and Gaber M Hisham. *Pyramids of Egypt Made of Man-Made Stone, Myth or Fact?* Symposium on Archeometry 1984, Smithsonian Institution, abstract 26-27. Washington, D.C., USA, 1984.

[1094]. Davies, Nartin. *The Gutenberg Bible.* London, The British Library, 1996.

[1095]. Degrassi, A. *Fasti Capitolini.* 1954; I Fasti consolari dell'impero romano, 1952.

[1096]. Delambre, J. B. *Histoire de l'Astronomie.* 2 Volumes. Paris, 1817.

[1097]. Delambre, J. *Histoire de l'Astronomie moderne.* 2 Volumes. Paris, 1821.

[1098]. *Della origine et ruccessi degli Slavi, oratione di M. V. Pribevo, Dalmatino da Lesena, etc. et hora tradotta della lingua Latina nell'Italiana da Bellisario Malaspalli, da Spalato.* Venetia, 1595.

[1099]. *Der Marienschrein im Dom zu Aachen.* Die Publikation dieses Sonderheftes erfolgt durch die Grünenthal GmbH, Aachen. Domkapitel, 2000.

[1100]. *Description de l'Égypte.* Publiée sous les ordes de Napoléon de Bonaparte. *Description de l'Égypte ou recueil des observations et des recherches qui ont été faites en Égypte pendant l'expédition de l'Armée francaise publié sous les ordes de Napoléon Bonaparte.* Bibliothèque de l'Image. Inter-Livres. 1995.

[1101]. Desroches-Noblecourt, Christiane. *Life and Death of Pharaoh Tutankhamen.* London, Penguin Books, 1963.

[1101:1]. *Deutschland. Germany. Allemagne. Germania.* Euro Map. Halwag AG, Bern, Printed in Switzerland-Germany 4-26 AK.

[1102]. Dheily, J. *Dictionaire Biblique.* Ed. Desclec. Tournai, 1964. 193.

[1103]. *Dialogus Historicus Palladii episcopi Helenopolis cum Theodoro.* Patrologiae Cursus Completus. Patrologiae Graecae. T. LVII. J.-P. Migne, 1858.

[1104]. *Die Bibel. Oder die Ganze Heilige Schrift des Alten and Neuen Testaments.* Nach der Überzetzung Martin Luthers. Württembergische Bibelanstalt, Stuttgart. 1967.

1105. *Die Weihnachtsgeschichte. Nacherzählt in Bildern aus der Biblioteca Apostolica Vaticana.* Stuttgart, Zürich, Belser Verlag, 1993.

[1106]. *Dom Betrachtung.* Die Hochgräber im Kölner Dom. 4. Herausgeber, Dompfarramt – Dompfarrer Rolf Breitenbruch, Domkloster 3, 50667, Köln.

[1107]. Douais, C. *L'Inquisition, ses origines, sa procédure.* Paris, 1906.

[1108]. Dreyer, J. L. E. *On the Origin of Ptolemy's Catalogue of Stars.* Monthly Notices of the Royal Astronomical Society, No. 77 (1917): 528-539.

[1109]. Dreyer, J. L. E. *On the Origin of Ptolemy's Catalogue of Stars.* Second Paper. Monthly Notices of the Royal Astronomical Society, No. 78 (1918): 343-349.

[1110]. Duden. *Ethymologie: Herkunfswörterbuch der deutschen Sprache.* Mannheim, Wien; Dudenverlag, Zürich, 1989.

[1111]. Duncan, A.J. *Quality Control and Industrial Statistics.* NY, Irwin, 1974.

[1112]. Dupont-Sommer, A. *Les écrits essentiens decouverts près de la Mer Morte.* Paris, 1957.

[1113]. Dupuis, C. *The Origin of All Religious Worship.* New Orleans, 1872.

[1114]. Duvernoy, Jean. *Le catharisme.* Volume I: *La religion des Cathares.* Volume II: *Histoire des Cathares.* Toulouse, Private, 1976 and 1979. Re-published 1986.

[1115]. Duvernoy, Jean, Paul Labal, Robert Lafont, Philippe Martell, and Michel Roquebert. *Les Cathares en Occitanie.* Fayard, 1981.

[1116]. Van Ermen, Eduard. *The United States in Old Maps and Prints.* Wilmington USA, Atomium Books, 1990.

[1116:1]. Égypte. Large album with photographs. Paris, Molière, Art Image, 1998.

[1117]. Eichler, Anja-Franziska. *Albrecht Dürer. 1471-1528.* Cologne, Könemann Verlagsgesellschaft GmbH, 1999.

[1118]. *Encyclopaedia Britannica; or, a Dictionary of Arts and Sciences, compiled upon a new Plan. In which the different Sciences and Arts are digested into distinct Treatises or Systems; and the various Technical Terms, etc. are explained as they occur in the order of the Alphabet. Illustrated with one hundred and sixty copperplates. By a Society of Gentlemen in Scotland. In 3 volumes.* Edinburgh, A. Bell and C. Macfarquhar, 1771.

[1118:1]. *Encyclopaedia Britannica.* On-line version, 2001.

[1119]. Evans, James. *On the Origin of the Ptolemaic Star Catalogue*. Part 1. *Journal for the History of Astronomy*, Volume 18, Part 3, No. 54 (August 1987): 155-172.

[1120]. Evans, James. *On the Origin of the Ptolemaic Star Catalogue*. Part 2. *Journal for the History of Astronomy*, Volume 18, Part 4, No. 55 (November 1987): 235-277.

[1121]. Liebermann, F., and R. Pauli, Eds. *Ex Annalibus Melrosensibus*. MGH SS, T.XXVII. Hannoverae, 1885. 439.

[1121:1]. Winship, Betsy, and Sheila Stoneham, eds. *Explosives and Rock Blasting*. Field Technical Operations. Atlas Rowder Company. Dallas, Texas, Marple Press, 1987.

[1122]. Fatih, Cimok. *Hagia Sophia*. Istanbul, A turizm yayinlari, 1995.

[1123]. Fatih, Cimok. *Hagia Sophia*. Istanbul, A turizm yayinlari, 1985.

[1124]. Fergusson, G. I. *Reduction of Atmospheric Radiocarbon Concentration by Fossil Fuel Carbon Dioxide and the Mean Life of Carbon Dioxide in the Atmosphere*. London, Proc. Royal Soc., 243 A, pages 561-574. 1958.

[1125]. Filarete, Antonio Averlino. *Tractat über die Baukunst*. Vienna, 1890.

[1126]. Fischer, Fr. *Thucydidus reliquiae in papyris et membranis aigiptiacis servatae*. Lipsiae, 1913.

[1127]. Verlag, Dr. Ludwig Reichert. *Flüsse im Herzen Europas. Rhein-Elbe-Donau*. Kartenabteilung der Staatsbibliothek zu Berlin. Preussischer Kulturbesitz. Wiesbaden, 1993.

[1128]. Fomenko, A.T. *The Jump of the Second Derivative of the Moon's Elongation. Celestial Mechanics,* Volume 29 (1981): 33-40.

[1129]. Fomenko, A. T. *Some New Empirico-Statistical Methods of Dating and the Analysis of Present Global Chronology*. The British Library. Department of Printed Books. Cup. 918/87. 1981.

[1130]. Fomenko, A.T. *New Empirico-Statistical Dating Methods and Statistics of Certain Astronomical Data*. The theses of the First International Congress of the International Bernoulli Society for Mathematical Statistics and Probability Theory. Volume 2. Moscow, Nauka, 1986. 892.

[1131]. Fomenko, A.T. *Duplicates in Mixed Sequences and a Frequency Duplication Principle. Methods and Applications*. Probability theory and mathematical statistics. Proceeding of the 4th Vilnius Conference (24-29 June 1985). Volume 16. Utrecht, Netherlands, VNU Science, 1987. 439-465.

[1132]. Fomenko, A.T. *Empirico-Statistical Methods in Ordering Narrative Texts. International Statistical Review*, Volume 566, No. 3 (1988): 279-301.

[1133]. Fomenko, A. T., V. V. Kalashnikov, and G.V. Nosovskiy. *When was Ptolemy's Star Catalogue in "Almagest" Compiled in Reality?* Preprint. No. 1989-04, ISSN 0347-2809. Dept. of Math., Chalmers Univ. of Technology, The University of Goteborg. Sweden.

[1134]. Fomenko, A. T., V. V. Kalashnikov, and G.V. Nosovskiy. *When was Ptolemy's Star Catalogue in "Almagest" Compiled in Reality? Statistical Analysis*. Acta Applicandae Mathematical. Volume 17. 1989. 203-229.

[1135]. Fomenko, A. T. *Mathematical Statistics and Problems of Ancient Chronology. A New Approach.* Acta Applicandae Mathematical. Volume 17. 1989. 231-256.

[1136]. Fomenko, A. T., Kalashnikov V. V., Nosovskiy G. V. *Geometrical and Statistical Methods of Analysis of Star Configurations. Dating Ptolemy's Almagest.* USA, CRC Press, 1993.

[1137]. Fomenko, A. T. *Empirico-Statistical Analysis of Narrative Material and its Applications to Historical Dating.* Volume 1: *The Development of the Statistical Tools.* Volume 2: *The Analysis of Ancient and Medieval Records.* The Netherlands, Kluwer Academic Publishers, 1994.

[1138]. Fomenko, A. T., V. V. Kalashnikov, and G.V. Nosovskiy. *The dating of Ptolemy's Almagest based on the coverings of the stars and on lunar eclipses.* Acta Applicandae Mathematicae. Volume 29. 1992. 281-298.

[1139]. Fomenko, A. T., V. V. Kalashnikov, and G.V. Nosovskiy. *Statistical analysis and dating of the observations on which Ptolemy's "Almagest" star catalogue is based.* In: *Probability theory and mathematical statistics.* Proc. of the Fifth Vilnius Conference. Volume 1. Moklas, Vilnius, Lithuania. VSP, Utrecht, The Netherlands, 1990. 360-374.

[1140]. Fomenko, A. T., and S. T. Rachev. *Volume Functions of Historical Texts and the Amplitude Correlation Principle.* Computers and the Humanities. Vol. 24. 1990. 187-206.

[1141]. Manuel, Frank E. *Isaac Newton, the Historian.* Cambridge, Massachusetts, The Belknap Press, 1963.

[1142]. Franke, Peter Robert, and Ilse Paar. *Die Antiken Münzen der Sammlung Heynen. Katalog mit Historischen Erläuterungen.* Landschaftsmuseum Krefeld-Burglinn. Rheinland-Verlag, Köln, in Kommission bei Rudolf Habelt Verlag, Bonn. 1976.

[1143]. de Landa, Friar Diego. *Yucatan before and after the Conquest.* Translated with notes by William Gates. San Fernando, Atrio de San Francisco, 1993.

[1144]. Fricke, W., and A. Koff *FK4.* No.10. Heidelberg, Veröf. Astr. Inst., 1963.

[1145]. Fuchs, W. *Nach allen Regeln der Kunst. Diagnosen über Literatur, Musik, bildende Kunst. Die Werke, ihre Autoren und Schöpfer.* Stuttgart, Deutsche Verlags-Anstalt., 1968.

[1146]. Fuchs, W. *Mathematical Theory of Word-Formation.* London, 1955.

[1147]. Fulton, Alexander. *Scotland and her Tartans. The Romantic Heritage of the Scottish Clans and Families.* Colour Library Books Ltd., Sandbach, Cheshire; Godalming, Surrey, 1991.

[1148]. Fussbroich, Helmut. *St. Maria Lyskirchen in Köln.* Rheinische Kunststätten. Heft 60. Rheinischer Verein für Denkmalpflege und Landschaftsschutz. Köln, Neusser Druckerei und Verlag GmbH, 1992.

[1149]. Gabovitsch, Eugen. *Newton als geistiger Vater der Chronologiekritik und Geschishtsrekonstruktion (neben Hardoin).* Bemerkungen zum Artikel von Uwe Topper in Synesis Nr. 4/1999. Efodon-Synesis (Germany) Nov/Dez. 1999, Nr. 6/1999, S. 29-33.

[1150]. Gabovitsch. Eugen. *Die Grosse Mauer als ein Mythos: Die Errichtungs-geschichte der Chinesischen Mauer und ihre Mythologisierung.* Efodon-Synesis (Germany), Nov/Dez. 1999, Nr.6/1999, S. 9-21.

[1151]. Gadol, J. *Leon Battista Alberti.* Chicago, London, 1969.

[1152]. Gassendi. *Nicolai Coppernici vita.* A supplement to the edition titled *Tychonis Brahei, equitis Mani, astronomorum copyrhaei vita.* XDCLV.

[1152:1]. El Gayar, El Sayed, and M. P. Jones. *Metallurgical Investigation of the Iron plate found in 1837 in the Great Pyramid at Gizeh, Egypt.* In: *Journal of the Historical Metallurgy Society,* Volume 1 (1989): 75-83.

[1153]. Gingerich, O. *Ptolemy Revisited: A Reply to R. R. Newton. Quarterly Journal of the Royal Astronomical Society,* No.22 (1981): 40-44.

[1154]. Ginzel, F. K. *Spezieller Kanon der Sonnen- und Mondfinsternisse für das Ländergebiet der klassischen Altertumswissenschaften und den Zeitraum von 900 vor Chr. bis 600 nach Chr.* Berlin, Mayer & Müller, 1899.

[1155]. Ginzel, F.K. *Handbuch der Mathematischen und Technischen Chronologie.* Bd. I–III. Leipzig, 1906, 1911, 1914.

[1156]. Ginzel, F. K., and A. Wilkens. *Theorie der Finsternisse.* Encykl. der Wissenschaftten. Bd. VI, 2. S. 335. 1908.

[1157]. Girou, Jean. *Simon de Monfort.* Paris: La Colombe, 1953.

[1158]. Della Fina, Giuseppe M., *Luoghi e tempi Etruschi schede di ricerca.* Firenze: Fatatrac, 1989.

[1159]. Gladwin, H. *Men out of Asia.* NY, 1949.

[1160]. Goss, John. *Kartenkunst: Die Geschichte der Kartographie.* Deutsche Asgabe: Braunschweig, Georg Westermann Verlag, 1994. German translation of the English edition: Goss, John. *The Mapmaker's Art. A History of Cartography.* London, Studio Editions Ltd.

[1160:1]. Granier, J., and S. Gagnière. *Avignon. (The city at Sunset. The Popes' Palace. The Saint Benezet bridge).* English edition. Éditions du Boumian, Monaco.

[1161]. Grasshoff, Gerd. *The History of Ptolemy's Star Catalogue.* New York, Springer Verlag, 1990.

[1162]. Grienberger, C. *Catalogus Veteres affixarum longitudiues et latitudines cum novis conferens.* Romae apud B. Zannetum, 1612. (The Pulkovo Observatory Library.)

[1163]. Grierson, Philip. *Coinage and Money in Byzantine Empire.* Spoleto, 1961.

[1164]. Grierson, Philip. *Monnaies du Moyen Âge.* Fribourg, 1976.

[1165]. Grimme, Ernst Günther. *Der Dom zu Aachen. Architektur und Ausstattung.* Aachen, Einhard-Verlag, 1994.

[1166]. Grollenberg, L. N. *Atlas of the Bible.* NY, 1956.

[1167]. Gualberto, Zapata Alonzo. *An Overview of the Mayan World. With a Synthesis of the Olmec, Totonac Zapotec, Mixtec, Teotihuacan, Toltec and Aztec Civilizations.* Mexico, Merida, 1993.

[1167:1]. *Guide to Edo-Tokyo Museum* (English edition). Edited by Edo-Tokyo Museum. Japan Broadcast Publishing Co., Ltd. Printed in Japan by Toppan Printing Co., Ltd.

[1168]. *Gutenberg-Bibel. Geschichtliche Bücher des Alten Testaments.* Die biblio-philen Taschenbücher. Dortmund, Harenberg Kommunikation, 1977.

[1169]. *Gutenberg Bibel (1452-1455).* Reprinted 1968 by Verlag Konrad Köbl. 8022 Grünwald bei München, Huberttusstrasse 13. Firma Elektra, Reprograf-ischer Betrieb, Kjeld Höjring, Niedernhausen/Ts. Printed in Germany.

[1170]. Schneider, Dr. Cornelia. *Gutenberg-Dokumentation. Information Mit-telalter. Das Buch vor Gutenberg (I).* Gutenberg-Museum Mainz, 1990.

[1171]. Schneider, Dr. Cornelia. *Gutenberg-Dokumentation. Information Mit-telalter. Das Buch vor Gutenberg (II).* Gutenberg-Museum Mainz, 1990.

[1172]. *Haack Geographisch-Kartographischer Kalender.* Germany, Haack Gotha, VEB Hermann Haack Geographisch-Kartographische Anstalt Gotha, 1983.

[1172:1]. *Haack Geographisch-Kartographischer Kalender.* Germany, Haack Gotha, VEB Hermann Haack Geographisch-Kartographische Anstalt Gotha, 1988.

[1173]. Hagek, W. *Kronyka Czeska.* Prague, 1541.

[1174]. Hans, Peter. *Der Dom zu Köln. 1248-1948.* Düsseldorf, Verlag L. Schwann, 1948.

[1175]. Hansen, P. *Ecliptische Tafeln für die Konjunktionen des Mondes und der Sonne.* Leipzig, 1857.

[1176]. Hansen, P. *Theorie der Sonnenfinsternisse und verwandten Erscheinun-gen.* Leipzig, 1859.

[1177]. Harley, J. B., and David Woodward. *The History of Cartography. Volume 1. Cartography in Prehistoric, Ancient and Medieval Europe and the Mediterra-nean.* Chicago & London, The University of Chicago Press, 1987.

[1178]. Harvey, Arden. *Who Owns Our Past? National Geographic,* Volume 175, No.3 (March 1989): 376-393.

[1179]. Hauvette, A. *Herodote historien des guerres midiques.* Paris, 1894.

[1180]. Haveta, E. *La modernité des prophètes.* Paris, 1891.

[1181]. Hazirlayan, H. H. Aliy Yalcin (Hz. Yusa Camii Imam-Hatibi). *Hazreti Yusa (Aleyhisselam).* Istanbul. Brochure written by the prior of the temple at the grave of St. Iusha at the outskirts of Istanbul.

[1182]. Hearnshaw, J .B., and D. Khan. *An Analysis of the Magnitude Data in Pto-lemy's Almagest.* Southern Stars. Journal of the Royal Astronomical Society of New Zealand (Wellington), Volume 36, Nos. 5-6 (December 1955): 169-177.

[1183]. Heath, T. L. *Aristarchus of Samos, the Ancient Copernicus; a History of Greek Astronomy to Aristarchus, together with Aristarchus' Treatise on the Sizes and Distances of the Sun and Moon.* Oxford, Clarendon Press, 1913.

[1184]. Heine-Geldern, R., and G.Ekholm. *Significant parallels in the symbolic arts of Southern Asia and Middle America.* In: *Selected Papers of the 29th International Congress of Americanists,* Volume 1. Chicago, 1951. 306.

[1185]. Heinsohn, Gunnar. *Assyrerkönige gleich Perserherrscher! (Die Assyrien-funde bestätigen das Achämenidenreach).* Gräfelfing, Mantis Verlag, 1996.

[1186]. Heinsohn, Gunnar, and Heribert Illig. *Wann lebten die Pharaonen? (Archäologische and technologische Grundlagen für eine Neuschreibung der Geschichte Ägyptens und der übrigen Welt.)* Gräfelfing, Mantis Verlag, 1997.

[1187]. Heintze, C. *Objects rituels, croyances et dieux de la Chine antique et de l'Amérique.* Antwerpen, 1936.

[1188]. Heis. *Die Finsternisse während des pelop. Krieges.* Progr. d. Fried. Wilh. Gimn. Köln, 1834.

[1189]. Herbert, Ewe. *Abbild oder Phantasie? Schiffe auf historischen Karten.* Rostock, VEB Hinstorff Verlag, 1978.

[1190]. [Herodotus]. *The History of Herodotus.* London, 1858.

[1191]. Hignett, C. *Xerxes Invasion of Greece.* Oxford, 1963.

[1192]. Hincks, E. *The Egyptian Dynasties of Manetho.* The Journal of Sacred Literature. London, 1864.

[1193]. Hipparchus. *Hipparchi in Arati et Eudoxi Phenomena Commentarium.* Ed. and German trans. C. Manitius. Leipzig, 1894.

[1194]. *Historiae bysantinae scriptores post Theophanem. Patrologiae cursus completus. Series graeca posterior.* T.CIX. J.-P. Migne, 1863.

[1195]. Hochart. *De l'authenticité des Annales et des Histoires de Tacite.* Paris, 1890.

[1196]. Hodge, K.C., and G.W.A. Newton. *Radiocarbon Dating. Manchester Museum Mummy Project. Multidisciplinary Research on Ancient Egyptian Mummified Remains.* Edited by A. Rosalie David. Published by Manchester Museum. Manchester, England, 1979. 137-147.

[1197]. Hofflit, D. *The Bright Star Catalogue.* New Haven Connecticut, USA, Yale Univ. Obs., 1982.

[1198]. Hoffman. *Sämtliche bei griechishen und lateinschen Schriftstellern des Altertums erwähnte Sonnen- und Mondfinsternisse.* Trieste, 1885.

[1199]. Horster, M. *Brunelleschi und Alberti in ihrer Stellung zur römischen Antike.* Florence, 1973.

[1200]. Horus. *The Enigma Surrounding the Sphinx.* An Egyptian Magazine, April/June 1999.

[1201]. Hoster, Joseph. *Der Dom zu Köln.* Köln, Greven Verlag, 1965.

[1202]. Huddleston, L.E. *Origin of the American Indian. European Concepts, 1492-1729.* Austin, 1967.

[1203]. Hütt, Wolfgang. Altdorfer. *Maler und Werk.* Eine Kunstheftreihe aus dem VEB Verlag der Kunst. Dresden, 1976.

[1204]. Hugot, Leo. *Aachen Cathedral.* Aachen, Germany, Einhard Verlag, 1988.

[1205]. Ideler, L. *Handbuch der mathematischen und technischen Chronologie.* Band 1-2. Berlin, 1825-1826.

[1206]. Ilhan Aksit. *The Topkapi Palace.* Istanbul, Aksit Kultur Turism Sanat Ajans Ltd., 1995.

[1207]. Ilhan Aksit. *The Museum of Chora. Mosaics and Frescoes.* Istanbul, Aksit Kultur Turism Sanat Ajans Ltd., 1995.

[1208]. Illig, Heribert. *Hat Karl der Große je gelebt? (Bauten, Funde und Schriften im Widerstreit).* Gräfelfing, Mantis Verlag, 1996.

[1208:1]. *Irish Dictionary.* Collins Gem. English-Irish. Irish-English. Seamus Mac Mathuna and O Corrain (University of Ulster). Harper Collins, 1999.

[1209]. Isidori Junioris. *Hispalensis episcopi: De responsione mundi.* 1472. (The Pulkovo Observatory Library.)

[1210]. Islam. *Kunst und Architektur.* Herausgegeben von Markus Hattstein und Peter Delis. Köln, Könemann, 2000.

[1211]. *Istanbul and the Marmara Region. A Tale of two Continents.* Turkey, The Ministry of Tourism, Istanbul, 1994.

[1212]. Janin, R. *Constantinople Byzantine.* Paris, 1950.

[1213]. Jirku, A. (Jurku, A.) *Ausgrabungen in Palästina-Syrien.* Halle, 1956.

[1214]. Johnson, Edwin. *The Rise of English Culture.* Williams and Norgate. London-New York, Putnam, 1904.

[1215]. Johnson, Edwin. *The Rise of Christendom.* London, Kegan Paul, Trench, Trubner, & Co. Ltd., 1890.

[1215:1]. Johnson, Paul. *The civilization of Ancient Egypt.* London, Seven Dials, Cassel & Co., 2000.

[1216]. Joubert, Pierre. *L'Heraldique. Les guides practiques.* Editions Ouest-France, 1984.

[1217]. Keegan, John. *A History of Warfare.* New York, Vintage Books, 1994.

[1218]. *Katalog dawnych map Rzeczypospolitej Polskiej w kolekcji Emeryka Hutten Czapskiego i w innych zbiorach.* Wroclaw, Warszawa, Krakow, Gdansk: Zaklad Narodowy im. Ossolinskich, Wyd. Polskiej Akademii Nauk. Instytut Geografii i Przestrzennego Zagospodarowania. Ossolineum. N.1. Mapy XV–XVI wieku. 1978.

[1219]. Keller, W. *Und die Bibel hat doch Recht.* Düsseldorf, 1958.

[1220]. Kenyon, K. M. *Digging in Jericho.* London, 1957.

[1221]. *Kings & Queens of England. A set of picture cards.* Great Britain, Fax Pax Ltd., 1988.

[1222]. Kinoshita, H. *Formulas for Precession.* Smithsonian Inst. Astrophys. Observatory. Cambridge, Massachussets, 1975.

[1223]. Sale, Kirkpatrick. *The Conquest of Paradise. Christopher Columbus and the Columbian Legacy.* New York, Penguin Books, 1990.

[1224]. Knobel, E.B. *British School of Archaeology in Egypt and Egyptian Research Account.* London, 1908.

[1225]. Knobel, E.B. *The Chronology of Star Catalogues.* Memoirs of the Royal Astronomical Society. No.43 (1877): 1-74.

[1226]. Kobold, H. *Finsternisse. Handwörterbuch der Astronomie.* Herausg. von W. Valentiner. Bd. I. Breslau, 1897.

[1227]. Koeva, Margarita. *Rila Monastery.* Sofia, Borina, 1995.

[1228]. *Köln in historischen Stadtplänen. Die Entwicklung der Stadt seit dem XVI Jahrhundert.* Berlin, Argon, 1995.

[1229]. *Kostbarkeiten der Buchkunst. Illuminationen klassischer Werke von Archimedes bis Vergil.* Herausgegeben von Giovanni Morello. Stuttgart-Zürich, Belser Verlag, 1997.

[1230]. Krishnaiah, P. and B. Miao. *Review about Estimation of Change-Points.* In: *Handbook of Statistics,* Volume 7. 1988. 375-402.

[1231]. *Krönungen, Könige in Aachen. Geschichte und Mythos.* Vom 12. Juni bis 3.Oktober 2000 in Rathaus, Domschatzkammer und Dom, Aachen. (Annette Fusenig M. A. und Barbara Jacobs M. A.). From 12th of June to 3rd October 2000 in Town Hall, Cathedral Treasury and Cathedral, Aachen. Kurzführer zur Ausstellung. Guide to the exhibition. Printed in Germany by Verein Aachener Krönungsgeschichte e. V.

[1232]. Mittelstädt, Kuno. *Albrecht Dürer.* Henschelverlag Kunst und Gesellschaft. Arkady, Warszawa-Berlin, 1977.

[1232:1]. *Kunst des Mittelalters in Armenien.* Burchard Brentjes, Stepan Mnazakanjan, Nina Stepanjan. (Kultur. Architektur. Plastik. Wandmalerei. Buchmalerei. Angewandte Kunst). Union Verlag, Berlin, 1981

[1233]. Lafuente, Jesús Precedo. *Visitor's Guide. The Cathedral of Santiago de Compostela.* Spain: Aldeasa, División Palacios y Museos, Estudios Gra'ficos Europeos, 1998.

[1234]. Kurth, Willi. *The Complete Woodcuts of Albrecht Dürer.* With an introduction by Campbell Dodgson, M.A., C.B.E. New York, Dover Publications, Inc., 1963.

[1235]. Lajta, Edit. *Malarstwo Francuskie od Gotyku do Renesansu.* Wydawnictwa Artystyczne i Filmowe-Warszawa. Drukowano na Wegrezech, 1979. Drukarnia Kossuth, Budapeszt. Wspolne wydanie wydawnictw Corvina, Budapest i WAiF, Warszawa.

[1236]. *L'art de vérifier les dates faites historiques.* Ed. par des Bénédictines. 1 ed., Paris, 1750; 2 ed., Paris, 1770; 3 ed., Paris, 1783, 1784, 1787.

[1237]. Laclotte, Michel (Director, Musée du Louvre). *Treasures of the Louvre.* New York, London-Paris, Abbeville, 1993.

[1238]. Langeteau, C. *Tables pour le calcul des syzygies ecliptiques, Connaissanse des Temps pour 1846.* Paris, 1843, 1850.

[1239]. Layamon. *Brut, or the Chronicle of Britain.* Ed. F. Madden. Volume II. London, 1847. 525-526, vv. 22589-22602.

[1240]. Stegena, Lajos, ed. *Lazarus Secretarius. The First Hungarian Mapmaker and His Work.* Budapest, Akademiai Kiado, 1982.

[1240:1]. Lecoq-Ramond, Sylvie, and Béguerie Pantxika. *Le Musée d'Unterlinden de Colmar.* Musées et Monuments de France. Paris, Schongauer & Albin Michel, 1991.

[1241]. Leland, C. *Fusang or discovery of America by Chinese Buddhist priests in the 5th century.* London, 1875.

[1242]. Dal Maso, Leonardo B.. *Rome of the Caesars.* Firenze, Bonechi Editioni Il Turismo, 1974, 1992.

[1243]. *Le Saint voyage de Jérusalem de seigneur d'Anglure.* Paris, F. Bonnardot and A. Longnon, 1878.

[1244]. *Le Wallraf-Richartz Museum de Cologne.* Munich, Scala, C. H. Becksche Verlagbuchhandlung (Oscar Beck), 1992.

[1245]. Lehmann, P. *Tafeln zur Berechnung der Mondphasen und Sonnen- und Mondfinsternisse.* Berlin, 1882.

[1245:1]. *Les Grandes Civilisations Disparues.* Sélection du Reader's Digest. Paris-Bruxelles-Montréal-Zurich, 1980.

[1246]. *Les Manuscripts de la Mer Morte. Aux origines du christianisme.* Les Dossiers d'Archéologie, No. 189 (Janv. 1994).

[1247]. de Austria, Leupoldus. *Compilatio de Astrorum Scientia,* cuts. 1489. (The Pulkovo Observatory Library.)

[1248]. Lhotsky, A. *Auf Satze und Vortrage.* Halle, 1970-1972.

[1249]. Lichtheim, Miriam. *Ancient Egyptian Literature.* Volumes 1-3. USA, University of California Press, 1975.

[1250]. Libby, W.F. *Radiocarbon dating.* 2nd edition. Chicago, Univ. of Chicago Press, 1955.

[1251]. Lilly, W. *An Introduction to Astrology.* London, G. Bell, 1939.

[1252]. Linde, A. v. d. *Gutenberg. Geschichte und Erdichtung.* Stuttgart, 1878.

[1253]. Linde, A. v. d. *Geschichte der Buchdruckerkunst.* Berlin, 1886.

[1254]. Lokotsch, K. *Etymologisches Wörterbuch der europäischen Wörter.* Heidelberg, 1927.

[1255]. Longhi, Roberto. *Caravaggio.* Die Italienische Malerei. Dresden: Editori Riuniti Rom, VEB Verlag der Kunst, 1968

[1256]. Lubienietski, S. *Theatrum Cometicum, etc.* Amstelodami, 1666-1668. (The Pulkovo Observatory Library.)

[1257]. Lubienietski, S. *Historia universalis omnium Cometarum.* Lugduni Batavorum, 1681. (The Pulkovo Observatory Library.)

[1258]. *Lucas Cranach d. Ä.* Herausgegeben von Heinz Lüdecke. Welt der Kunst. Henschelvarlag Kunst und Gesellschaft. Berlin, 1972.

[1259]. Magi, Giovanna, and Giuliano Valdes. *All of Turkey.* Firenze, Casa Editrice Bonechi, 1990.

[1260]. Manuel, Chrisoloras. *Manuels Chrisolorae Vita et scripta.* Patrologiae cursus completus. Series graeca posterior. T.CLVI. J.-P. Migne, 1866.

[1261]. Manuel II Palaeologus. *Laudatio funebris fratris sui Theodori Palaeologi Despotae.* Patrologiae cursus completus. Series graeca posterior. T. CLVI. J.-P. Migne, 1866.

[1261:1]. *Maps of the Ancient World. 2002 Calendar.* From The Huntington Library. Avalanche Publishing, Inc., 2001.

[1262]. *Mapy severni a jizni hvezdne oblohy.* Praha, Kartografie Praha, 1971.

[1263]. Marco Polo. *Le Livre des Merveilles.* La Renaissance du Livre. Collection Références. Extrait du Livre des Merveilles du Monde (Ms. fr. 2810) de la Bibliotheque nationale de France. 1999 Ultreya srl, Milan. 1996 Faksimile Verlag Luzern pour les textes et les images. 1999 La Renaissance du Livre, Tournai pour l'edition francaise. Belgique.

[1264]. Marco Polo. *The Travels of Marco Polo.* The Complete Yule-Cordier Edition. With a Total of 198 Illustrations and 32 Maps and Site Plans. Three Volumes Bound as Two. Volumes 1,2. Including the unabridged third edition (1903) of Henry Yule's annotated translation, as revised by Henry Cordier; together with Cordier's later volume of notes and addenda (1920). New York, Dover, 1993.

[1265]. Maria Da Villa Urbani. *Basilica of San Marco*. Milan, Editions KINA, 1993.

[1266]. Martin Behaim's 1492 *Erdapfel*. A paper version of our earliest surviving terrestrial Globe. First made in Nuremberg in 1492. Follow Marco Polo and the quest for spice on this unique medieval relic. Greaves & Thomas, London, England. Registered design & Patents Pending. Artwork & Globe Gores, 1997. (A selection of facsimile globes from the Greaves & Thomas collection. Spanning cartographic history from 1492 to the present day.)

[1267]. Maso Finiguerra. *A Florentine Picture-Chronicle*. Reproduced from the originals in the British Museum by the Imperial Press, Berlin. A critical and descriptive text by Sidney Colvin, M. A. Keeper of the prints and drawings of the British Museum. New York, Benjamin Blom, 1970.

[1268]. [Paris, Matthew] *The Illustrated Chronicles of Matthew Paris*. Cambridge, Corpus Christi College, 1993.

[1268:1]. McKenzie, John L., S. J. *Dictionary of the Bible*. G. Chapman, London, 1985 (1965 by Macmillan Publishing).

[1269]. Meier, H. *Deutsche Sprachstatistik*. Hildesheim, 1964.

[1270]. de la Garza, Mercedes. *The Mayas. 3000 years of civilization*. Mexico, Monclem Ediciones; Florence, Casa Editrice Bonechi, 1994.

[1271]. *Germany*. Michelin et Cie, 1996.

[1272]. *Paris*. Michelin et Cie, 1996.

[1273]. Michell, J. A. *Little History of Astro-Archaeology: Stages in the Transformation of a Heresy*. London, 1977.

[1273:0]. Michov, H. *Weitere Beiträge zur älteren Kartographie Russlands*. Mit 1 Textabbildung und 5 Karten. Sonderabzug aus den Mitteilungen der Geographischen Gesellschaft in Hamburg, Band XXII. Hamburg: L.Friederichsen & Co. Inhaber: Dr. L. Friederichsen, 1907.

[1273:1]. Migne, J.-P. *Patrologiae Cursus Completus etc.* Paris: Petit-Montrouge, 1800-1875.

[1274]. Miller, W. *The Latins in the Levant. A History of Frankish Greece in 1204-1566*. London, 1908.

[1275]. Mommsen, T. *Die Römische Chronologie bis auf Caesar*. Berlin, 1859, 2 Aufl.

[1276]. Montucla, J. E. *Histoire des Mathématiques*. T.IV. Paris, 1802.

[1277]. Montucla, J. E. *Histoire des Mathématiques*. 4 vols. Paris. 1799-1802.

[1278]. *Musée Royal de Naples: Peintures, bronzes et statues érotiques du cabinet secret, avec les explanations de M. C. F. (César Famin)*. Paris, 1857.

[1279]. *Museum. Gutenberg Museum Mainz*. Braunschweig, Georg Westermann Verlag, 1980. (3 Auflage 1994.)

[1280]. Myres, J. *Herodotus. Father of History*. Oxford, 1953.

[1281]. Ahmed Kardy. *Finding a Pharaoh's Funeral Bark*. National Geographic, Vol. 173, No. 4 (April 1988): 513-546.

[1282]. Peter Miller. *Riddle of the Pyramid Boats*. National Geographic, Vol. 173, No. 4 (April 1988): 534-546.

[1282:1]. Rick Gore. *The Eternal Etruscans. National Geographic,* Volume 173, No. 6 (June 1988): 696-743.

[1283]. *National Geographic,* Volume 176, No. 4 (October 1989).

[1284]. Nelli René. *Ecritures cathares.* Complete Cathar writings translated into French. Planete, 1968.

[1285]. Neugebauer, O. *Astronomische Chronologie.* Berlin and Leipzig, 1929.

[1286]. Neugebauer, O. *Specieller Kanon der Sonnenfinsternisse.* Ergänzungsheft, Astron. Nachr. 8, 4. Kiel, Verlag der Astronomischen Nachrichten, 1931.

[1287]. Neugebauer, O. *A History of Ancient Mathematical Astronomy.* 3 Vols. New York-Berlin, Springer-Verlag, 1975.

[1288]. Neugebauer, O. *The Exact Sciences in Antiquity.* 2nd edition. Providence, Rhode Island, Brown University Press, 1957.

[1289]. Neugebauer, Otto and Richard A. Parker. *Egyptian Astronomical Texts.* 3 vols. Providence and London: Lund Humphries for Brown University Press, 1960-1969.

[1290]. Neugebauer, O., and H. B. Van Hoesen. *Greek Horoscopes.* Philadelphia, The American Philosophical Society, 1959.

[1290:1]. Neugebauer, O., and R. A. Parker. *Egyptian Astronomical Texts.* Vols. 1-3. London, Brown University Press, 1964.

[1291]. Neugebauer, O., R. A. Parker, and D.Pingree. *The Zodiac Ceilings of Petosiris and Petubastis. Denkmäler der Oase Dachla. Aus dem Nachlass von Ahmed Fakhry.* Bearbeitet von J. Osing, M. Moursi, Do. Arnold, O. Neugebauer, R. A. Parker, D. Pengree und M. A. Nur-el-Din. Archäologische Veröffentlichungen 28 Deutsches Archäologisches Institut. Abteilung Kairo. Mainz am Rhein, Verlag Philipp von Zabern, 1982.

[1292]. Neugebauer, P. V. *Tafeln zur astronomischen Chronologie.* 3 Volumes. Leipzig, 1912.

[1293]. Neugebauer, P. V. *Abgekürzte Tafeln der Sonne und großen Planeten.* Berlin, 1904.

[1294]. Newcomb, S. *On the reccurence of solar eclipses with tables of eclipses.* Astronomical Papers (Washington). Vol. 1, No. 1 (1882).

[1295]. Newcomb, S. *Tables of the Motion of the Earth on its Axis and around the Sun.* Astronomical Paper. V.VI, Pt.1. 1898.

[1296]. Newmann, Dianne. *The Pergamon Altar.* Staatliche Museen zu Berlin, Preussischer Kulturbesitz, 1993.

[1297]. Newton, Isaac. *Abregé de la chronologie de I. Newton* fait par lui-même, et traduit sur le manuscript Angloise [par Nicolas Freret]. Paris: Gavelier, 1725.

[1298]. Newton, Isaac. *The Chronology of Ancient Kingdoms Amended. To which is Prefix'd, A Short Chronicle from the First Memory of Things in Europe, to the Conquest of Persia by Alexander the Great.* London: J. Tonson, 1728. Re-edited in 1988 by Histories and Mysteries of Man Ltd.

[1299]. Newton, Isaac. *La Chronologie des Ancien Royalmes Corrigée, Martin u.a.* Translation F. Granet. Paris, 1728.

[1300]. Newton, Isaac. *Kurzer Auszug aus der weltberühmten Isaac Newtons*

Chronologie derer alten Königreiche: worinnen 4 Haupt-Periodi veste gestellt u. aus d. Antiquität eruiert werden...; wobei zugl. gezeiget wird, wie d. dunckle Histoire d. alten verfallenen Königreiche... in e. richtige chronolog. Ordnung zu bringen sei... Aus d. Engl. Von Philipp Georg Hübner. Meiningen, 1741.

[1301]. Newton, Isaac. *Abrégé de la chronologie des ancien royaumes.* Trad. Deel Anglois de Mr. [Andrew] Reid. Geneve, 1743.

[1302]. Newton, Isaac. *Kurzer Auszug aus der I.Newtons Chronologie.* Von Pf. Georg Hübner, Hilburgshausen u. a. 1745.

[1303]. Newton, R. R. "Astronomical evidence concerning non-gravitational forces in the Earth-Moon system." *Astrophysics and Space Science,* Volume 16 (1972): 179-200.

[1304]. Newton, R. "Two Uses of Ancient Astronomy." *Philosophical Transactions of the Royal Society of London,* Series A., 276 (2 May 1974): 99-115. DOI: 10.1098/rsta.1974.0012.

[1305]. Newton, Robert R. *The Origins of Ptolemy's Astronomical Tables.* The Johns Hopkins University Applied Physics Laboratory. The Center for Archaeoastronomy, University of Maryland. USA, 1985.

[1306]. Newton, R. R. *Ancient Astronomical Observations and the Accelerations of the Earth and Moon.* Baltimore and London, John Hopkins University Press, 1970.

[1306:1]. Newton, R. R. *The Moon's Acceleration and Its Physical Origin.* Baltimore, John Hopkins University Press, 1979.

[1307]. Newton, Robert R. *On the fractions of degrees in an ancient star catalogue.* Quarterly Journal of the Royal Astronomical Society, Volume XX (1979): 383-394.

[1308]. Newton, Robert R. *The origins of Ptolemy's planetary parameters.* The Johns Hopkins University Applied Physics Lab. The Center for Archaeoastronomy. 1982. 86-90.

[1309]. *Nicolai Copernici Thorunensis de Revolutionibus Orbium Coelestium Libri VI.* Ex. auctoris autographio recudi curavit Societas Copernicana Thorunensis. Berolini, 1873.

[1310]. Nikulin, N. *Lucas Cranach. Masters of World Painting.* Leningrad, Aurora Art, 1976.

[1311]. Nilsson, M. P. *Primitive Time-Reckoning. A Study in the Origins and the First Development of the Art of Counting Time among the Primitive and Early Culture Peoples.* Lund, Gleerup, 1920.

[1312]. Noth, M. *Die Welt des Alten Testaments.* Berlin, 1957.

[1313]. Oertel, F. *Herodots ägyptischen Logos und die Glaubwürdigkeit Herodots.* Berlin, 1970.

[1314]. Olston, A. B. *The Story of Time.* Chicago, Jarvis Universal Clock Co., 1915.

[1315]. Oppolzer, Th. *Kanon der Sonnen- und Mondfinsternisse.* Wien: K. K.Hof- und Staatsdruckerei, 1887.

[1316]. Oppolzer, Th. *Tafeln zur Berechnung der Mondfinsternisse.* Wien, 1883.

[1317]. Oppolzer, Th. *Syzygientafeln für den Mond.* Leipzig, Astronomische Gesellschaft, 1881.

[1318]. Orbini, Mauro. *Origine de gli Slavi & progresso dell'Imperio loro.* Pesaro, 1606.

[1319]. Orontij, Finai Delphinatus. *Canonum Astronomicum.* 1553. (The Pulkovo Observatory Library.)

[1320]. Orontii, Finaei Delphinatis. *Fine Oronce, etc.* 1551. (The Pulkovo Observatory Library.)

[1321]. Orr, M. A. *Dante and the Early Astronomers.* London, Gall and Inglis, 1913.

[1321:1]. Otero, Gloria. *El Arte Romanico en España. Romanesque Art in Spain.* Subdireccion General de Promocion Exterior del Turismo. Turespaña, Spain, 1995.

[1322]. Otero, José Carro. *Santiago de Compostela.* Second edition. Leon, Spain, Editorial Everest S.A., 1999.

[1323]. Ostrowski, W. *The ancient names and early cartography of Byelorussia.* London, 1971.

[1324]. Owen, G. F. *Archaeology and the Bible.* NY, 1961.

[1325]. Page, E. S. *Continuous inspection schemes. Biometrika,* Volume 41, No.1 (1954): 100-115.

[1326]. Page, E. S. *A test for a change in a parameter occurring at an unknown point. Biometrica,* Vol. 42, No.4 (1955): 523-527.

[1327]. Paladilhe, Dominique. *Simon de Monfort et le Drame Cathare.* France: Librairie Académique Perrin, 1997.

[1328]. Pannekoek, A. *A History of Astronomy.* New York, 1961.

[1329]. *Paris. Tourist Guide.* Paris: Guide Michelin, 1992.

[1330]. Parker, Richard A. *Ancient Egyptian Astronomy.* Philosophical Transactions of the Royal Society of London, Ser. A, 276 (1974): 51-65.

[1331]. Pastoureau, Michel. *Traité d'Héraldique.* Bibliothèque de la Sauvegarde de l'Art Francais. 3e éd. Paris, Grands manuels Picard, 1997.

[1332]. Venetus, Paulus. *Philisiphiae naturalis compendium clarissimi philosophi Pauli Veneti: una libro de compositione mundi, etc.* Paris, J. Lambert (s. d.), n.d.

[1333]. Pearce, A. *The science of the stars.* London, Glen & Co., 1898.

[1334]. Pearce, A. *The text-book of Astrology.* London, Glen & Co., 1911.

[1335]. Pedersen, O. *A survey of the Almagest.* Odence, 1974.

[1335:1]. Pelloutier, S. *Histoire des Celtes.* Paris: Quillan, 1771.

[1336]. Perrier, Jacques. *Notre-Dame de Paris.* Association Maurice de Sully, Paris, 1996.

[1337]. Petavius, D. *De doctrina temporum.* Vol. 1. Paris, 1627. (Petau, D. *Opus de doctrina temporum, etc.* Volume 1. Antwerpiae, M. DCCV.)

[1338]. Petavius, D. *Petavii Avrelianensis e Societate Iesu, Rationarium Temporum in Partes Dvas, Libros tredecim distributum.* Editio Ultima. Parisiis, Apud Sebastianum Cramoisy, Regis, & Reginae Architypographum: Gabrielem Cramoisy. M.DC.LII. Cvm Pivilegio Regis.

[1339]. Peters, C. H. F., and E. B. Knobel *Ptolemy's Catalogue of Stars. A Revision of the Almagest.* Publ. No. 86. Washington, The Carnegie Inst. of Washington, 1915.

[1340]. Petrarca, Francesco. *Familiarum rerum libri.* Editione critica per cura di Vittorio Rossi. Firenze, 1968.

[1340:1]. Petrie, Flinders W. M. *Athribi* Mem. of British School of Archaeology in Egypt. Volume 14. 1902.

[1340:2]. Petrie, Flinders. *Wisdom of the Egyptians.* London, British School of Archaeology in Egypt and Bernard Quaritch Ltd., 1940.

[1341]. Pfeil, Ulrich. *Trier. A tour of the most famous sights.* Kunstverlag Weick. Passau, 1996.

[1342]. Philip, A. *The Calendar: Its History, Structure and Improvement.* Cambridge University Press, 1921.

[1343]. *Philipp Apian und die Kartographie der Renaissance.* Bayerische Staatsbibliothek. Anton H. München, Konrad Verlag, 1989.

[1344]. [Phrantzae, Georgius] *De Vita et Acriptus Georgii Phrantzae.* Patrologiae cursus completus. Series graeca posterior. T. CLVI. J.-P. Migne, 1866.

[1345]. Pingre, A. *Chronologie des eclipses qui ont été visibles depuis le pole boréal jusque vers l'equateur pendant les dix siècles qui ont précedé l'ère Chrétienne.* Paris, 1787.

[1346]. Pogo, A. *Additions and corrections to Oppolzer's Kanon der Mondfinsternisse. Astron. Journal,* V. 43 (1937): 45-48.

[1347]. Pokorny, J. *Indogermanisches etymologisches Wörterbuch.* In 2 Bd. Tübingen. Basel: Francke Verlag, 1994 (3. Aufl.).

[1348]. Goetz, Delia and Sylvanus G. Morley. *Popol Vuh. The Sacred Book of the Ancient Quiché Maya.* From the translation of Adrian Recinos. Volume 29 in the "Civilization of the American Indian" series. Norman and London, Univ. of Oklahoma Press, 1950. (13th edition in 1991).

[1349]. Portal, Charles. *Histoire de la ville de Cordes (Tarn), 1222-1799.* Toulouse, 1902.

[1350]. Priese, Karl-Heinz. *The Gold of Meroe.* The Metropolitan Museum of Art, New York. Mainz, Verlag Philipp von Zabern, 1993.

[1351]. Prowe, L. *Nicolaus Copernicus.* 3 Bde. Berlin, 1883-1884.

[1352]. [Ptolemaeus, Claudius]. *Phelusiensis Alexandrini philosophi et matematici excellentissimi Phaenomena stellarum 1022 fixarum ad hanc aetatem reducta, atque seorsum in studiosorum gratiam. Nunc primum edita, Interprete Georgio Trapezuntio.* Excessum Coloniai Agrippinae. Anno 1537, octavo Calendas 5 Septembers.

[1353]. [Ptolemaeus, Claudius]. *Geographia.* Ed. Sebastian Münster. Basel, 1540. Reprint: Series of Atlases in Facsimile. Amsterdam: Theatrum Orbis Terrarum Ltd., 1966.

[1354]. [Ptolemaeus, Claudius]. *Clavdii Ptolemaei Pelusiensis Alexandrini omnia quae extant opera, praeter Geographiam, etc.* Baseliae, 1551.

[1355]. Ptolemy. *The Almagest.* (Great Books of Western World, V. 16). Encyclopaedia Britannica, 1952.

THE ISSUE WITH ANTIQUITY

[1356]. Ptolemy, C. *Claudii Ptolemaei opera quae exstant omnia.* Ed. J. L.Heiberg et al. 3 volumes. Leipzig, 1898-1903,.

[1357]. Ptolemy. *Tetrabiblos.* Ed. and trans. F. E. Robbins. Harvard, 1940.

[1358]. *Ptolemy's Almagest.* Transl. and annot. by G. J. Toomer. London, 1984.

[1359]. Putnam, James. *Mummy.* London, New York, Eyewitness Books. 1993.

[1360]. Putnam, James. *Pyramid.* London, New York, Eyewitness Books. 1994.

[1361]. Radini (Radinus), Tedeschi. *Sideralis abyssus.* Luteciae, Impressum opa T. Kees. (The Pulkovo Observatory Library). 1514 (1511?).

[1362]. Ramet, Henri. *Histoire de Toulouse.* Toulouse, Le Pérégrinateur Editeur, Queray, 1994.

[1363]. Ranson, C. L. *A Late Egyptian Sarcophagus.* Bulletin of the Metropolitian Museum of Art. 9 (1914): 112-120.

[1364]. Raska. *Chronologie der Bibel.* Berlin, 1878.

[1365]. Rawlins, Dennis. *An investigation of the ancient star catalog.* Publications of the Astronomical Society of the Pacific. Volume XCIV. 1982. 359-373.

[1365:1]. Reade, Julian. *Assyrian Sculpture.* British Museum. British Museum Press, London, 1983, 1988.

[1366]. Reeves, Nicholas. *The Complete Tutankhamun. The King. The Tomb. The Royal Treasure.* New York, Thames and Hudson, 1990, 1995.

[1367]. Reeves, Nicholas, and Nan Froman. *Into the Mummy's Tomb. The Real-Life Discovery of Tutankhamun's Treasures.* Toronto: A Scholastic/Madison Press Book, 1993, 1994. 1st published in the United States by Scholastic, 1992.

[1368]. *Rembrandt Harmensz van Rijn.* Tableaux dans les musées de l'Union Soviétique. Leningrad, Aurora, 1981, 1987.

[1369]. Robert, C. *Archäologische Hermeneutik.* Berlin, 1919.

[1370]. Roberts, J. M. *The Pelican History of the World.* England, Penguin Books, 1984.

[1371]. Robertson, J. M. *Pagan christs; studies in comparative hierology.* London, Watts & Co, 1911.

[1372]. Roche, Déodar. *Le Catharisme.* 2 Volumes. Narbonne, Cahiers d'Études Cathares, 1973 and 1976.

[1373]. Rogov, Alexander. *Alexandrov. (Alexandrovskaya Sloboda, or, literally, "The Freemen's Village of Alexander").* Museum Cities. Leningrad, Avrora, 1979.

[1374]. Grafton, Anthony, ed. *Rome Reborn.* The Vatican Library and Renaissance Culture. Washington: Library of Congress; New Haven, London: Yale University Press; Vatican City: Biblioteca Apostolica Vaticana, 1993.

[1375]. Romero, Anne-Marie. *Saint-Denis. La montée des pouvours.* Caisse Nationale des Monuments Historiques et des Sites. Paris, CNRS, 1992, 1993.

[1376]. Roquebert, Michel. *Cathar Religion.* Toulouse, Editions Loubatières, 1994.

[1377]. Roquebert, Michel. *L'épopée Cathare, 1209-1229. (On the Crusade against the Albigeois).* 3 volumes. Toulouse: Private, 1970, 1977 and 1986.

[1378]. Rosalba, Manzo. *New Castle Museum. Naples City Hall. Joint to the major for culture.* D. E. C. Artistical and Museums Patrimony Service. Naples, n.d.

310

[1378:1]. Rose-Marie, Rainer Hagen. *Egypt. People, Gods, Pharaohs.* Köln: Benedikt Taschen Verlag GmbH, 1999.

[1379]. Ross. *Tacitus and Bracciolini. The Annals forged in the XVth century.* London, 1878.

[1380]. Rostovzeff, M. *Social and Economic History of the Roman Empire.* Paris, 1957.

[1381]. Rowley, H. H. *The Old Testament and Modern Study.* Oxford, 1961.

[1382]. *Rundsicht der Stadt Wien zur Zeit der Türkenbelagerung, 1529, Niklas Meldemann, Nürnberg 1530.* HM Inv. Nr. 48068. Faksimile 1994, Museen der Stadt Wien Druckerei Gert Herzig, Wien. (Mediaeval plan of Vienna of the XVI c. depicting the siege of Vienna by the Turks in 1529.)

[1383]. Sacro, Bosco J. de. *Opusculum Johannis de Sacro busto spericum, cu figuris optimus ei novis textu in se, sive ambiguitate declarantibus.* Leipzig, 1494. (The Pulkovo Observatory Library.)

[1384]. Sacro, Bosco J. de. *Sphera materialis.* (The Pulkovo Observatory Library). Nürnberg, Gedruckt durch J. Getkneckt, 1516.

[1385]. Sacro, Bosco J. de. *Opusculu de Sphaera . . . clarissimi philosophi Ioannis de Sacro busto.* (The Pulkovo Observatory Library). Viennae Pannoniae, 1518.

[1386]. Sayce. *Herodotus I–III. The ancient empire of the East.* London, 1883.

[1387]. Scaliger, I. *Opus novum de emendatione temporum.* Lutetiac. Paris, 1583. (Thesaurum temporum, 1606).

[1388]. Schaarschmidt, K. *Die Sammlung der Platos Schriften zur Schreidung der echten von den unechten untersucht.* Bonn, 1866.

[1389]. Schäfer, Heinrich. *Ägyptische und heutige Kunst und Weltgebäude der alten Ägypter. Zwei Aufsätze.* Berlin, Walter de Greyter, 1928.

[1390]. Schlafke, Jakob. *La Cattedrale di Colonia.* Editione Italiana. Bonechi Verlag Styria, Casa Editrice Bonechi, Graz, Lahn Verlag, Limburg/Lahn, 1990.

[1391]. Schliemann, Heinrich. *Ilios. Stadt und Land der Trojaner. Forschungen und Entdeckungen in der Trojas und besonders auf der Baustelle von Troja.* Leipzig, 1881.

[1392]. Schliemann, Heinrich. *Troja. Ergebnisse meiner neuesten Ausgrabungen auf der Baustelle von Troja, in der Heldengräbern Bunarbaschi und an anderen Orten in der Trojas im Jahre 1882.* Leipzig, 1884.

[1393]. Schilgen, Jost, and Martina Wengierek. *So schön ist Trier.* Grasberg, Sachbuchverlag Karin Mader, 1994.

[1394]. Schjellerup, H. C. F. G. *Description des étoiles fixes composée au milieu du Xe siècle de notre ère par l'astronome persan abd-Al-Rahman Al-Sufi.* St. Petersburg, 1874.

[1395]. Schram, R. *Tafeln zur Berechning der naheren Umstände der Sonnenfinsternisse.* Wien, 1886.

[1396]. Schram, R. *Reductionstafeln für den Oppolzerischen Finsternis Kanon zum Übergang auf die Ginzelschen Correctionen.* Wien, 1889.

[1396:1]. Schedel, Hartmann. *La chronique universelle de Nuremberg.* L'édition de

Nuremberg, colorée et commentée. (L'édition 1493, colorée et commentée). Introduction et Appendice par Stephan Füssel. Taschen GmbH. (Köln). Köln, London, Madrid, New York, Paris, Tokyo, 2001.

[1397]. Schram, R. *Kalendariographische und chronologische Tafeln.* Leipzig, 1908.

1398 Schroter, J. *Spezieller Kanon der zentralen Sonnen- und Mondfinsternisse.* Kristiania, 1923.

[1399]. Schulten, Walter. *Der Schrein der Heiligen drei Könige im Kölner Dom.* Luthe-Druck Köln, 1995.

[1400]. Schwahn, P. *Mathematische Theorie der astronomischen Finsternisse.* Leipzig, 1910.

[1401]. Schwegler, T. *Die Biblische Urgeschichte.* München, 1960.

[1402]. Serrus, Georges. *Montségur.* Toulouse, Editions Loubatières, 1994.

[1403]. Serrus, Georges, and Michel Roquebert. *Cathare Castles.* Toulouse, Editions Loubatières, 1993.

[1404]. Severy, Merle. *The world of Suleyman the Magnificent. National Geographic*, Volume 172, No.5 (1987): 552-601.

[1405]. Siebeck, H. *Zur Chronologie der platonischen Dialoge.* Halle, 1873.

[1405:1]. Simon, J. L., P. Bretagnon, J. Chapront, M.,Chapront-Touze, G. Francou, and J. Laskar. Software for the calculation of heliocentric coordinates, radial vectors and immediate speeds for the 8 main planets of the Solar System (the PLANETAP program, Fortran 77) *Astron. Astrophys.*, 282, 663 (1994).

1405:2 Sivaramamurti, Calambur. *The Art of India.* India Book House, Bombay, 1977. Published by Harry N. Abrams, Inc., New York.

[1406]. Shaban, S. *Change-point problem and two-phase regression: annotated bibliography. International Statistical Review*, Volume 48 (1980): 83-86.

[1407]. *Speyer. Die Kaiserstadt am Rhein.* KINA Italia Mailand, Kaiserdom-Pavillon Renate Hahn am Domplatz, ATD Mailand, 1994.

[1408]. *Speyer Cathedral.* Regensburg, Verlag Schnell & Steiner GmbH Regensburg, 1997.

[1409]. Spielberg, W. *Die Glaubwürdigkeit von Herodots Bericht über Ägypten.* Berlin, 1926.

[1410]. Staccioli, Romolo A. *Storia e civiltà degli Etruschi. Origine apogeo decadenza di un grande popolo dell'Italia antica.* Rome, Newton Compton editori, 1981.

[1411]. Stancheva, Magdalina. *Veliki Preslav.* Sofia, Zlatostrouy, 1993.

[1412]. Steeb, J. *Coelum sephiroticum Hebraeorum, etc.* (The Pulkovo Observatory Library). Mainz, 1679.

[1413]. Stephan, Beissel S. J. *Kunstschätze des Aachener Kaiserdomes. Werke der Goldschmiedekunst, Elfenbeinschnitzerei und Textilkunst.* M. Gladbach. Druck und Verlag von B. Kühlen. Anstalt für Christliche Kunst. 1904.

[1414]. Stevens, Henry N. *Ptolemy's Geography. A brief account of all printed editions down to 1730.* Amsterdam, Theatrum Orbis Terrarum Ltd. Meridian Publishing Company, 1972.

[1415]. Stierlin, Henri. *The Pharaohs Master-Builders.* Paris, Finest S.A./Éditions Pierre Terrail, 1992.

[1416]. *St. Lorenz. Sagen + Geschichten.* 73. Verein zur Erhaltung der St. Lorenz-kirche in Nürnberg (E.V.). Herausgegeben von Gerhard Althaus und Georg Stolz. Nürnberg. Nr. 15/3, unveränderte Auflage, 1998.

[1417]. *St.Lorenz. Türme + Glocken.* 81. Verein zur Erhaltung der St. Lorenz-kirche in Nürnberg (E. V.). Herausgegeben von Gerhard Althaus und Georg Stolz. Nürnberg. Nr.25/2, verbessterte Auflage, 1998.

[1418]. *St. Lorenz. Wappen in Fülle. Wappenkunde. Wappenkunst und Wappen-recht.* 86. Verein zur Erhaltung der St. Lorenz-kirche in Nürnberg (E.V.). Herausgegeben von Gerhard Althaus und Georg Stolz. Nürnberg. NF.Nr.31, 1986.

[1419]. *St. Lorenz. Ich bin das Licht der Welt. Grosse und kleine Lichter.* 90. Verein zur Erhaltung der St. Lorenzkirche in Nürnberg (E.V.). Herausgegeben von Gerhard Althaus und Georg Stolz. Nürnberg. NF.Nr.35, 1990.

[1420]. *St. Lorenz. Sand-Sandstein. Steinsand-Sand.* 91. Verein zur Erhaltung der St. Lorenzkirche in Nürnberg (E. V.). Herausgegeben von Gerhard Althaus und Georg Stolz. Nürnberg. NF. Nr. 36, 1991.

[1421]. *St. Lorenz. Behelmt, behütet und bedacht.* 92. Verein zur Erhaltung der St. Lorenzkirche in Nürnberg (E. V.). Herausgegeben von Gerhard Althaus und Georg Stolz. Nürnberg. NF. Nr. 37, 1992.

[1422]. *St. Lorenz. Mein Auge schauet was Gott gebauet.* 93. Was Verein zur Erh-altung der St. Lorenzkirche in Nürnberg (E. V.). Herausgegeben von Gerhard Althaus und Georg Stolz. Nürnberg. NF. Nr. 38, 1993.

[1423]. *St. Lorenz. Ecce Panis Angelorum. Das Sakramentshaus des Adam Kraft.* Verein zur Erhaltung der St. Lorenzkirche in Nürnberg (E. V.). Herausgege-ben von Gerhard Althaus und Georg Stolz. Nürnberg. NF. Nr. 39, 1994.

[1424]. *St. Lorenz. 500 Jahre Sakramentshaus: Erklärung – Verklärung, Deutung – Umdeutung.* 96. Verein zur Erhaltung der St. Lorenzkirche in Nürnberg (E. V.). Herausgegeben von Gerhard Althaus und Georg Stolz. Nürnberg. NF. Nr. 41, 1996.

[1425]. *St. Lorenz. Türen. Tore. Portale.* 97. Verein zur Erhaltung der St. Lorenz-kirche in Nürnberg (E.V.). Herausgegeben von Gerhard Althaus und Georg Stolz. Nürnberg. NF. Nr. 41, 1997.

[1426]. *St. Lorenz. Wandfresken. Bestand. Restaurierung. Erhaltung.* 98. Verein zur Erhaltung der St. Lorenzkirche in Nürnberg (E. V.). Herausgegeben von Gerhard Althaus und Georg Stolz. Nürnberg. NF. Nr. 43, 1998.

[1427]. *St. Lorenz. Im Blickpunkt das Kreuz. Kruzifix-Darstellungen.* 99. Verein zur Erhaltung der St. Lorenz-kirche in Nürnberg (E. V.). Herausgegeben von Gerhard Althaus und Georg Stolz. Nürnberg. NF. Nr. 44, 1999.

[1428]. Struve, O. *Libroram in biblioteca Speculae Pulcovensis catalogus systemat-icus.* Petropoli, 1860.

[1429]. Stryjkowski, Maciej. *O Poczatkach, wywodach....* Of the Beginnings, Sources, the Deeds of the Knights and the Home Affairs of the Glorious Peoples of Lithuania, Zhmuda, and Russia, an Original Tale Inspired by the Lord and the Author's Own Experience. Warszawa, 1978.

[1430]. Suckow, Hähel. *Stadtführer Halle. Sehenswertes in Halle.* Halle, Druckhaus Schütze, 1998.

[1431]. Suess, H. *Secular variations. Journal of Geophysical Research,* Volume 70, No. 23 (1965).

[1432]. Suess, H. *Bristlecone Pine. Radioactive Dating and Methods.* Vienna, 1968.

[1433]. Suess, H. *Bristlecone Pine Calibration of the Radiocarbon.* XII Nobel Symposium on Radiocarbon Variations and Absolute Chronology. Uppsala, 1969.

[1434]. Sueton. *Die zwölf Caesaren, nach der Übersetzung v. A. Stahr neu hrsg.* München, Leipzig, 1912.

[1435]. Suhle, A. *Mittelalteriche Brakteaten.* Leipzig, 1965.

[1436]. Swerdlow, N. M., and O. Neugebauer. *Mathematical Astronomy in Copernicus' De Revolutionibus.* 2 vols. Berlin, 1984.

[1437]. *Sztuka Egipska. Piramidy i mastaby.* Mala Encyklopedia Sztuki. 23. Warszawa, Arkady, 1976.

[1438]. *Sztuka Egipska. Luksor.* Opracowal Kazimierz Michalowski. Mala Encyklopedia Sztuki. 25. Warszawa, Arkady, 1976.

[1438:1]. Tabov, Jordan. *Chronological Distribution of Information in Historical Texts.* Computers and the Humanities, 2003, Volume 37, pages 235-240.

[1439]. Targuebayre, Claire. *Cordes en Albigeois.* Toulouse, Editions Privat, 1988.

[1440]. Tesnierio, Ioanne. *Opus Matematicum octolibrum.* (The Pulkovo Observatory Library.) Coloniae Agrippinae, apud J. Birckmannum & W. Richwinum, 1562.

[1441]. Teutsch Astronomei. *Astronomia.* Woodcuts, 1545. (The Pulkovo Observatory Library.)

[1442]. *The Anglo-Saxon Chronicle.* London: Everyman's library, J. M. Dent. Sons Ltd., 1990.

[1443]. Wright, G. E., ed. *The Bible and the Ancient Near East. Essays in Honour of W.F.Albright.* NY, 1961.

[1444]. *The Cambridge medieval history. IV. The Byzantine Empire.* Cambridge Univ. Press, 1966-1967.

[1445]. *The Cathedral of St.Stephen in Vienna.* Graz, Verlag Styria, Casa Editrice Bonechi, 1992.

[1446]. Gransden, A., ed. *The Chronicle of Bury St. Edmunds, 1212-1301.* London-Edinburgh, 1964.

[1447]. *The Concise Columbia Encyclopedia.* USA, Columbia University Press, 1983.

[1448]. *The Egyptian Book of the Dead. The Book of Going Forth by Day.* The first authentic presentation of the complete papyrus of Ani. Featuring full color images. Transl. by Dr. R. Faulkner. San Francisco, Chronicle Books, 1994.

[1449]. *The English version of the polyglot Bible with a copies and original selection of references to parallel and illustrative passages.* London, S. Bagster and Sons.

[1450]. *The Holy Bible, containing Old and New Testaments: Translated out of the original tongues; and with the former translations diligently compared and revised, by His Majesty's special command. Appointed to be read in Churches.* London, British and Foreign Bible Society, Instituted in London in the Year 1804.

[1451]. *The Holy Bible, containing Old and New Testaments: Translated out of the original tongues; and with the former translations diligently compared and revised, by His Majesty's special command. Authorized King James version.* Salt Lake City, Utah, Church of Jesus Christ of Latter-Day Saints, 1992.

[1452]. *The New Encyclopaedia Britannica.* Volume 16. 1987.

[1453]. *The place of astronomy in the ancient world.* A discussion organized jointly for the Royal Society and the British Academy. Philos. Trans. of the Royal. Soc. of London, Ser. A., Volume 276 (1974): 1-276.

[1454]. Farid, Shafik, ed. *The Pyramids of Giza.* Book 1. Simpkins Splendor of Egypt. Salt Lake City, Utah, Simpkins Souvenirs, 1982.

[1455]. *The R. C. Church of St. Karl. Vienna.* Salzburg, Christiche Kunststätten Österreichs, Nr.20 E. Verlag St. Peter, 1994.

[1456]. Werber, Eugen. *The Sarajevo Haggadah.* Svjetlost, Sarajevo. Printed by Mladinska Knjiga, Ljubljiana, 1999.

[1457]. *The Shrine of Torreciudad. Guide.* Oficina de Información, 22391 Torreciudad (Huesca), España.

[1458]. Farid, Shafik, ed. *The Temple of Luxor.* Book 3. Simpkins Splendor of Egypt. Salt Lake City, Utah, Simpkins Souvenirs, 1982.

[1458:1]. *The Treasures of the Valley of the Kings. Tombs and Temples of the Theban West Bank in Luxor.* Edited by Kent R.Weeks. The American University in Cairo Press. Cairo, Egypt, 2001. White Star, S. r. l. Vercelli, Italy.

[1459]. *The World Encompassed.* An exhibition of the history of maps held at the Baltimore Museum of Art October 1 to November 23, 1952. Baltimore, Maryland, The Trustees of the Walters Art Gallery, 1952.

[1460]. Thierry, Amedee. *St. Jean Chrysostome et l'impératrice Eudoxie.* Paris, 1872.

[1460:1]. Thoren, Victor E. *The Lord of Uraniborg. A Biography of Tycho Brahe.* With contributions by John R. Christianson. Cambridge, New York, Port Chester, Melbourne, Sydney, Cambridge University Press (1994?).

[1461]. Thorndike, L. H. D. *A History of Magic and Experimental Science. (During the first thirteen centuries of our era).* Volumes 1,2. NY, 1923., New York, Columbia University Press, 1943, 1947, 1958.

[1462]. Topper, Uwe. *Die Große Aktion. Europas Erfundene Geschichte. Die planmäßige Fälschung unserer Vergangenheit von der Antike bis zur Aufklärung.* Tübingen, Grabert-Verlag, n.d.

[1463]. Topper, Uwe. *Erfundene Geschichte. Unsere Zeitrechnung ist falsch. Leben wir im Jahr 1702?* München, F. A. Herbig Verlagsbuchhandlung GmbH, 1999.

[1464]. Turhan, Can. *Istanbul, Gate to the Orient.* Istanbul, Orient, 1995.

[1465]. Turhan, Can. *Topkapi Palace.* Istanbul, Orient, 1995.

[1466]. Eco, Umberto. *Serendipities. Language and Lunacy.* Weidenfeld & Nicolson (UK). NY, Orion/Columbia Univ. Press. 1999.

[1467]. *Venice.* Venezia, Storti Edizioni, 1993.

[1468]. Vesconte, Pietro. *Seekarten.* Mit einem Geleitwort von Otto Mazal. Einfürung von Lelio Pagani. Edition Georg Popp Würzburg. 1978. Grafica Gutenberg, Bergamo, 1977.

[1469]. Vidal-Quadras, José A. *Torreciudad.* Imprenta Moises Barbasto, Spain, 1987.

[1470]. Vidal-Quadras, José A. *Torreciudad. A shrine to Our Lady.* Office of Information Torreciudad, Spain, n.d.

[1471]. Villehardouin, Geoffroy de. *La conquète de Constantinople.* Historiens et chroniqueurs du Moyen Âge. Ed. A. Pauphilet. Paris, 1963.

[1472]. Virgil, Mocanu. *Tintoretto.* Clasicii Picturii Universale. Bucuresti, Editura Meridiane, 1977.

[1473]. Vries, Hesselde. *Variation in concentration of radiocarbon with time and location on Earth.* Koninkl. Nederlandse Akad. Wetensch. Proc. 1958, ser. B. 61, pages 1-9.

[1474]. *Wallraf-Rischartz-Museum der Stadt Köln. Vollständliges Verzeichnis der Gemäldesammlung.* Köln/Mailand, 1986.

[1475]. Waterfield, R. L. *A Hundred Years of Astronomy.* NY, Macmillan, 1938.

[1476]. Wehli, Tünde. *A Középkori Spanyolország Festészete.* Budapest, Corvina Kiadó, 1980.

[1477]. Wenzler, Claude. *L'Héraldique.* Rennes, Editions Ouest-France, 1997.

[1478]. Werner, H., and F. Schmeidler. *Synopsis der Nomenklatur der Fixsterne.* Wissensch. Stuttgart, Verlags-Gesellschaft 1986.

[1478:1]. Wigal, Donald. *Anciennes Cartes Marines. A la Découverte des Nouveaux Mondes. 1290-1699.* New York, Parkstone Press, 2000.

[1479]. Williams, John. *Observations of Comets from B.C.611 A.D. to 1640, extracted from the Chinese Annals.* 1871.

[1480]. Willis, E. H., H. Tauber, and K. O. Münnich. *Variations in the atmospheric radiocarbon concentration over the past 1300 years. Radiocarbon,* Volume 2 (1960): 1.

[1481]. Wissowa, Pauly. *Real-Encyclopädie der Klassischen Altertumwissenschaft in alphabetischer Ordnung.* Hrsg. von Kroll. Stuttgart, 1839-1852.

[1482]. Wittkower, R. *Architectural Principles in the Age of Humanism.* Paris, 1960.

[1483]. Wolf, R. *Handbuch der Astronomie, ihrer Geschichte und Literatur.* Bd. II. Zürich, 1892.

[1484]. Wooley, L. *Excavation at Ur.* NY, 1955.

[1485]. Woronowa, Tamara, and Andrej Sterligov. *Westeuropäische Buchmalerei des 8. bis 16. Jahrhunderts in der Russischen Nationalbibliothek, Sankt Petersburg. (Frankreich. Spanien. England. Deutschland. Italien. Niederlande).* Augsburg: Bechtermünz. Genehmigte Lizenzausgabe für Weltbild Verlag, 2000. England, Parkstone/Aurora, 1996.

[1486]. Wright, G. E. *Biblical Archaeology.* Philadelphia, London, 1957.

[1487]. Altet, Xavier Barral. *Compostelle de Grand Chemin.* Découvertes Gallimard Réligions. Gallimard, 1993.

[1488]. Zadkiel. *The Grammar of Astrology.* London, J. Cornish, 1849.

[1489]. Zarnecki, George, Florence Deucher, and Irmgard Hutter. *Neue Belser Stilgeschichte. Band IV. Romantik, Gotik, Byzanz.* Stuttgard, Zürich, Belser Verlag, 1986.

[1490]. Zech, J. *Astronomische Untersuchungen über die wichtigeren Finsternisse, welche von den Schriftstellern des klassischen Altertums erwähnt werden.* Leipzig, 1853.

[1491]. *Zeitensprünge.* Interdisziplinäres Bulletin. Sonderdruck. September 1996. Thema Absolutdatierung. Mantis Verlag, Germany.

[1492]. Zevi, B., E. Battisti, E. Garin, and L. Malle. *Alberti. Enciclopedia universale dell'arte.* Vol. I. Venezia, Roma, 1958.

Made in the USA
Columbia, SC
19 June 2022

61943224R00190